WHAT
COLLEGE ON YOUR OWN
IS ALL ABOUT

"This book is a part of today's movement toward life-long learning. It opens doors to self-study in college arts–and–science fields for interested American adults—those bold, ambitious new learners who are proving to be a new frontier in American higher education."

—Oluf M. Davidsen,
President,
American College Testing Program

PART I tells you why you should get a college education—and how you can get it at home. It tells you how to use a library, where to get popularly priced paperback classics, and how to find and register for the many programs—including the "CLEP" examinations—which award credits and degrees for independent study.

PART II helps you decide *what* you want to learn. It provides you with a unique study guide to contemporary college subjects, including basic and advanced level reading lists recommended by leading educators from the top colleges and universities in the country.

Whether you use COLLEGE ON YOUR OWN to get a degree or to seek knowledge as its own reward, you will learn a great deal—about other people, about the world, and especially about yourself.

WITH CONTRIBUTIONS BY
LEADING EDUCATORS FROM MAJOR UNIVERSITIES

Bennington College * Brandeis University * Columbia University * City University of New York * DePaul University * Kent State University * Massachusetts Institute of Technology * Northeastern University * Stanford University * State University of New York at Binghamton * State University of New York College at Purchase * Swarthmore College * University of Michigan * Vassar College

COLLEGE ON YOUR OWN

How You Can Get a
College Education at Home

Gail Thain Parker and Gene R. Hawes

A Hudson Group Book

RLI: $\dfrac{\text{VLM 12 (VLR 11-12)}}{\text{IL 12+}}$

COLLEGE ON YOUR OWN
A Bantam Book / March 1978

ISBN 0-553-01092-1

Published simultaneously in the United States and Canada

Bantam Books are published by Bantam Books, Inc.
Its trademark consisting of the words "Bantam Books"
and the portrayal of a bantam, is registered in the
United States Patent Office and in other countries.
Marca Registrada. Bantam Books, Inc.,
666 Fifth Avenue, New York, New York 10019.

PRINTED IN THE UNITED STATES OF AMERICA

0 9 8 7 6 5 4 3 2 1

ACKNOWLEDGMENTS

Editorial associates of the authors who made very substantial contributions to this book by carrying out exacting tasks of research, coordination and manuscript preparation and editing are Alys Bohn, Elizabeth Hawes, Mark Hawes and Roberta Hawes. Assisting with bibliographic research were Betsy Behnke, Hayden Carruth, Charlotte Green, Jane McGinness and Alice Rosenthal. Long stretches of the manuscript were typed by Andrea Freund, Joni Stern and Florence Wise. Mylas Martin helped draft and provided valuable suggestions on certain sections. The work of each of these able and congenial co-workers is greatly appreciated.

Very special thanks beyond their identifications at the head of each Part 2 chapter are due the scholars who served as Editorial Advisors on major fields of college study. The book would not have been possible without their enthusiastic and most capable collaboration. Readers no less than the authors of the book are much in their debt.

An equally indispensable collaborator is Toni Burbank, the senior editor at Bantam Books who joined whole-heartedly in creating the book all the way from original definition through design and production of finished volumes. We are grateful in addition for the generous help of her associates at Bantam, Joëlle Delbourgo and Barbara Whiteman.

G. T. P. and G. R. H.

COLLEGE ON YOUR OWN

How You Can Get a
College Education at Home

CONTENTS

PART 1
New Reasons—
and New Opportunities—
for Pursuing College On Your Own   1

Chapter 1.   Current College Learning: 3
          Intellectual Excitement, Human Values

Chapter 2.   People Who Now Pursue   7
          College Studies on Their Own

Chapter 3.   How You Can Do It—   12
          For Yourself

Chapter 4.   How You Can Do It—   29
          For Credits and Degrees

PART 2
A Guide to Contemporary Fields
of College Study   39

Introduction: The Arts and Sciences: 41
          Using These Chapters

Interdisciplinary Areas

Chapter 5.   East Asian Civilizations: 43
          ". . . different ways of thought and life"
          Editorial Advisor:
          Lillian M. Li, Swarthmore College

Chapter 6.   Environmental Studies: 56
          ". . . understanding and working toward
          the solution of environmental problems"
          Editorial Advisor:
          David B. Sutton, The Antaeus Group

Chapter 7.   Western Civilization: 77
          ". . . broad understanding of an entire
                    cultural tradition"
                    Editorial Advisor:
          Mary E. Payer, Columbia University

Chapter 8.   Women's Studies: 121
          ". . . independent action
                    and bold departure"
                    Editorial Advisor:
                    Mary P. Ryan
          State University of New York
                    at Binghamton

                    The Social Sciences   139

Chapter 9.   Anthropology: 141
          ". . . the study of human nature and possibilities"
                    Editorial Advisor:
          Michelle and Renato Rosaldo,
                    Stanford University

Chapter 10.   Economics: 161
          ". . . the physical needs
                    and wants of people"
                    Editorial Advisor:
          Rosalind S. Seneca, Columbia University

Chapter 11.   History—American: 176
          ". . . patterns of culture and the reactions
          of individuals to historical situations"
                    Editorial Advisor:
          James Shenton, Columbia University

Chapter 12.   History—Black American: 200
          ". . . to correct large
                    and long-standing omissions"
                    Editorial Advisor:
          James Shenton, Columbia University

Chapter 13.   Political Science: 219
          ". . . what human beings should
          make of their common life together"
                    Editorial Advisor:
          Mary L. Shanley, Vassar College

Chapter 14. Psychology: 233
" . . . who we are and
why we act the way we do"
Editoral Advisor:
Susan Carey
Massachusetts Institute of Technology

Chapter 15. Sociology: 257
". . . a systematic attempt to
understand social behavior and society"
Editorial Advisor:
Charlotte Weissberg, Brandeis University

The Humanities 277

Chapter 16. Art History: 279
". . . a coherent and rich language of forms"
Editorial Advisor:
Eugene Santomasso
City University of New York

Chapter 17. American Literature: 297
". . . our native sense of life"
Editorial Advisor:
William Alexander, University of Michigan

Chapter 18. English Composition/Creative Writing: 314
". . . clarity and expressive power"
Editorial Advisor:
Jesse H. McKnight III, Kent State University

Chapter 19. English Literature: 320
". . . a long and rich portrayal of life"
Editorial Advisor:
William Alexander, University of Michigan

Chapter 20. Film: 338
". . . sound, lighting, and choice of image"
Editorial Advisor:
William Alexander, University of Michigan

Chapter 21. Philosophy: 346
". . . much more important than
what philosophers have said"
Editorial Advisor: Ned Block
Massachusetts Institute of Technology

The Sciences and Mathematics   363

Chapter 22.   Biology: 365
". . . the marvelous diversity of life"
Editorial Advisor:
Madeleine Swindlehurst, Bennington College

Chapter 23.   Chemistry: 379
*". . . atoms, molecules, and
their interactions"*
Editorial Advisor:
Dennis R. Aebersold, Bennington College

Chapter 24.   Earth Sciences: . 384
*". . . rocks, minerals, and the processes
that form and rework these materials"*
Editorial Advisor:
Richard S. Naylor, Northeastern University

Chapter 25.   Mathematics: 391
*". . . No laboratory is necessary;
just paper and pencil and patience"*
Editorial Advisor:
Susanna and Helmut Epp, DePaul University

Chapter 26.   Physics: 409
*". . . explaining phenomena from the
cosmic scale down to the level of the atomic"*
Editorial Advisor:
James Currin
State University of New York College
at Purchase

Part One

New Reasons—
and New Opportunities—
for Pursuing College
On Your Own

Chapter One

CURRENT
COLLEGE LEARNING
Intellectual Excitement, Human Values

Americans have long believed that a college education was in itself the key to success. College graduates earned more and, apparently, lived better than those who entered the work force at an early age. Faith that a degree could make all the difference in a person's life has fueled the enormous growth of higher education since World War II. If a B.A. was the prerequisite for realizing the American dream, then clearly it was "un-American" not to make degree programs available to all who were interested.

Recently, however, there are signs that faith in the power of the bachelor's degree is severely shaken. As more and more people received B.A.s, higher degrees became necessary for advancement in a number of fields. The old statistics which seemed to show that the possession of a college degree greatly increased a worker's lifetime earnings no longer appear valid. Indeed, many now feel that the reason college graduates have in the past tended to earn higher incomes was not related to anything they learned; rather, it was because of who they were when they went to college—the children of prosperous families or unusually ambitious individuals themselves. Moreover, everyone has seen reports of unemployed college graduates in today's depressed economy and projections of simply not enough jobs to go around in years ahead. One large recent study found that economic success in the United States hinges less on education than on luck.

With all these gloomy predictions, why write a book called *College On Your Own*? Frankly, we feel that the current cynical view of college education represents a wholly predictable reaction to the American tendency to equate value with cash value. Having a college education is not in itself going to guarantee financial success. The point is not how much money you may or may not earn, but the difference an educated mind can make to you as a human being.

For many people there is and will be no substitute for the experience of four years of college. For others the desire to get a degree is preeminent—and for good reasons, ranging from a much needed job qualification to "something I've always wanted to do for myself." And for still others, the degree is irrelevant, but the pleasures of learning a subject thoroughly are in themselves a supreme value.

College On Your Own has been written with all these groups in mind. For those who anticipate going to college or those who are already enrolled, the brief introductions to contemporary areas of college study and the annotated bibliographies should provide a way of exploring possible areas of specialization—majors—as well as a means of supplementing current studies. High-school students can use the guide to gain a clearer idea of what will be expected of them. College students may want to continue work in areas in which they have taken an introductory course. Alternately, they may want to "read ahead" to anticipate what is involved in a given specialty. Those who have already graduated may wish to go back and study a field they ignored as undergraduates or to keep up with some of the latest research in their former majors. Of the twenty-two chapters in Part 2, several represent lines of investigation that were not being taught to undergraduates ten, much less twenty, years ago.

This book may also be of help to those who were unable to go to college right after high school and who now discover that they need a degree in order to advance in their chosen careers. It may also aid people who now find that they can return to school, whether full-time or part-time, to fulfill a long-standing ambition. It can help them prepare themselves for the demands that will be placed on them by faculty members once they are enrolled. It can help them explore possible majors. Chapter 4 lists programs through which students can earn recognized course credits toward a college degree and can even complete all work for a degree by learning on their own.

For those of you who are less interested in a degree than in satisfying an old or new curiosity, *College On Your Own* provides a way of beginning at the beginning and working at your own pace through a field of study. A great deal has been written about life on a small planet. Surely one of the most appropriate (and ecological) measures any of us can take is to develop our inner resources and learn to find our greatest pleasures, not in motor boats and jet planes, but in the movement of our minds. Henry David Thoreau said that he had traveled widely in Concord; all of us have an opportunity for the most significant adventure in an area bound on one side by our own homes and on the other by the local library, museum, or institution of higher education.

In Part 2 you will, accordingly, find chapters on human behavior, social structure, and history, on masterworks of literature and art, on the development of writing skills, on philosophy and film. You will also find chapters on the natural world, on quantitative and spatial relationships, and several devoted to new interdisciplinary areas— East Asian civilizations, environmental studies, Western civilization, and women's studies.

Needless to say, much has been left out. Studies of languages and literatures other than English and European history are among the most obvious omissions. Space limitations have further made it impractical to include areas of undergraduate professional study: teacher education, engineering, agriculture, journalism, and business. However, students in all these professional areas also study in the liberal-arts areas we have outlined. Students entering medicine, dentistry, law, government administration, the ministry, social work, library service, or college teaching itself generally finish bachelor's degree programs in the liberal arts before going on to professional schools.

Intellectual excitement and emphasis on human values are two qualities that seem especially characteristic of liberal education today. That intellectual excitement stems in part from continued rapid growth in the total quantity of knowledge. Half of all the scientists who have ever lived are alive and producing new findings today. Substantial recent growth marks field after field—although quantity in research is obviously no substitute for quality.

The explosive growth of knowledge in recent decades has included a number of epochal discoveries. "Plate tectonics" in geology—the theory that the continents are part of vast plates of solid material floating on the earth's molten core—has revolutionized our understanding of the earth's history. The discovery of DNA, the basic material that transmits inherited characteristics in all forms of life, has opened new vistas in biology. Similar discoveries have created hotly debated new issues in such fields as learning psychology, political science, and philosophy.

One consequence of the knowledge explosion is that such older academic disciplines as biology, psychology, and geology have grown into broad subject areas with branches each roughly comparable in extent to its parent discipline at, say, the turn of the century. Biology, for example, is now often referred to as the biological sciences and includes such broad specialties as genetics (the study of heredity), ecology, evolution, microbiology, and molecular biology.

Newer fields—such as biochemistry, geophysics, and economic history—cut across the borders of older disciplines. Vigorous new interdisciplinary areas integrating knowledge from many fields have been created. Techniques of scholarship in literature and the arts have been extended to new areas, as in the case of film.

Intellectual excitement in college studies today stems, in addition, from recent attempts made to comprehend vast social changes. Many academic areas resemble battlefields as major syntheses are being questioned by a new generation of professionals. In anthropology, sociology, economics, political science, and history the battlelines are constantly being drawn and redrawn, making the situation at once more confusing and more exciting for the serious student. Long-accepted methods and presuppositions have become hot issues; formulations that served their purpose for years no longer seem adequate to explain current events.

Changing social attitudes and priorities are reflected in the new interdisciplinary fields of women's studies and Black studies, where traditional conceptions of women and Blacks are methodically questioned. Research investigations in the social sciences reflect an increasing sense of urgency about the problems of the disadvantaged; a new branch of economics, for instance, focuses on welfare economics. Historians are increasingly interested in social history of the sort that portrays the lives and analyzes the historic influence of ordinary people.

In itself the development of many new opportunities for Americans to acquire the kind of learning traditionally dispensed by colleges without going to college, whether through continuing-education programs or competency testing, reflects changing national priorities. More than 90,000 people a year now take examinations in the College-Level Examination Program (CLEP) of the College Board. They take these tests to receive regular college course credit for subjects they can learn on their own before their examination sessions. More than 1,700 colleges and universities across the country grant course credits on the basis of CLEP examinations according to policies specified by the individual college.

Many hundreds of persons have already received college degrees, and thousands more are registered in the Regents External Degree Program of New York State, Empire State College of the State University of New York, and Thomas A. Edison College of New Jersey. In all three institutions adults of any age can enroll and do all of their studying for their degrees without attending any college classes if they so choose. This can also be done in the college degree programs of the still newer Connecticut Board for State Academic Awards.

Thousands of others have entered similar programs enabling them to complete studies largely on their own offered by many individual colleges. Among them are the "university without walls" programs of more than twenty schools across the country, the independent studies program of Syracuse University, the bachelor of liberal studies program of the University of Oklahoma, and various external degree programs of the California state universities and colleges.

Closer to home, so to speak, the professional college teachers and scholars who made this book possible by serving as editorial advisors invariably believe that the books they recommend can be mastered by serious general readers such as yourself.

"College on your own" is not simply a slogan; it is a real possibility. Chapter 2 tells more about people who have explored this possibility for themselves. Chapter 3 suggests ways to use this book to benefit from individual college studies. Chapter 4 gives basic information on programs awarding course credits and degrees for individual study. Part 2 of the book provides the reader with a study guide paralleling the offerings of a good liberal arts college today. You may want to work toward a degree, or you may feel that knowledge itself is its own best reward. Either way, we feel sure that you will learn more about your own inner resources in the course of your studies.

Chapter Two

PEOPLE WHO NOW PURSUE COLLEGE STUDIES ON THEIR OWN

"I think it's a marvelous opportunity for someone like myself," Diane Edwards observed recently. A thirty-nine-year-old mother of three, she was commenting on how the reading and study she had done on her own had earned her credit for more than a year of college. At eighteen she had finished one year of college, and twenty years later she turned to the Harrisburg campus of Pennsylvania State University to complete work for her degree. There she discovered a way to win further credit toward the degree. She took the CLEP "general examinations" (in English composition, humanities, mathematics, natural sciences, and social sciences-history).

To her delight, she was awarded more than a year's worth of credit on the basis of her CLEP marks in addition to credit for the first year she had completed long before. Thanks to what she had learned herself and the examinations, she could get her degree in the following year through part-time study. "It saved me time," she said. "It would have taken me another year and a half of money and time to get where I am now."

Not only had Pat W. Warren never gone to college; at the age of fifteen he had dropped out of high school. Now in his forties, he recently earned a bachelor's degree from Southwest Texas State University— very largely on the basis of learning on his own.

A staff master sergeant with more than a quarter-century's service in the Air Force, Pat Warren had earned his high-school equivalency diploma through tests before talking to a Southwest Texas State counselor. At the time, he was a course chief with the department of security police training at Lackland Air Force Base. The Armed Forces courses he had completed, plus career experience, would be worth 40 of some 120 credits he would need to qualify for a bachelor's in occupational education with an emphasis on law enforcement, the counselor explained. Sergeant Warren then arranged for the military education officer at the base to give him examinations through which he could qualify for the further credits he needed for his degree. Thirty-four were "end-of-course" examinations in the United States Armed Forces Institute program; five were CLEP examinations.

For some time Pat Warren studied intensively; he took the thirty-nine different examinations during his lunch hours. He was able to meet all the requirements in only fifteen months right on the base and was awarded the degree with honors.

Diane Edwards and Pat Warren are only two of the 90,000 or more persons a year who currently demonstrate in CLEP examinations what academic course material they have mastered on their own. Joan Stefanchik at forty-one felt she had no hope for college whatever. Her father's death had forced her to leave high school before graduating. By the time she reached her forties, she and her husband were living with their five children in New Jersey, and she was working full-time. She nevertheless somehow made time to read and learn, and she took examinations for her high-school equivalency diploma.

Her marks in these were so high that Montclair State College wanted her to try for its "second careers program," in which persons over twenty-five begin with advanced standing earned on CLEP examinations and go on to earn bachelor's degrees. Very largely on her own, she prepared for the CLEP examinations and learned the equivalent of two years of full-time college study. She qualified for junior-year standing at Montclair and majored in psychology as background for a subsequent career in guidance counseling.

William Calder is still another example of someone who learned quite a lot on his own as evidenced on CLEP as well as other examinations. He had taken two years of part-time extension study in engineering in the 1930s before lack of money during the Depression forced him to stop. On his own he later studied for and passed the examinations for a Pennsylvania state license in engineering. At fifty-nine, a professional civil engineer with the state's Public Utility Commission, he felt an urge to study business administration. "It was sort of a personal desire to keep abreast of the times," he said. "I'm studying business administration but not for monetary considerations, just personal desire." Before resuming his college studies, he was able to earn enough credit on CLEP tests to finish work for the bachelor's in business in about three years of night and Saturday classes.

By learning on her own in an intensive schedule, Anita Ferrari was able to complete in just nine months much of the learning that normally takes students four years. In that nine months she met all the requirements for the bachelor's degree at the University of Oregon. Aged thirty-eight, she entered the university as a freshman in the spring of 1974. By the end of the year she had finished all her requirements for the degree.

What she had learned before, plus some brushing up, got Ms. Ferrari off to a running start with 27 credits earned on the CLEP general examinations. At Oregon, students also can take the university's own "challenge" examinations for credit instead of attending courses. She accepted the challenge, earning more than 100 additional credits.

One signal advantage was that, as a native of Europe who had long lived and worked in various countries, she had already learned five languages. She took examinations in them all—Italian, French, Spanish, Portuguese, and English (her weakest)—for a total of some 70 credits. But her remaining 30-odd challenge credits were in subjects she learned on her own, from the ground up, during that nine months while also attending classes for about 50 credits more. (Oregon, on a quarter-term calendar, requires around 180 quarter-hours of credit for the bachelor's degree.)

What Ms. Ferrari accomplished did not hinge on any superior abilities of hers, she insists. "Am I academically gifted?" she asked when interviewed. "No. I refuse that. I've been told that so many times. I utterly reject it. I'm fairly curious, and I'm interested in life, that's all."

Almost anyone with interest and determination can do much the same, she emphasized. "I find that people are generally afraid of things like this. I'm thirty-eight and I have a fairly organized mind. I was pushy enough to go around to the various offices and ask questions. Most students don't have the kind of aggressiveness that I found was needed. That's especially true of the younger students, but it's even true of many of the older ones."

Ms. Ferrari went at learning on her own with an energetic and systematic attack. Before any one examination, she spent a couple of weeks in general preparation. Then she usually put in two weeks studying for up to six hours a day, most often in the university library. (Others learning on their own need not put in such heavy blocks of time.) During her concentrated four-week preparations she was independently learning the content of quarter-courses or two-quarter-courses normally absorbed over periods of three or six months.

"Many people can get to the heart of a subject without a teacher at all," she said. "It can be done if you read enough books, if you get into the subject deeply enough."

One of the newer programs in which individuals do carry out extensive learning without being taught is that of Empire State College, the "nonresidential" college of the State University of New York. Donald Wentworth began his Empire State studies at the age of thirty-four, when he was also an assembly-line worker at a Ford plant and a union officer and bargaining representative of thirteen years' standing. He continued full-time in that career and, like all Empire State students, met periodically with his faculty advisor (called a "mentor"). The students usually meet with their individual mentors once every few months to review and evaluate completion of tasks agreed on in a previous "learning contract" and to plan the tasks of the next contract. Mentors are located at twenty-five "learning centers" and units throughout the state.

Concentrating on the history of the American labor movement, Mr. Wentworth carried out his own ambitious program of readings. The demanding topics he studied independently included the thought of Karl Marx and Friedrich Engels, reports on the lives of workers in the early industrial period, the history of early labor organizations, and labor's response to modern industrialism.

Among other Empire State students who similarly learn without attending college classes, Ruth Van Zandt, a twenty-eight-year-old nursery school teacher, read widely in American history and literature toward the goal of teaching those subjects in high school. Charles Booth, twenty-three and a Marine Corps veteran, planned close study of such philosophers as Plato, Kant, Hegel, Husserl, Heidegger, and Marcuse in connection with his aim of eventually starting an experimental school. Robert Lenard, twenty, launched into a sequence of independent studies combining Mediterranean travel with exploration of Spanish archaeology and culture and Greek history through a reading list of more than thirty books in those fields. Carol Tartaglia focused on political science after volunteer work had led to a paid job as administrative assistant to a state senator when she was in her thirties. Reading deeply in New York history was part of the degree studies she designed to help realize her hope of some day running for political office.

By now, more than five thousand people have received associates' degrees (ordinarily earned after two years' full-time college study), and bachelors' degrees in the Regents External Degree Program of New York State. This was the country's earliest program in which degrees could be earned entirely by examination, without the students' ever attending a college class or even consulting a professor.

In fact, more than one in every ten of its graduates have earned their degrees completely by examination. Because it offers no instruction and imposes no attendance requirements, the program can be and has been entered by persons anywhere in the country and around the world.

Many people have carried out very ambitious learning on their own through the Regents External program. Among them is a twenty-seven-year-old businessman in Hong Kong, who earned the associate's degree entirely through examinations. A sixty-year-old woman earned an associate's degree in liberal arts studies and planned to head into a second career by going on for the Regents External associate's degree in nursing, which qualifies recipients for taking the state Registered Nurse licensure examinations.

One thirty-two-year-old housewife, who had left school at fourteen, completed work for both her high-school equivalency and her external associate's degree within two years and thought she would continue on into graduate school. A fifty-one-year-old grandfather in Tennessee completely qualified for the bachelor of science in business administration by learning on his own and taking examinations, as did a thirty-eight-year-old housewife.

At sixty, a retired public-relations executive and former mayor of Hillsdale, N. J., used credit both from some college courses taken long before and from current examinations to meet requirements for the business B.S. degree. A Louisiana husband and wife worked for their degrees together. A twenty-nine-year-old man who had been imprisoned at sixteen for a shotgun murder that he later attributed to "a twisted and immature mind" became the first inmate to earn the program's associate in arts degree; he subsequently went on to receive its bachelor of arts degree, and not long after won an early parole.

Still others may learn a great deal on their own simply for their own pleasure and benefit. One such person was Martin Radtke, who came to the United States from Lithuania in 1913 at the age of thirty. For many years he worked as a gardener in New Jersey. But he began going to the New York Public Library, particularly to read works on economics and finance. Armed with this knowledge, he began to invest his small savings during the 1930s. In 1973 library officials were astounded to learn that he had bequeathed their institution $358,000.

Today, if you go to the main lobby of that great library, you will see the names of its largest benefactors inscribed on its walls, from John Jacob Astor on down. But you will find only one memorial plaque set into its floor. On it you can read the words from Martin Radtke's will:

I had little opportunity for formal education as a young man in Lithuania, and I am deeply indebted to The New York Public Library for the opportunity to educate myself. In appreciation, I have given the library my estate with the wish that it be used so that others can have the same opportunity made available to me.

Chapter Three

HOW YOU CAN DO IT—
FOR YOURSELF

You can use the extensive reading guides of Part 2 in many different ways, depending on the background and interests you bring to this book. If you already know which areas you want to study or catch up in, you can simply start right there. On the other hand, you may want to go through the chapters of Part 2 as a guide to the breadth of study usually expected of a college undergraduate. The outlined readings parallel the course offerings of many liberal arts colleges, where students are expected to plan programs that generally include

introductory courses in several different areas often including English composition;
followed by intermediate work, again in several areas;
culminating in advanced work in at least one "major" field or in an interdisciplinary area.

The chapters of Part 2 provide reading guides to works ranging from introductory to advanced. Together, they represent broad guides to undergraduate programs in any one of more than twenty major fields, plus varieties of interdisciplinary combinations readers may choose to pursue, such as American history and literature, women's studies and sociology, or economics and mathematics.

Even if you want to use Part 2 as a guide to an entire four-year college education, you would study only a relatively small proportion of all the books listed. Do not be overwhelmed by the chapters; each cites many more books than any one person would be expected to read.

You might begin by picking two or three widely different fields (perhaps one each in the social sciences, the humanities, and the sciences, or one in an interdisciplinary area). In addition to reading a number of the introductory books listed in each field you choose, you may want to work on improving your writing skills with the help of one or more books in the chapter on English composition. Gradually you will get an idea of where your preferences lie and where you will want to work your way through to the advanced level.

Further guidance offered to help you make the most of this book is given in the rest of the chapter. First, it tells how to get the books cited in the extensive reading lists of Part 2. Next it outlines different ways of studying the texts that interest you—ways used by college students in the range of reading they do for their courses. Finally, it illustrates in detail how you can plan your reading and study so that they will parallel representative college programs today, describing the numbers and kinds of books that will most effectively convey the information typically covered in a four-year college education.

ACQUIRING YOUR READING

Bookstores were envisioned as the main source for your reading materials. Wherever possible, the bibliographies list paperback editions, which are widely and inexpensively available and are used very extensively in college courses today. College students commonly buy and own the books in which they do most of their studying, and we thought you might want to do the same. (Many people find it helps to mark and dog-ear the books that mean most to them.)

If you do want to get your books primarily from bookstores rather than libraries, try to use a store with a large stock of higher-priced or "quality" paperbacks; a bookstore at a college in your town will be especially helpful. Be patient rather than discouraged on the occasions when the bookstore does not carry a particular work you want. Bookstores easily can and will order a book for you at no extra charge if you identify it by author, title, and publisher. Since it often takes two to four weeks for special-order books to arrive, you should try to plan ahead (or use library copies in the interim).

If by chance the first bookstore you try cannot or will not help you, talk to the manager of a second or third bookstore about your interests until you find one who will provide the service you want. Many bookstore people will be enthusiastic about your endeavor and glad to assist.

In print and out of print are important terms. Books "in print" are ones available from their publishers' stocks. A book is "out of print" if its publisher has run out of copies and decided against reprinting. Almost all the books given in the Part 2 bibliographies were in print as this book went to press. Any of those identified as out of print may be obtained through libraries or second-hand book dealers.

Books In Print, published annually, is a multi-volume directory that lists every book published in the United States that is in print (and hence available for new-copy purchase) at that time. You will be able to consult a copy of it in almost any library or bookstore. With a library copy, you can use the list of publishers' addresses to order books directly from the publishers. In this case, however, you would have to do the corresponding yourself, and you might not receive books quite as quickly as if you ordered them through a bookstore. Some publishers, regrettably, ignore individual orders for copies of their books.

In the case of well-known works originally written in English, you need not get precisely the edition identified in Part 2. Our editorial advisors at times specified particular editions because they thought the introductions or other critical commentary especially good. But ordinarily little is lost if you study other editions of such works—so long as they are not abridged. However, it will be worth some searching on your part to get a particular translation recommended in Part 2. Poor or outdated translations can be misleading or obscure.

Rather than buying some or all of the books recommended in Part 2, you can, of course, read library copies. Even a small public library should be able to provide most of the books listed if it joins in a regional system of "interlibrary loan." These systems, which are very common, make it possible for all the public and college libraries in a given area to provide borrowers at one library access to books held by any others.

Most librarians are pleased to assist the ambitious endeavors of library users. You might, therefore, do well to explain your interests to a sympathetic librarian, either for help in locating books or just for kindred enthusiasm about books and learning. A librarian might grant extended-loan privileges for works you want to study an unusually long time. And any librarian will explain how to use the card catalog and book collections, as well as guide you to pamphlets and books on the use of libraries.

College libraries in your vicinity may be especially attractive to you, not only for their atmosphere, but also for the character of their collections. Some college libraries charge a modest fee for the use of their facilities by community residents; but you can be certain of access to the library at any college where you enroll even for only one part-time course. A number of the books you may want from a college library, however, may be held "on reserve" and consequently available only for use in the library or for overnight loan. This is true particularly for books required in college courses.

One last aspect of relying on libraries deserves mention. You should not be surprised if a library's copy of a book has the same author, title, and copyright year as are cited in the Part 2 bibliography entry but is issued by a different publisher. Libraries usually acquire hardcover editions of books (for durability) rather than the paperback editions identified in Part 2, and the hardcover and paperback publishers of a book often differ.

SUGGESTIONS ON STUDY TECHNIQUES

Once you are familiar with the various ways in which to obtain books recommended in Part 2, basic suggestions about techniques for studying them may be helpful regardless of your overall study plan. Reading done by capable college students ranges from minutely detailed study and near-memorization to very rapid skimming of whole groups of books—depending on the subject and purpose (and, in the students' case, the time available). College students do not study everything they read at the same pace and with the same concentration.

Books presenting completely new material in the sciences and mathematics or other closely reasoned and technical works in a social science (for example, economics) or one of the humanities (such as philosophy) tend to demand very close, reflective reading. Such detailed attention is also required by major works of literature. You would want to read books like these slowly and thoughtfully, underlining and making marginal notes (if you are using your own copy), pausing to reflect or reread, possibly making notes on separate sheets or cards as you go along, and working problems or answering questions as you come upon them in order to test your comprehension.

Depending on your own purposes, however, it is, often appropriate to read more rapidly and selectively. If, for example, your primary, interest is in the American involvement in the two World Wars, you may need to understand domestic developments between the World Wars, in the decades of the 1920s and 1930s. You might then get half a dozen varied histories on each decade—works in social, economic, and political history—within the United States. These you can skim, going through each group of books in several hours, looking especially at contents listings, introductions, and major conclusions and dipping into selected passages as they catch your interest.

Different reading speeds and degrees of thoroughness are commonly indicated on reading lists given students for college courses. Often such lists are divided into "central" (or "required") and "collateral" (or "supplementary") readings. Students are expected to have thorough knowledge of the matter contained in the central readings but to assimilate collateral readings only in a general or partial way. In your case it will be largely your own interests and study plans that determine which readings will be the most important (central) and which less important (collateral).

After you have absorbed the broad outlines and major features of a given field, you can look forward to mastering other introductory works in it much faster and more readily than at the outset. You should also find it possible to move easily and even enjoyably through more advanced works.

As you do such varied reading, you may wonder whether you will be handicapped by not having the assignments, lectures, class discussions, tests, papers, and other features of traditional college classes. While there may be some drawbacks, much can still be gained from books alone by resourceful and determined readers. Ultimately learning is an internal process, whether you are in a classroom or in your own home; you have the advantage of a special excitement and satisfaction (not to mention flexibility, convenience, and economy) in mastering ideas on your own.

You are likely to want to rely on your own judgment in deciding when you really understand what is covered in any group of books you have chosen from Part 2. Depending on your own judgment is quite defensible. Essentially it is what people do in all their practical and professional reading. Should you, however, want to test your knowledge, a great many widely used examinations are available to determine if people have satisfactorily learned the substance of actual college courses on their own. Two extensive series of them (and where you can write for full information on them) are described in Chapter 4—those in the "College-Level Examination Program" and the "College Proficiency Examination Program." They include tests in English composition, should you want to assess your writing skills.

Still another series of tests may appeal to you; these are the "advanced tests" in the Graduate Record Examinations series. Each of these tests is designed for college graduates who have majored in a given subject; among them, for example, are tests in biology, chemistry, economics, geology, history, English literature, mathematics, philosophy, political science, psychology, and sociology. Many graduate schools require the tests for applicants seeking to earn advanced degrees. Anyone interested may take the "GREs" anywhere in the United States. Information about them may be obtained from Graduate Record Examinations, Educational Testing Service, Box 955, Princeton, N.J. 08540.

Just as you can dispense with examinations, you need not be anxious about your lack of professors to give you the "true secrets" of how to study. There really are no secrets that hold true for all or even most learners. Study skills and methods are highly individual, and most college students develop their own idiosyncratic ways of studying with little help from their teachers. Those who really want to and can understand college readings will also, over time, develop their own study techniques. Moreover, because professors often assume that their students already know how to study (except for those enrolled in specially designated programs), they concentrate their teaching on the substance of the course, usually supplementing and discussing the readings in the light of their own thinking, and rarely say anything about study methods.

If you like, however, you can read one of the various books on study skills often found in bookstores and libraries. You may pick up some ideas or find it interesting to compare your approach with others. Two such works issued in paperback are Robert A. Carman and W. Royce Adams, Jr., *Study Skills: A Student's Guide for Survival* (Wiley, Self-Teaching Guide series, 1972); and Eugene H. Ehrlich, *How to Study Better and Get Higher Marks* (Apollo, 1961; revised T. Y. Crowell hardcover edition, 1976).

You may expect, however, that study skills effective for you will grow rather naturally as you progress in your learning. And as you progress, you will naturally develop habits of analysis that can equal in value the content of what you have learned. These habits or skills will enable you to explore new bodies of material.

You probably stand a particularly good chance of developing newly disciplined habits of thought because of your interest in learning on your own. Students attending college may be goaded into learning by the pressure of quizzes, exams, and assignments and fail to develop confidence in their own ability to continue to learn.

PLANNING YOUR OWN PROGRAM OF STUDY

Now, how might you structure study plans of your own (drawing on chapters in Parts 2) that will be roughly equivalent to typical four-year college programs? How many and what types of books should you select? This may sound like bookkeeping, but it parallels the elaborate systems of academic bookkeeping that colleges often use in setting degree requirements.

As a preliminary step let's consider the overall shape of an undergraduate education. One essential dimension is often described as "breadth." Breadth is generally translated into particular degree requirements often referred to as "distribution requirements."

These requirements commonly call for undergraduates to take one (or more) one-year introductory course in at least two of the three broad liberal arts areas (humanities, social sciences, sciences-mathematics, as indicated by the sections in Part 2). Some colleges require in addition (or instead) completion of courses on the intermediate or advanced levels in one of the liberal arts areas outside the student's major. In meeting these distribution requirements, interdisciplinary courses (such as women's studies or Western civilization) may often be substituted for similar courses in individual subjects.

Other degree requirements outside the major may include physical education or proficiency in reading and writing a foreign language. Many colleges today tend to have lower "breadth" requirements than those outlined above, so that students may tailor their programs of study to individual interests. But equivalent breadth requirements still remain in force at what may be a majority of American colleges.

"Depth" is the other essential dimension of a typical degree program. It is realized largely through requirements for the student's "major" (area of major concentration of study). Requirements for majors in the different subjects are usually set by each college's faculty department in that subject (or by interdepartmental committees). Studies in the major usually occupy at least a fourth to a third of a student's total degree program (that is, of the student's total time spent in classes and studying). Moreover, to assure that the student will know the major area in some depth, major requirements very often call for from two to four courses each on the intermediate and advanced levels. Often some or all the courses are specified.

In recent years many colleges have introduced marked flexibility in requirements for certain kinds of majors. With faculty approval, students may pursue "double" majors (combining work in two departments), interdisciplinary majors (combining work in several departments in order to concentrate in such areas as environmental studies or East Asian studies), or "self-designed" majors (usually interdisciplinary majors along lines not previously established by the faculty). Some work on advanced levels is expected in each of these newer kinds of majors.

In short, a program designed to parallel a typical four-year college program today would have two main parts—the major, for knowledge in depth; and general education choices, for breadth. In addition, you will almost certainly want to make forays into other areas, choosing what for regularly enrolled students are often called "electives." It may be worth noting that students at colleges frequently decide on their majors after getting experience in different fields through courses in general education and electives. You may want to proceed similarly if at first you are undecided on a major field.

Colleges differ widely in the ways they allow students to design their programs. Minimum requirements for a given major tend to be similar, but even these (as well as options for interdisciplinary majors) differ widely; some colleges have strong major offerings and more stringent requirements in certain fields than do many other colleges. But colleges differ far more widely in their general education or distribution requirements and in the proportion of electives they permit.

The University of California at Berkeley seems to represent one extreme, having reduced many of its earlier distribution requirements in 1970. Before that date, its requirements had included four courses in the sciences and four courses of a foreign language. Roderic B. Park, dean of Berkeley's undergraduate college, observed in the mid-1970s, "The language requirement was dropped to two quarters and there was no rule about biological or physical sciences. This means that in a department like history, where some of the classes are listed under humanities, you can take an entire program and graduate and never get outside the major. It's that extreme."

Harvard similarly has few requirements outside the major, and many flexible options for special majors. Henry Rosovsky, dean of the Faculty of Arts and Sciences, observed that the Harvard College curriculum has more and more "tended to multiply options and reduce requirements." He then posed the question, "Will this faculty be satisfied with a B.A. degree that is basically a 'certificate of attendance' at Harvard? It can be—indeed, it has been—argued that whatever our rules and regulations say, we are very close to providing such a degree at the present time."

Columbia College illustrates the other extreme of heavy general education requirements. Peter R. Pouncey, dean of the college, has stated, "The college retains the most structured curriculum left in the country: 52 of the 124 points [credits] prescribed for the degree must go to meeting requirements apart from the major, whether in specific courses such as humanities or contemporary civilization, or in a range of options such as the language requirement [two full years of one of 60 foreign languages]."

You thus have distinguished precedents for shaping your study plan of readings from Chapters in Part 2 in widely varying ways and still accomplishing the kind and amount of study completed by students to earn bachelor's degrees. In an approach like the one taken at Berkeley you might draw almost all your readings from any one chapter in Part 2 (on a subject or area), and read only a few works listed in chapters of other sections of Part 2. In a method similar to the Harvard plan you might read widely from many chapters of Part 2 (probably also doing advanced readings in several areas and organizing your readings around an intellectual interest—for example, science and civilization, or the arts in different cultures and eras). Or, in following an approach such as Columbia's you can do a third or more of your readings in introductory-intermediate books across humanities and social science chapters (and Western civilization) and go on into many advanced works in a chapter (or chapters) you choose as your major.

Now for some bookkeeping details. How many volumes should you study in order to conclude that you have acquired the learning of a typical four-year college education? Using the Berkeley mode as a touchstone, you might do most of your readings in the works listed in a chapter of Part 2 you have selected as your major. Almost all of these cite readings of a scope you would find characteristic of rather strong major offerings in each field at one or another college. These chapters vary in the number of books they include; those in the sciences and mathematics each tend to list some 30 to perhaps 75 books (all calling for very close, detailed study), while chapters in the humanities and social science areas tend to list from 100 to 150 or more books.

Speaking generally, you will have acquired knowledge typical of that gained by students majoring in a given field if you know rather thoroughly between half to two-thirds of the books across the full range of an extensive chapter and if you sample or skim some of the other books in the chapter. In your major, then, you would master from 15 to perhaps 40 books in the case of a science or from 50 to 80 or 100 or more books in one of the humanities or social sciences. (In a science you should actually take some college laboratory courses if you want to parallel very closely the work of student work in college.)

The Berkeley model also included some work outside the major. For these general education and elective studies, you may want to choose two or three areas (chapters) distinctly different from your major and get to know well from 10 to 20 or more books on the introductory and possibly intermediate levels in each. If you want more breadth in your learning, you can plan your studies to include some readings from each of the three broad liberal arts areas (the humanities, social sciences, and sciences-mathematics).

If you are seriously interested in learning on your own, you will presumably want to go beyond the minimal requirements and explore for yourself. It is not our intention to justify the idea that a college degree consists of a certain number of books read or courses taken, but rather to give you a realistic sense of what current degree requirements may include. The best undergraduates almost always do more than what is required—they venture into allied fields, they write senior essays (theses) or design special projects; in short, they are "on their own" even when they are enrolled in college.

You may be wondering how much time you would or should spend to get a college education of the kind roughly outlined here. There is no single answer to this question. The amount of time needed or spent in individual study varies enormously from college to college and even from student to student in the same course at the same college.

As a very general rule of thumb, colleges often suggest that students study one or two hours outside class for each hour of class instruction. Some students manage to earn the bachelor's degree with an average of only one hour's outside study or less; other students want to, or must, put in four or more hours' study for each hour of classroom instruction, either in some courses or throughout their college years.

Converting these facts into total hours, we find that a typical student taking a full-time program will be enrolled for some 400 to 450 hours of instruction in class through an academic year (15 hours a week for 27 to 30 weeks). Outside study in readings would accordingly range from 400 to 900 hours a year. Over a four-year college education, outside study would run to a total of 1,600 to 3,600 hours.

The likelihood of your having time of this order depends on what you like and what you want, as well as on your day-to-day schedule. If you now spend an hour or more a day on reading newspapers while commuting to work, or on watching television programs simply to pass time, and if you were to spend no more than that time on serious, exciting books to enlarge your intellectual powers, you would be spending 300 or 400 hours a year in study. In about four years, while still doing everything else you are now about in your life, you would then be able to complete most or all of the studying in books carried out in a typical college education. You would have acquired the essential or central learning of a college education—an education to which college graduates would have had to devote most of their efforts over the same four years.

This four-year estimate hinges on the lower, 1,600-hour end of the range of total hours spent in college study, as you will note. This amount may be reasonable because you are presumably more highly motivated than typical college students, and possibly more experienced in managing your time. Unlike students whose goal is purely a degree, you should have the satisfaction of knowing that any part of college learning you accomplish is a positive gain, valuable and interesting in itself. This factor can buoy your enthusiasm and keep it up through an effort of any length—one lasting for only a few weeks, or one going on year after year as an integral part of your intellectual life.

You may be interested in seeing some concrete, detailed examples of full four-year college programs at specific colleges outlined in terms of readings from chapters in Part 2. Three such examples are given in the rest of this chapter. They involve colleges with widely typical bachelor's requirements, which go from the extreme of slight demands outside the major (as in the earlier Berkeley and Harvard illustrations) to heavy demands (as at Columbia).

The first example outlines a program that a student majoring in sociology can follow in meeting requirements for the Bachelor of Arts degree at the College of Letters and Science at the University of Wisconsin-Madison. This illustrative program, framed according to requirements as they stood in the early 1970s, assumes that the student had developed intermediate-level proficiency in a foreign language (a B.A. requirement) while still in high school.

The choice of specific courses shown in the program can be varied greatly according to a student's interests and still satisfy the requirements of a major in sociology. Wisconsin's B.A. requirements include a total of 120 credits, 40 of which must be distributed (for "breadth")

...anities, social sciences, and sciences; for "depth," the ...r requirement is 30 credits, with a number of specified courses or areas, plus at least 20 credits in other social sciences and at least 80 credits outside sociology. As you can see, these Wisconsin requirements tend toward the extreme of heavy demands in general education outside the major.

We are reproducing the program with actual course numbers and titles as they might appear on the student's college transcript (complete academic record) from freshman through senior year. (In the listing below, the approximate average of three credits per course is assumed number of later courses are given. An asterisk after the course follows the with a second listing which translates the program of courses, into the form of readings in Part 2.

ONE POSSIBLE SOCIOLOGY MAJOR'S PROGRAM FOR THE B.A.— COURSE NUMBERS & TITLES

College of Letters and Science, University of Wisconsin-Madison

FRESHMAN YEAR

Eng. 101	Freshman English
Soc. 210*	An Introduction to Sociology
Bio. 101	Concepts in Biology
Anth. 101	General Anthropology
Phil. 101	Introduction to Philosophy
Psych. 201	Introduction to Psychology
Hist. 101	American History 1607–1865
Soc. 134*	Problems of American Minority Groups
Soc. 450*	Introduction to Social Theory
Eng. 200	Introduction to Literature

SOPHOMORE YEAR

Art 141	Ancient & Medieval Art
Phys. 101	General Physics
Soc. 357*	Methods of Sociological Inquiry
Stat. 201	Principles of Statistics
Eng. 205	English Literature
Geol. 100	General Geology
Art 102	Renaissance to Modern Art
Soc. 538*	Small Groups
Soc. 640*	Sociology of the Family
Econ. 101	General Economics

JUNIOR YEAR

Soc. 476*	Contemporary Social Thought
Soc. 543*	Collective Behavior
Anth. 200	Cultural Anthropology
Soc. 624*	Political Sociology
Anth. 330*	Topics in Ethnology
Hist 111	Ancient History
Eng. 253	Studies in Narrative Literature
Psych. 530	Introductory Social Psychology
Psych. 538	Group Dynamics

SENIOR YEAR

Anth. 349	Culture Contact and Acculturation
Stat. 202	Principles of Statistics
Soc. 644*	Capitalism & Socialism
Soc. 677*	Urbanism and Urbanization
Poli Sci 476	Political Leadership
Hist. 127	The World in the 20th Century
Soc. 537*	Social Behavior Dynamics
Soc. 648*	Sociology of Education
Env. 101	Forum on the Environment
Econ. 366	Comparative Economic Systems

The same sociology major's program can be translated into specific readings, drawn from chapters in Part 2. Major headings in this listing correspond to section titles and subordinate headings are chapter titles in Part 2. Each chapter title is followed by the topic subheadings given in the bibliographies. The order of suggested readings generally proceeds from introductory to advanced within each field but otherwise does not reflect any recommended sequence for your study.

After each topic a number indicates how many books you might want to study as central or basic readings. These roughly estimated numbers represent our judgment of the minimum number of books students at colleges are generally expected to read in a course which approximately corresponds to each topic. (The estimates most definitely do not represent books on actual course reading lists used at the University of Wisconsin.)

Our estimates reflect a frequent departure of reading lists in Part 2 from college practice. Introductory courses at colleges often center around a single textbook (and may also include a number of collateral or supplementary readings in other books). By contrast, lists in Part 2 generally omit college texts, instead recommending introductory books that have been written for general readers by recognized scholars. In the listing below we accordingly often show a few such general books to be read as introductory to a field instead of a single textbook.

In addition, our estimates do not reflect a feature commonly found in course reading lists—that of identifying only certain chapters or parts of some books to be read, in either central or collateral books. As suggested in the earlier section of the chapter on different ways of reading, you can limit yourself to parts of some books in the light of your own interests and of notes on the books in Part 2 reading lists.

The estimated numbers of books (in this and the two following listings) should be viewed as only the most general of guides. Professors naturally tend to want students to read widely in any course and often give students lists citing many more books than are indicated in our estimates; some of the best students among those for whom a given course is especially important will do a great deal of the reading recommended by a professor. But because the ability and time of many students are limited, professors develop a realistic idea of the minimum learning any student must have to pass the course. Our estimated numbers reflect roughly such minimum learning. You should, of course, feel free to read widely beyond the scope indicated here, for your own central readings and especially for your collateral readings.

ONE POSSIBLE
SOCIOLOGY MAJOR'S PROGRAM—
PART 2 READINGS

College of Letters and Science,
University of Wisconsin-Madison

Part 2 Section/Chapter/topic	Central Readings (approximate no. of books)
SECTION B. THE SOCIAL SCIENCES	
Chapter 15. Sociology	
introductory sociology	3
small groups	3
class and stratification (minority groups)	4
sociology of the family	3
selected theoretical works	3
social psychology	3
modern works	3
collective behavior/social movements	3
political sociology	3
urban studies	3
sociology of education	3
the new critics	2
selected general works	4
Chapter 9. Anthropology	
general and historical anthropology	3
social organization	2
cultural anthropology	3
ethnographies	4

Chapter 10. Economics
    introductory works   3
    comparative economic systems   3
Chapter 11. American History
    colonial development to a nation divided   7
    1900–the present   7
Chapter 12. Black American History
    surveys   1
    civil rights   1
    Black militancy and the Black now   3
Chapter 13. Political Science
    the executive   1
    international relations and organization   2
Chapter 14. Psychology
    introductory psychology   2
    social psychology   3
    interpersonal communication   2
    social motivation   1

SECTION C. THE HUMANITIES
Chapter 18. English Composition
    general work   1
Chapter 17. American Literature
    selected works   8
Chapter 19. English Literature
    selected works   8
Chapter 16. Art History
    ancient & medieval art   3
    renaissance to modern art   3
Chapter 21. Philosophy
    introductory philosophy   2

SECTION A. INTERDISCIPLINARY AREAS
Chapter 7. Western Civilization
    ancient history   2
    the twentieth century   5
Chapter 6. Environmental Studies
    introductory and selected works   4

SECTION D. THE SCIENCES AND MATHEMATICS
Chapter 22. Biology
    introductory works   2
Chapter 25. Mathematics
    probability and statistics   2
Chapter 26. Physics
    basic physics   2

The second example will be of special interest to someone who prefers acquiring the knowledge of a science major. It outlines the Part

2 readings approximately equivalent to the knowledge gained by a student who has earned the B.A. degree with a major in biology at the University of Redlands in Southern California.

This listing is patterned to reflect studies meeting Redlands' requirements of the early 1970s for such a degree. Those requirements call for a total of 120 "units" (credits), with at least six units in each of the three broad liberal arts areas (the humanities, social sciences, and sciences) plus fulfillment of major requirements. They represent roughly an intermediate position between the extremes of slight and heavy demands outside the major. Redlands also offers options for B.A. "nonmajor" programs in which a student (with faculty approval) would not have to meet requirements for a major with heavy concentration in one area as shown here. Johnson College of Redlands (distinct from its Main Campus) provides for still more flexible bachelor's degree programs.

ONE POSSIBLE
BIOLOGY MAJOR'S PROGRAM—
PART 2 READINGS

Main Campus, University of Redlands

Part 2 Section/Chapter/Topic	Central Readings (approx. no. of books)
SECTION D. THE SCIENCES AND MATHEMATICS	
Chapter 22. Biology	
general biology—introductory works	2
general biology—introductory & intermediate works in topics:	
molecules and cells	1
physiology	1
genetics and evolution	1
plants and environment	1
animal kingdom	1
populations and behavior	1
ecology (intermediate)	1
embryology (intermediate)	1
genetics (intermediate)	1
cell biology (intermediate)	1
population genetics (advanced)	2
Chapter 24. Physics	
introductory physics	1
Chapter 25. Mathematics	
precalculus with introduction to analysis	2
calculus	1
computer programming	1

SECTION B. THE SOCIAL SCIENCES

Chapter 15. Sociology
   introductory sociology   3
Chapter 9. Anthropology
   introductory anthropology   3
Chapter 14. Psychology
   introductory psychology   2
Chapter 13. Political Science
   American government and politics   5
   political structure and processes   2
   international relations—general books   1
   classic works   3
Chapter 11. American History
   the colonial period   5
Chapter 12. Black American History
   1900 to the present   4

SECTION A. INTERDISCIPLINARY AREAS

Chapter 7. Western Civilization
   Europe since 1945   5
Chapter 8. Women's Studies
   selected works (introductory; comprehensive)   4

SECTION C. THE HUMANITIES

Chapter 16. Art History
   20th century art (survey works)   2
Chapter 19. English Literature
   selected works (different periods)   7
Chapter 21. Philosophy
   introductory philosophy   4
   ethics   3
   alternative conceptual schemes (phil. of science)   2

A third and last example shows a body of readings in Part 2 to illustrate a widely popular major—English. The listing is designed to reflect requirements for the B.A. with a major in English at Grinnell College in Iowa in the early 1970s.

After Grinnell abolished its former course and distribution requirements in 1970, it called for the completion of 124 credits of study as almost its only formally stated requirement for awarding the B.A. It thus represents a college which requires few courses outside the major. The school, however, urges each student to carry out at least basic studies in each of the three broad liberal arts areas. This recommendation is reflected in the listing. Because Grinnell considers psychology a science, the listing cuts across all three areas as Grinnell defines them.

Grinnell also expects each student to select one of three types of majors—conventional (in an individual subject; chosen by a large majority of Grinnell students), interdisciplinary (such as American studies or general science) or independent (that is, student-designed).

Requirements for a major in English at Grinnell call for 32 or more credits, 8 of which may be earned in related departments.

ONE POSSIBLE
ENGLISH MAJOR'S PROGRAM—
PART 2 READINGS
Grinnell College

Part 2 Section/Chapter/Topic	Central Readings (approx. no. of books)
SECTION C. THE HUMANITIES	
Chapter 19. English Literature	
Medieval literature	2
Renaissance literature	3
Shakespeare (plays and criticism)	5
the British novel	14
basic critical readings	3
further critical readings	4
Chapter 18. English Composition/Creative Writing	
introductory study and practice	1
intermediate study and practice	3
advanced study and practice	3
Chapter 20. American Literature	
poetry (major poets of different periods)	3
fiction before 1890	7
fiction since 1890	7
Chapter 16. Art History	
introductory survey, Europe and America	3
Chapter 21. Philosophy	
introductory philosophy	4
SECTION A. INTERDISCIPLINARY AREAS	
Chapter 5. East Asian Civilizations	
introductory study (survey, ancient times to the present)	8
Chapter 6. Environmental Studies	
introductory study (focus on influence of science and society on the environment)	2
Chapter 7. Western Civilization	
introductory study (survey, ancient times to the present)	8
Chapter 8. Women's Studies	
women's roles in American history and literature	3

SECTION B. THE SOCIAL SCIENCES

Chapter 9. Anthropology
    introductory anthropology   2
    cultural anthropology   4
Chapter 10. Economics
    introductory economics   2
    economic development   3
Chapter 11. American History
    introductory study (broad survey)   2
    colonial period   3
    Federal period through the Civil War   4
Chapter 12. Black American History
    introductory study (broad survey)   2
Chapter 13. Political Science
    political thought in the 20th century   4
Chapter 14. Psychology
    introductory psychology   2
    developmental psychology   3
Chapter 15. Sociology
    introductory sociology   2
    social psychology   2
    economic and political sociology
      (urban emphasis)   5

We hope that these three examples will give you an idea of the kind of study plan you can make for yourself if you want to gain the breadth and depth of knowledge acquired by a typical college undergraduate. As you can see, the three listings each amount to only small fragments of all the learning possible by using the chapters in Part 2, to say nothing of all the learning you may ultimately wish to do.

This realization (both now and as you go along) should not be disheartening—being aware of what you do not know is surely as important as being aware of what you do know. True education is a humbling experience.

Chapter Four

HOW YOU CAN DO IT— FOR CREDITS AND DEGREES

Many avenues are open today to anyone wishing to earn course credits and degrees as recognition of studies carried out independently. The following pages contain a brief guide to such degree programs. If you do enter one of them, you will want to follow its specific recommendations as to what to read. The reading guides in this book were designed by the individual editorial advisors, and no effort was made to have the readings reflect the recommendations or practice of any one program or college.

EXAMINATION PROGRAMS
TO EARN CREDIT FOR STUDY ON YOUR OWN

COLLEGE-LEVEL EXAMINATION PROGRAM
COLLEGE ENTRANCE EXAMINATION BOARD
888 SEVENTH AVENUE
NEW YORK, NY 10019

Very widely available means of earning college credits on your own are offered by CLEP—the College-Level-Examination Program of the College Entrance Examination Board. About 1,700 colleges and universities in all 50 states have their own policies for awarding credits on the basis of CLEP scores. Many will grant credit equivalent to one year or two years of full-time study for satisfactory performance on CLEP examinations. It is not uncommon for persons past their early twenties to receive a year's worth of credits on CLEP examinations and then pursue degrees through part-time study at colleges.

CLEP itself awards no credit. It only provides examinations that may qualify the student for credit from specific colleges or programs that recognize the CLEP method.

You can prepare for CLEP examinations on your own (or test to see if you are already prepared for some) with the help of a substantial booklet ordered from the program, *CLEP General and Subject Examinations; Descriptions and Sample Questions.* The booklet describes topics and points covered in each examination, but it does not identify specific books to be studied. It includes many practice questions with explanations of correct answers.

You can take CLEP examinations at one of 800 test centers at colleges throughout the country; they are offered monthly. If you are on active duty in military service, you can also arrange to take them at any military installation around the world. Civilians outside the United States can also make advance arrangements for testing at a location convenient to them. Fees range from $20 for one examination to $40 for five and $80 for nine taken in the same monthly period of several testing days. The applicant must register to take examinations three or more weeks in advance.

Each CLEP general examination lasts an hour and offers multiple-choice questions. Adults who have already read widely can often do well on these with little further study. Scores above minimum levels stipulated by the college can be worth almost a year's course credits at a number of colleges (as examples in Chapter 2 illustrate). The five examinations are in the areas of English Composition, Humanities, Mathematics, Natural Sciences, and Social Sciences and History. (Revised versions of these five—each with a ninety-minute time limit— will be introduced in the fall of 1978.)

CLEP also offers many "subject" examinations (47 in 1977). Each typically covers the work of a specific college course in a liberal arts or professional subject. Each 90-minute examination contains multiple-choice questions. Many offer additional 90-minute essay examinations, but you would take these only at the request of a college from which you want credit. Among the subject examinations are

Accounting, Introductory
Afro-American History
American Government
American History
American Literature
Anatomy, Physiology, Microbiology (for nursing students)
Behaviorial Science for Nurses
Biology
Business Law, Introductory
Business Management, Introduction to
Calculus with Analytic Geometry
Chemistry, General
College Algebra
College Algebra-Trigonometry
Computer Programming, Elementary: Fortran IV
Computers and Data Processing
Economics (3 examinations: Introductory Macroeconomics, Introductory Microeconomics, Introductory Micro- and Macroeconomics)

Educational Psychology
English Composition
English Literature
Freshman English
Fundamentals of Nursing
Geology
History of American Education
Human Growth and Development
Literature, Analysis and Interpretation of
Marketing, Introductory
Medical-Surgical Nursing
Medical Technology (4 examinations: Clinical Chemistry, Hematology, Immunohematology and Blood Banking, Microbiology)
Money and Banking
Psychology, General
Sociology, Introductory
Statistics
Tests and Measurements
Trigonometry
Western Civilization

CLEP was introduced in 1965 by the association of 2,000 colleges and secondary schools that is often informally called the College Board. CLEP was a natural outgrowth of the College Board's Advanced Placement Program (AP), through which able students go on into college-level courses given in their high schools and take AP examinations to receive credit from colleges they later attend.

COLLEGE PROFICIENCY EXAMINATION PROGRAM
STATE EDUCATION DEPARTMENT
99 WASHINGTON AVENUE
ALBANY, NY 12230

or, outside New York State nation-wide
ACT PROFICIENCY EXAMINATION PROGRAM
AMERICAN COLLEGE TESTING PROGRAM
BOX 168
IOWA CITY, IOWA 52240

You also have nation-wide opportunities for earning college credits on your own through the large examination program known as "CPEP" in New York State and "PEP" throughout the rest of the country. (The program's formal name in New York State, which introduced it, is the College Proficiency Examination Program; its name outside New York is the Proficiency Examination Program.)

Examinations covering knowledge typically learned in college courses in a wide variety of subjects are offered in CPEP/PEP. Most examinations are about three hours in length. A large majority of colleges in New York State and many colleges in other states have policies for awarding credit on the basis of these examinations. They are given nation-wide by the American College Testing Program (ACT), which offers college entrance tests and related services used by thousands of colleges and schools and more than a million students a year.

CPEP/PEP examinations are offered at test centers throughout the country during two-day test administrations scheduled four times a year, in February, May, August and November. Fees range from $20 to $50 for most of the examinations.

Detailed descriptions of the examinations, and study guides suggesting specific books as helpful in preparing for each examination, are available on request. Among CPEP/PEP examinations are the following.

ARTS AND SCIENCES
African and Afro-American History
American History
American Literature: The Beginnings to the Civil War
American Literature: The Civil War to the Present
Anatomy and Physiology
Applied Music (voice or instrumental performance, judged by a panel of college music teachers)
Biology
Earth Science
European History
Freshman English
Shakespeare

CRIMINAL JUSTICE
Introduction to Criminal Justice
Criminal Investigation

BUSINESS
Accounting (3 examinations: Levels I, II, III)
Finance (Levels I, II, III)
Management of Human Resources (Levels I, II, III)
Marketing (Levels I, II, III)
Operations Management (Levels I, II, III)
Business Environment and Strategy

EDUCATION
Educational Psychology
History of American Education
Philosophy of Education
Reading Instruction in the Elementary School
Corrective and Remedial Instruction in Reading
Diagnosis and Remediation of Reading Problems

HEALTH EDUCATION SCIENCES
Health I: Personal Health—Physical Aspects
Health II: Personal Health—Emotional-Social Aspects
Health III: Public-Environmental Health

FOREIGN LANGUAGES
(the Proficiency Tests for Teachers and Advanced Students of the Modern Language Association, a two-part examination in each language)
French
German
Italian
Russian
Spanish

NURSING CPEs
Adult Nursing
Fundamentals of Nursing
Maternal and Child Nursing (Associate Degree and Baccalaureate Degree Levels)
Medical-Surgical Nursing
Psychiatric-Mental Health Nursing

ASSOCIATE IN NURSING REGENTS EXTERNAL DEGREE EXAMINATIONS
Commonalities in Nursing Care: Areas I and II
Differences in Nursing Care: Areas I, II and III
Nursing Health Care
Occupational Strategy (Nursing)
Clinical Performance (a two-and-a-half day examination)

CPEP was established by the Board of Regents of The University of the State of New York in 1961 and its first examinations were given in 1963. Its success led to the founding of the Regents External Degree Program in 1970.

PROGRAMS OFFERING CREDITS AND DEGREES FOR STUDY THAT CAN BE DONE ENTIRELY ON YOUR OWN

BOARD FOR STATE ACADEMIC AWARDS
340 CAPITOL AVENUE
HARTFORD, CT 06115

You can earn an associate in arts or associate in science degree (normally awarded on graduation from a two-year college after study in the arts and sciences), or the bachelor of arts or bachelor of science degree, entirely by examination in the program of the Board for State Academic Awards. Introduced as the newest unit of the Connecticut state system of higher education in 1973, it provides means for you to earn recognized college degrees entirely by self-study. You can also meet some or all of its degree requirements by credit from college courses you have taken (or will take) as well as from courses and examinations taken in military service.

Examinations recognized for credit in the program include CLEP and PEP. Provision is also made for awarding credit by special assessment examination in areas of learning for which no established examinations are available. Anyone located in any part of the country or the world may enroll if the person seems likely to be able to meet degree requirements through examinations or completion of courses.

Information booklets and pamphlets are available at public libraries throughout Connecticut as well as from the Board's office. Study guides identifying specific books helpful in preparing for the examinations are provided on request. Fees are modest (currently, $50 for enrollment, $25 for annual records maintenance after the first 18 months, $10 for graduation).

REGENTS EXTERNAL DEGREE PROGRAM OF THE UNIVERSITY OF THE STATE OF NEW YORK
99 WASHINGTON AVENUE
ALBANY, NY 12230

You can qualify for any one of a variety of associate's and bachelor's degrees entirely through study on your own by making use of the Regents External Degree Program. The earliest program to open this possibility, in 1970, it is also the largest such program, having by now awarded more than 5,000 degrees and grown to a current enrollment of more than 13,000 persons.

Among the degrees for which it now offers programs are

Associate in Arts
Associate in Science
Associate in Applied Science (nursing)
Associate in Science (nursing)
Bachelor of Arts
Bachelor of Science
Bachelor of Science (business administration)
Bachelor of Science (nursing)

Anyone may enroll. Persons in all parts of the country are registered in the program.

Examinations recognized for credit include CLEP, CPEP, and RED examinations, the extensive series of examinations provided by the Armed Forces especially for their personnel, and the Graduate Record Examinations administered by Educational Testing Service.

Credits are also awarded for appropriate course work done in colleges, military service, or even corporate employment. Credit thus earned in a wide variety of ways may be centrally recorded and made available in transcript form by using the program's "Regents credit bank." Learning at the college level in areas for which appropriate examinations are not available can be evaluated and awarded credit through "special assessment" carried out by college faculty members.

A major source of information about the program is its extensive annual catalog, *College Proficiency Examinations; Regents External Degrees*. Examination study guides identifying specific books to consult are also available on request. Current fees are $50 for enrollment, $25 for annual records maintenance after the first year, and $10 for graduation.

The Regents of The University of the State of New York, a governmental body unique to New York State, sponsors the program. The Regents board is responsible for all education in the state. Colleges and universities derive their authority to grant degrees from charters and approvals issued by the Regents.

THOMAS A. EDISON COLLEGE
FORRESTAL ROAD
PRINCETON, N.J. 08540

Identifying itself as "The New Jersey State College for External Degrees," Edison College offers various degrees available entirely through self-study. These include

Associate in Arts
Associate in Applied Science in Management
Associate in Applied Science in Radiologic Technology
Bachelor of Arts
Bachelor of Science in Business Administration

Edison was established and enrolled its first student in 1972. Imposing no entrance requirements, it has attracted registrants from many parts of the country and the world. If you are in or near New Jersey, you may find it helpful to meet with one of the Edison College academic counselors at widespread locations throughout the state. They can furnish informal evaluation of your previous education and help in planning further education either on your own or at other New Jersey colleges.

Edison recognizes both course work (in military service and employment as well as in colleges) and performance on examinations for credit. Among types of examinations for which it awards credit are CLEP, CPEP, College Board Advanced Placement, special Armed Forces series, and those of a recently introduced examination program of its own, TECEP (Thomas Edison College Examination Program, which initially includes examinations in business administration, foreign languages, and radiologic or x-ray technology).

Examination study guides identifying specific books and detailed descriptions of examinations are provided on request. Individual assessment can be used to evaluate the value in credits of learning for which appropriate examinations are not available. Full current information about Edison College is given in its annual catalog.

Edison was founded as the ninth state college in New Jersey by the state's Board of Higher Education; it operates under its own board of trustees.

PROGRAMS OFFERING CREDITS
AND DEGREES FOR STUDY THAT CAN BE
DONE SUBSTANTIALLY ON YOUR OWN

Individual colleges in increasing numbers are introducing programs in which substantial parts of the student's degree-credit study can be carried out off-campus, without conventional class attendance but under the general supervision of faculty members. These programs are offered for students of the traditional 18-to-22 college age who prefer independent study as well as for older people who find it difficult to attend classes.

This section accordingly identifies and characterizes only a few of the larger and better-known programs of this kind. Similar programs may exist in your own vicinity.

EMPIRE STATE COLLEGE OF
THE STATE UNIVERSITY OF NEW YORK
SARATOGA SPRINGS, NY 12866

You can complete work for a degree entirely on your own, except for meeting monthly or every few months with a faculty advisor, through Empire State College. Empire State has no campus and conducts no classes, but it makes its advisors available at some 20 learning centers and units of the college throughout the state. It accordingly enrolls students throughout New York as well as ones from other states and even foreign countries who can manage to meet periodically with their advisors.

Flexible programs for associate's and bachelor's degrees can be carried out by Empire State students. They progress and are awarded credit through "learning contracts" worked out with their advisors (called "mentors"). These contracts define programs of study to be completed in a specified time. The programs can, for example, include conventional courses at other colleges, individual study validated by written papers or examinations, independent research reports in connection with work or travel, and work in the creative arts. Students may register for working on a full-time, half-time or quarter-time basis.

EXTERNAL DEGREE PROGRAM OF THE
CALIFORNIA STATE UNIVERSITY AND COLLEGES
5670 WILSHIRE BOULEVARD
LOS ANGELES, CA 90036

At least eight of the nineteen campuses of the California State University and Colleges system allow students to enroll in external-degree programs designed for Californians who are not within easy commuting distance of the campus or whose schedules do not permit them to spend large amounts of time attending classes. Some seminars, meetings, and classes on campus are required, however. Campuses offering such programs (for the bachelor of arts in business administration, unless otherwise noted) include:

California State University, Chico; Chico, CA 95926
California State University, Hayward; Hayward, CA 94542
California State University, Sacramento; Sacramento, CA 95819
San Francisco State University; San Fransisco, CA 94132
San Jose State University; San Jose, CA 95192
California State College, Dominguez Hills (B.A., M.A. in the Humanities); Dominguez Hills, CA 90747
California State University, Long Beach (M.A. in Vocational Education); Long Beach, CA 90840
California State College, Sonoma (B.A. in Liberal Arts); Rohnert Park, CA 94928

UNIVERSITY WITHOUT WALLS
UNION FOR EXPERIMENTING COLLEGES AND UNIVERSITIES
ANTIOCH COLLEGE
YELLOW SPRINGS, OH 45387

Some 30 colleges or centers across the country have developed individual versions of the "university without walls" program, coordinated by a central office. UWW programs at individual colleges vary greatly in focus and provisions, but a feature common to all is the opportunity to carry out significant amounts of work toward the degree away from campus (in field work, social service, special research, or action projects and travel, as well as in reading and study). Union Graduate School at the central office makes it possible to earn masters' and doctoral degrees through equally diverse activities.

Information about UWW programs may be obtained either from the central office or from a participating college. Among colleges and centers with UWW programs are

University of Alabama, New College; University, AL 35486
Antioch College/West; 3663 Sacramento St., San Francisco, CA 94118
Antioch College/Philadelphia; 1227 Walnut St., Philadelphia, PA 19107
Bard College; Annondale-on-Hudson, NY 12504
University Without Walls/Berkeley; 2700 Bancroft Way, Berkeley, CA 94704
Chicago State University; 95th and King Dr., Chicago, IL 60628
University Without Walls/Flaming Rainbow; P.O. Box 154, Tahlequah, OK 74464
Florida International University/Miami Dade Community College; 300 N.E. Second Ave., Miami, FL 33132
Franconia College; Franconia, NH 03580
Friends World College; Plover Lane, Huntington, NY 11743
Goddard College; Plainfield, VT 05677
Hispanic International University; 3602 Navigation, Houston, TX 77003

Hofstra University; Hempstead, NY 11559
Johnston College, University of Redlands; Redlands, CA 92373
Loretto Heights College; 3001 S. Federal Blvd., Denver, CO 80236
University of Massachusetts; Amherst, MA 01022
University of Minnesota; Minneapolis, MN 55455
Morgan State College, Urban Regional Learning Center; Baltimore, MD
    21212
Northeastern Illinois University; Bryn Mawr at St. Louis Avenues,
    Chicago, IL 60625
University of the Pacific; Stockton, CA 95204
Pitzer College; Claremont, CA 91711
Roger Williams College; 35 Richmond St., Providence, RI 02903
Shaw University; Raleigh, NC 27602
Skidmore College; Saratoga Springs, NY 12866
Stephens College; Columbia, MO 65201
Westminster College; Fulton, MO 65251
University of Wisconsin at Green Bay; Green Bay, WI 54302
Universidad Boricua; 1766 Church St., Washington, DC 20036
Universidad de Campesinos Libres; 841 W. Belmont Ave., Fresno, CA
    20036

OTHER SOURCES FOR COLLEGE LEARNING
SUBSTANTIALLY ON YOUR OWN

There are still many other sources from which you can obtain college
credits and degrees for learning substantially on your own. Again,
programs such as those described above are spreading steadily, and
one or more colleges in your vicinity may have similar offerings. Two
pioneer programs of this kind are the independent study program of
Syracuse University (Syracuse, NY 13202) and the College of Liberal
Studies Programs at the University of Oklahoma (Norman, OK 73069).
The University of Maryland, Rutgers University, and the University of
Houston recently introduced programs offering American adaptations
of the Open University, Britain's nonresidential college for adults. The
State University of Nebraska has begun an ambitious "SUN" program
to make largely nonresidential college studies available to adults
across a group of Midwestern states.

If you feel you want the help of lesson-by-lesson guidance and
evaluation in your self-study, you may be interested in correspondence
courses offered by many colleges (including Empire State). A full list of
those colleges and the correspondence courses they offer can be ordered from Independent Study Division, National University Extension Association, One Dupont Circle, Suite 360, Washington, DC
20036.

Clearly, many different avenues are open today to college learning
on your own. One of the most satisfying ways of all, though, begins on
the next page.

Part Two

A Guide to Contemporary Fields of College Study

THE ARTS
AND SCIENCES
Using These Chapters

The Arts and Sciences

For several centuries what might be called the core knowledge of our civilization has been organized in fields of learning generally called the arts and sciences (or liberal arts and sciences). Thought in these fields seems fundamental or central to more specialized forms of human inquiry, as biology is to medicine, for example, or economics to business. This guide to fields of college study today extends across the arts and sciences, presenting chapters on them in customary groupings.

The section called Interdisciplinary Areas presents guides to several of the fields especially popular among students who choose to do much of their learning in areas that integrate knowledge and techniques drawn from a number of traditionally distinct scholarly specialties. Such interdisciplinary areas treated here are East Asian civilizations, environmental studies, Western civilization, and women's studies. The section on the social sciences includes fields in which human societies are studied in the spirit of the "physical" or "natural" sciences—including anthropology, economics, history, political science, psychology (sometimes classified as a science), and sociology. The section dealing with the traditional humanities includes chapters on modern descendants of fields that flourished some five centuries ago in the European Renaissance, the fields of human-centered (rather than theologically centered) learning called humane or humanistic learning. The humanities at present include studies of the arts, literature and philosophy.

Perhaps the most familiar category is the remaining one, sciences. Among them are biology, chemistry, geology and other earth sciences, physics, and mathematics (which is often grouped with the sciences, though it is unique in several respects).

These Chapters

Each introduction to a chapter in Part 2 has been written to present a general idea of the field treated in the chapter. These brief essays characterize the fields as they are typically studied by undergraduates today, identifying major branches or bodies of knowledge encompassed by the field. To help guide your study, the essays often outline typical sequences in which students advance in the field or suggest sequences you may choose to follow. Points that may be helpful to you in learning on your own are noted when they seem particularly important to the subject. Some essays sketch historical perspectives or schools of thought in the field. Essays frequently include explanatory comments on special features of the subsequent bibliographies.

Bibliographies in each chapter extend from typical freshman-year studies through advanced works for majors (except for the shorter chapters on English Composition/Creative Writing and film, which present relatively fewer advanced works). Wherever feasible, the books listed in the bibliographies are available in paperback editions. Paperbacks, used extensively by students today, are generally inexpensive and widely available.

A bookstore that does not stock any of the books you want should be able to order them. You can also order any of them directly from their publishers, obtaining the proper addresses with the help of a reference librarian (one source is *Books in Print,* Bowker, annual editions). You can, of course, find many of the books in libraries, which should also be able to help you locate any of the few articles in scholarly journals that are cited. You will have to depend on libraries (or second-hand book dealers) for any of the few out-of-print books.

Throughout each bibliography, notes comment on or characterize each book; occasionally a note applies to more than one book. Some bibliographies contain notes introducing sections within the bibliography; they serve to enlarge on the explanation of the field given in the introductory essay.

When commenting on individual books, notes deliberately tend to avoid superlatives—terms such as excellent, superb, definitive, classic, masterful. Editorial advisors for the chapters selected the best book they knew of in each case, over many others they might have chosen. Every book has some special excellence or importance to recommend it. Many books are widely viewed as classics in their spheres. On the other hand, judgments differ, and we cannot help but have omitted some works considered classics by other authorities.

The order in which books are listed in each bibliography suggests one sequence in which you may want to pursue your learning. Within sections of each bibliography, works are very rarely given in the conventional bibliography order—alphabetically, by the authors' last names. Rather, the order essentially follows a reading sequence recommended by the editorial advisor. Only when such a natural sequence for study is not important are books listed alphabetically.

We hope that the ways in which the chapters are presented will help substantially as you set out in college learning on your own.

Chapter Five

EAST ASIAN
CIVILIZATIONS
". . . different ways of thought and life"

Editorial Advisor:
Lillian M. Li
Department of History, Swarthmore College

INTRODUCTION

In recent years China and Japan have captured the interest of many Americans. This concern stems in part from the recognition of the increasing importance of these East Asian nations in world politics and economics, but in large measure it arises from a recognition of the important perspective different ways of thought and life can throw on our own way of life. The technological efficiency of Japan and the revolutionary social doctrines of Maoism, as well as the mysticism of Taoism, have all found their admirers in this country.

American scholarship on Asia is largely a legacy of the Second World War. Many of the senior scholars in the field received their language training while serving in the armed forces during the war. Under their leadership both the quantity and quality of scholarship produced in the United States in the postwar period has reached impressive proportions. In the prewar years European Sinology had tended to concentrate on translation, literary criticism, and textual analysis, but postwar Western scholarship, both European and American, has broadened its outlook and methodology and shifted its emphasis to modern history and the social sciences.

American scholarship was further stimulated by the Cold War. Just as Russian studies were generously supported by government and private foundation grants in the 1950s, Asian studies benefited from similar support in the 1960s. And though the upsurge of public attention had begun to diminish by the early 1970s, the major graduate schools had already produced a significant number of young scholars, most of whom were well trained in languages and had traveled and studied in Asia.

In Chinese studies the United States has assumed a leading role, not only in comparison to Europe, but also—ironically and probably temporarily—in comparison to China itself. Since 1949, and especially since the early 1960s, the political situation in China has tended to discourage scholarship in modern history and other fields that are politically sensitive. It is in these disciplines that American scholars have filled a vacuum. Attempts to set up exchange programs for Chinese and American scholars have so far met with no success.

On the Japanese side, however, no such vacuum in scholarship exists. Japanese scholars have not failed to live up to their own previous standards of scholarship, thoroughness, and productivity. Whereas American scholars are sometimes faced with insufficient secondary sources on Chinese subjects, they are invariably overwhelmed by quantities of secondary materials on almost every Japanese topic.

In the past ten or fifteen years interest in Asia has been reflected in undergraduate education as well as in graduate schools and the scholarly world. Asian studies were initially offered only in major universities, but now many colleges include courses on Asia among their offerings in history, religion, art, political science, and other subjects. Asian studies can roughly be divided into three broad areas: East Asia (China, Japan, Korea, and Vietnam); South Asia (India, Pakistan, Bangladesh, and Sri Lanka, formerly called Ceylon); and Southeast Asia. Since not even the major universities can be strong in all these areas, this chapter makes no pretense at being comprehensive, restricting itself to books on China and Japan.

The works listed in the bibliography have been chosen for their scholarly insight as well as for their suitability to general readers and their availability in paperback. Each of the bibliography's two main divisions (China and Japan) begins with studies that trace the history of each civilization. Subsequent sections are arranged topically, pointing out further sources of information on philosophy and religion, art, and literature.

Should your interest in East Asian studies lead you to go beyond this bibliography, you may wish to consult the standard bibliographies in the field. They list specialized works available only in hard-cover editions as well as a variety of articles. For general purposes, Charles O. Hucker's China: A Critical Bibliography (Univ. of Arizona Press, 1962) and Bernard Silberman's Japan and Korea: A Critical Bibliography (Univ. of Arizona Press, 1962) are best. For more recent publications, consult the annual Bibliography of Asian Studies published by the Journal of Asian Studies and The Cumulative Bibliography of Asian Studies, 1941–1965, 8 vols. (G. K. Hall & Co., 1970), and The Cumulative Bibliography of Asian Studies, 1966–70, 6 vols. (G. K. Hall, 1970).

Quite a few colleges now offer Chinese or Japanese language instruction as part of their programs in Asian Studies. Readers who would like to learn Chinese and/or Japanese may find the following two textbook series most helpful. For Chinese: De Francis, John, Beginning Chinese (1963), Character Text for Beginning Chinese (1964), Beginning Chinese Reader (2 parts, 1966), Intermediate Chinese (1964), Character Text for Intermediate Chinese (1965), Intermediate Chinese Reader (2 parts, 1967), Advanced Chinese (1966), Character Text for Advanced

Chinese (1966), *Advanced Chinese Reader* (1969), *Index Volume: Beginning, Intermediate, and Advanced Texts in Spoken and Written Chinese* (1970). For Japanese: Jorden, Eleanor H., and Hamako I. Chaplin, *Beginning Japanese* (part 1, 1962; part 2, 1963). Both series are published by Yale University Press.

The Peking government has also issued an elementary Chinese textbook series with records: *Elementary Chinese 1, Elementary Chinese 2.* Foreign Languages Press, 1974. These are available from China Books and Periodicals, 125 Fifth Ave., New York, N.Y. 10003.

BIBLIOGRAPHY

NOTE Works listed below are introductory unless designated otherwise. Each section begins with anthologies and general works. Other books are given in roughly chronological order where chronology is relevant. As a rule, only books available in paper editions are listed; exceptions are made only where a title is of critical importance.

Chinese names in the bibliography are presented with the surname (family name) first, followed immediately—without comma—by the individual's given name (as in Chinese-language usage and predominant American publishing style). Japanese names are treated like English-language names (as in predominant American publishing style).

CHINA

General

Fairbank, John K., Edwin O. Reischauer, and Albert M. Craig, *East Asia: Tradition and Transformation.* **Houghton Mifflin (hard cover), 1973.** A textbook developed from Harvard University's introductory and interdisciplinary course in Chinese and Japanese civilizations (a course affectionately and irreverently called "the rice paddies" by students).

Gentzler, J. Mason, *A Syllabus of Chinese Civilization.* **Columbia Univ. Press, 1972.** A useful study guide developed in Columbia's extensive Asian Studies program. Gives outlines of history and major subjects, annotated reading lists, and questions for discussion.

Dawson, Raymond, ed., *The Legacy of China.* **Oxford Univ. Press, 1971.** Collection of essays by specialists on various aspects of traditional Chinese civilization and culture.

Fairbank, John K., *The United States and China,* **3rd ed., Harvard Univ. Press, 1971.** More about China than the U. S. One of the best short introductions to modern China.

Bianco, Lucien, *Origins of the Chinese Revolution, 1915–1949.* **Stanford Univ. Press, 1971.** An interpretation of recent history that stresses underlying social changes.

Early History

Watson, William, *Early Civilization in China.* **McGraw-Hill, 1966.** Brief discussion of archaeological findings, illustrated with color plates.

Treistman, Judith M., *The Prehistory of China.* **Doubleday (Natural History), 1972.** Reconstruction of life in prehistoric and ancient China based on archaeological evidence.

Hsu Cho-yun, *Ancient China in Transition: An Analysis of Social Mobility, 722–222 B.C.* **Stanford Univ. Press, 1965.** Treats society and politics in the Eastern Chou period. ADVANCED.

Levenson, Joseph R., and Franz Schurmann, *China, An Interpretive History: From the Beginning to the Fall of Han.* **Univ. of California Press, 1969.** A provocative discussion of key issues in early Chinese history.

Loewe, Michael, *Everyday Life in Early Imperial China.* **Harper & Row, 1970.** An account of life in Han China.

Gernet, Jacques, *Daily Life in China on the Eve of the Mongol Invasion, 1250–1276.* **Stanford Univ. Press, 1962.** An excellent and absorbing description of life in the Southern Sung capital of Hangchow.

Polo, Marco, *The Travels of Marco Polo.* **Dutton, 1954.** Marco Polo's description of his travels profoundly influenced the European view of China.

Ho Ping-ti, *The Ladder of Success in Imperial China.* **Columbia Univ. Press (out of print), 1962.** An analysis of the civil service examinations as a channel for social mobility in the Ming and Ch'ing periods, 1368–1911. ADVANCED.

Elvin, Mark, *The Pattern of the Chinese Past.* **Stanford Univ. Press, 1975.** A controversial treatment of Chinese history from the perspective of technological and economic changes. ADVANCED.

Van Der Sprenkel, Sybille, *Legal Institutions in Manchu China.* **Humanities, 1962.** Discusses the role of law in traditional Chinese society. ADVANCED.

Lattimore, Owen, *Inner Asian Frontiers of China.* **Beacon (out of print), 1962.** The classic treatment of the interaction of the nomadic cultures of frontier with sedentary Chinese civilization.

Fairbank, John K., ed., *Chinese World Order: Traditional China's Foreign Relations.* **Harvard Univ. Press, 1968.** Collection of essays about the myths and realities of the Chinese tributary system.

Modern History

Fairbank, John K., *The United States and China* (see under "General" above).

Bianco, Lucien, *Origins of the Chinese Revolution, 1915–1949* (see under "General," above).

Spence, Jonathan, *To Change China: Western Advisers in China, 1620–1960*. Little, Brown, 1969. Brief biographies of Westerners, from the Jesuits to Stilwell, who in one way or another tried to transform Chinese life.

Fay, Peter Ward, *The Opium War, 1840–1842*. Norton, 1976. A lively account of the Opium War, based on Western sources.

Chang Hsin-pao, *Commissioner Lin and the Opium War*. Norton, 1970. An analysis of the causes of the Opium War, based on Chinese and Western sources.

Teng Ssu-yu and John K. Fairbank, ed., *China's Response to the West: A Documentary Survey, 1839–1923*. Atheneum, 1963. Translations showing the attitudes toward the West of influential Chinese intellectuals and leaders.

Chesneaux, Jean, *Peasant Revolts in China, 1840–1949*. Norton, 1973. Modern China surveyed from the perspective of the peasantry.

Michael, Franz, *The Taiping Rebellion: History*, vol. 1 (of 3 vols.). Univ. of Washington Press, 1971. A survey of Taiping origins, organization, and military strategy.

Wright, Mary C., *The Last Stand of Chinese Conservatism: The T'ung-chih Restoration, 1862–1874*. Stanford Univ. Press, 1957. Although outdated in its treatment of certain subjects, this book remains a classic in the field.

Cohen, Paul A., *China and Christianity: The Missionary Movement and the Growth of Chinese Antiforeignism*. Harvard Univ. Press (hard cover), 1963. Treats the impact of Western missionaries on Chinese society in the mid-nineteenth century.

Schwartz, Benjamin, *In Search of Wealth and Power: Yen Fu and the West*. Harper, 1969. An intellectual biography of Yen Fu, translator of many important Western works of philosophy and political theory into Chinese. ADVANCED.

Levenson, Joseph R., *Liang Ch'i-ch'ao and the Mind of Modern China*, 2nd ed. Univ. of California Press, 1959. Biography and study of the thought of modern China's most influential intellectual. ADVANCED.

Tan, Chester C., *Boxer Catastrophe*. Norton, 1971. The standard account.

Schiffrin, Harold Z., *Sun Yat-sen and the Origins of the Chinese*

Revolution. Univ. of California Press, **1968.** The most up-to-date treatment of Sun, but covers only his early career up to 1905.

Sharman, Lyon, *Sun Yat-sen, His Life and its Meaning: A Critical Biography.* **Stanford Univ. Press, 1934.** Not as scholarly as Schiffrin, but a complete biography of Sun.

Wright, Mary C., ed., *China in Revolution: The First Phase, 1900–1913.* **Yale Univ. Press, 1968.** Essays on various aspects of the revolution of 1911, which toppled the Manchu dynasty.

Pruitt, Ida, ed., *A Daughter of Han; The Autobiography of a Chinese Working Woman.* **Stanford Univ. Press, 1945.** The memoirs of a lower-class Chinese woman whose life spanned the turbulent years of the late nineteenth and early twentieth centuries.

Sheridan, James E., *Chinese Warlord: The Career of Feng Yü-hsiang.* **Stanford Univ. Press, 1966.** Biography of one of the major warlords. The first chapter has an excellent discussion of warlordism in general.

Chow Tse-tsung, *The May Fourth Movement: Intellectual Revolution in Modern China.* **Stanford Univ. Press, 1960.** The standard work on this important intellectual and social movement.

The Communist Movement and Contemporary China

Schwartz, Benjamin I., *Chinese Communism and the Rise of Mao.* **Harper & Row, 1951.** The classic account of the ideological and power struggles which brought Mao Tse-tung to power in the Chinese Communist Party.

Schram, Stuart, *Mao Tse-tung.* **Penguin, 1968.** The best biography of Mao; also gives an overview of the development of the Communist Party.

Schram, Stuart, ed., *The Political Thought of Mao Tse-tung.* **Praeger, 1969.** A useful selection of Mao's writings, with an excellent introduction by the editor.

Snow, Edgar, *Red Star over China,* **rev. ed. Grove, 1968.** A classic; the first report by an American about the origins of the Communist Party.

Selden, Mark, *The Yenan Way in Revolutionary China.* **Harvard Univ. Press, 1971.** An excellent study of the formative years of the Communist Party at Yenan.

Johnson, Chalmers A., *Peasant Nationalism and Communist Power: The Emergence of Revolutionary China, 1937–1945.* **Stanford Univ. Press, 1962.** A controversial study showing how the Communists used anti-Japanese nationalist sentiments to extend their influence among the Chinese peasantry.

White, Theodore H., and Annalee Jacoby, *Thunder Out of China.*

Apollo Editions, 1975. A famous piece of wartime reporting that throws an unfavorable light on the Nationalist government's war efforts.

Tsou Tang, *America's Failure in China, 1941–1950,* 2 vols. Univ. of Chicago Press, 1963. A monumental study of American involvement in the Chinese civil war.

Isaacs, Harold R., *Images of Asia.* Harper & Row, 1973. A study of American images of Chinese and Indians.

Yang C. K., *Chinese Communist Society: The Family and the Village.* MIT Press, 1965. Study of transition in a South China village, based on field work.

Hinton, William, *Fanshen: A Documentary of Revolution in a Chinese Village.* Random House, 1968. Land reform in a Chinese village, as seen by an observer.

Myrdal, Jan, *Report from a Chinese Village.* Random House, 1972. Absorbing account of the impact of the Communist victory on one village.

Vogel, Ezra R., *Canton under Communism.* Harper & Row, 1971. Analyzes how shifts in party policy since 1949 have affected this major Chinese city.

Schurmann, Franz, *Ideology and Organization in Communist China,* rev. ed., Univ. of California Press, 1968. An important study of the role of ideology and organization in China.

Lewis, John Wilson, ed., *Party Leadership and Revolutionary Power in China.* Cambridge Univ. Press, 1970. Collection of essays on various aspects of party leadership.

Philosophy and Religion in China

Chan Wing-tsit, ed., *A Source Book in Chinese Philosophy.* Princeton Univ. Press, 1963. Translations of selections from major Chinese thinkers, with useful cross-references.

DeBary, William Theodore, et al., ed., *Sources of Chinese Tradition,* 2 vols. Columbia Univ. Press, 1960. Covers a wider range of thinkers than Chan, but each selection is shorter. Very useful anthology.

Mote, Frederick W., *Intellectual Foundations of China.* Knopf, 1971. A succinct and masterful treatment of classical Chinese thought.

Fung Yu-lan, *A Short History of Chinese Philosophy,* ed. Derk Bodde, abr. ed. Macmillan (Free Press), 1953. A standard and reliable survey by an eminent Chinese scholar.

Creel, Herrlee, *Chinese Thought from Confucius to Mao Tse-tung.*

Univ. of Chicago Press, 1971. Brief, somewhat popularized, introductory survey.

Munro, Donald J., *The Concept of Man in Early China.* Stanford Univ. Press, 1969. A provocative treatment of the concept of equality in ancient Chinese thought.

Waley, Arthur, ed., *Three Ways of Thought in Ancient China.* Doubleday, 1956. Selections from Mencius, Chuang-tzu, and the Legalists, with comments by Waley.

Wilhelm, Hellmut, *Change: Eight Lectures on the "I Ching."* Princeton Univ. Press, 1972. Scholarly discussion of the ancient classic of divination, which has become popular in the United States.

Wright, Arthur F., *Buddhism in Chinese History.* Stanford Univ. Press, 1959. Brief and lucid history of Buddhism in China.

Nivison, David S., and Arthur F. Wright, eds., *Confucianism in Action.* Stanford Univ. Press, 1959. Essays on various aspects of Confucianism as manifested in cultural and institutional history.

Art in China

Sullivan, Michael, *A Short History of Chinese Art,* rev. ed. Univ. of California Press, 1970.

Sze, Mai-mai, *The Way of Chinese Painting;* abr. reprint of *The Tao of Painting: A Study of the Ritual Disposition of Chinese Painting.* Random House, 1973.

Sickman, Laurence, and Alexander Soper, *The Art and Architecture of China,* 3rd ed. Penguin Books, 1971. Handsomely illustrated with black and white plates.

Literature in China

Birch, Cyril, ed., *Anthology of Chinese Literature: From Early Times to the Fourteenth Century; Anthology of Chinese Literature: From the Fourteenth Century to the Present.* Grove, 1965, 1972. Selections from various genres of Chinese literature throughout the centuries.

Bynner, Witter, and Kiang Kang-hu, *The Jade Mountain: A Chinese Anthology.* Random House, 1964. Translation of the famous collection, *300 T'ang Poems.*

Liu, James J. Y., *The Art of Chinese Poetry.* Univ. of Chicago Press, 1962. A brief and informative discussion of Chinese poetry.

Ts'ao Hsueh-ch'in, *Dream of the Red Chamber,* tr. Wang Chi-chen. Doubleday, 1958. Famous novel of the fortunes of a great family of the early Ch'ing period. Although not necessarily the best or most complete translation, this edition provides a convenient introduction to this lengthy work.

Wu Ching-tzu, *The Scholars,* tr. Yang Hsien-yi and Gladys Yang. Grosset, 1974. A famous novel satirizing scholars and the "examination life" in the eighteenth century.

Jenner, W. J. F., ed., *Modern Chinese Stories.* Oxford. Univ. Press, 1974. A good selection of twentieth-century short stories.

Silent China: the Selected Writings of Lu Xun, ed. and tr. Gladys Yang. Oxford Univ. Press, 1974. A collection of stories by modern China's best-known writer and satirist.

Pa Chin (pseud. for Li Fei-kan), *Family.* Doubleday, 1931. Novel depicting the effects of modern life on a traditional Chinese family.

JAPAN

General

Fairbank, John K., Edwin O. Reischauer, and Albert M. Craig, *East Asia: Tradition and Transformation.* Houghton Mifflin (hard cover), 1973. See beginning of bibliography.

Varley, H. Paul, *A Syllabus of Japanese Civilization.* Columbia Univ. Press, 1972. A useful study guide developed in Columbia's extensive Asian Studies program. Gives outlines of history and major subjects, annotated reading lists, and questions for discussion.

Hall, John Whitney, *Japan: From Prehistory to Modern Times.* Dell, 1971. Text suitable for both elementary and advanced levels.

Reischauer, Edwin O., *Japan: The Story of a Nation,* rev. ed., Knopf, 1974. One of the best general, short introductions to Japan.

Reischauer, Edwin O., *The Japanese.* Harvard Univ. Press (hard cover), 1977. An introduction to contemporary Japanese society with less emphasis on historical background than *Japan: The Story of a Nation.*

Early History

Duus, Peter, *Feudalism in Japan.* Knopf, 1969. Concise explanation of the development of Japanese political and social institutions.

Morris, Ivan, *The World of the Shining Prince.* Penguin, 1969. A fascinating description of court life in the late Heian period. Should be read in conjunction with *The Tale of Genji* (see "Literature").

Sansom, George B., *The Western World and Japan.* Random House, 1973. On Western contacts with Japan from the earliest times to the late nineteenth century; by the dean of Japanese historical studies.

Keene, Donald, *Japanese Discovery of Europe, 1720–1830,* rev. ed. Stanford Univ. Press, 1969. A study of the influence of Dutch learning, particularly through the experience of Honda Toshiaki (1744–1821).

Smith, Thomas C., *The Agrarian Origins of Modern Japan*. Stanford Univ. Press, **1959**. Describes the improvements in agricultural technology during the Tokugawa period and the critical social changes which accompanied them. ADVANCED.

Bellah, Robert N., *Tokugawa Religion: The Values of Preindustrial Japan*. Beacon, **1970**. A sociologist's attempt to find something comparable to the Protestant ethic in Japanese religion. ADVANCED.

Hall, John W., and Marius B. Jansen, eds., *Studies in the Institutional History of Early Modern Japan*. Princeton Univ. Press, **1968**. Scholarly articles on the Tokugawa period. ADVANCED.

Jansen, Marius B., *Sakamoto Ryōma and the Meiji Restoration*. Stanford Univ. Press, **1961**. A biography of one of the leaders of the Meiji Restoration in Tosa; good background for the Restoration itself.

Modern History

Fukuzawa, Yukichi, *The Autobiography of Yukichi Fukuzawa*. Schocken, **1972**. The delightful memoirs of Japan's most influential proponent of westernization in the early Meiji period.

Dower, John, ed., *The Origins of the Modern Japanese State: Selected Writings of E. H. Norman*. Pantheon, **1975**. The works of a leading prewar Western scholar of modern Japanese history, based on Japanese Marxist interpretations.

Jansen, Marium B., ed., *Changing Japanese Attitudes Toward Modernization*. Princeton Univ. Press, **1965**. A collection of scholarly articles on various aspects of the problem of modernization.

Lockwood, William W., *The Economic Development of Japan: Growth and Structural Change, 1868–1938*, rev. ed. Princeton Univ. Press, **1969**. The standard work on Japan's economic history.

Maruyama, Masao, *Thought and Behavior in Modern Japanese Politics*. Oxford Univ. Press, **1969**. Essays by Japan's most eminent political theorist. Maruyama's interpretation of Japanese fascism is particularly important.

Iriye, Akira, *Across the Pacific: An Inner History of American-East Asian Relation*. Harcourt Brace Jovanovich, **1969**. Survey of relations between the U. S., China, and Japan, primarily in the twentieth century.

Morley, James W., ed., *Dilemmas of Growth in Prewar Japan*. Princeton Univ. Press, **1974**. Scholarly essays discussing the social and economic context for the rise of militarism in the 1930s. ADVANCED.

Borg, Dorothy and Shumpei Okamoto, eds., *Pearl Harbor as History: Japanese-American Relations, 1931–1941*. Columbia Univ. Press, **1974**. Essays based on the most recent scholarship on this subject.

Butow, Robert J., *Tojo and the Coming of the War*. Stanford Univ. Press, 1961. Provides insights into the Japanese decision-making process that led to Pearl Harbor.

Contemporary Japan

Benedict, Ruth, *The Chrysanthemum and the Sword: Patterns of Japanese Culture*. NAL, 1967. Although regarded as outdated in some respects, this analysis of the Japanese "character" still provides important insights.

Nakane, Chie, *Japanese Society*. Univ. of California Press, 1970. A widely acclaimed analysis of Japanese social structure.

Vogel, Ezra F., *Japan's New Middle Class: The Salary Man and His Family in a Tokyo Suburb,* rev. ed. Univ. of California Press, 1971. On middle-class life and values; very readable.

Dore, Ronald P., *City Life in Japan: A Study of a Tokyo Ward,* 2nd ed. Univ. of California Press, 1958. A detailed study of one section of Tokyo in the early 1950s.

Dore, Ronald P., *British Factory—Japanese Factory: The Origins of National Diversity in Employment Relations.* Univ. of California Press, 1973. The author skillfully compares British and Japanese industrial organization and demonstrates that modernization and Westernization are not necessarily identical.

Cole, Robert E., *Japanese Blue Collar: The Changing Tradition.* Univ. of California Press, 1971. A study of Japanese workers.

Beardsley, Richard K., John W. Hall, and Robert E. Ward, *Village Japan.* Univ. of Chicago Press, 1969. Based on field work done in a Japanese village during the 1950s.

Scalapino, Robert A., and Junnosuke Masumi, *Parties and Politics in Contemporary Japan.* Univ. of California Press, 1962. Japanese politics up to 1960.

Thayer, Nathaniel B., *How the Conservatives Rule Japan.* Princeton Univ. Press, 1969. A detailed study of the Liberal Democratic Party.

Ike, Nobutaka, *Japanese Politics: Patron-Client Democracy.* Knopf, 1972. An interpretation of Japanese politics by a well-known political scientist.

Hellmann, Donald C., *Japan and East Asia: The New International Order.* Praeger, 1972. Analyzes Japan's international position.

Philosophy and Religion

DeBary, William Theodore, Ryusaku Tsunoda, and Donald Keene, eds., *Sources of Japanese Tradition,* 2 vols. Columbia Univ. Press,

1958. Selections from major thinkers and writers from the earliest times to the twentieth century.

Earhart, H. Byron, *Japanese Religion: Unity and Diversity,* **2nd ed. Dickenson, 1974.** Useful survey of the major Japanese religions.

Saunders, E. Dale, *Buddhism in Japan: with an Outline of Its Origins in India.* **Univ. of Pennsylvania Press, 1971.** Brief account of the historical development of Buddhism in Japan.

Dumoulin, Heinrich, *A History of Zen Buddhism.* **Beacon, 1969.** Historical survey of the development of Zen in China and Japan.

Suzuki, Daisetz T., *Zen and Japanese Culture.* **Princeton Univ. Press, 1964.** The impact of Zen Buddhism on aspects of Japanese culture, by one of the best-known interpreters of Zen to the western world. (Further reading may also be done in the same author's *Essays in Zen Buddhism,* **Grove, 1961,** and *Introduction to Zen Buddhism,* **Grove, 1964.**)

McFarland, H. Neill, *Rush Hour of the Gods: A Study of New Religious Movements in Japan.* **Harper & Row, 1970.** Popular account of postwar Japanese religious groups, including Sōka Gakkai.

Hori, Ichiro, *Folk Religion in Japan: Continuity and Change.* **Univ. of Chicago Press, 1968.** Discussion of popular religious practices in Japan.

Art

Warner, Langdon, *The Enduring Art of Japan.* **Grove, 1958.** A brief and excellent introduction.

Munsterburg, Hugo, *The Arts of Japan: An Illustrated History.* **C. E. Tuttle, 1956.** Also convenient as an introduction; well illustrated.

Soper, A., and Robert T. Paine, *Art and Architecture of Japan.* **Penguin, 1974.** Places special emphasis on Japan's distinctive architectural styles.

Literature

Keene, Donald, ed., *Anthology of Japanese Literature: Earliest Era to Mid-Nineteenth Century; Modern Japanese Literature: An Anthology.* **Grove, 1956.** The two Keene anthologies provide a wide range of genres and a sample of the best of Japanese literature through the centuries.

Keene, Donald, *Japanese Literature: An Introduction for Western Readers.* **Grove, 1955.** A brief and very useful introduction.

Manyōshō: The Nippon Gakujutsu Shinkōkai Translation of One Thousand Poems, **ed. Donald Keene. Columbia Univ. Press, 1969.** This eighth-century anthology of Japanese poems reveals much about ancient life and attitudes.

Lady Murasaki, *Tale of Genji*, tr. Arthur Waley. Doubleday, 1955. This famous Japanese novel of courtly romance and intrigue in the eleventh century has never failed to delight its readers. This volume presents its first section.

***Confessions of Lady Nijō*, tr. Karen Brazell. Doubleday, 1973.** A first-hand account of court life in the thirteenth century.

Waley, Arthur, tr., *The Nō Plays of Japan*. Grove, 1957. Classic plays translated by the most famous translator of Chinese and Japanese literature into English.

Keene, Donald, tr., *Four Major Plays of Chikamatsu*. Columbia Univ. Press, 1964. Chikamatsu Monzaemon (1653–1725) was the most important figure in the development of the Japanese theater.

Natsume, Soseki, *Kokoro*, tr. Edwin McClellan. Regnery, 1967. An important twentieth-century novel depicting the passing of the Meiji era.

Tanizaki, Junichiro, *Some Prefer Nettles*, tr. Edward C. Seidensticker. Berkeley Pub., 1955. A novel showing the conflicts between the old and new in prewar Japan.

Mishima, Yukio, *Temple of the Golden Pavilion*, tr. Ivan Morris. Berkeley Pub., 1959. Translations of many of Mishima's novels are available in paperback. This is one of his best-known works.

Chapter Six

ENVIRONMENTAL STUDIES

". . . understanding and working toward the solution of environmental problems"

Editorial Advisor:
David B. Sutton
The Antaeus Group

INTRODUCTION

During the last decade, concern over the state of the natural environment has led to widespread citizen action, new legislation, new government agencies, and a flood of monographs and books. Many Americans have begun to see the urgent need of reevaluating their attitudes toward nature and one another. As a result, colleges and universities across the country have rapidly developed new programs of ecological or environmental studies.

Environmental Studies seems the better and increasingly popular name for these programs. Ecology is that branch of the biological sciences that deals with the total network of material interactions between all forms of life and their native settings (see the chapter on Biology). By contrast, Environmental Studies as a field is generally understood to include not only basic ecology but also knowledge of many other fields that bear directly on understanding and working toward the solution of environmental problems.

Economics, political science, psychology, and philosophy are among the disciplines that can contribute to the understanding of environmental problems. Given the many-faceted nature of those problems, Environmental Studies is of necessity an interdisciplinary pursuit. Many colleges have added some environment content to existing courses in economic geography, geology, and biology. Comprehensive majors in Environmental Studies are offered by a small but growing number of schools. These programs often feature flexible curricula, individualized learning, the presentation of study materials in newer formats, and interdisciplinary faculty teams.

The Environmental Studies bibliography that follows includes the works typically studied during the undergraduate years in these comprehensive programs. It can help you acquire the knowledge mastered by college majors in Environmental Studies today.

The bibliography reflects the fact that the area represents a new approach by integrating academic fields through stress on those aspects of each field that contribute to an understanding of the basic interactions of humanity and the total environment. Its broad aim is to build understanding of those qualities of the environment that enhance the well-being of present and coming generations.

A more detailed statement of the purposes of this course of study has been made by the environmental education staff of the U. S. Office of Education. The statement characterizes environmental education as

> . . . a life-long process . . . that is a way of looking at life, fostering awareness of other life and interrelationships, learning to recognize the effects (good and bad) we have on physical surroundings, and the responsibilities we must accept for the mere fact of our presence and of our activities in our environment. It should enable us to make value judgments and act accordingly. It is acceptance of life values and ways of living which minimize destruction and maximize those relationships that enhance life. It is learning how to contribute to the quality of life, and the constructive use, rather than exploitation, of the environment.

In keeping with this view, college programs seek to develop environmentally informed and responsible citizens who understand and accept the challenge of earth stewardship. Their purpose is not to train professionals who will work in environmental fields, although these college programs represent important preprofessional preparation. (Readers interested in finding out about careers in the area may consult: J. G. Ferguson editorial staff, *Career Opportunities: Ecology, Conservation and Environmental Control*, Doubleday, 1972; or Odum Fanning, *Opportunity in Environmental Careers*, Vocational Guidance Manuals, % Data Courier, Louisville, Ky., hard cover, 1972.)

As a study area designed to develop effective and informed individuals rather than professional specialists, Environmental Studies stands in the centuries-old tradition of liberal college education— education not just for a livelihood but for living.

THE GENERAL CHARACTER OF ENVIRONMENTAL STUDIES PROGRAMS

Many different approaches can be taken in designing a college program in environmental studies, but all approaches have as a common goal the acquisition of basic ecological concepts and an understanding of how these concepts relate to human socioeconomic systems and the quality of life. Many college programs follow the same general pattern. Once students have mastered essential scientific background, they begin to understand how they affect and are affected by natural ecosystems. They can then pursue the more technical aspects of this interaction. Through reading and the application of various analytic techniques they can study the nature of pollution and resource depletion and the alternative means of controlling these problems.

But these analyses are incomplete until students have gained insight into the causes that have allowed these conditions to develop. Lasting solutions will result only from correcting root causes. Relevant aspects of philosophy, literature, and other subjects in the humanities and social sciences must therefore be explored if students are to learn about the full range of the environmental crisis.

For example, in examining the socioeconomic roots of environmental problems, students must deal with the fact that increasingly serious problems of pollution grow out of our patterns of consumption and resource exploitation as well as the complex body of laws and customs underlying them. They must think through questions and priorities that involve basic issues of philosophy and public policy. They must consider historical precedents for possible alternatives. And they must analyze future forecasts and prospects, for by now our responsibility for the well-being of future generations has become only too clear.

ILLUSTRATIVE PROGRAMS OF STUDY

For an extensive program of individual study, you may work with the books in the following bibliography either in the sequence in which they are listed or by selecting books from the various categories in an order of your own design.

A Program Following the Bibliography Sequence

If you choose to follow the sequence of the bibliography, you will first be introduced to the books (relatively few as yet) that span the whole range of concerns in Environmental Studies today. The next two sections will guide you to works on the scientific thought underlying environmental analyses—basic ecology, earth sciences and human and animal biology. These naturally parallel some of the works identified in the chapters of this book on Biology and Earth Sciences, which can supplement related readings here.

Human interaction with the environment is explained in the works of the following section. They provide substantial background for the subsequent section on specific environmental problem areas and forms of environmental degradation.

With the help of the sections that follow, the reader can gain further perspectives on related values and attitudes, social responses, political institutions, economics, and technology. Significant forecasts of the future and debates about them are listed in the section on, "Images of the Future." Closing sections identify periodicals and organizations with which you can continue to keep informed in this area of vital public concern.

A Program Selecting From the Bibliography Sequence

One suggested course of study in which you would work with books selected from the bibliography sections in a different sequence is typical of an undergraduate major in highly developed programs of Environmental Studies. It is outlined below. After each block of study is briefly characterized, the pertinent works in the bibliography are identified by the name of a bibliography section, and the last names of the authors of the works in that section are given in parentheses.

Because human impact on the environment can best be judged against the backdrop of natural processes, you may want to begin by setting the biophysical scene upon which human activity may be later imposed. The external physical environment can be viewed as a complex of interacting systems that maintain the dynamic unity of the land, air, and water. ("Basic Ecology and Earth Sciences": Parsegian; Rumney; Tarling and Tarling.)

The interplay of the geologic cycle has determined North American land forms, and upon this basic geologic substratum a series of additional components (such as soil type, water resources, and climatic patterns) can be added to complete the physical setting. ("Basic Ecology and Earth Sciences": Edinger; Farb; Rumney.)

This set of physical characteristics provides a unique place for the development of North American life forms. You may move on to the study of biological and ecological systems, defining their components and their interaction. ("Basic Ecology and Earth Sciences": Grobstein; Laszlo; McHale; Parsegian; Sutton.)

Exploration of the dynamics of ecosystems considers the development and succession of the biotic community, with special reference to changes occurring in community structure, complexity, and stability. The organizing influences of energy flowing through the system, as well as the self-replenishing nature of the biogeochemical cycles, would be considered. ("Basic Ecology and Earth Sciences": Clapham; Miller; Scientific American Books; Sutton.)

Homo sapiens is a biological species that is part of and dependent upon ecological systems. It is important to realize that past and ongoing development of the species is inescapably tied to the functioning of these natural systems. Human beings are a product of their environment as well as its major modifier. You may move on to study the evolving human animal as it adapts to its ever-changing ecological situation. ("Human and Cultural Evolution": Campbell; Dobzhansky; Dubos; Hardin.)

With primitive human beings, a new ecological dominant emerges. The elaboration of the unique biological traits of homo sapiens can be traced as the species is seen to assert its dominance. ("Human and Cultural Evolution": Bates; Boughey; Campbell.)

The human species' most distinctive characteristic, however, is its capacity for learning; through this capability it has been able to develop the unique mode of cultural adaptation to its environment. ("Human and Cultural Evolution": Dobzhansky; Dubos; Goldschmidt.)

The use of language, insight, and generalization should all be considered as the antecedents to social arrangements, the transmission of culture, and the formation of a body of philosophy and ethics—all of which have a fundamental impact on actions that alter the environment. ("Values, Attitudes and Institutions": Baier and Rescher; Barbour; Ornstein; Tuan.) The evolution of culture may also be viewed as the development and adaptation of social institutions to the needs of society. ("Human and Cultural Evolution": Fried; Giesbrecht; Goldschmidt.)

Given this general background, you may want to study Native American cultures in their aboriginal settings to acquire specific examples of human beings adapting to their environment. ("Human and Cultural Evolution": Farb; Service; Smith.) European immigrants, on the other hand, bringing with them another set of cultural baggage, assumed quite different patterns of environmental interaction. ("General Surveys and Anthologies": Detwyler; Marsh; Thomas.) Indeed, their imprint remains with us today, and many of our contemporary problems can be traced to the continuing influence of this "frontier mind" on American culture. ("Values, Attitudes and Institutions": English and Mayfield. "Social Responses": Pursell; Udall.)

In this perspective, current examples of environmental degradation can be seen to have their origins in deeply rooted attitudes and values, in human nature itself. It is in this context that you will place the more detailed study of each environmental problem. ("Environmental Problem Areas"; "Land Use"; "Environmental Degradation.") These fundamental considerations will also introduce the motivations for the different schools of conservation thought. Utilitarian, aesthetic, and ecological conservation can be investigated in light of their differing scientific, economic, political, and philosophical approaches. ("Social Responses": Nash, Pursell, Udall.)

In the political arena groups espousing differing ideologies compete for natural resources now as in the past. Many of the factors preventing corrective action are the result of people's prevailing pioneer attitudes of superabundance ("General Surveys and Anthologies": Ehrlich. "Images of the Future": Meadows), rugged individualism ("Social Responses": Nash. "Political Institutions": Davies; Pirages), and cowboy economics ("Economics and the Environment": Boulding; Daly).

Solutions to environmental problems must be developed in light of present environmental realities. Exponential rates of change strain at the political, educational, and social structure of our nation. Coming to terms with environmental problems may require drastic institutional change. The need for immediate action is clear, for "the future," as Alvin Toffler notes, "is coming faster all the time." ("Images of the Future": Toffler.) It is important therefore to heed the thought of futurists and modern environmental planners if we are to prepare for the changes required in the future ("Images of the Future").

SIGNIFICANCE OF ENVIRONMENTAL STUDIES FOR THE FUTURE

The environmental crisis represents a complex and interrelated set of problems which will continue to face us in the future. People will be called upon continually to decide how the world community should deal with problems of energy and mineral scarcities, food, water, and land allocation, pollution, and related environmental impact problems, and population dynamics. There are no simple solutions. Future generations will not be able to make intelligent decisions about these matters unless the job of preparing them begins now. Environmental studies provides a way of enriching the educational process with a subject matter of critical social significance.

If solutions to environmental problems are not themselves to become future problems, they must be evaluated from broad intellectual foundations, where solutions are seen not only in terms of engineering simplicity and economic return, but in the quality and richness of human life. Lacking comprehensive approaches, we will continue to be overwhelmed by short-range problems perceived as separate crises, and we will continue to be burdened with the ultimate high cost of short-sighted responses.

The following readings are intended to provide a breadth of concepts and skills from many disciplines needed to deal with the many complex environmental issues. It is hoped that they will be a suitable beginning for the life-long pursuit of environmental studies.

BIBLIOGRAPHY

GENERAL SURVEYS AND ANTHOLOGIES

NOTE   As yet, only a few general books encompass the entire range of environmental studies. Some are anthologies of articles; others are comprehensive treatments interweaving many environmental themes. Works of both types are noted below to provide a good general introduction. After reading through sections of the bibliography, you may also want to return to several of the more advanced general works listed here to tie all your readings together.

Dasmann, R. F., *Environmental Conservation*, 3rd ed. Wiley, 1972. Treats land use, both past and present, and presents guidelines for the future.

Detwyler, T. R., ed., *Man's Impact on Environment*. McGraw-Hill, 1971. Reprints 52 articles that chronicle man's recent impact on the atmosphere, climate, water, land, vegetation, and animals.

Ehrlich, P. R., and A. H. Ehrlich, *Population, Resources, Environment: Issues in Human Ecology*, 2nd ed. Freeman (hard cover), 1972. An analysis of the worldwide crisis of rapid population growth and the resulting demands on food, resources, and the environment. Argues that ultimately there are no technological panaceas, but that dramatic and rapid changes in personal attitudes are required. A good sourcebook to have; comprehensive and detailed, extremely well-written, great breadth.

Greenwood, N., and J. M. B. Edwards, *Human Environments and Natural Systems: A Conflict of Dominion.* Duxbury, 1973. A readable, nontechnical introduction to environmental studies.

Marsh, G. P., *Man and Nature: The Earth as Modified by Human Action.* Harvard Univ. Press, 1965. An early plea (first issued in 1864) to halt the wholesale destruction of the resources of the land before they are irretrievably lost. Influenced many environmentalists.

Miller, G. T. Jr., *Living in the Environment: Concepts, Problems and Alternatives,* Wadsworth, (hard cover), 1975. The broadest treatment to date.

Murdoch, W. W., ed., *Environment: Resources, Pollution, and Society,* Sinauer Associates, Inc. (hard cover) Stamford, Conn., 2nd ed., 1975. A collection of essays; each was originally written for this volume by a leading expert on a specific environmental issue. Among essays of particular interest that relate to subsequent bibliography sections are: Preston Cloud, "Mineral Resources in Fact and Fancy"; W. T. Edmonson, "Fresh Water Pollution"; E. Cook, "Ionizing Radiation"; L. K. Caldwell, "Environment and Administration: The Politics of Ecology"; V. J. Yannacone, Jr., "Environment and the Law"; and K. E. Boulding, "Environment and Economics."

Southwick, C. H. *Ecology and the Quality of our Environment.* Van Nostrand Reinhold, 1972. An introduction to human ecology tracing the roots of the science and of our environmental problems.

Thomas, W. L., ed., *Man's Role in Changing the Face of the Earth.* Univ. of Chicago, 1956. A work of over 1100 pages dealing with the process of environmental modification; gives past and present examples, as well as prospects for the future. A classic in the field.

Sutton, D. B., and N. P. Harmon, *A Content Analysis of Environmental Studies.* John Muir Institute, Berkeley, Calif., 1975. Lists the concepts from biology, physics, economics, political science, philosophy, and the many other disciplines making up environmental studies. The conceptual scheme is sequentially ordered and offers a contextual framework for programs in Environmental Studies.

BASIC ECOLOGY AND EARTH SCIENCES

NOTE See also chapters dealing with Biology and Earth Sciences.

Clapham, W. B., Jr., *Natural Ecosystems.* Macmillan, 1973. A good intermediate level introduction to the study of natural ecosystems; outlines basic components and their interactions showing how they operate as dynamic, integrated systems.

Edinger, J. G. *Watching for the Wind: The Seen and Unseen Influences of Local Weather.* Doubleday, 1967. A book on meteorology which will allow you to see order in the seemingly chaotic phenomena that constitute our weather; well-written, easy to read.

Farb, P., *Face of North America: The Natural History of a Continent.* **Harper & Row, 1963.** Combines insights from both the earth sciences and the life sciences to describe how each major feature of the continent came to be and what influences are altering it. Written for a popular audience without sacrificing technical accuracy.

Grobstein, C., *The Strategy of Life,* **2nd ed. Freeman, 1974.** Explains what modern biology has to say about life—what it is, where it came from, and where it is expected to go; an outstanding statement.

Laszlo, E., *The Systems View of the World.* **Braziller, 1973.** Explores the new world view of systems thinkers, particularly as it applies to man and nature.

McHale, J., *World Facts and Trends.* **Collier, 1972. Contains charts and diagrams from** *The Ecological Context,* **by McHale (Braziller, 1970).** *The Ecological Context* deals with the "life support" systems of the physical environment. Through graphs and charts it depicts the state of our ecological systems of energy and materials. A nice contextual overview.

Miller, G. T., Jr., *Energetics, Kinetics, and Life: an Ecological Approach.* **Wadsworth, 1971.** An introduction to thermodynamics and its application to life processes; interesting, not overly technical.

Parsegian, V. L., *This Cybernetic World of Man, Machines and Earth Systems.* **Anchor, 1973.** A discussion of cybernetics for the layman, with many examples of how cybernetics works in living and inanimate systems.

Rumney, G. R., *The Geosystem: Dynamic Integration of Land, Sea and Air.* **Wm. C. Brown, 1970.** Treats the earth as a single planetary system integrated through the exchange of energy, matter and momentum. INTERMEDIATE.

Russwurm, L. H., and E. Sommerville, eds., *Man's Natural Environment: A Systems Approach.* **Duxbury, 1974.** A collection of articles on the study of various systems in physical geography. INTRODUCTORY.

Scientific American Books, *The Biosphere.* **Freeman, 1970.** An excellent introduction to chemical cycling and energy flow.

Sutton, D. B., and N. P. Harmon. *Ecology: Selected Concepts.* **The Antaeus Group, Stanford, CA, 1976.** A self-teaching guide presenting the basic concepts of ecology from four points of view—energy, cycles, populations, and ecosystems. A good way to learn the basics.

Tarling, D., and M. Tarling, *Continental Drift: A Study of Earth's Moving Surface.* **Doubleday, 1971.** An outline of the evidence for and examples of continental drift, including its relation to volcanoes, earthquakes, and the location of minerals.

BASIC HUMAN BIOLOGY

NOTE   See also the chapter dealing with Biology.

Barnett, A., *The Human Species: A Biology of Man.* Penguin, 1961. Supplies the essentials of the biological sciences needed to understand human biology. Comprehensive and enjoyable reading.

Clegg, E. J., *The Study of Man: An Introduction to Human Biology.* American Elsevier, 1968. Ann introduction for the general reader to the study of human variation.

Sears, R. R., and S. S. Feldman, eds., *The Seven Ages of Man.* Kaufmann, 1973. Provides a balanced and accurate view of human development (physical, personality, and ability) from infancy to old age.

Volpe, E. P., *Human Heredity and Birth Defects.* Pegasus, 1971. A lucid overview of the exciting area of fetal development; accurate and highly readable.

HUMAN AND CULTURAL EVOLUTION

Bates, M., *Man in Nature.* Prentice-Hall, 1964. An overview of the evolution and natural history of man.

Billings, W. B., *Plants, Man, and the Ecosystem,* 2nd ed. Wadsworth, 1970. Defines the "rules of the ecological game" that man must follow if he is to prosper. Emphasizes the importance of plants to ecosystem structure and function.

Boughey, A. S., *Man and the Environment: An Introduction to Human Ecology and Evolution.* Macmillan, 1971. An introductory text that provides an ecological account of human origins and the development of modern society with all of its environmental problems.

Campbell, B. G., *Human Evolution: An Introduction to Man's Adaptations,* 2nd ed. Aldine, 1974. A book written for readers with no previous knowledge of biology. Presents a picture of those human adaptations that distinguish man from his fellow primates.

Dobzhansky, T., *Mankind Evolving.* Yale Univ. Press, 1962. A comprehensive discussion of man's biological and cultural adaptations.

Dubos, R., *Man Adapting.* Yale Univ. Press, 1971. Dubos' dominant theme is that the states of health or disease are the expressions of the success or failure of the human organism to respond adaptively to environmental challenges; interestingly written.

Farb, P., *Man's Rise to Civilization,* rev. ed. Dutton (hard cover), 1978. A volume that uses the "living laboratory of North America" to explore the evolution of complexity in human society. Through the analysis of the band, tribe, chiefdom, and state as expressed in various North American cultures, Farb digs for the roots of modern industrialized society.

Fried, M. H., *The Evolution of Political Society: An Essay in Political Anthropology*. Random, 1967. Describes a unified theory of the emergence of ranking, social stratification, and the state; a bold attempt.

Giesbrecht, M. G., *The Evolution of Economic Society*. Freeman, 1972. An introduction to economics that portrays man's economic behavior as an integral part in the development of society; lively.

Goldschmidt, W., *Man's Way: A Preface to the Understanding of Human Society*. Holt, Rinehart & Winston, 1959. An anthropologist's account of the evolutionary sequence of man adapting his social institutions to meet the changing exigencies of growing communities and technical advance. A nice overview.

Hardin, G., *Nature and Man's Fate*. NAL, 1959. A general introduction to evolutionary theory and the dynamics of human evolution for the lay reader; also explores some crucial social, political, and ethical issues from the vantage point of the evolutionary biologist.

McClary, A., *Biology and Society: The Evolution of Man and His Technology*. Macmillan, 1975. An introduction to how and why our technological society evolved; a good overview.

Rhinelander, P. H., *Is Man Incomprehensible to Man?* Freeman, 1974. An essay on the philosophy of man. Outlines the different images of man and views of human nature. Points out the importance of clarifying the implicit assumptions that we make.

Service, E., *The Hunters*. Prentice-Hall, 1966. Examines the technology, economic relations, and status of property of most primitive bands of hunter-gatherers. By comparing their societies to those of primate and modern man, it is possible to gain insight into the basic elements of human society.

Smith, R. L., ed., *The Ecology of Man: An Ecosystem Approach*. Harper & Row, 1972. A select number of articles on human ecology with commentaries by the editor; excellent.

ENVIRONMENTAL PROBLEM AREAS

NOTE Most efforts to resolve environmental problems center on a relatively few basic issues and concerns. In order to provide a balanced perspective, the readings below represent the views of those on both sides of various environmental issues. Many of the general readings listed above contain sections on each of these problem areas as well.

Population and Food

Baker, H. D., *Plants and Civilization*, 2nd ed. Wadsworth, 1970. Illustrates the profound influence that plants have had on man's economic, cultural, and political history. INTRODUCTORY.

Borgstrom, G., *The Food and People Dilemma.* Duxbury, 1973. A nontechnical summary of the population-food issue, clearly focused on its historical and biological dimensions; excellent.

Borgstrom, G., *Too Many: An Ecological Overview of Earth's Limitations.* Collier, 1969. Points out the fundamental biological laws of life and the dictates of common sense that impose limits on the many schemes to greatly increase available food supply.

Boughey, A. S., *Ecology of Population,* Macmillan, 1973. An introduction to the principles of population ecology, with a brief treatment of their applications to human population.

Brown, L., and E. P. Eckholm, *By Bread Alone.* Praeger, 1974. An interdisciplinary analysis of future world food-production prospects, concluding that global food scarcity is already demanding a stabilization of world population and diet changes, with a reduction in grain-intensive livestock products.

Burnett, M., and D. O. White, *Natural History of Infectious Disease.* Cambridge Univ. Press, 1972. Infectious disease was a part of the general picture of how life evolved and continues to influence the development of man today.

Callahan, D., ed., *The American Population Debate,* Doubleday, 1971. A collection of articles on the question of overpopulation in the United States.

Commission on Population Growth and the American Future, *Population and the American Future.* NAL, 1972. An investigation by the President's Commission; outlines the problems of population growth and their legal and moral implications.

Hardin, G., ed., *Population, Evolution and Birth Control: A Collage of Controversial Ideas,* Freeman, 1969. A collection of readings dealing with the social impact of biology, with the author's usual insightful editorial comment.

Lappe, F. M., *Diet for a Small Planet.* Ballantine, 1971. Promotes a way of eating that makes the most of the earth's capacity to supply vital proteins.

Williams, R. J., *Nutrition in a Nutshell.* Dolphin, 1962. This book by a well-known biochemist and nutritionist presents in layman's terms the fundamentals of nutrition; delightful.

Hardin, G., *Birth Control.* Pegasus, 1970. A very readable summary of birth-control methods.

Havemann, E., *Birth Control.* Time-Life Books, 1967. A special report, beautifully illustrated.

Food. Science, May 9, 1975, Vol. 188 (4188). Entire issue of magazine devoted to the topic. Rather technical.

Energy

Clark, W., *Energy for Survival*. Doubleday, 1975. A comprehensive overview of our energy-dependent society, prospects for its future, and alternative sources of power.

Holdren, J., and P. Herrera, *Energy—A Crisis in Power*. Sierra Club, 1971. Summarizes the scientific and political aspects.

Lechie, J. O., ed., *Other Homes and Garbage: Design for Alternative Life Styles*. Sierra Club, 1975. A do-it-yourself alternative-energy supply book, includes introductory discussion on theory as well.

Lowins, A. B., Soft Energy Paths: Towards a Durable Peace, Balinger, 1977. One of the strongest statements on U.S. energy policy.

Odum, H. T., *Environment, Power and Society*. Wiley-Interscience, 1971. A technical discussion of energy use and human society.

Energy Policy Project of the Ford Foundation, *A Time to Choose*. Ballinger, 1974. An analysis of energy issues and policies, including the important options of developing new energy sources, reducing energy consumption, and increasing international cooperation.

Steinhart, C. E., and J. S. Steinhart, *Energy: Sources, Use and Role in Human Affairs*. Duxbury, 1974. A good overview.

Depletion of Natural Resources

National Research Council, *Resources and Man*. Freeman, 1969. An authoritative source on our resources.

Skinner, B. J. *Earth Resources*. Prentice-Hall, 1969. A brief survey.

Clawson, M., *America's Land and its Uses*. Johns Hopkins, 1972. An overview on land use by one of the nation's experts.

Darling, F. F., and J. P. Milton, eds., *Future Environments of North America: Transformation of a Continent*. Doubleday (Natural History), 1966. Articles by 34 ecologists, regional planners, economists, jurists, and conservationists evaluating ecological criteria in regional planning and tracing the decision-making process as it affects our relation to the environment.

Heller, A., ed., *The California Tomorrow Plan*. Kaufman, 1972. A comprehensive land-use plan for the state of California. A rare example of an integrated ecological approach to land-use planning.

McHarg, I. L., *Design With Nature*. Doubleday (Natural History), 1959. Describes an ecological approach to land-use planning.

Reilly, W. K., ed., *The Use of Land: A Citizen's Policy Guide to Urban Growth*. Crowell, 1973. Report of task force sponsored by the

Rockefeller Brothers' Fund, calling for "a changed attitude toward land."

Whyte, W. H., *The Last Landscape*. Doubleday, 1960. An outstanding analysis of land use and the problem of open space.

ENVIRONMENTAL DEGRADATION

General

Brubaker, S., *To Live on Earth*. NAL, 1972. A comprehensive overview of pollution and its causes.

Dasmann, R. F., *The Conservation Alternative*. Wiley, 1975. A brief summary prepared to provide a quick grasp of the scope and significance of current environmental problems. Excellent.

Grayson, M. H., and T. R. Shepard, Jr., *The Disaster Lobby: Prophets of Ecological Doom and Other Absurdities*. Follett, 1973. Described by Garrett Hardin as "an exercise in Freudian denial." A rather naive discounting of the earth's finite limits and the progressive and irreversible damage being done to natural ecosystems.

Institute of Ecology, *Man in the Living Environment*. Univ. of Wisconsin Press, 1972. A report prepared by 50 scientists to present their views of global ecological problems for the 1972 United Nations Conference on the Human Environment.

Maddox, J., *The Doomsday Syndrome*. McGraw-Hill, 1972. A rather uninformed attack on the environmental "alarmist" with a few valid points, unfortunately, its own extremism distorts the real issues.

Neuhaus, R., *In Defense of People: Ecology and the Seduction of Radicalism*. Macmillan, 1971. An evocative polemic against the ecology movement.

Air

Battan, L. J., *The Unclean Sky*. Doubleday, 1966. A meterologist describes the causes of air pollution and examines some possible paths to improvement; a good introduction.

Brodine, V., *Fundamentals of Air Pollution*. Addison-Wesley, 1973. A more advanced textbook for those who would like to investigate air pollution in detail.

Water

Marx, W., *The Frail Ocean*. Ballantine, 1967. Treats ocean pollution; a beautiful little book.

McCaull, J., and J. Crossland, *Water Pollution*. Harcourt Brace Jovanovich, 1972. Explains water pollution and its control.

Radiation

Bryerton, G., *The Nuclear Dilemma.* **Ballantine, 1970.** A balanced overview of the risks and benefits of nuclear power.

Gofman, J. W., and A. A. Tamplin, *Poisoned Power: The Case against Nuclear Power.* **Rodale, 1971.** A hard-hitting attack on nuclear power plants by two prominent nuclear scientists; a popularized account for the lay reader.

Seaborg, G. T. and W. R. Corliss. *Man and Atom.* **Dutton, 1971.** A good summary of the case for nuclear power; Seaborg is a former chairman of the Atomic Energy Commission.

Chemicals

Carson, R., *Silent Spring.* **Fawcett Crest, 1962.** Sounded the first warning about pesticides and is generally credited with awakening public concern. Clearly would qualify for an Environmental Books Hall of Fame.

Maxwell, K. E., ed., *Chemicals and Life.* **Dickerson, 1970.** A collection of readings on how natural and man-made chemicals affect our lives.

Rudd, R. L., *Pesticides and the Living Landscape.* **Univ. of Wisconsin Press, 1964.** Treats for lay readers the biological competitors of humankind and the prices paid for the methods used to combat them; an eloquent work.

Noise

Environmental Protection Agency, *Report to the President and Congress on Noise.* **Government Printing Office, 1971.** An excellent summary.

Still, H., *In Quest of Quiet.* **Stackpole, 1970.** A popular account of noise and the problem of its control.

Taylor, R., *Noise.* **Penguin, 1970.** A more technical treatment of noise for the lay reader.

Health

Benarde, M. A., *Our Precarious Habitat.* **Norton, 1973.** Examines the existing and potential threats to health within our environment; extensive, balanced.

Insel, P. M., and R. H. Moss, ed., *Health and the Social Environment.* **Heath, 1974.** A rather advanced treatment of the effects of the psychosocial environment on health.

World Health Organization, *Health Hazards of the Human Envi-*

ronment. **The Organization, 1972.** Contains an enormous amount of concentrated and technical information dealing with the effects of environmental influences on physical and mental health.

Dubos, R., *Man, Medicine and Environment.* **NAL, 1972.** Outlines changing views on health and the ecological aspects of disease; brief.

Endangered Species

Ehrenfeld, D. W., *Biological Conservation.* **Holt, Rinehart & Winston, 1970.** A concise introduction to conservation of wildlife.

Ziswiler, V., *Extinct and Vanishing Animals: A Biology of Extinction and Survival.* **Springer, 1967.** A popular summary.

VALUES, ATTITUDES AND INSTITUTIONS

Baier, L., and N. Rescher, eds., *Values and the Future.* **Macmillan (Free Press), 1969.** In 18 essays philosophers join with social scientists to define our values and trace the impact of technology on them.

Barbour, I. G., ed., *Western Man and Environmental Ethics: Attitudes Toward Nature and Technology.* **Addison-Wesley 1973.** Articles dealing with the philosophical and institutional roots of our environmental crises; probably the best collection of its kind.

English, P. W., and R. C. Mayfield, eds., *Man, Space, and Environment.* **Oxford Univ. Press, 1972.** Readings on the cultural landscape, environmental perception, and behavior from an ecological view.

Hardin, G., *Exploring New Ethics for Survival: The Voyage of the Spaceship Beagle.* **Penguin, 1972.** An extension of Hardin's classic article, "The Tragedy of the Commons"; a hard-hitting book by one of the best writers in the field. That article is probably the most important one published for lay readers on the use of common resources.

Hardin, G. and J. Baden, eds., *Managing the Commons,* **Freeman, 1977.** An anthology of readings that discusses the concept of the Commons, and ways in which the potentially destructive cultural norm of independent individual action may be changed to promote human welfare.

Ornstein, R. E., *The Psychology of Consciousness.* **Freeman, 1972.** Traces the connections between environmental awareness and self-awareness in individuals and societies. It attempts to reconcile analytical and intuitive approaches to knowledge. An invaluable bridge to understanding differing views of reality. Extremely important.

Tuan, Yi-Fu, *Topophilia: A Study of Environmental Perception, Attitudes and Values.* **Prentice-Hall, 1974.** Explores how and why humans vary in their perceptions, attitudes, and values toward their environment; essays highly original in thought.

Tzu, Lao, *Tao Te Ching,* tr. D. C. Lau. Penguin, 1963. The ancient Taoist classic that still has much to offer the environmentalists.

Kozlovsky, D. G., *An Ecological and Evolutionary Ethic.* Prentice-Hall, 1974. Argues that we will not have a world beautiful to live in until we acquire a naturalistic philosophy.

SOCIAL RESPONSES

Anderson, D. D., *Sunshine and Smoke: American Writers and the American Environment.* Lippincott, 1971. Chronicles the concern of American writers, from colonial times to the present, for nature and the quality of the environment; a beautiful volume.

Burch, W. R., *Daydreams and Nightmares: A Sociological Essay on the American Environment.* Harper & Row, 1971. This provocative but rather difficult synthesis examines the social consequences of man-environment interactions.

Burch, W. R., Jr., N. H. Cheek, Jr., and L. Taylor, eds., *Social Behavior, Natural Resources, and the Environment.* Harper & Row, 1972. A collection of essays concerned with how man approaches the physical environment through culture and social organization.

Leopold, A., *A Sand County Almanac.* Oxford Univ. Press, 1949. Essays by a man who was thinking ecologically before there was a body of science to support such thought; evocative and poetic.

Nash, R., *Wilderness and the American Mind.* Yale Univ. Press, 1973. The classic study of American attitudes toward wilderness over the last three centuries.

Nash, R., ed., *Environment and Americans: The Problem of Priorities.* Holt, Rinehart & Winston, 1972. Readings that document the ambivalence of American attitudes toward the environment, past and present.

Pursell, C., ed., *From Conservation to Ecology: The Development of Environmental Concern.* Crowell, 1973. A collection of articles tracing the beginnings of environmental concern and the development of the various conservation movements.

Udall, S. L., *The Quiet Crisis.* Discus, 1964. A fresh insight into the men and the forces that have shaped our pattern of land use in the United States; beautifully written.

Ekirch, A. A., Jr., *Man and Nature in America.* Univ. of Nebraska Press, 1973. A historical narrative tracing the change and conflict in public opinion concerning the relationship between Americans and their environment.

POLITICAL INSTITUTIONS

Caldwell, L. K., *Environment: Challenge to Modern Society.* **Natural History Press, 1970.** A prominent social scientist discusses how and why the ecological crisis should be made a major concern of public policy. This thorough analysis outlines the policy needed to alter the government's and individual citizen's use of the environment.

Davies, C. J., III, *The Politics of Pollution.* **Pegasus, 1970.** Analyzes governmental regulation and control of pollution; a fine general account.

Douglas, William O., *A Wilderness Bill of Rights.* **Little, Brown, 1965.** A conservationist and former U. S. Supreme Court Justice proposes a plan to preserve our waning heritage of natural resources.

The Leonardo Scholars, *Resources and Decisions.* **Duxbury, 1975.** A group of prominent scholars from many disciplines analyzes how and why environmental decisions are made, an excellent insight.

Ophuls, W., *Ecology and the Politics of Scarcity,* **Freeman, 1977.** A probing analysis of the political and social implications of the environmental crisis.

Pirages, D. C., and P. R. Ehrlich, *ARK II: Social Response to Environmental Imperatives.* **Freeman, 1972.** Argues that drastic political, social, and economic changes will be needed to solve problems of overpopulation, resource depletion, inflation, political corruption, and continuous warfare.

Sax, J. L., *Defending the Environment: A Strategy for Citizen Action.* **Knopf, 1971.** Goes beyond political activism and demonstrates how environmental controversies can be taken into court.

Stone, C. D., *Should Trees Have Standing? Toward Legal Rights for Natural Objects.* **Kaufman, 1974.** A bold argument for recognizing the value of the environment, this work was prepared as a legal treatise in the controversial Mineral King-Disney-Sierra Club suit. The U. S. Supreme Court opinions in that case are included.

ECONOMICS AND THE ENVIRONMENT

Clarke, R. O., and P. C. List, *Environmental Spectrum: Social and Economic Views of the Quality of Life.* **Van Nostrand Reinhold, 1974.** Adds the views of sociologists and humanists to the debate on the relation of economic growth to the quality of life.

Crocker, T. D., and A. J. Rogers, III, *Environmental Economics.* **Dryden, 1971.** A whimsical introduction to environmental economics.

Daly, H. E., ed., *Toward a Steady State Economy.* **Freeman, 1973.** Articles arguing for the means by which our industrial society can begin to make the extensive changes needed to prevent its collapse. These contributors believe that "re-tooling," not just "fine tuning" of our economic systems, is necessary.

Dasmann, R. F., J. P. Milton, and P. H. Freeman, *Ecological Principles for Economic Development.* **Wiley, 1973.** Calls for an interdisciplinary understanding of international development, in terms of human and natural resources as well as economic indicators.

Freeman, A. M., R. H. Haveman, and A. V. Kneese, *The Economics of Environmental Policy.* **Wiley, 1973.** A more advanced treatment of pollution control. Deals in some detail with tax, subsidy, and regulation solutions.

Goldman, M. I., ed., *Ecology and Economics: Controlling Pollution in the 1970s.* **Prentice-Hall, 1972.** An introductory collection of essays balancing theory with specific case studies. Shows that production processes in the U. S. A., Europe, Japan, and the U. S. S. R., all have adverse environmental effects which must be accounted for.

Mishan, E. J., *Technology and Growth: The Price We Pay.* **Praeger, 1969.** A rather popularized challenge to growth economists.

Schumacher, E. F., *Small is Beautiful: Economics As If People Mattered.* **Harper & Row, 1973.** A British economist calls for a different sort of economics that will lead, not to mass production, but to production by the masses.

TECHNOLOGY AND SOCIETY

Commoner, Barry, *The Closing Circle: Nature, Man and Technology.* **Bantam, 1971.** A popular account of man's misuse of technology and the resulting ecological damage.

Engineering Concepts Curriculum Project, Polytechnic Institute of Brooklyn, *Man and His Technology.* **McGraw-Hill, 1972.** Presents the basic engineering concepts needed to understand modern technology; easily understood.

Farvar, M. T., and J. P. Milton, eds., *The Careless Technology: Ecology and International Development.* **Doubleday (Natural History; hard cover), 1972.** An extensive treatment (over 1,000 pages) documenting numerous cases of ecological backlash resulting from misplaced technology.

Ferkiss, V., *The Future of Technological Society.* **Braziller, 1974.** An analysis of present-day problems much the same as Heilbroner's *An Inquiry into the Human Prospect* except that the author is optimistic that a new "ecological humanism" will arise, based on a more naturalistic and wholistic view of technological society, and that it will renew planetary order.

Fuller, Buckminster, *Utopia or Oblivion: The Prospects for Humanity.* **Bantam, 1969.** Bursting with technological optimism, the author believes that information and energy "increasing without any foreseeable limit" can solve all of humankind's problems.

Mesthene, E. G., *Technological Change: Its Impact on Man and Society.* **NAL, 1970.** Argues that the accelerating rate of technological change is outstripping the traditional institutions and values of society and that society must respond positively in order to make human beings the masters rather than the slaves of their own inventions.

IMAGES OF THE FUTURE

Cole, H. S. D., C. Freeman, M. Jahoda, and K. L. R. Pavitt, eds., *Models of Doom: A Critique of "The Limits to Growth."* **Universe, 1973.** A detailed critical analysis of the M.I.T. world model (Meadows et al., The Limits to Growth; see below) by a British systems-analysis team. Ends with a response by the original Meadows team reflecting several ideological differences between the two groups of researchers.

Ehrlich, P. R., and A. H. Ehrlich, *The End of Affluence.* **Ballantine, 1974.** Predicts an inevitable defection from the "American Way of Consumption," with new life styles shaped by scarcities.

Harman, W. W., *An Incomplete Guide to the Future,* **Freeman, 1977.** An enthralling book outlining Harmon's belief that Western society will undergo a pervasive transformation in the years ahead.

Heilbroner, R. L., *An Inquiry into the Human Prospect.* **Norton, 1974.** A rather gloomy view of the global predicament of humankind today as it is confronted with runaway population growth, nuclear weaponry, and mounting environmental problems.

Meadows, D. H., D. L. Meadows, J. Randers and W. W. Behrens, III, *The Limits to Growth.* **NAL, 1974.** Current rates of population growth and industrial production are driving world ecosystems to collapse, this controversial study found. It was made with a world simulation model developed by an M.I.T. research group. Public debate has revealed many unstated assumptions on both sides.

Oltmans, W. L., *On Growth.* **Capricorn, 1974.** A series of 70 interviews with prominent people in a wide range of disciplines on the "Limits to Growth" debate.

Toffler, A., ed., *Learning for Tomorrow: The Role of the Future in Education.* **Random House, 1974.** An urgent plea for "education in the future tense," based on the view that we must understand the nature of the future for which we are preparing.

Toffler, A., *Future Shock.* **Bantam, 1970.** A popular book that says the human race must begin to exercise some degree of control over its future or be overwhelmed by exponential rates of change.

Watt, K. F., *The Titanic Effect: Planning for the Unthinkable.* **Sinaur Associates, 1974.** A look at the tendency of individuals and societies to ignore problems until they become crises. To most people the possibility of enormous disasters is simply "unthinkable." Watt argues that without intelligent planning for the future, humankind is headed for disaster.

KEEPING UP TO DATE

NOTE Readers interested in continuing to keep well-informed on environmental issues may do so by reading relevant articles in the following periodicals. Each has a different emphasis and point of view but, collectively, they provide a balanced treatment of environmental developments. They can be found in almost any good-sized library.

Periodicals

Audubon. Published six times a year by the National Audubon Society, 950 Third Ave., New York, NY 10022.

Bioscience. Published twice monthly by the American Institute of Biological Sciences, 3900 Wisconsin Ave. N. W., Washington, DC 20016.

The Ecologist. Published monthly, 73 Molesworth Street, Wadebridge, Cornwall, England.

Environment. Published ten times a year by the Committee for Environmental Information, 438 N. Skinner Boulevard, St. Louis, MO 63130.

Environmental Conservation. Published quarterly by Elsevier Sequoia, S. A. Box 851, 1001 Lausanne 1, Switzerland.

Environmental Science and Technology. Published monthly by the American Chemical Society, 1155 Sixteenth St. N. W., Washington, DC 20036.

The Futurist. Published bimonthly by World Future Society, P. O. Box 19285, Twentieth Street Station, Washington, DC 20036.

Human Ecology: an Interdisciplinary Journal. Published quarterly by Plenum Publishing Corporation, 227 W. 17 St., New York, NY 10011.

Impact of Science on Society. Published quarterly by UNESCO Publishing Center, P. O. Box 433, New York, NY 10016.

The International Journal of Environmental Studies. Published quarterly by Gordon and Breach Science Publishers, Inc., 440 Park Ave. South, New York, NY 10016.

Science. Published weekly by the American Association for the Advancement of Science, 1515 Massachusetts Ave., N. W., Washington, DC 20036.

Scientific American. Published monthly, 415 Madison Ave., New York, NY 10017.

Technology and Culture. Published quarterly by the Univ. of Chicago Press, 5801 Ellis Ave., Chicago, IL 60637.

Zygon, Journal of Religion and Science. Published quarterly by the Univ. of Chicago Press, 5801 Ellis Ave., Chicago, IL 60637.

Environmental Organizations and Institutes

NOTE The following environmental organizations may not publish subscription periodicals, but they are active in generating both new research and educational, political, and legal activity. You may keep informed of their activities and interests by becoming a member.

The Antaeus Group, P.O. Box 4050, Stanford, CA 94305. A newly formed multidisciplinary group involved in environmental education and research.

Environmental Defense Fund, Inc., 162 Old Town Road, East Setauket, NY 11733. A group of scientists, lawyers, and other citizens who defend environmental concerns aggressively and effectively before the courts and regulatory agencies.

Friends of the Earth, 30 E. 42 St., New York, NY 10017. Well known for its activity in public campaigns to protect the environment; issues a news periodical, *Not Man Apart.*

John Muir Institute for Environmental Studies, 2118-C Vine St., Berkeley, CA 94709. Seeks solutions to environmental problems through research and education.

National Audubon Society, 950 Third Ave., New York, NY 10022. Promotes the conservation of wildlife and the natural environment; issues reports to members in addition to the *Audubon* magazine.

The Nature Conservancy, Suite 8000, 1800 N. Kent St., Arlington, VA 22209. Dedicated to preservation of natural areas for present and future generations.

Population Reference Bureau, 1755 Massachusetts Ave., N. W. Washington DC 20036. Involved in in-depth analyses of population-related problems. Publishes a bulletin eight times a year and a world population data chart every year.

Resources for the Future, Inc., 1755 Massachusetts Ave., N. W., Washington DC 20036. Works to advance the development, conservation and use of natural resources.

The Sierra Club, 1050 Mills Tower, San Francisco, CA 94104. A very powerful environmental group. It publishes a monthly bulletin.

Chapter Seven

WESTERN CIVILIZATION:
"... broad understanding of an
entire cultural tradition"

Editorial Advisor:
Mary E. Payer
Contemporary Civilization Staff
Columbia College, Columbia University
and Department of Philosophy Columbia University

INTRODUCTION

In the last half-century, hundreds of American colleges have introduced special interdisciplinary courses taught jointly by professors in a variety of academic fields, including history, philosophy, economics, religion, political science, and sociology.

When they are rigorously developed, these courses serve two primary purposes. They can provide an introduction to a wide range of later studies, and they can convey a broad understanding of an entire cultural tradition better than can courses in any single academic field.

One of the oldest and most influential programs of this kind is the Contemporary Civilization program developed at Columbia College, Columbia University. This section is based on the work done by generations of scholars who have taught in the program since its introduction in 1917, as it is interpreted and taught by a current staff member.

Originally begun as an attempt to explain the issues involved in the First World War, the program has long since been broadened to encompass the interdisciplinary study of the ideals, origins, and characteristic elements of Western (as distinct from Eastern, or Asian) society. Today the program allows the perceptive student to grasp the rich, subtle, and often contradictory elements of the Western tradition.

WHAT IS "WESTERN CIVILIZATION"?

Although the title "Western Civilization" is straightforward enough, it is a difficult and challenging task to determine what, precisely, is implied in defining and understanding the reality of that sociopoliticocultural entity which is both uniquely "Western" and has the unity of structural, functional, and conceptual characteristics which give it a claim to being a "civilization."

Consequently, an awareness of the necessity of considering many elements simultaneously has been, and must continue to be, part of the study of Western Civilization. The difficulty, then, is to understand the need to make sense of the concepts, issues, and historical problems involved without distorting them by translating them into wholly contemporary terms.

This difficulty has led to the debate over what is involved in the understanding of Western Civilization. Is it purely history, in which we trace the development of concepts of major importance in the Western tradition—such as "justice," "the person," or "authority"? Or is it the achronological analysis of problems and issues, without particular concern for their historical and developmental implications?

It is my feeling that the study of Western civilization demands that we recognize the importance of all approaches to understanding, and that we exploit these approaches when and where they are useful and germane. It is never possible to merely "do history"; by the very fact that we have chosen to study wars rather than slavery, for example, we are selectively creating the history we study. The same can be said of Western civilization: we create it by defining it in a certain way, and we should be conscious of this fact in our approach.

With respect to the history of ideas, it is important to develop an awareness of the temptation to create spurious continuities by smoothing over, or ignoring, terminological or conceptual differences in the great ideas of Western culture.

Finally, it is necessary to preserve an analytic approach to what is read. In the study of Western Civilization, a healthy skepticism is one of the most fruitful attitudes to maintain (as it is in the study of almost anything): it will go a long way toward enabling us to separate truth from fantasy and to ferret out the ideological notions embedded in so-called matters of fact.

RELATIONSHIP OF OURSELVES TO THE MATERIAL

This consideration brings us quite naturally to the question of how independent readers should approach the study of Western Civilization. My introductory remarks on the complexity of the topic were not intended to scare, nor to make the task seem difficult (or, indeed, a task). Rather, they were made in order to point out the pitfalls of certain prevalent academic approaches and to alert readers to biases existing among scholars.

The study of Western Civilization should be richly rewarding, for the civilization is rich; and it should be challenging, and often something like detective work. There are very few clues that explain the triumph of certain ideas and norms and the decline of others.

Why is it, for example, that Western civilization is patriarchal in its major outlines? Why is individualism such a matter of concern? Was a woman a person in ancient Rome (where six women in the same family might have the same name, and so exist in only a roughly identified fashion) in the same way that a man was a person? When did the dominance of reason occur (if ever) in the West? And so on. These are the parts of a great puzzle that can be put together only slowly; the parts, moreover, often come in surprising shapes and forms.

All these points can be made with relative ease when the course is taught in the classroom, face-to-face. For independent readers, however, the situation is somewhat different; guidance is therefore built into the arrangement of the appended bibliography. Roughly, the bibliography takes the following form.

Meta-Concerns

The second section of the bibliography is titled "History and Ideology: Thinking About What We Are Doing." It is intended to illustrate that there are different notions of history, that there is an ideological problem to consider in understanding Western (or any other) civilization, and that the function of ideology itself must be understood in order to make sense of the past.

Organization

The bibliography is arranged chronologically because there is a great value to seeing the development of ideas over time. Within each chronological (or roughly chronological) section, important topics, issues, and developments are listed separately. In addition to this general structure, I have placed introductory or background discussions at the start of each section. Consequently the reader should be able to move from more general to more specific consideration of each chronological period and each topic of interest.

Debate

Debate often occurs in classroom discussion. In order to make it clear to independent readers that there is room for disagreement I have wherever possible included articles or books which present different opinions or conflicting interpretations of major topics—for example, the role of slavery in Greece and Rome; debate on the standard of living during the Industrial Revolution; the problem of madness in the age of reason. The book by Kaplow, listed in the first section of the bibliography, is invaluable as a source of well-argued opposing views.

BRIEF CHRONOLOGICAL GUIDELINES

To provide the reader with a broad summary view, each title of a main section in the following bibliography is given here with a brief characterization of major developments covered in the readings for that section.

The Ancient World—Greece and Rome

Important as seat of Western culture; development of canons of rationality and scientific method; important theories of the state, ethics, politics; notion of the person as necessarily and naturally part of the state; low status of women; slavery a fact of life.

The Medieval World

Inheritance of classic tradition; modification of this tradition by Judaeo-Christian world view; establishment of Christianity in the West; dominance of the Pauline tradition; Christian theory of history—progress toward an end, a goal set by God (as opposed to Greek cyclical theories of rise and decay); the growth of science; development of feudal society and change of legal and political norms; the barbarian influence; the problem of church and state; the importance of millenial Christianity; early peasant revolts; development of cities as trade grew and increased; medieval attitudes toward rationality—more flexible than those of later centuries; heresy and persecution.

Early Modern Europe

The Renaissance, and rediscovery of the pagan world; the influence of humanism on all aspects of life and culture; narrowing attitudes toward rationality; foundations of early European states, and development of more rational politics of power (Machiavelli); economic growth and expansion; early imperialism and colonization (Spain and the New World).

The Reformation

Revolution in theology; end of the Roman Catholic Church's era of dominance in religion, secular ideology, and politics; development of Lutheran and Calvinist traditions; splinter sects, in revolt from Lutheran and Calvinist domination of the reformation; the alliance of reformation theology and politics (see Engels, *The Peasant War*); development of individualism consonant with Lutheran notions of justification and personal relationship to God; personal conscience as opposed to mediation of The Church; relationship of Protestant world view to growth of capitalism (see Weber).

The Seventeenth Century

Consolidation of monarchies; the debate over constitutionalism (Hobbes, Locke); social contract theory—scientific theories of the origin and growth of the state, and its justification; growth of individualism, and its relationship to the growth of a market economy; the gradual transformation of rural to urban society; the revolution in science and philosophy (Galileo, Descartes, Newton); development of a century yields new theories of mind, nature, and science, in which the world becomes more mechanical, the person more rational.

The Enlightenment

The triumph of reason; the problem of dealing with Christian and pagan influences in Enlightenment thought (see Gay); the continued tendency to dehumanize the insane intensifies; knowledge and morality become more complex areas of debate (Hume, Kant); the importance of freedom in morality and political theory (Kant, Rousseau); the development of theory of the ego (Kant); the market system is given a theory (Adam Smith).

Eighteenth-Century Revolutions

Theories of revolution; the American Revolution; the French Revolution; importance of Enlightenment ideals to the revolutionaries; conflicting interpretation of the French Revolution; conservative critique of revolution (Burke).

The Industrial Revolution

The revolution in methods of manufacturing, and the consequent restructuring of society; the impact of the industrial revolution upon day-to-day life and upon Britain's place in the world economy; the traumatic effects of industrialization upon families and individuals; the optimist-pessimist debate over improvement in standard of living; the gloomy prognostications of Malthus.

Restoration, Revolution, and Nationalism

Restoration of monarchy after collapse of the French Revolution of 1789; the mid-nineteenth-century revolutions and their failure; the growth of European liberalism; nationalist sentiment increases; reform movements collapse as the revolutions of the 1840s fail.

The Advance of Capitalism—Programs for Reform

The second phase of British capitalism, and the growing industrial power of Germany; criticism of the effects of industrialization within Britain—debate over social reform (Mill, Bentham, utilitarian philosophy); Mill's theory of individualism, and its impact upon British political theory and social legislation (importance of general educational system; free speech); Mill and early support (liberal variety) for feminism.

The Growth of Socialism

Utopian Socialism of Owen, Fourier, Saint-Simon; critique of Utopian Socialism (Marx and Engels); the Communist Manifesto; Marx—

theories of human nature, alienation, relationship of human and societal development to economic base; critique of capitalism; Socialist feminism, critique of the bourgeois family.

Science, Philosophy, and Technology in the Nineteenth Century

Darwin and the theory of evolution; impact of Darwin upon all aspects of intellectual life; social Darwinism; Hegel—the phenomenology of mind: growth of theory of consciousness; Nietzsche—critique of traditional moral theory; early explorations in human consciousness and psychology; the growth of technology seen as a problem (*Frankenstein*); continuing encroachment upon the rights of the insane; development of scientific attitudes toward madness.

Friends and Enemies of Capitalism

Critique of capitalist theory; Marx—*Kapital*; friends—Carnegie and "The Gospel of Wealth"; critique of Marx (Wicksteed); Lenin on the role of the intellectual in bringing about the overthrow of the capitalist state.

The Unified Nation-State

Mature nation-states in Europe; their growing power after the collapse of the 1848 revolutions; consolidation of law within countries; development of increasing tensions between countries; impending collapse of international relations as tensions increase.

Imperialism

Expansion of European and United States economies into the underdeveloped countries; colonialism and its relationship to needs of the developed economies; justification of imperialism (Disraeli, T. Roosevelt; see Schumpeter); Lenin's critique of imperialism, and its important role in critique of developed capitalism; continuing debate over imperialism.

The Twentieth Century

Revolutions continue; colonialism continues; critique of the psychologically devastating effects of colonialism (see Fanon); feminism grows in its critical power (see Rowbotham); Fascism and counterrevolution as a fact of twentieth-century life; Nazism as an economic, social, and psychological phenomenon; continuing defense and critique of capitalism (see Friedman; Marcuse); the ecological crisis and its vast proportions (see *The Limits to Growth*); the growth and influence of psychoanalytic theory (Freud; Erikson); important revisions to psychoanalytic theory (Reich, Laing, Erikson, Marcuse); development of theories of the self: Freud, and the recognition of the unconscious; critics of Freud's theory of the person (see Marcuse, *Eros*); Freud's critique of repressive society; Marcuse's advancement of this critique; critique of psychology, and development of behaviorist theories (Skinner); the critique of science (Kuhn).

BIBLIOGRAPHY

This rich and long bibliography is designed in a special way to serve as your reading and study guide. In the bibliographies of other sections, most individual entries refer to an entire book that the entry cites and comments on. Many entries in this bibliography, by contrast, refer to parts of books that are identified and commented on.

Since specific chapters and sections of books have thus been singled out in order to give you more complete guidance, you do not have to cope unaided with massive tomes spanning many centuries and epochal controversies.

Books that present large collections of source documents and essays and that are repeatedly cited in the entries are given in the bibliography's opening section. Appearing first (before the author's name) in the entry for each collection is the abbreviation or key word used to identify the book in later citations.

If you like, you can read only these bulging collections for a respectable introduction to the complex heritage of Western Civilization; they are widely used as basic reading in college courses. Most entries, however, refer to full works in paperbacks as well as to the briefer and introductory selections or treatments from these collections. As a result, you can go well beyond a mere snippet or taste of any subject or age that deeply interests you.

All the collections are available in paperback editions except for the first two listed (each of which is a relatively expensive, two-volume work, issued only in hard covers). But since the later entries most often give alternates for selections in these two works, it is not absolutely necessary to use them.

Notations at the end of many entries indicate the level of difficulty of the reading, as follows (no notation is given if the level is evident from the entry itself).

BASIC   College freshman-sophomore level. Introductory material; little or no background needed for understanding.

INTERMEDIATE   College sophomore-junior level. Even if introductory, not understandable without some effort, background data, or knowledge of more basic material.

ADVANCED   College senior level or for penetrating readers. Theoretically demanding, complex; may assume exposure to some understanding of many issues or deeper understanding of one. The most challenging level of work and, potentially, the most rewarding.

After listing the books of collections, the bibliography presents a group of readings (on history and ideology) that can deepen your understanding of almost all works subsequently listed. The bibliography finally portrays the vast and intricate sweep of European-American civilization chronologically, as it unfolded in time.

COLLECTIONS OFTEN REFERRED TO IN LATER ENTRIES (ABBREVIATIONS OR KEY WORDS USED FOR LATER REFERENCE GIVEN FIRST)

ICCW. **Contemporary Civilization Staff of Columbia College,** *Introduction to Contemporary Civilization in the West,* **3rd ed., 2 vols. Columbia Univ. Press (hard cover), 1961.** A source book, chronologically arranged, presenting selections which document most major topics in Western Civilization—such as political theory, social theory, science, religion, history, and economics. The selections are copious but often quite brief. Thus, while chronologically extensive (ancient world through early twentieth century), the collection is limited by brevity; it should therefore be used as an "introductory" vehicle. Presents very little on slavery, women, and radical movements; must be supplemented by other sources for full documentation.

CWC. **Contemporary Civilization Staff of Columbia College,** *Chapters in Western Civilization,* **3rd ed., 2 vols. Columbia Univ. Press (hard cover), 1962.** The companion book to *ICCW, CWC* is a collection of essays by distinguished scholars, encompassing the areas mentioned above and designed to provide "a clear understanding of contemporary institutions through the study of the past." The essays—lucid and comprehensive without being forbiddingly difficult—are an excellent introduction to the general period or topic to be studied. However, the essays end with the early twentieth century and closely follow the "limited" approach described above.

Kaplow. **Kaplow, Jeffry,** *Western Civilization: Mainstream Readings and Radical Critiques,* **2 vols. Knopf, 1973.** This book has four merits. It supplements *ICCW* and *CWC,* both in time covered (up to the Cold War), and in topics included (social stratification, fascism, and so on). It discusses the notion of radical history. It presents a generally balanced debate by radical and nonradical historians for each topic covered. And its selections are not so short as to be unusable. Truncation of selections is somewhat troublesome but can be compensated for by reading entire sections (as opposed to individual chapters). No treatment of women or psychology; weak treatment of Greece; excellent on Reformation, Industrial Revolution, Russian Revolution.

LD. **Cherniavsky, Michael, and Arthur T. Slavin,** *Social Textures of Western Civilization: The Lower Depths,* **2 vols. Xerox College, 1972. (Vol. 2 by Cherniavsky, Slavin, and Stuart Ewen.)** While this collection provides a rich selection of contemporary sources and documents, it is limited by the extreme brevity of most selections. Comparatively extensive material on urban and rural life, women, and "psychic experience" (reason; consciousness of self). Very sparse on early modern Europe; less sparse but not extensive coverage of the French revolution.

OS. Chodorow, Stanley, and Peter N. Stearns, eds., *The Other Side of Western Civilization; Readings in Everyday Life*, 2 vols. Harcourt Brace Jovanovich, 1973. The focus of this collection is "everyday life," as illustrated through the study, for example, of leisure events, sports; short, often specialized articles on crime, the working class, and hygiene (as typical examples) abound. The very narrow focus is limiting; however, there are articles on women and on family life, and these are a plus, if a somewhat qualified one.

EE. Mitchell, Allan, and Istvan Deak, *Everyman in Europe; Essays in Social History*, 2 vols. Prentice-Hall, 1974. Another collection which aims to comprehend the life of the poor men and women who have always been the majority in Western society. Arguing that the poor and uneducated are more readily comprehended as "types" (such as peasant, woman) than are individuals (such as Louis XIV), the authors present a chronologically organized series of type-problems, focusing mainly on women, slaves-serfs, urban-rural issues, industrialization and youth. Selections are of uneven length, and most are excerpted from much longer books. As usual, the collection is limited by its specialized aim and by the brevity of articles. It is recommended for its inclusion of material on slaves, women, youth, old and new social types, and conflicts in standards of morality.

ISS. Blackburn, Robin, *Ideology in Social Science*. Random House, 1973. Some of the most recent writing by radical scholars in the field of social theory. Important articles present a critique of dominant ideologies in the social sciences, especially economics, history, *political science*, and sociology. In the section titled "Key Problems," important problems in recent capitalism are discussed, and the characteristics of American imperialism are differentiated from those of European imperialism. While this is not a basic collection, it is invaluable for the study of ideology and ideological issues and for the more advanced reader seeking critiques of Western civilization.

ST. Fried, Albert, and Ronald Sanders, *Socialist Thought*. Doubleday, 1964. This anthology, a "documentary history" of European socialism, is designed to present a comprehensive picture of the development of socialism which is neither too diffuse nor misleadingly brief. As a result, the readings are extensive (covering the period from the early communism of the French Revolution through twentieth-century socialism) and cover topics from "Utopian Socialism" through "Anarchism," "Revisionism," and "Bolshevism." While the selections are extracted from the major documents of socialism, and while the range of authors is broad (Babeuf, Fichte, Millerand, C.A.R. Crosland), they are unfortunately brief (some only one or two pages). The book is therefore best used as a basic introduction, to be followed by more lengthy readings.

Revolutions. Kaplan, Lawrence, ed., *Revolutions; A Comparative Study from Cromwell to Castro.* Doubleday, 1973. It is difficult to find satisfactory treatments of the subject of revolution, and this anthology does not completely suffice. It is implicitly (through topical and chronological listing) rather than explicitly comparative. There is a useful first part, presenting three articles defining revolution; parts five and six provide welcome coverage of twentieth-century revolutions in Russia, China, Vietnam, Mexico, Algeria, and the French universities. Articles are for the most part long and substantial. INTERMEDIATE.

Anarchy. Krimerman, Leonard I., and Lewis Perry, eds. *Patterns of Anarchy; A Collection of Writings in the Anarchist Tradition.* Doubleday, 1966. A comprehensive presentation of the anarchist position through topics of central importance: definition of anarchism, its philosophical foundations, anarchism's critique of society as it is, anarchist alternatives, theories of education, the critique of socialism, and the question of the 'soundness' of anarchism. An excellent collection, limited only by the brevity of many selections. Useful as both an introduction and as a more advanced focus of discussion for specialized topics such as education, the individual, and the critique of socialism. An excellent companion to *ST,* above.

HISTORY AND IDEOLOGY:
THINKING ABOUT WHAT WE ARE DOING

Hegel, G. W. F., *Reason and History.* Bobbs-Merrill, 1953. "The Three Methods of Writing History," pp. 3–10). On the three methods of treating history—as original, reflective, or philosophical. Philosophical history is to Hegel "the thoughtful contemplation of history." BASIC-INTERMEDIATE.

Jones, Gareth Stedman, "History: The Poverty of Empiricism," in *ISS,* pp. 96–115. Examination of recent schools of history and critique of historical conclusions based only on the "facts" and drawn in the absence of a comprehensive theory of history or society. INTERMEDIATE.

Kaplow, Jeffry, "The Meaning of Radical History," in *Kaplow,* Vol. I, pp. xiii–xx. A straightforward and lucid argument for the necessity of "radical history" which, while preserving the truth, refuses "to make the truth dispassionate." BASIC.

Mannheim, Karl, *Ideology and Utopia: An Introduction to the Sociology of Knowledge.* Harcourt Brace Jovanovich, 1955. Ch. I, "Preliminary Approach to the Problem," pp. 1–54; Ch. II, "Ideology and Utopia," pp. 55–108; Ch. IV, The Utopian Mentality," pp. 192–263. A difficult but rich study of the nature of ideology, its evaluative and nonevaluative senses; treats: the need to understand the function of ideology in order to understand the true roots of social consciousness and self-understanding (Ch. I); false consciousness and the dangers of conscious or unconscious self-delusion (Ch. II); the relationship of what is called "Utopian" to what is called "real" (Ch. IV). ADVANCED, but fulfilling to the more sophisticated reader, in its critique of "unconscious social existence." Relation to Western Civilization: To what extent do we understand history, society, existence in society? To what extent are we the victims of ideological distortion, knowingly or unknowingly?

Erikson, Erik, *Childhood and Society,* rev. ed. Norton, 1964. Ch. 8, Reflections on the American Identity." A psychological investigation of the development of uniquely American roles or prototypes, such as "Mom" (the dominant, authoritarian mother) and John Henry ("the equal of any machine"); the influence of "the machine" on values which become important in individual development; and the relationship of "national identities" to individual ego-formation. Suggestive in its demonstration that "ideological" notions have psychologically important implications. INTERMEDIATE, but assumes knowledge of psychology.

THE ANCIENT WORLD: GREECE AND ROME

General

Marrou, Henri, "The Heritage of the Ancient World," in CWC, Vol. I, Ch. I. Importance of Greece as direct ancestor of the modern West— Greece as the seat of science, philosophy, and rationality in the ancient world.

Greece, Source Works

Plato, *The Republic,* tr. F. M. Cornford. Oxford Univ. Press, 1945. The source of most important issues in Western political theory: the nature of the state and of justice; the concept of justice and its definition; relationship of the person to the state; definition of the person; and relationship of ability to social class. Justification of theory of the state through theory of knowledge (Theory of Ideas). Important discussions of education, communism, the role of women, and censorship. An absolutely necessary reading in Western Civilization. INTERMEDIATE, except for theory of knowledge (ADVANCED).

Aristotle, *The Politics,* tr. A. T. Sinclair. Penguin, 1970. A continuation of the Platonic debate, improved by Aristotle's blend of empirical data with theoretical assertions. Critique of Plato. Theory of revolutions. Classification of types of state, from best to worst. Critique of democracy as we know it, and defense of "oligarchic democracy." The state seen as responsible for producing the highest moral life possible in humans. Slavery is justified, women are seen as less rational than men. INTERMEDIATE. Introductory selections in *ICCW*, Vol. I, pp. 30–59, BASIC.

Aristotle, *Nichomachean Ethics,* tr. Martin Ostwald, Bobbs-Merrill, 1962. Aristotle's classic work in moral theory, in which he argues that politics is part of ethics, the science of the good. Good, justice, responsibility, and free will are among the important moral concepts defined. Completes the theoretical underpinning to Aristotle's arguments on the good life and the good state presented in the *Politics*. Books I and X, The Good, BASIC. The book as a whole, INTERMEDIATE to ADVANCED.

Greece, Secondary Works

Barker, Ernest, *The Political Thought of Plato and Aristotle.* **Dover, 1959.** Classic. Ranges from the Pre-Socratics through the influence of Greek political theory on later ages. INTERMEDIATE.

Bernal, J. D., *Science in History,* **Vol. I,** *The Emergence of Science.* **M.I.T. Press, 1974.** Bernal traces the emergence of science from its archaic origins and traditions through the Middle Ages. A superb introductory section discusses the complexity of the term "science," demonstrating that science is a concept with many senses (technique, methodology, tradition), all important if we are to understand what science is, does, and implies. With this background, Part 2 documents the course of science in the ancient world and its interrelationship with historic and societal development. Chapter 4 is devoted to the Iron Age and to Greek science and technology in particular.

Jaeger, Werner, *Paidaea: The Ideals of Greek Culture,* **3 vols. Oxford Univ. Press. Vol. 1, 1974; Vol. 2 (hard cover), 1943; Vol. 3 (hard cover), 1944.** A work of genius, in which Jaeger traces the development and shaping of the Greek character through the historical processes by which character was formed and through intellectual processes by which the ideal human personality was constructed. Rich material on the heroic and classical ideals, the age of Plato, the struggle for the establishment of rationality as a standard, and the reconstruction of Greek culture (and conflict of cultural ideals) after the decline of the Athenian empire. ADVANCED.

Kitto, H.D.F., *The Greeks.* **Pelican, 1969.** Clear and comprehensive discussion of the major aspects of Greek life and thought, especially politics, philosophy, "the Greek mind," urban-rural relations, and the importance of the fifth century B.C. Very easy to read. BASIC.

Slater, Philip E., *The Glory of Hera; Greek Mythology and the Greek Family.* **Beacon, 1968.** Reconstruction of the pattern of interpersonal relations in the Greek family and analysis of elemental psychological conflicts mediating and constituting these relationships; the reflection of Greek family relationships in the figures of Greek mythology. Excellent material on mother-son relationships; the psychic consequences of the social repression of Greek women and their isolation in the home; the establishment of male defense reactions against "the threat of ambivalent mothers." Knowledge of some psychoanalytic theory is necessary in order to fully exploit Slater's work. An important contribution to the understanding of the complete Greek psyche and of the exploitation of women in Greece. INTERMEDIATE to ADVANCED.

Kaplow, J., "I / Ancient Greece: Slavery and Science," in *Kaplow,* Vol. I, pp. 1–32. Two articles, one on slave labor in Greece, the other on the problem of the halt of science in the fifth century B.C. In both articles it is argued that domination (of persons in one case, nature in the other) was a leitmotif of classical Greek culture; and that, paradoxically, freedom, rationality, and slavery advanced hand in hand. BASIC.

Rome

Kaplow, J., "II / The End of the Roman Empire in the West," in *Kaplow,* Vol. I, pp. 33–67. In this group of three articles, which should be read as a unit, Kaplow presents varying explanations for the fall of Rome—one arguing that Rome fell when the upper "classes" were absorbed by the lower (involving a lowering of standards); another, that Rome fell when the sociopolitical structure was strained beyond its limits, and could no longer hope to be rescued by devices and institutions such as slavery; and finally, the argument that successive barbarian incursions produced indirect pressures which altered the forces of production, the balance of power, and the old regime (including the regime of slavery). Taken as a whole, the articles throw light on the important issue of slavery and class in the Roman Empire. INTERMEDIATE.

THE MEDIEVAL WORLD

The Early Development of Christianity—General

Latourette, Kenneth Scott, "Medieval Thought: Christian Conceptions of Life," in *CWC,* Vol. I, Chapter II. This article stresses the debt of the Middle Ages to early Christianity, the late Roman world, and Augustine. The following entries present further background material and major sources on early Christianity and Augustine as bases for understanding the Medieval World.

Kaplow, J., "III / The Early History of Christianity," in *Kaplow,* Vol. I, pp. 69–102. The two articles in this section analyze the myth of Jesus and ideological notions surrounding the development of early Christian "legend" and the social basis of Christianity. Both Pauline Christianity and the Christianity which finally "triumphed" in once-pagan Rome are seen as products of social change which coincided with religious change. BASIC to INTERMEDIATE.

The Early Development of Christianity—Sources

Paul of Tarsus, Epistles to the Romans, Galatians, Corinthians, in *The New Testament of the Jerusalem Bible,* Doubleday, 1969. The need to live by the Spirit, the role of a Christian, the relationship of a Christian to the state, the life of faith, and the doctrine of justification by faith—all important aspects of the Christianity of Augustine and

Luther—are presented in moving and direct fashion by Paul, the most influential of the early Christian apostles. Note the "mood" as well as the content of these letters. Basic.

Augustine, The *Confessions,* tr. R. S. Pine-Coffin. Penguin, 1961. The first great autobiography written by a Western thinker, the *Confessions* is an impassioned narrative of Augustine's movement from pagan to Christian life. Important sections on sin, free will, God's grace; the meaning of time and its relation to consciousness; Christian love. Reflecting a mixture of Pauline theology and neo-Platonic philosophy, with strong doses of Augustine's original psychologizing, the *Confessions* is a "mirror of the age." Basic to Intermediate. Sections in Book XI, on time, more Advanced.

Augustine, *The City of God,* ed. David Knowles, Pelican, 1972. Augustine's refutation of the argument that Christianity caused the decay of Rome. The two cities—that of God and that of the world—are contrasted; and history is seen as the story of the progress of the struggle between the forces of God and forces of the devil. Shaped debate on government, society, and Christianity for centuries. Profound "Christian pessimism": hope for secular happiness is an empty dream. Intermediate.

Science and Learning in the Middle Ages

Claggett, Marshall, "The Growth of Learning in the West," Ch. III, in *CWC,* Vol. I. Background of medieval scientific and scholarly activity and its relationship to Greek culture. Basic.

Bernal, J. D., *Science in History,* Vol. 1, *The Emergence of Science* (see above). In Chs. 5 and 6, Bernal continues his masterful exploration of the interrelationship of the paths of science and history. He traces the influence of Islam upon early medieval science; discusses the clash between theology and science; and documents the development (dogma notwithstanding) of autonomous scientific traditions, methods, and institutions in the Middle Ages.

Medieval European Society—General

Mundy, John Hine, "European Society in the Middle Ages," in *CWC,* Vol. I, Ch. IV. Basic background discussion of the development of medieval society, the classes constituting it, the Christian ideology, and the power of the church.

Kaplow, J., "IV / Barbarian Society," in *Kaplow,* Vol. I, pp. 103–136. Two brief articles discuss the impact of barbarian upon Roman society and justice. The role of the clan and its centrality to the Germans is analyzed; and the blood feud as a means of administering justice and controlling violence is examined. The latter article is a convenient introduction to the notion of alternate systems of justice and the problem of the control of violence in the absence of a central state authority. Basic to Intermediate.

Kaplow, J., "V / Feudalism," in *Kaplow*, Vol. I, pp. 137–170. Two brief excerpts by Bloch and by Parain introduce the problem of defining feudalism; Kaplow contrasts Bloch's complex but "somewhat artificial" definition with Parain's more strongly economic one. Parain bases his concept of feudalism on the existing relationships of production and the resultant class structures (the feudal lord has property in the land and limited property in the serf as well.) A good debate, if somewhat advanced. Readers desiring more should move on to Bloch, below.

Heer, Friedrich, *The Medieval World, Europe 1100–1350*. NAL, 1964. A *tour de force* in which Heer lucidly and comprehensively sweeps through all important aspects of medieval life, from politics and religion through university life, science, and history. Read *in toto*, advanced; but well worth the effort. Note especially Chapter 13, "Jews and Women."

Bloch, Marc, *Feudal Society*, tr. L. A. Manyon, 2 vols. Univ. of Chicago Press, 1961. A work of major importance for the understanding of medieval society as a comprehensive whole, including environment—conditions of life and "mental climate"; the ties of kinship and their social function; the relationship of vassalage, and its socioeconomic implication; classes in medieval society; social organization; and feudalism as a particular and persistent type of society. The book as a whole is advanced, but sections—such as those on the impact of the barbarian invasions, kinship ties, and social classes—may be read separately to supplement more basic readings in these areas (such as the introductory essays in *CWC*). A great work of scholarship.

Medieval European Society—Sources

Louis the Pious, *Capitulare de Villis*, excerpts in *ICCW*, Vol. I, pp. 326–334. A list of instructions composed shortly before 800 A.D. for the royal stewards in the properties of Carolingian Gaul, in which many important concerns of the manor—such as justice for its inhabitants and fiscal responsibility in day-to-day operations—are illustrated. BASIC.

Anonymous, *The Annals of Xanten*, excerpts in *ICCW*, Vol. I, pp. 334–341. A brief extract from ninth-century history, illustrating the sense of devastation and chaos caused by famine and the plunder of the Northmen. BASIC.

Power, Eileen, *Medieval People*, Barnes & Noble, 1963. A well-chosen selection of six "sketches" illustrating "various aspects of social life in the Middle Ages and various classes of historical material." The selections span the experiences of a peasant, Bodo; Marco Polo; a prioress (Chaucer's Mme. Eglantine in real life); a wealthy housewife; a wool merchant; and a clothier. The reality of day-to-day existence is clearly grasped through the reading of these selections, as is the more subtle fabric of implications of class and role. BASIC, and an excellent book of its kind.

Marcus, J. R., ed., *The Jew in the Medieval World*, Atheneum, 1969.
A source book of documents illustrating the life experiences, social
existence, and persecution of medieval European Jews. Selections from
this book on the persecution of the Strasbourg Jews and the protection
of Jews by Papal decree appear in *LD*, Vol. I, pp. 322–325. Selections
are BASIC.

Medieval European Society—Secondary Works

**Aries, Philippe, *Centuries of Childhood, A Social History of Family
Life*, Random House, 1962.** In this unique work Aries demonstrates
that, until relatively recently, "childhood life" was unknown. The
book spans the period extending from the Middle Ages to the
seventeenth century and discusses family, school, and discipline as
well as the child. As Aries proceeds in an order which is topical (the
idea of childhood; dress; education; the college; the family; and so on)
rather than chronological, the reader must skip through the book ex-
tracting those portions germane to the Middle Ages. However, the first
three chapters, Part I, serve as an excellent introduction to the problem
of defining childhood; and the introductory chapters to the sections on
scholastic life and the family also discuss the medieval situation. The
book is a pioneering venture in an important but hitherto uninvesti-
gated aspect of social history. BASIC to INTERMEDIATE.

Politics in the Middle Ages—Introduction and Sources

**Strayer, Joseph R., "Medieval Political Institutions," in *CWC*, Vol. I,
Ch. I.** A basic introduction to the political history of the Middle Ages,
from the fifth to the fifteenth centuries.

**Aquinas, Thomas, *The Pocket Aquinas*, ed. Vernon J. Bourke.
Pocket Books, 1960.** The sections on moral life and ethics; usury and
credit sales; society and political philosophy (the nature of the state;
the desirability of rule by one person; the function of the state) provide
an accurate and comprehensive picture of the political views of
Aquinas, who became the greatest name in thirteenth-century intellectual life and who is known today as the foremost medieval philosopher.
Evident in these selections is Aquinas' awareness of the problems of
political existence, the need to find new solutions to new problems
(usury and expanding trade, for example), and the influence of Aristotelianism upon one of the most probing and comprehensive thinkers
ever to write in the west. INTERMEDIATE.

**Gui, Bernard, *Manual of the Inquisitor*. Selections in *ICCW*, Vol. I,
pp. 257–265.** A brief extract from the translated *Manual* illustrating the
medieval church's preoccupation with heresy, its extreme concern for
"wayward souls," and the fate of those who chose to remain true to
their variant theological views. BASIC.

**Tierney, Brian, ed., *The Crisis of Church and State, 1050–1300*.
Prentice-Hall, 1964.** This collection, with commentary, includes selec-

tions from all major participants in the battle over the proper relationship between church and state, and the question of ultimate supremacy of either pope or emperor. INTERMEDIATE.

Politics in the Middle Ages—Secondary Works

Kaplow, J., "Religion, Revolt, and Social Struggles in the Late Middle Ages," in Kaplow, Vol. I, pp. 171–214. Three selections which focus attention on an important but too often neglected part of medieval politics—the rebellions of the poor and the way in which radical politics and radical religion joined hands to struggle for the attainment of the equality and dignity before God, promised to all by the Gospels. An excellent if brief introduction to the issues of milleniarist Christianity and its social force. The article by Cohn can serve as an introduction to The Pursuit of the Millenium, below. INTERMEDIATE.

Cohn, Norman, The Pursuit of the Millenium, rev. ed. Oxford Univ. Press, 1970. A classic history of anarchic sects in the twelfth to sixteenth centuries in Europe. Especially valuable is Cohn's exhaustive treatment of the connection between radicalism in religion and the struggles of the poor. A good book to read in conjunction with Engels's The Peasant War in Germany. INTERMEDIATE.

The Economy in the Middle Ages

Clagett, Marshall, "The Medieval Economy", in CWC, Vol. I, Ch. V. A brief introduction to the importance of trade to the growing medieval economy; the development of the guilds; and agriculture and feudalism.

Pirenne, Henri, Medieval Cities: Their Origins and the Revival of Trade. Princeton Univ. Press, 1970. In this highly debated book written in 1925, Pirenne argues that it was the closing of the Mediterranean Sea by the Moslems, and not the invasions of the barbarians, that ruined the ancient world and shattered the Roman empire. This "Moslem lake" theory is the center of much recent controversy. But other parts of the book present an excellent discussion of the necessary relationship of urban growth to active and profitable commerce. Two thorough chapters cover the origins of the merchant and middle classes. BASIC.

EARLY MODERN EUROPE

General

Burckhardt, Jacob, The Civilization of the Renaissance in Italy, 2 vols., Harper & Row, 1958. Burckhardt's lucidly and tightly written masterwork on the Italian Renaissance, written in 1860, is still the standard reference work on that period's manners, morals, society, learning, and life. While the book as a whole is advanced, smaller sections can be read as rewarding, self-contained units which serve as introductions to such topics as "discovery of the individual," "equality of men and women," "the connection of ridicule and wit with individualism," and "general spirit of doubt." Highly recommended as itself one of the outstanding examples of Western Civilization.

Foucault, Michel, *Madness and Civilization; A History of Insanity in the Age of Reason*, NAL, 1965. Ch. 1, "Stultifera Navis," examines the identification of "madmen" as scapegoats in the period following the extermination of leprosy (lepers formerly having been the medical pariahs) and the beginning of a "modern" attitude toward the "mad"—discomfort rooted in the knowledge that the power of the mad is their indifference to reason, and fascination based upon the unapproachable freedom of the "mad." This is not a simple book, but its refusal to accept the lot of the "mad" as a fact and its probing beneath the surface of culture, in an attempt to explain changing attitudes toward the mentally deviant, make it an important part of any Western Civilization course.

Early Modern Europe—Politics

Bouwsma, William J., "Politics in the Age of the Renaissance," in *CWC*, Vol. I, Ch. VII. A basic discussion of politics in and among the Italian city-states, problems of consolidation of local governments into nations throughout Europe, and international relations in the Renaissance.

Rice, Eugene F., Jr., *The Foundations of Early Modern Europe, 1460–1559*, Norton, 1970. In chapters on science, technology, humanism and art, as well as chapters on economic and political development, Rice traces the important movements in the foundation of early modern Europe. A compact yet highly readable presentation. Chapter 4, "The Formation of the Early Modern State," sketches important factors in the emergence of sovereign states. BASIC.

Machiavelli, Niccolo, *The Prince and Selected Discourses*, ed. and tr. Daniel Donno. Bantam, 1971. In *The Prince* Machiavelli presented a theory of political leadership which stressed the possession and maintainence of power and split off politics from morality. Exit Aristotle, Plato, and Aquinas; enter the modern world of politics. Since its presentation, *The Prince* has been a major text in the attempted justification of "power politics." In his *Discourses* Machiavelli describes the positive aspects of republican government. A more optimistic view of human nature and the state emerges, often in contradiction to his cynical observations in *The Prince*. BASIC.

More, Thomas, *Utopia*, in Milligan, Burton A., ed., *Three Renaissance Classics*. Scribner's, 1971. A satiric attack on the acquisitiveness of More's society, coupled with a highly Platonic argument that the community was necessarily intended to realize moral as well as political ends. More attacks the disease of incessant desire for profit and asserts that primitive communism, leading to a society in which luxury, wealth, and poverty are eliminated, is the only cure acceptable for rational and moral human beings. Excerpts, which can be used for an introduction to More, are in *ICCW*, Vol. I, pp. 647–676.

Early Modern Europe—Economic Expansion

Braudel, Fernand, "European Expansion and Capitalism: 1450–1650," in CWC, Vol. I. Expansionism, economic and demographic; the growth of business and trade; economic crises. BASIC.

Rice, Eugene F., Jr., Chs. 1 and 2 of Foundations (above, "Early Modern Europe—Politics"). Technology, discovery, and the economic expansion of Europe. BASIC.

Hilton, R. H., "Capitalism—What's in a Name?", in Kaplow, Vol. I., pp. 247–257. In an unfortunately brief article, Hilton questions the orthodox thesis of continuous economic advance associated with the "movement toward capitalism" and argues that the continued dominance of old classes in early modern Europe points to relatively unchanged economic conditions. INTERMEDIATE.

de las Casas, Bartolomeo, The Devastation of the Indies; A Brief Account, tr. Herma Briffault. Seabury, 1974. This translation of the treatise written by the Spanish friar de las Casas gives the eye-witness account of Spain's devastation and dehumanization of the Indians found in the New World. Issues discussed by Casas include the capability of the Indians, the value of their customs and way of life, the Indian character, and the enslavement of the Indians by Spain. An indictment of early European tendencies to devalue "barbarian" civilizations and primitive peoples, and to exploit whenever possible. BASIC.

Early Modern Europe—Humanist Culture

Rice, Eugene F., Jr., Ch. 3, "Renaissance Society and Humanist Culture," in Foundations (above, "Early Modern Europe—Politics"). BASIC.

Kristeller, Paul Oskar, "The Moral Thought of Renaissance Humanism," in CWC, Vol. I, Ch. IX. A lucid discussion of the nature and implications of humanism which corrects Burckhardt and others who underestimate the importance of moral theory among Renaissance humanists and which seeks to define humanism more precisely. INTERMEDIATE.

Cassirer, Ernst, Paul O. Kristeller, and J. H. Randall, Jr., eds., The Renaissance Philosophy of Man. Univ. of Chicago Press, 1965. Critical introductions to, and selected texts of Petrarch, Valla, Ficino, Pico della Mirandola, Pomponazzi, and Vives. A superb collection marked by the breadth and depth of the selected texts. The important traditions of Humanism, Platonism, and Aristotelianism are presented, and major problems common to all schools appear and reappear. Free will, the nature of the Good, the end of desire, human dignity, the problem of freedom, immortality of the soul, are all discussed and debated; the diffusion of important Renaissance ideas outside Italy is illustrated in the selection from Vives. These selections are intermediate to advanced and demand some background knowledge both of the Renaissance itself and of classical philosophy.

THE REFORMATION

Introductory

Bainton, Roland H., "The Reformation," in *CWC,* **Vol. I, Ch. X.** A compact discussion, in which the background of the Reformation is traced and the major Reformation movements led by Luther and Calvin are analyzed; some mention is made of "splinter" sects, the Reformation outside of Germany, and the social consequences of the Reformation. BASIC.

Rice, Eugene F., Jr., in chs. 5 and 6 of *Foundations* **(above, "Early Modern Europe—Politics").** Rice presents a somewhat more complete discussion of the Reformation than Bainton, including sections on peasants, burghers, and freedom-liberty as a politicoreligious issue. He also questions Engels' assertion that a correspondence exists between theological preference and economic class during the Reformation, but he does not substantiate with convincing data his argument that the Reformation at crucial moments was class-blind. INTERMEDIATE.

Kaplow, J., "IX / The Reformation in Germany," in *Kaplow,* **Vol. I, pp. 295–333.** In a trio of excerpts from works by Joseph Lortz, Ernst Bloch, and Roy Pascal, Kaplow asks us to consider the question of why the Reformation began in Germany and of the social presuppositions of the Reformation. Lortz argues that there was dissatisfaction in the Catholic church in Germany but offers no greater explanation than ultimate appeals to "a history of dissatisfaction." Bloch and Pascal probe deeper, arguing that class is an important factor in explaining the success of the Reformation in Germany; that religious-class alliances did exist, and that milleniarist reform movements were of particular importance to peasants as they attempted to express their material and moral suffering and remedy their woeful conditions of existence. Though these selections are not basic, they are a good introduction to the issue of religion and social class. They nicely supplement Engels.

The Reformation—Sources

Hillerbrand, Hans, ed., *The Protestant Reformation.* **Harper & Row, 1969.** Selections from Martin Luther, Zwingli, the Anabaptists, Calvin, and the English Reformation are presented. Wide scope of coverage of the Reformation.

LUTHER Selections illustrate the main Lutheran doctrinal points—justification through faith alone, the notion of righteousness, Christian freedom as freedom rooted in love and faith, and the authority of the scriptures; the Lutheran argument that church and state must be separate; Luther's ambivalence toward the German peasants (who were in revolt against the princes partly because of Luther's early encouragement); and the peculiarly Pauline flavor of Luther's crisis-theological approach to sin and the problem of human depravity. INTERMEDIATE.

CALVIN Selections from the *Reply to Sadoleto, Institutes,* and *Ordinances* present the main tenets of Calvinism. Especially important: the notion of predestination; the theological reasonableness of the notion that humans are "depraved"; the necessity for church order and discipline; and the organization of Calvin's church on lines of authority which reenforce class and sex difference. INTERMEDIATE.

NOTE **Excerpts from Lutheran texts also in *ICCW*, Vol. I, pp. 700–730; from Calvin's *Institutes,* same volume, pp. 731–751.**

The Reformation—Secondary Works

Engels, Frederick, *The Peasant War in Germany*. International Pub. Co., 1966. In this small book Engels analyzes the revolt of the German peasants in 1522—"the first great democratic struggle which heralded the dawn of a new era"; contrasts the revolutionary Muenzer with the opportunist Luther; and, in his analysis of the causes of the failure of the peasant revolution, establishes the principles necessary for successful revolutionary action. Excellent not only for its analysis of the social role of religion, but also for its recognition of the revolutionary role of the peasants. BASIC.

Weber, Max, *The Protestant Ethic and the Spirit of Capitalism*. Scribner's, 1958. Although the empirical evidence upon which Weber's theses are based is now dated and the point of view is highly selective, Weber's *Protestant Ethic* remains required reading in any attempt to answer the question of the relationship of religion to society and economics. Weber argues that Protestantism is more favorable to capitalism than are other great creeds (such as Catholicism) and that certain Protestant notions ("the calling") were highly influential in the molding of characters open to related capitalist notions (a "life-task," to be pursued with a conviction of success). While the notion of "calling" is debatable and the question of explaining economic advance in Catholic countries remains, the central point which emerges from Weber cannot be ignored: Just as Marx understood, and stressed, the economic forces sustaining religious ideology, Weber understood the subtle ideological notions to be found in religion which can reinforce certain economic systems. INTERMEDIATE.

THE SEVENTEENTH CENTURY

Emergence of a States System

Wolf, John B., "The Emergence of the European States-System", in ***CWC,*** **Vol. I, Ch. XI.** An examination of the movements in seventeenth-century political events resulting in the creation of political institutions which became the framework for modern political experience. The political effects of the Reformation are discussed, and a sketch of seventeenth-century wars is presented. BASIC.

Elliot, J. H., "Revolution and Continuity in Early Modern Europe," **in** ***Revolutions,*** **pp. 49–75.** A well-constructed attack upon the commonly held notion (among scholars of the seventeenth century) that the century was one of continual and severe crisis. Limiting his critique to "political revolutions," Elliot demonstrates the possibility for error which attaches to projecting modern notions back into the seventeenth century and ending up with significant "revolutions" when, in fact, the traditional societal structures, and the aristocratic-monarchical state, remained. INTERMEDIATE.

Constitutionalism—Introductory

Ashley, Maurice, "Constitutionalism and the Sovereign State in the Seventeenth Century," in *CWC,* **Vol. I, Ch. XII.** The basic discussion of constitutionalism in England and of the political events and revolutions which served as background for the leading political theorists of the time—Filmer, Hobbes, Harrington, John Milton, and Locke.

Woolrych, Austin, "The English Revolution, 1640–1660," in ***Revo-*** ***lutions,*** **pp. 77–111.** A recent essay (1971), which questions earlier, pat theories of the English Revolution in the light of new evidence on wealth, power, and social class in seventeenth-century England. BASIC.

Constitutionalism—Source Works and a Secondary Work

Hobbes, Thomas, ***Leviathan,*** **ed. C. B. Macpherson. Pelican, 1968.** The first "scientific" theory of the state. An attempt to contractually base the almost total power of the sovereign in the actualities of political existence, the exigencies of survival. Imaginary "state of nature" as basis for deductions. Note the mechanistic theory of the person presented in Part I and the assumption that social existence implies "the war of all against all" in "the state of nature." INTERMEDIATE.

Locke, John, ***Two Treatises of Government,*** **ed. Peter Laslett. NAL,** **1965.** A social-contract theory in which "nature" guarantees perfect freedom but freedom is limited by reason (and not by fear, as Hobbes had argued). Individual desires in conflict, and the lack of any established source of authority, lead to the contract out of which issues government, the duty of which is to protect life and property of its citizens. Government is a trust, and governments can be replaced for betrayal of trust. Consent of the people is the sole basis of the sovereign's authority. A major text in Anglo-American political theory, theory of liberalism. INTERMEDIATE.

Macpherson, C. B., *The Political Theory of Possessive Individualism, Hobbes to Locke.* Oxford Univ. Press, 1962. A "fundamental reinterpretation of political theory from Hobbes to Locke," emphasizing the importance of "possessiveness" in theories of the person and the state and attempting to root the notion of possessive individualism in an economic environment dominated by the market system. Controversial, but important for its exposure of the error of expressing freedom of the individual as a function of possession—a flaw embedded in modern liberal-democratic theory and the source of unending social contradiction. ADVANCED.

Society in the Seventeenth Century

Laslett, Peter, *The World We Have Lost.* Scribner's, 1965. A study of the contrasts in English society before and after the coming of industry in the seventeenth century. Rich chapters consider the contrasts in pre- and post-industrial existence; the 'one-class' society in pre-industrial England and its accompanying status-system; life in the village community; authority in the traditional world; and the question of the economic condition of the peasants (Did the Peasants Really Starve? Chapter 5). BASIC.

NOTE Mousnier and Vilar (below) will give the more advanced student a sense of the political and social inertia which persisted throughout a crisis-ridden seventeenth century, thwarting and hindering social and economic change even when (as in the case of Spain) it was desirable.

Mousnier, Roland, "The Society of Orders and the Society of Classes," in *Kaplow*, Vol. I, Ch. 23, pp. 339–355. A short but suggestive selection, in which Mousnier argues that the theory of class difference cannot explain seventeenth-century change because classes were not well differentiated; and that rank and status were much more important to the society of seventeenth-century France. He further argues that groups themselves, by consensus, determine those social functions and ranks to be placed at the top of the social hierarchy.

Vilar, Pierre, "1598–1620: The Crisis of Spanish Power and Conscience," in *Kaplow*, Vol. I, Ch. 25, pp. 373–383. An unfortunately brief selection, in which the paradox of economic crisis in imperial Spain is linked to the persistence of a government which was parasitic upon developing enterprise and to the continuation of feudalism in a world which could no longer be dealt with "feudally."

Science and Philosophy in the Seventeenth Century—
Introductory

Nagel, Ernest, "The Development of Modern Science," in *CWC,* **Vol. I., Ch. XIII.** The transition from medieval to "modern" science—establishment of Copernican astronomy; the continued mathematicization of "nature"; the birth of the science of "dynamics" and, with it, modern physics. Galileo, Descartes, Newton, and Bacon, and their influence upon the development of scientific method. BASIC.

Butterfield, Herbert, *The Origins of Modern Science.* **Macmillan (Free Press), 1965.** A basic, highly readable history of the origins of modern science, which goes back to the 1300s in order to demonstrate the historical importance of medieval astronomy to the development of seventeenth-century science; illustrates the tendencies of scientists to see only what they look for (in a compact discussion of problems in explaining the circulation of the blood before Harvey); and ends with a brief discussion of the connection of the idea of progress with the emergence of scientific theories of evolution. BASIC.

Foucault, Michel, *Madness and Civilization.* **NAL, 1965.** Chs. II-IV: These chapters discuss the "Great Confinement" that occurred in the seventeenth century, when the insane were incarcerated in enormous numbers and social and political developments in England and on the continent continued to erode the freedom to be significantly different. Interesting discussion as well of the use of confinement for political ends (especially in France, where at one time in the seventeenth century one out of every ten Parisians was confined); and the growing discomfort of the "age of reason" with the unreasonable delirium, and the nonreasonable passion of the insane. Excellent supplement to the "age of reason." (What did it mean to be "reasonable" in the 1600s?)

Science and Philosophy in the Seventeenth Century—
Source Works

Bacon, Francis, *The New Organon,* **ed. Fulton H. Anderson. Bobbs-Merrill, 1960.** (A good edition, which also contains *The Great Instauration* and other important Baconian works.) Here we have the equation of Knowledge and Power, which became so important in the development of the modern scientific-technologic attitude. Further; there is Bacon's analysis of "the idols of tribe, cave, market, and theater"—an early penetration of the ideological veils masking our interpretations of "truth"; essays on the inductive method as the only proper method of science; and a critique of the *a priorism* of medieval science. BASIC. **Bacon selections in ICCW, Vol. I, pp. 780–785.**

Galilei, Galileo, *Dialogue Concerning the Two Chief Systems of the World,* **ed. Stillman Drake. Univ. of California Press, 1967.** In this work Galileo mounts an important attack upon the Ptolemaic system of astronomy and Aristotelian physical theory. In a three-sided debate among a Copernican, an Aristotelian-Ptolemaic, and an impartial candidate for conversion to either view, the Copernican wins. Introduced here is the notion of *uniformity*—like effects from like causes—taken for granted in today's science, but then a matter of debate. INTERMEDIATE. Selections from the above work, as well as from the *Assayer*, the records of the trial of Galileo, *The Dialogue Concerning Two New Sciences*, and correspondence on the nature of science, appear in *ICCW*, Vol. I, pp. 786–811.

Descartes, René, *Discourse on Method and Meditations*, tr. L. J. Lafleur. Bobbs-Merrill, 1962. This edition contains the *Discourses* and the *Meditations*, both of vast importance in shaping "modern" attitudes toward science and scientific method; the utility of the mathematical method in science; the nature of mind; the problem of self and self-consciousness: and the positive function of methodological skepticism. Important: The "I think, therefore I am" argument of the *Meditations*; and the origin of the mind-body problem in Descartes' assertion that mind is something other than, and superior to, the mechanical body. INTERMEDIATE to ADVANCED. (Selections from the *Discourse* in *ICCW*, Vol. I, pp. 813–835; BASIC.)

Newton, Isaac, *Newton's Philosophy of Nature*, tr. H. Standish Thayer. Hafner, 1953. Included in this edition are the *Principia Mathematica*, as well as selections from Newton's other major scientific works. In the *Principia* Newton established the theoretical basis for modern science. This important work represents the fruition of the seventeenth-century scientific revolution: the empiricism of Galileo and the formalism of Descartes merge, and the new science of physics is conceptually and methodologically established in a comprehensive theory explaining both celestial and terrestrial motion. "Gravity" emerges as a central explanatory concept in physical theory. (Basic selections from the *Principia* and other works in *ICCW*, Vol. I, pp. 837–852.)

THE ENLIGHTENMENT

Background and Ideals

Ford, Franklin L., "The World of the Enlightenment," in *CWC*, Vol. I, Ch. XIV. A brief sketch of the major themes of the Enlightenment—confidence in the supreme value of analytic rationality; the importance of experience for all knowledge; increased faith in the reasonableness of "nature"; the deemphasis of the importance of religion; increased concern for personal responsibility as the basis of morality; development of the notions of taste and beauty; and the justification of classical economics through appeal to its "supreme rationality." BASIC.

Gay, Peter, *The Enlightenment, An Interpretation: The Rise of Modern Paganism*. Random House, 1968. In this major work Gay analyzes the Enlightenment as a coherent and comprehensive whole in order to determine its true nature and "rescue it from its admirers nearly as much as its detractors." While considering the deep differences in point of view which separated major Enlightenment figures, Gay argues that certain general ideas and strategies common to the period as a whole can, and must, be acknowledged. Using numerous examples, he argues that the Enlightenment can best be summed up in the two words *criticism* and *power;* and that the moving force of the philosophers was their desire to gain autonomy through liberation from the conflicting Christian and pagan strands of their intellectual, cultural, and social inheritance. ADVANCED, but indispensable. The Preface, Overture, and Chapter One can be read as more basic material. (An excellent Bibliographical Essay is appended.)

Foucault, Michel, *Madness and Civilization.* NAL, 1965. Review Chs. III and IV, and go on to Chs. V–VIII. Note especially the discussion of the great "dread of unreason" which, as part and parcel of the Enlightenment ideology, led to increased social and psychological separation of the insane from their "rational" brethren.

The Enlightenment—Source Works

Locke, John, "Essay Concerning Human Understanding," abridged in *The Empiricists.* Doubleday (Anchor), 1969. The theory of knowledge presented here blew like a fresh wind through the Enlightenment, freeing human thought from supernatural authority in its argument that all knowledge was the result of experience and that there were no innate ideas (as postulated by Descartes), God-given or otherwise. The implications for political theory were clear and seen as such by Enlightenment theorists: Neither Adam's sin nor lowly birth could be appealed to in explaining what one became. Another boost for the nascent theory of individualism is implicit. The introductory chapters of Books I, II, and IV are BASIC. As a whole, the book is ADVANCED. (Selections in *ICCW*, Vol. I, pp. 1057–1069.)

Kant, Immanuel, "What Is Enlightenment?" in Lewis White Beck, ed., *On History.* Bobbs-Merrill, 1963. (This edition contains several of Kant's works on the philosophy of history.) The essay is a brief but profound meditation on the true meaning of Enlightenment: "Having the courage to use one's own mind, without the guidance of others." A succinct statement of the tasks facing those who wish to become enlightened, and the rewards, seen as freedom and true human dignity. BASIC and necessary. (The essay is presented in its entirety in **ICCW, Vol. I, pp. 1071–1076, with extracts from Perpetual Peace, pp. 1076–1087.)**

The Enlightenment—Knowledge and Morality

Hume, David, *Selections,* ed. Charles W. Hende, Jr. Scribners, 1971. A selection of major portions of the most influential works of Hume— *A Treatise of Human Nature; Enquiry Concerning Human Understanding; Enquiry Concerning the Principles of Morals; The Natural History of Religion;* and *Dialogues Concerning Natural Religion.* A comprehensive presentation of Hume's theory of knowledge, which stresses the uncertainty of all knowledge and the consequent importance of convention in human society and which demonstrates the inability of empiricism to establish causality in nature as a law; his moral theory, which stressed the importance of convention and usefulness in testing moral concepts, his consistent and thoroughgoing skepticism; and his critique of religion, which attacked "religious proofs" as ultimately either unfounded or self-contradictory. (Selections from the *Enquiry Concerning the Principles of Morals and Dialogues* in *ICCW*, Vol. I, pp. 1145–1164, 1214–1235; BASIC. Hume's philosophy as a whole, ADVANCED.)

Kant, Immanuel, *The Critique of Pure Reason,* tr. Norman Kemp Smith. St. Martin's, 1965. The pinnacle of Kant's philosophical system, in which he attempts to demonstrate that knowledge is neither innate (against the Rationalists), nor entirely empirical (against Hume and Empiricism), and in so doing, founds modern theory of knowledge and grounds human freedom in our epistemological responsibility for creating, not passively receiving, knowledge. The foundation stone of the modern concept of the ego, the person, and human freedom. Extremely difficult; but the Prefaces and Introduction can be read with profit by students with some knowledge of Empiricist and Rationalist philosophy.

Kant, Immanuel, *Groundwork of the Metaphysic of Morals,* tr. H. J. Paton. Harper & Row, 1964. One of the most important books in the history of moral theory. A trenchant critique of a totally empirical moral theory (such as Hume's) and an argument that moral reasonableness demands adherence to objective and universal standards of morality and goodness. Establishes the notion of a categorical imperative to moral action and duty (so important in later German thought) as reverence for the law. INTERMEDIATE. (Selections in *ICCW*, Vol. I, pp. 1165–1186.)

The Enlightenment—Politics and Economics

Rousseau, Jean-Jacques, *Discourse on the Origin of Inequality,* in *The Social Contract and Discourse on the Origin of Inequality,* ed. Lester G. Crocker. Pocket Books, 1971. Highly readable and prophetic critique of society, in which Rousseau anticipates Marxist and Freudian themes, arguing that human beings in the state of nature were happier; that society is built upon the lie of private property and only serves to reinforce presocietal inequalities of wealth and power; that so-called progress has led to moral depravity and the intensification of standards of reason at the cost of pity and sympathy; and that we must return to "natural values" in order to overcome the alienation which has beset the "civilized" world. BASIC.

Rousseau, Jean-Jacques, *The Social Contract,* ed. Charles Frankel. Hafner, 1954. In a brilliantly original essay, Rousseau argues that only by terminating natural existence and making a social contract can human beings trade merely natural freedom for civic and moral freedom. Citizenship is seen as inalienable once gained, and unanimity in political action is argued as necessary. This leads to the highly problematic notion of the General Will and the assertion that, if necessary, we must be forced to be free. Possibilities of manipulation and totalitarian implications have caused this to become one of the most strongly debated issues in Rousseau's theory. INTERMEDIATE. (Selections in *ICCW*, Vol. I, pp. 1269–1306.)

Smith, Adam, *The Wealth of Nations,* abridged ed. Bruce Mazlish. Bobbs-Merrill, 1961. A masterwork in political economy and dispassionate presentation of the theory of the market. Systematic exposition of the concepts of price, value, labor, and laissez faire. Important: the labor theory of value; the notion of laissez faire; the assumptions that the "capitalist" is above all rational, whether producer or consumer; and the notion of the "invisible hand," wonderfully working to insure equilibrium and satisfaction for all. There is also an excellent critique of mercantilism and shrewd insight into the tendencies of "the dealers" to move toward monopoly unless carefully watched. The assumption throughout is that the pure "market economy" (which has never existed in actuality) works to the maximum benefit of all. INTERMEDIATE. (Selections in *ICCW,* Vol. I, pp. 1313–1333.)

EIGHTEENTH CENTURY REVOLUTIONS

Theories of Revolution

Kaplan, Lawrence, ed., "I. Definitions of Revolution", in *Revolution,* pp. 3–46. In this section Kaplan presents three articles, all germane to the difficult problem of understanding the nature of revolution, the different kinds of revolutions that can and do occur; and recent views of revolution. ADVANCED, but useful to the student who, after reading about specific revolutions, wants to know more about their nature and genesis.

The American Revolution—Source Work

Hamilton, Alexander, James Madison, and John Jay, *The Federalist Papers,* ed. Clinton Rossiter. NAL, 1961. In these "papers" written between October 1787 and May 1788, three of the "conceptual fathers" of the American Revolution engage in a debate that shaped the principles of American constitutional theory. Important: critique of both direct democracy and a strong monarchy; and development of a theory of federalism and republican government. See especially Essay 10, by Madison, in which the essence of federalist theory is presented. BASIC.

The American Revolution—Secondary Works

De Tocqueville, Alexis, *Democracy in America,* 2 vols., ed. Andrew Hacker, tr. Henry Reeve. Pocket Books, 1971. Written by the French political philosopher in 1835, after a visit to the forty-year-old United States, this prophetic study acknowledges the universality of democratic ideals in America and predicts the "inevitability of democracy" for Europe. A dispassionate analysis of democracy as a social and political reality. BASIC. (Selections in *ICCW*, Vol. II, pp. 494–509.)

Wood, Gordon, "The American Revolution," in *Revolutions*, pp. 113–148. A recent discussion of the importance of ideas to the Revolution; support for the views of scholars such as Bailyn (see below), who argue that there was more to the American Revolution than an unwitting defense of American rights against the British crown or a political movement which succeeded in the absence of substantial ideology or theoretical content. BASIC.

Bailyn, Bernard, *The Ideological Origins of the American Revolution*, Harvard Univ. Press, 1967. A sophisticated and meticulously written analysis of the assumptions, beliefs, and ideas underlying the events which led up to, and were part of, the American Revolution. The "ideological origins" of the Revolution are found by Bailyn in innumerable pamphlets written and circulated during the revolutionary era. What issues is a strong sense of both the importance of major ideas—freedom, rights, political autonomy—and the unpredictability of the events of the time to those who were enmeshed in them. A major contribution to the understanding of the American Revolution. INTERMEDIATE to ADVANCED.

The French Revolution—Introductory and Source Works

Godechot, Jacques, "The French Revolution," in *CWC*, Vol. II, Ch. I. A brief introduction to the French Revolution of 1789. BASIC.

Hobsbawm, E. J., *The Age of Revolution, 1789–1848*, NAL, 1962. Part 1, Ch. 3, "The French Revolution," is a compact sketch of the historical events of the revolution. BASIC.

NOTE   All three of the documents below are brief and should be read as a unit to provide some sense of the demands and ideals of the French revolutionaries.

Sieyes, Joseph Emmanuel, "What Is the Third Estate?" in *ICCW*, Vol. II, pp. 27–32. One of the most eloquent tracts of the Revolutionary period, influenced by the political and moral ideas of the *philosophes* but founded in the political reality of the existence of the Third Estate. The three questions, stark and direct, summarize a major political problem of the time: What is the third estate? Everything. What has it been in the political order up to the present? Nothing. What does it demand? To become something.

***The Declaration of the Rights of Man and the Citizen*, in *ICCW*, Vol. II, pp. 33–35.** In addition to its declaration of individual rights demanded by the third estate, the Declaration included a commitment to the notion of private property; therefore, even though it became important as a symbol of opposition to the old regime, the Declaration was criticized by Robespierre for its implicit grant of latitude to the rich.

Robespierre, Maximilien, "In Favor of an Armed People, of a War Against the Vendée," in *ICCW,* **Vol. II, pp. 49–51.** Appeal to the *sans-culottes,* the poor of Paris, to retain their solidarity and become the nucleus of the Revolutionary army. Implicit in this appeal is exclusion of the moderates and the wealthier classes from the center of Revolutionary action.

Burke, Edmund, and Thomas Paine, *Reflections on the Revolution in France by Edmund Burke and the Rights of Man by Thomas Paine.* **Doubleday, 1969.** Burke's critique of the French Revolution was based on his general theory of conservatism—great respect for the embodied customs and traditions of a nation; reverence for the inheritance of the past; and denial of the notion that there are any absolute rights, rights not embedded in the gradually realized and developed laws of a nation. In *The Rights of Man* Paine defends the principles involved in the French Revolution, arguing from an Enlightenment faith in the importance of reason freed from the petrifaction of past custom and the conviction that revolution on behalf of "abstract rights" was a necessity in the France of 1789.

The French Revolution—Secondary Works

Lefebvre, Georges, *The Coming of the French Revolution.* **Princeton Univ. Press, 1971.** In this classic study of the events leading up to the Revolution, Lefebvre develops two important theses: that of "parallel revolutions," aristocratic, bourgeois, popular, and peasant; and that of the Revolution as essentially "bourgeois." The latter thesis has stimulated much debate on the importance of class struggle to the revolution and the question of the existence of a true bourgeois class; yet the book remains an important scholarly contribution to the understanding of the French Revolution. BASIC.

Kaplow, J., "I / The French Revolution," in *Kaplow,* **Vol. II, pp. 5–48.** Articles by leading scholars of the French Revolution—Taylor, Soboul and Kaplow himself. Taylor seeks to determine whether it can be asserted on any grounds that the Revolution was bourgeois and argues that the notion "bourgeois" must be redefined in the light of not only economic, but also juridical and political realities of the time. Soboul asserts that the *sans-culottes,* after thwarting a counterrevolution, defeated their own more radical ends by dissension and contradictions within their forces. And Kaplow discusses the living conditions and intense misery of the masses of urban poor who formed an intrinsic part of the Revolutionary forces of 1789. The first article is somewhat ADVANCED in its argument (demanding a knowledge of the debates involved). Soboul and Kaplow are BASIC.

THE INDUSTRIAL REVOLUTION

Introductory

Landes, David, "The Industrial Revolution: 1750–1850," in *CWC,* **Vol. II, Ch. IV.** A basic yet comprehensive discussion of the nature, preconditions, and implications of the Industrial Revolution in England; and a brief consideration of why Continental industrialization did not proceed at the same pace.

Hobsbawm, E. J., *Industry and Empire.* **Penguin, 1972.** Read Chs. 1–5. A thorough survey of the industrialization of Britain over the period from 1750 to the present. This book is a necessity for any reader seriously interested in the preconditions, nature, and development of industrialization; and the traumatic and often negative results that modernization can effect. See especially Ch. 4, "The Human Results of the Industrial Revolution," where Hobsbawm argues pessimistically that it is an assumption which remains to be proved that industrialization improved the standard of living of the British laboring classes. Suggested by this chapter is the important question: What is encompassed in a standard of living—material wealth alone, or other, more subtle values? INTERMEDIATE.

The Industrial Revolution—Source Works

Vorspan, Rachel, ed., *Industrialization and the Working Classes.* **Spectator Press, Columbia College** (available from Columbia University Bookstore, New York, NY 10027). A collection of nineteenth-century documents and excerpts from larger works, graphically illustrating the evils of the factory system as opposed to the domestic (cottage manufacture) system; the wretched living and working conditions of the British laboring class; implicit contempt for the working classes; the brutal reality of urbanization (that is, the creation of large urban slums); and the response of the working class through strikes and the Chartist movement. BASIC.

Malthus, Thomas Robert, *An Essay on the Principle of Population,* **ed. Anthony Flew, Penguin, 1971.** In the first edition (1798) of this gloomy classic, Malthus argued that, since population increases at a geometric rate and the food supply at an arithmetic rate, overpopulation, and with it the decline of progress, is inevitable unless population growth is checked by war, pestilence, or famine. In the furor that followed publication of the *Essay,* Malthus was forced to reexamine his evidence (such as it was) and conclusions. In the second (1803) edition he allowed that the numerous poor might limit their reproductive propensities (and so save the world from catastrophe) if their standard of living increased. But his argument was still seen by liberals as an attack upon the poor and by nonliberals as a defense of subsistence wages (to make conditions too attractive for the poor would encourage them to overreproduce, so that gains in living standards would be canceled by increases in population). Although limited by lack of data and Malthus's failure to consider the possible benefits of technology to the problem of agriculture, this work is still important, particularly today, when overpopulation and famine are a reality in many lands when supposedly reasonable economists suggest "triage" of the world's poorest countries, and when the question of the limits of technology is vital.

The Industrial Revolution—Comment and Debate

Kaplow, J., "II / The Industrial Revolution," in *Kaplow,* **Vol. II, pp. 49–119.** Presenting a series of four articles, which should be read as a unit, Kaplow illustrates the need of understanding the working class as a class with dignity and values of its own, not deserving of the contemptuous treatment which it inherited when it also inherited industrialization and the destruction of its traditional milieu. There is also an informative juxtaposition of articles on the stages of economic growth by Rostow and Hobsbawm, in which Hobsbawm argues that Rostow's five-stage argument explains nothing; and a debate on the standard of living during the Industrial Revolution between Hobsbawm and Hartwell, illustrating the difficulty confronting optimists and pessimists in settling on mutually accepted definitions of "improvement." The excerpt on the working class, by Thompson, is BASIC. The other articles are more ADVANCED and demand a deeper understanding of economic theory and the history of British industrialization.

RESTORATION, REVOLUTION, AND NATIONALISM

Restoration and Revolution

Mellon, Stanley, "Restoration and Revolution," in *CWC,* **Vol. II, Ch. II.** A short history of European resistance to the French Revolution, the growth of English liberalism, the French Restoration and its failure, and the Revolution of 1848. BASIC.

Hobsbawm, E. J., *The Age of Revolution.* **NAL, 1962.** Chs. 4–6: War, Peace, Revolutions. Basic background to the period 1792–1848.

Marx, Karl, "The Eighteenth Brumaire of Louis Bonaparte," in *The Marx-Engels Reader,* **ed. Robert C. Tucker pp. 436–525. Norton, 1972.** Marx argues here that it was the class struggle in France, and not the talent of Louis Bonaparte, which made the coup d'état of 1851 possible. The analysis, presented from the materialist viewpoint of history, is INTERMEDIATE.

Marx, Karl, *The Civil War in France,* **in Tucker (above), pp. 527–576.** In this pamphlet, written only two days after the collapse of the last resistance of the Paris Commune, Marx analyzed the reasons for its failure, arguing that the 72-day rule of this proletarian government was nevertheless of major importance as the first historical example of the "dictatorship of the proletariat." INTERMEDIATE.

Hamerow, Theodore S., "The German Revolution of 1848," in *Revolutions,* pp. 209–226. This short but rewarding excerpt argues that the Revolution of 1848 failed in Germany "not because of treason of the middle class, not because of weakness of the national character, not even because of the timidity of the leaders," but because nineteenth-century Germany lacked the mass despair necessary to produce an uprising and maintained an optimistic faith in the ability of the established institutions to solve its serious problems.

Nationalism

Krieger, Leonard, "Nationalism and the Nation-State System: 1789–1870," in *CWC,* Vol. II, Ch. III. In this basic article Krieger attempts to unravel the "puzzle of nationalism," placing its birth in the Jacobin sentiments of the French Revolution, discussing the nationalism of Napoleon, analyzing the reason for the split between liberalism and nationalism, and discussing the nationalism-romanticism connection. BASIC.

Fichte, J. G., *Addresses to the German Nation.* Harper & Row, 1968. A classic example of nationalist philosophy, in which Fichte argues that the Germans have a special character, a special spirit, and a unique capability to create a European culture. Important in this treatise is the notion of freedom as "consciousness of one's vocation" and the argument that identification of the will with the higher destiny of the nation can achieve the infinite. "Love of Nation" must transcend reason, according to Fichte, or it is nothing. Education is seen as the vehicle by which character can be altered so that vocation is realized, and national unity becomes possible. (Selections in *ICCW,* Vol. II, pp. 149–157. BASIC.)

Kaplow, J., "IV / The Risorgimento," in *Kaplow,* Vol. II, pp. 157–198. A pair of complex articles by Gramsci and by Rosario Romeo. Debate centers on the reason for failure of the left to achieve a more "bourgeois-democratic" government after the unification of Italy. Gramsci provides a Marxist analysis, which Romeo challenges. ADVANCED and specialized.

THE ADVANCE OF CAPITALISM AND PROGRAMS FOR REFORM

The Growth of Capitalism

Dillard, Dudley, "Capitalism after 1850," in *CWC,* Vol. II, Ch. VII. A brief discussion of the "golden age of capitalism," its expansion, and the development of forces (monopolies, cartels, unions) tending to undermine a free-market system. BASIC and uncritical.

Hobsbawm, E. J., *Industry and Empire.* Penguin, 1972. Chs. 6, 7, 8, and 9. In these chapters Hobsbawm discusses the second phase of British industrialization (coal and steel); the extinction of Socialism as affluence grew in the mid-nineteenth century; the "great Depression" of the 1860s and 1870s and its relationship to the growth of imperialism; improvements in standard of living in mid-century; and the beginnings of the decline of British industry at the end of the century. BASIC.

Programs for Reform

Mill, John Stuart, *On Liberty,* in *The Essential Works of John Stuart Mill,* ed. Max Lerner. Bantam, 1971. In this, his most famous book, Mill offers a liberal defense of individualism and argues that the rights of the person should be expanded as far as possible, barring only their interference with the rights of others. The tyranny of the majority is recognized as one of the most dangerous threats of democracy, and individual freedom is seen as our most precious possession. In basing his theory of liberty on a theory of personal development, Mill enriches the debate over the relationship of self-realization to society. The argument is weakened overall by Mill's perception, in true British-liberal fashion, of society as a collection of "individual atoms." (Selections in *ICCW,* Vol. II, pp. 592–619.)

Mill, John Stuart, *Utilitarianism,* in *Essential Works* (above). Mill extends the quantitative utilitarian theory of Bentham to a qualitative dimension: pleasure and pain become not only a matter of amount of happiness or suffering, but also of kind. This argument had an important effect on social debate, carrying the message of necessity of good education for all in order to produce moral and productive citizens. "The greatest happiness for the greatest number" was translated into a political principle in *Utilitarianism,* where a good society was designated an essential element in happiness. BASIC.

Mill, John Stuart, and Harriet Mill, *On the Subjection of Women,* in *Essays on Sex Equality,* ed. Alice S. Rossi. Univ. of Chicago Press, 1970. In this essay, Mill argues that women have been raised for subjection and that social conditioning molds and shapes their desires away from autonomy and toward subjection. Mill, influenced by his own relationship with Harriet Taylor, argued that marriage should be a matter of complementary partnership; however, he doubted correctly that few men of his day would recognize the justice of his claim. BASIC.

THE GROWTH OF SOCIALISM

Plamenatz, John, "Socialist Thought From Owen to Marx," in *CWC,* Vol. II, Ch. V. A discussion of Utopian, pre-Marxist, and Marxist socialism, with a brief critique of Marx. BASIC.

Fried, A., and R. Sanders, "Utopian Socialism," in *ST,* Ch. III. Brief commentary with selections from Saint-Simon, Fourier, and Owen (the founders of modern socialism). In their appeal to humankind as a whole and not to a particular class, and in appealing to the moral consciousness of humanity rather than promoting practical class-oriented programs for reform and revolution, these early social reformers were dubbed Utopian by Marx and Engels in the *Communist Manifesto*. BASIC.

NOTE   The six entries below concern selections in **Tucker, Robert C., ed., *The Marx-Engels Reader*. Norton, 1972.**

Marx, Karl, *Economic and Philosophic Manuscripts* (1844), in Tucker, pp. 53–103. In these early manuscripts Marx first develops the concept of a proletarian revolution. He sees the communism of the future, which will be won through this revolution, as the goal of all past and present historical process. The important notion of self-alienation is introduced here, as is the concept of species-being. Hegel's philosophy is criticized on the grounds of its abstraction from empirical reality. INTERMEDIATE. (The sections on Hegel are ADVANCED.)

Marx, Karl, and Friedrich Engels, *The German Ideology* (1845–46), in Tucker, pp. 111–164. In Part I, by Marx, the "materialist theory of history" is comprehensively developed. INTERMEDIATE.

Marx, Karl, and Friedrich Engels, *The Communist Manifesto* (1848), in Tucker, pp. 331–362. Application of the theory of classes to the needs of the proletariat, and a call for the proletariat to unite in order to advance the cause of Communism (as opposed to Utopian socialism) and to win material freedom. The program for Communism, including abolition of property, free education for all, and centralization of credit, is set forth in detail. BASIC.

Marx, Karl, *Wage, Labour and Capital* (1847), selections in Tucker, pp. 167–190. Embryonic presentation of the economic arguments later developed in full in *Capital*. Demonstration of the destructiveness of the capital-labor system in the bourgeois-capitalist socioeconomic system. INTERMEDIATE.

Marx, Karl, *Capital* (1867–1880), selections in Tucker, pp. 191–327. Marx's *magnum opus* and life's work—the critique of capitalism on which he worked for thirty years. The selections include a critique of profit on the grounds that it is extracted from the surplus value put into a product by the laborer; development of the notions of surplus-value and the fetishism of commodities; the strife between worker and machine; and the "General Law of Capitalist Accumulation." INTERMEDIATE to ADVANCED.

Engels, Friedrich, *The Condition of the Working-Class in England in 1844*, selection, "Working-Class Manchester," in Tucker, pp. 429–435. (The entire work, translated by W. O. Henderson and W. H. Chaloner, is published by Stanford Univ. Press, 1968.) "A blazing protest against the exploitation of the industrial working class." This work is based on Engels' own observation of the intense misery and social degradation of the laboring classes in Manchester. The case histories discussed by Engels are a horrifying testimony to the inhumanity of the British factory system and attitudes toward the poor. BASIC.

The Woman Question; Selections from the Writings of Karl Marx, Friedrich Engels, V. I. Lenin, and Joseph Stalin, rev. ed. **International Pub. Co., 1971.** Excerpts from *Capital,* the *Communist Manifesto, The Origin of the Family, Private Property and the State* (Engels), and *The Condition of the Working Class in England* present the Marxist theory of women. Important: Engels' argument, based on the controversial anthropological theories of Morgan, that early society was matriarchal and communistic and that the enslavement of women coincides with the rise of patriarchy and the holding of private property. Critique of bourgeois society as perpetuating the exploitation of women for economic ends, and condemnation of bourgeois marriage. BASIC.

Krimerman, Leonard I., and Lewis Perry, "Section II: Criticizing Socialism," in *Anarchy,* pp. 61–139. Six brief but interesting selections, in which anarchist writers identify the failures (from their point of view) of Utopian and Marxist Socialism. INTERMEDIATE.

SCIENCE, PHILOSOPHY AND TECHNOLOGY IN THE NINETEENTH CENTURY

Introductory

Himmelfarb, Gertrude, "Victorianism and Darwinism," in *CWC,* Vol. II, Ch. VI. A general discussion of the impact of Darwin upon science and society; the Victorian "ideology," and the revolutionizing effect of Darwin's theory of evolution on all aspects of intellectual life. An introduction to the theory which effectively replaced design in nature with chance, and dealt a death blow to those theories seeing nature as fixed, stable, or moving toward some "greater end." BASIC.

Darwin and Social Darwinism

Darwin, Charles, *The Origin of Species,* in *Darwin,* ed. Philip Appleman. Norton (Critical Edition), 1970. (This excellent paperback contains *The Descent of Man* as well as *Origin.* In addition, another section gives contemporary discussion and debate and recent critique. An epilogue by Appleman assesses the legacy of Darwin to the twentieth century.) In the *Origin* Darwin presents a two-part theory of descent—the theory of evolution and that of natural selection. Exit theological explanations for the origin of the human species. The Victorian world was both stunned and excited by this theory, and intense debate followed. BASIC. (Selections in *ICCW.* Vol. II, pp. 814–832.)

Spencer, Herbert, *Illustrations of Universal Progress,* selections in *ICCW,* Vol. II, pp. 835–842. Fully a decade before Darwin, Spencer blended Comte's positivism with a theory of the steady and organic evolution of society to develop a "Law of Progress." The progress of mankind is seen as lawful and inevitable and is evinced by increasing complexity in social development (just as increasing complexity and differentiation in nature indicates a higher evolutionary stage). BASIC.

Philosophy in the Nineteenth Century

Hegel, G. W. F., *The Phenomenology of Mind*, tr. J. B. Baillie. Harper & Row, 1967. The dialectical development of "spirit," moving from mere consciousness to self-consciousness; then to "objective" consciousness—social and moral activity; experience of natural religion; religion in the form of art; and ultimately, to absolute knowledge—in which the self knows not only itself, but also knows itself "as all existence." In this massive and complex work Hegel not only developed a philosophy of consciousness, but anticipated notions of self-consciousness, false consciousness, and guilt not fully explicated until Nietzsche and Freud later produced their analyses of psychological experience. Origin of the theory of Lordship and Bondage, and the notion of the "Unhappy Consciousness"—the "Alienated soul which is conscious of itself as a divided nature, a doubled and merely contradictory being." The reader is directed to Section B., "Self-Consciousness," for a relatively approachable introduction to these theories. Extremely ADVANCED.

Nietzsche, Friedrich, *On the Genealogy of Morals*, tr. Walter Kaufmann and R. J. Hollingdale. Random House, 1969. Nietzsche's major work on ethics, in which he uses psychology (and philology) to demonstrate the difference between "master" and "slave" morality and to argue that conventional morality is a device of resentment, by which the slaves, a majority, impose their inferior wills and standards upon the intellectual and spiritual "masters." Christianity and Judaism are seen as two such false moral theories. In the second essay of this treatise, Nietzsche analyzes the nature of guilt and bad conscience, in a prescient development of psychology which anticipates the later work of Freud. INTERMEDIATE, and rewarding in its originality.

The Other Side of Science and Reason in the Nineteenth Century

Shelley, Mary, *Frankenstein (or, The Modern Prometheus)*. Airmont, 1963. The implications of uncontrolled technology, and the disaster that follows upon going beyond the bounds of humanity in technological and scientific innovation. BASIC.

Foucault, Michel, *Madness and Civilization*. NAL, 1965. Chs. VIII and IX. The birth of the asylum; its flourishing in the nineteenth century, when behind the scientific facade of "medicine" patients were treated virtually as prisoners by the "philanthropist" Pinel; and, Tuke, who, in the name of Quaker principles of autonomy and reason, established a tyranny of self-imposed fear in his Retreat. Who is mad?

FRIENDS AND ENEMIES OF CAPITALISM

Friends

Carnegie, Andrew, *The Gospel of Wealth,* selection in *ICCW,* Vol. II, pp. 886–893. In this idyll, Carnegie (many times a millionaire) assures us that when the problem of the administration of wealth is solved, "the ties of brotherhood may still bind together the rich and poor in harmonious relationship." Wealth should be administered by the wise; charity should be administered, in the main, to those who would help themselves. BASIC.

Wicksteed, Philip, "The Marxian Theory of Value," in *ICCW,* Vol. II, pp. 938–952. A popular exposition of the economic theory of marginal value, in which Marx's theory of exploitation of labor is criticized. INTERMEDIATE.

Enemies

Bell, Daniel, "Critics of Capitalist Society: 1870–1917," in *CWC,* Vol. II, Ch. VIII. Discussion of the political and economic critique of the evils of capitalism by late-nineteenth-century thinkers—Marx, Lenin, Sorel, Bakunin. BASIC.

Marx, Karl, *Capital.* See above, *The Growth of Socialism.*

Lenin, V. I., "What Is To Be Done?" in Robert C. Tucker, ed., *The Lenin Anthology.* Norton, 1975. Responding to Kautsky, Lenin argues that the proletariat alone will never develop socialist consciousness; and, indeed, will only seek to better their own conditions, thereby perpetuating the status quo (trade unions do nothing more). Consequently, it is the business of the intellectuals to bring a theory of socialism to the proletariat from the outside. This assertion implicitly contradicts the orthodox Marxist assertion that the proletariat, by virtue of their conditions of existence, should develop class consciousness and socialist inclinations without the aid of the bourgeois intellectual.

THE UNIFIED NATION-STATE

Stern, Fritz, "The Maturing of the Nation-State," in *CWC,* Vol. II, Ch. IX. Consolidation of the internal power of European nations following the collapse of the revolutions of 1848. The growth of democratization and capitalism in the 1850s and 1860s. The establishment of law within countries with the concurrent maintenance of anarchy in external relations. The crisis in economics at the end of the century—the decline of England, rise of Germany, and intensification of imperial expansion. BASIC.

"The Unified Nation-State," in *ICCW,* Vol. II, pp. 989–1004, 1005–1019, 1030–1039, 1040–1044, 1045–1066. In a series of brief excerpts from the works of Treitschke, Bismarck, Jules Ferry, Maurice Barrès, and Charles Péguy, the editors present a wide variety of nationalist arguments, rationales, themes, and ideologies, ranging from the hard "Realpolitik" of Treitschke (who argued for the grandeur of war) through the cool rationality of Bismarck's defense of strong social legislation as a device for ensuring national allegiance to the extreme nationalism of Maurice Barrès. These excerpts are brief, and some are a bit exotic to the modern reader, who may choose to skip this section or merely sample the theories of Treitschke and Bismarck.

IMPERIALISM

Mansergh, Nicholas, "Imperialism: The Years of European Ascendency." in CWC, Vol. II, Ch. X. Discussion of various theories of imperialism and of the association of imperialism with colonialism. The assertion, unsubstantiated in the essay, is made that "The circumstances that produced nineteenth century imperialism no longer exist." Unduly optimistic with respect to the disappearance of imperialism. BASIC, but assumes knowledge of nineteenth-century economic development.

Disraeli, Benjamin, "Conservative and Liberal Principles" and "The Berlin Treaty," in ICCW, Vol. II, pp. 1111–1126. Insertion of imperialism into the platform of the British Conservative Party; discussion of the partitions of Turkey and Egypt, with not an iota of recognition of any other interest than Britain's desire to protect its imperial interests first. BASIC.

Roosevelt, Theodore, "The Strenuous Life," in ICCW, Vol. II, pp. 1128–1137. A protectionist-imperialist speech, in which T. R. affirms the necessity of "facing our tasks" as protector to the weaker and less developed nations, such as Cuba. We must, he argues, assume the mantle of guardian (and developer) of those countries not yet ready to stand independently. (The road to Vietnam is very old.) BASIC.

Schumpeter, Joseph, "The Sociology of Imperialism," in ICCW, Vol. II, pp. 1090–1109; also in Schumpeter, Imperialism and Social Classes, NAL, 1955. In this selection Schumpeter, one of the leading capitalist theorists of the twentieth century, argues that imperialism does not follow from pure capitalism (nor does export monopolism). He sees imperialism as a development supported by the forces of nationalism and militarism, both precapitalist in their origins. INTERMEDIATE.

Lenin, V. I., _Imperialism, The Highest Stage of Capitalism_, in Tucker, ed. (above, "Friends and Enemies of Capitalism"); selections also in ICCW, Vol. II, pp. 1079–1088. Lenin argues that imperialism is a necessary development of capitalism in its advanced stage, when all competitive advantages have been exhausted and the need for continued profit forces exportation of capital into backward countries, which have no internal possibilities for competition on equal ground. INTERMEDIATE.

Kaplow, J., "VI / Imperialism," in *Kaplow,* Vol. II, pp. 229–276. Two articles—one by a major critic of the Leninist theory of imperialism, and the other by a defender of the accuracy of the general theory expounded by Lenin—present the problem of understanding what imperialism is and what it implies economically and politically. These articles are advanced, but they outline most aspects of the debate over imperialism well.

THE TWENTIETH CENTURY

Exploitation and Revolution

Lenin, V. I., *State and Revolution (August–September 1917): The Marxist Theory of the State and the Tasks of the Proletariat in the Revolution,* in Tucker, ed. (above, "Friends and Enemies of Capitalism"). Lenin reemphasizes Engels' theory of the withering away of the state and the role of the proletariat in the destruction of the state, arguing that the transition is not intended to be gradual; freedom is to be seized by the proletariat, and the state is to be overthrown. This work was interrupted by the Russian Revolution. INTERMEDIATE.

Fanon, Frantz, *The Wretched of the Earth,* preface by Jean-Paul Sartre. Grove, 1968. Fanon, a psychiatrist assigned to an Algerian hospital while the Algerian rebels were being incarcerated and tortured by the French, examines the role of colonial violence and the cost to those who are its victims. The dilemma of divided consciousness among colonized peoples is analyzed, and the solution for colonial violence is presented. Violence, in return, alone can restore autonomy when all other roads are blocked. (Sartre: "Have the courage to read this book.") BASIC.

Kaplan, Lawrence, "Part V; Twentieth Century Revolutions," in *Revolutions,* pp. 265–404. In this section Kaplan presents material on twentieth-century revolutions which have succeeded because their leaders were able to combine the general theories of Marxism with an understanding of specific conditions which had to be met, whether in Lenin's Russia of 1917, Mao's China of the 1940s, or Ho's Vietnam of the 1950s. As a unit, these short essays provide the reader with a sense of the issues involved in twentieth-century revolutions and the tactics of successful revolutionary action in the modern world.

Rowbotham, Sheila, *Women, Resistance and Revolution.* Random House, 1973. Rowbotham's argument in this book, "the first narrative history of feminism," is strong and clear (and historically documented): The liberation of women has not been fully realized; but until it has, we cannot truthfully speak of human liberation. Tracing the history of women's oppression, and the resistance to the demands for equality advanced by "impudent lasses" of the seventeenth and eighteenth centuries, Rowbotham works her way to the twentieth century, demonstrating along the way that, again and again, revolutions (such as the French Revolution of 1789 and the Russian of 1917) awakened dreams of equality and autonomy in women, only to disappoint them as other goals took precedence. In two excellent chapters (3 and 6) the contribution of Marxism to feminist theory is presented, along with a central dilemma: while the theory demonstrates that women in bourgeois society must be oppressed, in practice recent Marxist systems see the problem of the emancipation of women as marginal. Chapter 5 ("Bread and Roses") analyzes the special problems of working women. And concluding chapters discuss the aspirations of women in China, Vietnam, Algeria, and Cuba.

Schneir, Miriam, ed., *Feminism: The Essential Historical Writings.* Random House, 1972. A collection of essays, letters, memoirs and other documents by the major feminist writers (including such male feminists as Mill, Ibsen, Veblen, Engels, and Bebel), designed to demonstrate the existence of women's movements starting in the eighteenth century and the fact that feminism is "one of the basic movements for human liberty." Selections, while short, are taken from original documents and illuminate both the problems faced by feminism and the movements designed to advance the struggle for female liberty. A final section deals with twentieth-century feminism but stops short of recent years. Nothing is presented from Marxist, Socialist, or radical Feminists (except for short selections from Bebel, Engels, and Goldman)—a serious lack.

Fascism and Counterrevolution in the Twentieth Century

Kaplow, J., "Fascism and Counterrevolution," in *Kaplow,* pp. 331–378. This section presents analyses of the phenomenon of fascism in the twentieth century which argue that no single cause can explain it (Bracher); that class relations were important in the rise of German fascism (Poulantzas); and that fascism, which appeals to the petit bourgeois, does not always satisfy him once it is established (Neumann). These articles should be read together, and their joint implications pondered. ADVANCED.

Reich, Wilhelm, *The Mass Psychology of Fascism.* Simon & Schuster, 1974. In this penetrating analysis, Reich sees fascism as multidimensional in its origins; not peculiar to any nationality; nor explainable in purely socioeconomic terms (Vulgar Marxism). He argues, rather, that it expresses the irrational character structure of the average repressed person, so that it can develop in any society in which there is significant repression. Important also are discussions of the power of ideology; the role of the authoritarian family in supporting the social ideals of fascism; and the argument that only when meaningful work is a possibility, can social repression and the development of irrational characteristics be avoided. ADVANCED, radical, and penetrating in its critique of society.

Erikson, Erik, *Childhood and Society,* 2nd ed. Norton, 1963. Chapter IX, "The Legend of Hitler's Childhood." Erikson argues that we can better understand the depravity of Hitler if we understand his failure to establish a positive identity during youth; and that, as a corollary, we can assume that political situations which hamper the development of personal identity, or bend it, are dangerous, not only to individuals, but also to the rational existence of society as a whole. INTERMEDIATE.

Economics in the Twentieth Century

Friedman, Milton, *Capitalism and Freedom*. Univ. of Chicago Press, 1970. A systematic exposition of the role of competitive capitalism by its foremost theoretical defender in the United States. Many modernized laissez-faire arguments, coupled with the conviction that private enterprise operating in the free market system is the optimal device for achieving economic progress while insuring political freedom. INTERMEDIATE.

Meadows, D. H., D. L. Meadows, J. Randers, and W. W. Behrens, III, *The Limits to Growth*. NAL, 1974. "A report on the predicament of mankind": if the world continues to use its resources and reserves at its present rate, the limits to growth on the planet Earth will be reached within the next 100 years. Unless there is systematic and comprehensive global planning and cooperation, catastrophe is inevitable. An ecological, economic, political and technological challenge: Can we create a society able to endure indefinitely *and* preserve civilization? Are the limits of technology soon to be reached? Even if technology is not "limited," can it solve problems of population, food, and environment before the world situation deteriorates? While the methodology of this study and its conclusions are the center of intense debate, the importance of its implications remains undebatable. BASIC.

Psychology in the Twentieth Century

Freud, Sigmund, *A General Introduction to Psychoanalysis*. Pocket Books, 1969. Freud's series of 28 lectures delivered at the University of Vienna in 1915 and 1917, in which he sets forth the major concepts of psychoanalytic theory, summing up almost 30 years of research. Limited only by the fact that Freudian theory continued to evolve until Freud's death in 1939, they are an excellent starting point for a serious beginner. BASIC to INTERMEDIATE.

Erikson, Erik, *Childhood and Society*. Norton, 1963. Erikson develops a genetic theory of personal development (the "Eight Stages of Man") in which the chance of meeting successfully the development criteria at any "stage" depends upon success in the prior stages and in which the social interaction of parents and children is crucial to the achievement of "ego development." In this theory is rooted Erikson's assertion that the bases of ego are not totally individual but are related to the society in which a person develops. A comprehensive analysis of "growing up." INTERMEDIATE.

Laing, R. D., *The Politics of the Family and Other Essays*. Random House (Vintage), 1972. In this often sketchy but brilliant book, Laing, a psychiatrist who is closer to Sartre and Marx than to Freud, argues that the term "family" is best defined as a system of reciprocal identities in which it is not possible to consider only one member as "disturbed" while all others are "normal." The complexity of the family as a psychological unit extending through generations of influence is analyzed, and the assertion is made that very few families actually understand what they think they are experiencing in day-to-day life. ADVANCED.

Self and Society in the Twentieth Century

Freud, Sigmund, *Civilization and its Discontents,* tr. and ed. James Strachey. Norton, 1962. The question: Can humans satisfy themselves and the demands of civilization simultaneously? If not, what does this imply for the ultimate well-being of the human race, which will not surrender civilization yet seeks satisfaction of desire, the elimination of repression, and the avoidance of psychic discomfort? Freud's answer—that the conflict is permanent and part of human nature—leaves him unable to offer any consolation to the human race in its discontent. A book of immense importance to the twentieth century, when psychic alienation grows and traditional remedies fail. (Think back to Rousseau's *Discourse on The Origin of Inequality;* look ahead to Marcuse's *Eros and Civilization.*) INTERMEDIATE.

Marcuse, Herbert, *Eros and Civilization; A Philosophical Inquiry into Freud.* Random House, 1962. In one of the most important analyses of Freud's theories to be written in this century, Marcuse criticizes Freud's theory of the person and the theory of civilization to which it is tied. The Freudian argument that civilization must be based on the "permanent subjugation of human instincts" is denied, on the grounds that implicit in Freud's theory is acceptance of questionable socioeconomic assumptions (the need for repression in order to accomplish the tasks of society, for one). Marcuse proposes a new notion of civilization, in which progress is not tied to repression: a socioeconomic system organized on neo-Marxist principles, in which the "surplus-repression" implicit in materialistic capitalism is eliminated and in which we move beyond the reality principle so important to Freud, to a society in which *rational* self-gratification is the rule and reason and instinct are united, not opposed. A massive challenge to current premises of sociopsychological and economic existence, called Utopian by Freudians and the only way to save humanity by Marcusians. ADVANCED.

Skinner, B. F., *Beyond Freedom and Dignity.* Bantam, 1971. One of the most important (and debated) critiques of contemporary notions of freedom, autonomy, and "human nature." Skinner argues that we must consciously design our culture ("arrange environments") and shape behavior, in order to avoid the pitfalls of a naive and misguided pseudohumanism and to preserve true human dignity. A thorough indictment of "prescientific" (that is, non-Skinnerian) theories and attitudes, which view "human nature" as the source of freedom, rather than understanding that the only truly human behavior must come from an understanding of the "technology of behavior." INTERMEDIATE.

Science and Technology in the Twentieth Century

Kuhn, Thomas S., *The Structure of Scientific Revolutions*. Univ. of Chicago Press, 1970. An argument that normal science is vastly different from the "science of crisis situations." Through appeals to history, Kuhn demonstrates that major changes in theories (such as the transition from Ptolemaic to Copernican astronomy) are never purely scientific and involve an entire reorientation of world view. The implication of this argument is that there is very little true continuity in science, a conclusion intuitively denied by most scientists who think in "normal-scientific" terms. Kuhn also argues that there are no "pure facts" and that the theory of choice colors the very perception and identification of so-called facts in science. ADVANCED.

Chapter Eight

WOMEN'S STUDIES
". . . independent action and bold departure"

Editorial Advisor:
Mary P. Ryan
Department of History
State University of New York at Binghamton

INTRODUCTION

Recent Origins, Current Extent

Few mentions of the study of women could be found in the literature of academic disciplines before 1968. Professors and students alike had casually taken it for granted that studies of "mankind" included women. But close examination disproved this assumption in field after field; it became evident that it was largely male experience that had been studied.

A survey of college textbooks in American history, for example, found none that devoted more than 2 percent of their pages to women. Sociologists had described American occupational structure and social mobility in terms of the income and status of men. In literature women writers tended to be treated as an exotic breed (as reflected in the term, "lady author") and to be criticized with condescension. Where sex differences were central, as in Freudian psychology, the study of women was built around a male model that reinforced the status quo of sex inequality.

Acting on their own, women faculty members and advanced graduate students began documenting and countering this widespread neglect in the mid-1960s. They realized that they had been ignoring the experiences of women as completely as any of their male colleagues did. When they put together the first Women's Studies courses, they reacted largely to their own need to know; together with undergraduates, they began to press colleges to introduce such courses of study.

By 1973 colleges were offering more than 2,000 Women's Studies courses in disciplines ranging from anthropology to psychology as well as in interdisciplinary fields. Scholars were launching specialized

121

classroom investigations into topics as diverse as Black Matriarchy and Woman as Intellectual in Modern European History. Today more than 200 colleges and universities have consolidated the new courses into Women's Studies programs, many offering an undergraduate major and several granting graduate degrees. In a very few years enough in the way of scholarly literature, teaching strategy, and conceptual framework has been developed to make the systematic study of women possible.

Attractions of This New Field for Students

Far more remains to be done, however. Great gaps in knowledge need to be filled, and more conclusive answers to fundamental questions need to be framed. A sense of urgent tasks ahead should serve to invite students to enter an exciting and challenging new field.

Independent action and bold departure from the conventions of academic life will continue to be the hallmark of Women's Studies. Today's scholars in the field are largely self-taught, and students have helped to build present course offerings through their own initiative. Women's Studies could well take as its motto, "On Your Own."

At the same time the pursuit of Women's Studies thrives on cooperation. As part of the current women's movement, its development has been marked by much sharing of knowledge, interchange among students, and joint work in collective projects. Consider planning your course of study in league with friends, within a consciousness-raising group, or in a community center.

Defining Women's Studies—and Woman

The subject matter of Women's Studies in current thinking and practice covers a very broad range. It extends over the whole experience of the female sex—woman's psychology, her economic status, her social role, her artistic accomplishments, her history, and on through all the areas of knowledge in which human (and largely male) experience has been studied.

Some skeptics challenge the validity of an enterprise so circumscribed. They claim that women's experience is not distinct enough to justify isolated treatment and that gender is an artificial criterion for categorizing human experience. Other critics maintain that isolated investigation of women's experience reinforces the concept of females as separate and, as things now stand, unequal.

Such views make it important at the outset to show that women have sufficiently distinctive characteristics to justify special study and that such study can be used to help end systematic inequality. To define woman, we might look first to biology for a characterization in terms of the reproductive system and secondary sex traits. But what of character and behavior? Does the female's physiological childbearing function mean she must assume sole responsibility for child care? Does the suggestion that male hormones carry aggressive tendencies determine that women behave more passively? Immediately we find ourselves in a maze through which biologists alone cannot guide us. Sociology offers some help. Harriet Hölter, for example, in *Sex Roles and Social Structure* (see below), maintains that biology signals the development of a "master status system," a fundamental standard for dividing human labor and for organizing and stratifying society. The profoundly distinctive set of roles, character traits, and experience ascribed to females in all human cultures is well worth intensive study. An understanding of the process of sex differentiation that has decreed the social subordination of women is essential to all of us who confront sex roles.

Describing Women—A Major Element in Women's Studies

In addition to a quest for sufficiently broad and deep definitions of women, Women's Studies is concerned extensively with describing all the varieties of female experience. For this purpose we turn to such disciplines as anthropology and history.

Cross-cultural studies in anthropology suggest that certain sex roles persist in most cultures—generally, that men engage in defense, that women care for children. But these typical roles and accompanying sex temperaments are not found in all societies (see Maccoby, below). No universal standard assigns such activities as weaving, field labor, or trade exclusively to men or women (see Boserup, Rosaldo, below); nor are aggressive masculinity and tender femininity universal standards of temperament (see Mead, below). Class, race, and ethnic origin are linked to further variations in womanhood within each society.

History gives additional testimony to the range of social roles and cultural images that have been assigned to women. American history reveals short-term changes—from hardy farmwomen through fragile Victorian belles to vivacious "working girls." Womanhood often changes within the life cycle of a single individual, and these changes can be studied in the literary testimony of both women and men.

The humanities and social sciences together can be used to examine that central institution, the family. Scholars in the field of Women's Studies pay particular attention to the changing functions and organization of the family and take care to recognize that the home alone should not and does not define women's social boundaries.

Women's Studies and the Academic Disciplines

Scholars in the new field of Women's Studies use methods and concepts from the established academic disciplines even while challenging each field to broaden and reform itself to include female experience. Political Science, for example, may not find women in leadership roles, as independent voting blocs, or actively engaged in politics; but this does not excuse its neglect of half the citizenry. Questions that political scientists must explore include the causes of women's apathy or failure to assume high office, the consequences of the limited political authority of women, and the unofficial and indirect ways in which women may influence political decisions. Social

Psychology, for example, may ask why, if women do not measure up on a scale of "achievement," this situation has occurred; we must reconsider the concept and investigate women's standards of success, their dreams and nightmares. Similar problems arise in the field of Economics. Enrollment in the paid labor force does not exhaust the category "work." How about housework? Shopping? Child care? In the area of History a massive effort is required to recover the records of women and devise techniques of uncovering their past. Art History and Literary Studies, in addition to considering works by women and determining any distinctive features of women's culture, must consider yet unrecognized aesthetic outlets for women: needlework, quilts, home decoration, letters, and the like. In sum, women's studies can revitalize and enrich the academic disciplines.

It is important, however, to remember that the broad questions and issues raised in Women's Studies have no simple answers or easy explanations. You will also find that some writing in the field employs the complex, technical methods (or intimidating jargon) of specialized academic disciplines. Should you wish to pursue advanced investigations in such fields, consult the appropriate sections of this volume for guidance.

Women's Studies and Women's Protest

To counteract the sense that women are hopelessly in bondage as the second sex, students will want to explore the long history of feminism as well as its contemporary theories and programs for change. Such covert acts of rebellion as witchcraft, crime, and "hen-pecking" as well as conscious feminism are worthy of attention, as are women's "support systems": bonds between female kin, neighbors, and coworkers.

Further Directions

Books such as those listed below do not raise all the questions relevant to Women's Studies. Most of them are but the first tentative attempts to study women. Other illuminating studies are scattered through periodicals or are still in the process of composition. But the numbers are growing; scan bookshelves frequently for a continuing supply of works. Continue to check the periodicals and bibliographic aids at the end of the booklist for ongoing, open-ended sources. Some projects in the meantime: start a journal of your readings and reactions, a family biography going generations back in women's experience, a local history of women in your community, or a survey of neighbors and coworkers. Design a Utopian children's book, outline a television series with dignified female characters, or construct a movie scenario full of exhilarating female exploits. In the last analysis, Women's Studies becomes integrated into everyday life as everything becomes a subject for scrutiny and a source of greater understanding.

BIBLIOGRAPHY

NOTE The works listed below have been chosen with readability in mind, but the readings do vary somewhat in difficulty. To aid the reader, the words INTRODUCTORY, INTERMEDIATE, or ADVANCED appear after appropriate entries. All books are available in paperback unless otherwise noted.

DEFINING WOMEN

Definitions in the Sciences and Social Sciences

Maccoby, Eleanor, ed., *The Development of Sex Differences.* Stanford Univ. Press (hard cover), 1966. Contains important data and methods for women's studies, taken from anthropology, biology, and psychology. ADVANCED.

Maccoby, Eleanor, and Carol Jacklin, *Psychology of Sex Differences.* Stanford Univ. Press (hard cover), 1975. Judicious, thorough summary of research on sex differences. ADVANCED.

Money, John, and Anke Ehrhardt, *Man and Woman, Boy and Girl: Differentiation and Dimorphism of Gender Identity.* Johns Hopkins Univ. Press, 1972. Quite technical but clear and cautious explanation of the biology of sex identity. ADVANCED.

Carroll, Berenice, ed., *Liberating Women's History: Theoretical and Critical Essays.* Univ. of Illinois Press, 1975. Addresses historical meaning of womanhood in wide range of times and places. INTERMEDIATE.

Herschberger, Ruth, *Adam's Rib: A Defense of Modern Woman.* Harper & Row, 1970. Old, but full of common sense and humor about obstinate categorization of sex differences. INTRODUCTORY.

Martin, M. Kay, and Barbara Voorhies, *The Female of the Species.* Columbia University Press, 1974. A good introduction to the anthropology of women with chapters on biology and sex differences among primates and in a variety of human cultures. INTRODUCTORY.

Rosaldo, Michelle Z., and Louise Lamphere, *Woman, Culture and Society.* Stanford Univ. Press, 1974. Contains some good theorizing about the anthropological origins of sex roles as well as interesting ethnographical information. INTERMEDIATE.

Hölter, Harriet, *Sex Roles and Social Structure.* Universitet (hard cover), 1970. Excellent in defining the sociology of sex roles, based primarily on Scandinavian data. ADVANCED.

Safilios-Rothschild, Constantina, ed., *Towards a Sociology of Women.* Wiley, 1972. Sociological introduction to women's studies. INTERMEDIATE.

Bardwick, Judith, M., *Psychology of Women: A Study of Biocul-*

tural Conflicts. **Harper & Row, 1971.** Introduces the major issues in the field, although it fails to resolve them or transcend some of the prejudices of the discipline. INTRODUCTORY.

Coser, Rose L., Ed., *The Family: Its Structure and Functions.* **St. Martin, 1964.** A thorough and technical study; includes articles on changing sex roles and alternatives to current American family organization. INTERMEDIATE.

Yorburg, Betty, *Sexual Identity: Sex Roles and Social Change.* **Wiley, 1974.** Rudimentary survey of sociology literature. INTRODUCTORY.

Watson, Barbara Bellow, *Women's Studies: The Social Realities.* **Harper's College Press, 1976.** This book can serve as an introductory text to Women's Studies as an interdisciplinary field. INTRODUCTORY.

Definitions in Political and Feminist Philosophy

Engels, Frederick, *The Origin of the Family: Private Property and the State.* **Path Press, 1972.** Although it draws on outdated anthropology and is limited by nineteenth-century views held by Engels when he was writing with Karl Marx, it presents an approach to the family and women that remains highly useful. INTERMEDIATE.

Zaretsky, Eli, *Capitalism, the Family, and Personal Life.* **Harper & Row, 1976.** Presents woman's place within the context of expanding private life; difficult but very important. ADVANCED.

Mitchell, Juliet, *Woman's Estate.* **Pantheon, 1972.** See especially Part Two for Mitchell's division of womanhood into its functional components. INTRODUCTORY.

Firestone, Shulamith, *The Dialectic of Sex.* **Bantam, 1971.** A radical feminist defines woman's predicament; very provocative. INTRODUCTORY.

Figes, Eva, *Patriarchal Attitudes.* **Fawcett-World, 1971. Greer, Germaine,** *The Female Eunuch.* **Bantam, 1972. Millett, Kate.** *Sexual Politics,* **Avon, 1971. Grace, Atkinson,** *Amazon Odyssey.* **Links Books, Quick Fox, 1974.** All present further definitions of women from the perspective of contemporary feminism. INTRODUCTORY.

Gould, Carol C., and Marx W. Wartofsky, eds., *Women and Philosophy: Toward a Theory of Liberation.* **Putnam, 1976.** Essays presenting philosophical approaches to women's position in history and in contemporary society. INTRODUCTORY.

DESCRIBING WOMEN HISTORICALLY AND CROSS-CULTURALLY

An Overview

Bullough, Vern L. and Bonnie Bullough, *The Subordinate Sex: A History of Attitudes towards Women.* **Penguin, 1974.** Solid survey of women in history. INTERMEDIATE.

DeBeauvoir, Simone, *The Second Sex.* **Random House, 1974.** Contains encyclopedic information about historical variations on the theme of women as "other." INTERMEDIATE.

O'Faolain, Julia, and Lauro Martines, eds., *Not in God's Image: A History of Women's Europe from the Greeks to the Nineteenth Century.* **Harper & Row, 1973.** Collections of documents detailing women's predicament from the ancients to the Victorians. INTRODUCTORY.

Goode, William J., *World Revolution and Family Patterns.* **Free Press, 1963.** Summarizes information on women and the family cross-culturally. INTERMEDIATE.

Iglitzin, Lynne B., and Ruth Ross, eds., *Women in the World, A Comparative Study.* **Clio Press, 1976.** Describes the contemporary status and struggles of women in developing countries as well as in the U.S. and Europe. INTERMEDIATE.

Spacks, Patricia Meyer, *The Female Imagination.* **Avon, 1976.** INTERMEDIATE.

Some Pre-Modern Cultures

Andreski, Iris, ed., *Old Wives' Tales: Life Stories of African Women.* **Schocken (hard cover), 1970.** First-person accounts of the lives of elderly women from the Ibibio tribe of Eastern Nigeria. INTRODUCTORY.

Boserup, Esther, *Women's Role in Economic Development.* **St. Martin's, 1970.** An essential work on patterns of labor in the Third World before and after the intrusion of Western culture and technology. INTERMEDIATE.

Fernea, Elizabeth W., *Guests of the Sheik: An Ethnology of an Iraqi Village.* **Doubleday, 1969.** Ethnography of an Iraqi Village that gives attention to women in households and harems. INTRODUCTORY.

Mead, Margaret, *Sex and Temperament.* **Dell, 1967.** Much-respected demonstration of the varieties of characteristics culturally assigned to men and women. INTRODUCTORY.

Lurie, Nancy, *Mountain Wolf Woman: Sister of Crashing Thunder; Autobiography of a Winnebago Indian.* **Univ. of Michigan Press (hard cover), 1961.** A distinctive experience of womanhood. INTRODUCTORY.

Wolf, Margery, *Women and the Family in Rural Taiwan.* **Stanford Univ. Press, 1972.** Describes the life cycle of women in a small agricultural village. INTERMEDIATE.

Reiter, Rayna R., ed., *Toward an Anthology of Women.* **Monthly Review Press, 1976.** Includes examples of the Marxist-Feminist perspective along with ethnographic studies. INTERMEDIATE.

PERCEPTIONS AND CONCEPTIONS OF WOMEN

Psychology Constructs the Female

Deutsh, Helene, *The Psychology of Women.* **Vol. I, Grune, 1944, Vol. II, Bantam, 1973.** Traditional Freudian model of female psychology constructed by Freud's disciple beginning in the 1940s; unchallenged until recently, it must be taken as documentation of attitudes toward women, not as "science." INTERMEDIATE.

Horney, Karen, *Feminine Psychology.* **Norton, 1973. Thompson, Clara, On Women. NAL, 1971.** Two foremost critics of Freudian theories of women struggling, not entirely successfully, to break free of Freudian concepts. INTERMEDIATE.

Miller, Jean B., ed., *Psychoanalysis and Women.* **Penguin, 1973.** Collection of criticism of Freudian tenets. INTERMEDIATE.

Mitchell, Juliet, *Psychoanalysis and Feminism.* **Pantheon (hard cover), 1974.** A difficult book, but worth reading for suggestions about the feminine unconscious and its future. ADVANCED.

Women in Literature and Art— Criticism

Heilbrun, Carolyn, *Toward a Recognition of Androgyny.* **Harper & Row, 1974.** Presents an important theory with illustrations from English literature. INTERMEDIATE.

Hardwick, Elizabeth, *Seduction and Betrayal: Women and Literature.* **Random House, 1974.** Analyses and critiques of the depiction of women in fiction. INTERMEDIATE.

Moers, Ellen, *Literary Women.* **Doubleday, 1977.** Analysis of French, English and American women writers. INTERMEDIATE.

Lakoff, Robin, *Language and Woman's Place.* **Harper & Row, 1975.** Presents the basic linguistics of sexism. INTRODUCTORY.

Millett, Kate, *Sexual Politics.* **Avon, 1971.** Pioneering criticisms of male writing about women. INTRODUCTORY.

Showalter, Elaine, *A Literature of Their Own: British Women Novelists from Brontë to Lessing.* **Princeton University Press (hard cover), 1977.** Examines women's distinctive literary tradition. INTERMEDIATE.

Woolf, Virginia, *A Room of One's Own.* **Harcourt Brace Jovanovich, 1929.** The classic on women and writing. INTRODUCTORY.

Hess, Thomas B., and Elizabeth C. Baker, *Art and Sexual Politics.* **Macmillan, 1973.** Essays offering explanation for paucity of women acknowledged to be great painters and sculptors. INTERMEDIATE.

Harris, Ann Sutherland, and Linda Nochlin, *Women Artists 1550–*

1950. L. A. County Museum of Art, 1976. Catalogue with color prints and critical treatment of the most extensive exhibition of women painters to date. INTERMEDIATE.

Women in Literature and Art—
Women Novelists and Poets

These sources are limitless. The following authors have been widely read in Women's Studies courses: Margaret Atwood, Jane Austen, George Eliot, the Brontës, Virginia Woolf, Doris Lessing, Emily Dickinson, Louisa May Alcott, Kate Chopin, Rita Mae Brown, Tillie Olsen, Marge Piercy, Sylvia Plath, Erica Jong, Mary McCarthy, Alix Kate Schulman, Agnes Smedley, Adrienne Rich, Maya Angelou. Various anthologies of poetry, short stories and drama are available in paperback.

Women in Literature and Art—
Women and Film

Haskell, Molly, *From Reverence to Rape: The Treatment of Women in the Movies.* Penguin, 1974. Critically reviews images of women in American cinema from its beginning to the present. INTRODUCTORY.

Rosen, Marjorie, *Popcorn Venus: Women, Movies, and the American Dream.* Avon, 1974. A hasty escapade through changing themes relating to women in American movie history, rather giddy but well stocked with titles and popular stars. INTRODUCTORY.

Mellen, Joan, *Women and Their Sexuality in the New Film.* Horizon, 1974. Focus on European directors with intense and often penetrating analysis. ADVANCED.

FEMINISTS AND FEMINISM

Wollstonecraft, Mary, *Vindication of the Rights of Women.* Norton, 1967. First explicit feminism in the Enlightenment tradition. INTERMEDIATE.

Flexner, Eleanor, *Mary Wollstonecraft.* Penguin, 1973. An acclaimed biography. INTERMEDIATE.

Mill, John Stuart, and Harriet Mill, *Essays on Sex Equality,* ed. Alice S. Rossi. Univ. of Chicago Press, 1970, Feminism born of nineteenth-century liberalism. INTERMEDIATE.

Freeman, Jo, *The Politics of Women's Liberation: A Case Study of an Emerging Social Movement and its Relation to Policy Process.* Longman, 1975. Provides a valuable perspective on the origins of the contemporary women's movement. INTRODUCTORY.

Rowbotham, Sheila, *Women, Resistance and Revolution: A History of Women and Revolution in the Modern World.* **Random House, 1973.** Fine study of women in revolt from sixteenth-century England to contemporary Vietnam. INTERMEDIATE.

Rossi, Alice S., ed., *The Feminist Papers: From Adams to de-Beauvoir.* **Bantam, 1974.** Collection of feminist writing from Abigail Adams to Simone deBeauvoir. INTRODUCTORY.

Lerner, Gerda, *The Grimke Sisters from South Carolina: Pioneers for Women's Rights and Abolition.* **Schocken, 1971.** Biography of the pioneers of American feminism and their engagement in abolitionism. INTRODUCTORY.

Sklar, Kathryn K., *Catharine Beecher: A Study in American Domesticity.* **Yale Univ. Press (hard cover), 1973.** The subject of this biography is not a conventional feminist, but a domestic reformer whose life and work provided a fulcrum of change in women's place, the implications of which are matter for argument. INTERMEDIATE.

Kraditor, Aileen S., *The Ideas of the Women's Suffrage Movement 1890–1920.* **Doubleday, 1971.** A major work on the American suffrage movement, very informative regarding feminist theories and policies. INTERMEDIATE.

O'Neill, William L., *Everyone Was Brave: The Rise and Fall of Feminism in America.* **Quadrangle, 1969.** Also an informative work on the suffrage and related women's movements in the late nineteenth and early twentieth centuries. INTERMEDIATE.

Davis, Allen F., *American Heroine: The Life and Legend of Jane Addams.* **Oxford Univ. Press (hard cover), 1973.** Jane Addams, the subject of this biography, was more a Progressive reformer than an avowed feminist, but she illustrated and furthered dramatic changes in women's status and roles at the turn of the century. INTERMEDIATE.

Stanton, Elizabeth C., *Eighty Years and More: Reminiscences 1815–1897.* **Schocken, 1971.** Fascinating story of the life of a nineteenth-century activist. INTRODUCTORY.

Parker, Gail, ed., *The Oven Birds: American Women on Womanhood, 1820–1920.* **Doubleday, 1972.** An anthology which examines how leading feminists and authors viewed themselves as women. INTERMEDIATE.

Gilman, Charlotte P., *Women and Economics: The Economic Factor between Men and Women as a Factor in Social Evolution.* **Harper & Row, 1970.** Most radical feminist theory of the suffrage era; still instructive. ADVANCED.

Kennedy, David M., *Birth Control in America: The Career of Margaret Sanger.* **Yale Univ. Press, 1970.** Thorough biography and plausible interpretation of the work and personality of a pioneer in the birth-control movement. INTERMEDIATE.

Rowbotham, Sheila, *Woman's Consciousness, Man's World*. Penguin, 1974. A small book expressing one woman's feminism and how it evolved from her experience in the 1960s and 1970s. INTERMEDIATE.

AMERICAN HISTORY

Surveys

Beard, Mary R., *Woman as a Force in History*. Macmillan, 1971. Scanty materials, but the approach deserves attention. INTERMEDIATE.

Buhle, Mary Jo, Anne Gordon, and Nancy Dye, *Women in American Society*. Pamphlet, published by Radical America. A brief tract setting up a social-economic and feminist framework for the study of American women's history. INTRODUCTORY.

Douglas, Ann, *The Feminization of American Culture*. Knopf (hard cover), 1977. Portrays the way in which American culture became sentimentalized and feminized in the nineteenth century and traces the roots of our consumer culture of today.

Banner, Lois W., *Women in Modern America: A Brief History*. Harcourt Brace Jovanovich, 1974. A brief, primarily descriptive, survey of American women's roles and images from the late nineteenth century forward. INTRODUCTORY.

Flexner, Eleanor, *Century of Struggle: The Women's Rights Movement in the United States*. Atheneum, 1968. For a long time the only history of American women emphasizing political, legal, and educational progress. INTERMEDIATE.

Lerner, Gerda, ed., *Black Women in White America: A Documentary History*. Random House, 1973. Copious documents on all aspects of Black women's past. INTERMEDIATE.

Smith, Page, *Daughters of the Promised Land: Women in American History*. Little, Brown, 1970. An idiosyncratic approach; will anger some feminists. INTERMEDIATE.

Sochen, June, *Herstory: A Woman's View of American History*. Alfred Pub., 1974. A quick jaunt through the highlights of women's history. INTRODUCTORY.

Ryan, Mary P., *Womanhood in America*. Franklin Watts (New Viewpoints), 1975. Attempts to sketch the social roles and cultural images deemed appropriate to women in each stage of America's socioeconomic development. INTRODUCTORY.

Monographs

Demos, John, *A Little Commonwealth: Family Life in Plymouth Colony*. Oxford Univ. Press, 1971. Case study of agricultural villages before commercial and industrial capitalism drove a wedge between home and work, male and female roles. INTERMEDIATE.

Morgan, Edmund S., *Puritan Family: Religion and Domestic Relations in Seventeenth Century New England.* Harper & Row, 1966. Supplies the attitudes toward women and literary evidence that Demos (above) lacks. INTERMEDIATE.

Cott, Nancy, *The Bonds of Womanhood: Women's Sphere in New England, 1780–1835.* Yale University Press (hard cover), 1977. Depicts the status and roles of women at a crucial period of social and historical change. INTERMEDIATE.

Spruill, Julia C., *Women's Life and Work in the Southern Colonies.* Norton, 1972. Packed full of information about women in the South into the eighteenth century. INTRODUCTORY.

Scott, Anne F., *The Southern Lady: From Pedestal to Politics, 1830–1930.* Univ. of Chicago Press, 1972. Explodes the familiar myth and charts the work and activism of upperclass white women from slavery through the Civil War into the progressive era. INTERMEDIATE.

Chafe, William H., *The American Woman: Her Changing Social, Economic, and Political Roles, 1920–1970.* Oxford Univ. Press, 1974. Clarifies much of recent history; best on women's entry into the work force in and after the Second World War. INTRODUCTORY.

Gordon, Linda, *Woman's Body/Woman's Right: A Social History of Birth Control in America.* Viking (hard cover), 1976. An important book on a crucial subject. INTERMEDIATE.

Women in the Labor Force

Smuts, Robert W., *Women and Work in America.* Schocken, 1971. Instructive survey of changing patterns of employment, primarily from the late nineteenth century to the mid-1920s. INTRODUCTORY.

O'Neill, William L., ed., *Women at Work.* Quadrangle, 1972. Contains Elinor Langer's fine study of women workers at the New York Telephone Company. INTRODUCTORY.

Baxandall, Rosalyn, Linda Gordon, and Susan Weberby, eds., *America's Working Women, A Documentary History—1600 to the Present.* Viking, 1976. This collection provides interesting and needed documentation of women workers. INTERMEDIATE.

Oppenheimer, Valerie K., *The Female Labor Force in the United States: Demographic and Economic Factors Governing its Growth and Changing Composition.* Greenwood Press, 1976. Contains numerous detailed, sometimes difficult, tables and statistics, but they provide crucial information about the age, marital status, and

childbearing history of women workers in the twentieth century. AD-
VANCED.

SOME COMPARATIVE EXCURSIONS
OUTSIDE THE UNITED STATES

Sullerot, Evelyne, *Woman, Society, and Change.* McGraw-Hill,
1971. Provides comparative data on women's changing roles. INTRO-
DUCTORY.

Vicinus, Martha, ed., *Suffer and be Still: Women in the Victorian
Age.* **Indiana Univ. Press, 1973.** Articles surveying Victorian
womanhood in England and on the continent. INTERMEDIATE.

Putnam, Emily J., *The Lady: Studies of Certain Significant Phases
of Her History.* **Univ. of Chicago Press, 1970.** Insights into the peculiar
plight of upperclass women. INTRODUCTORY.

Sidel, Ruth, *Women and Child-Care in China.* Penguin, 1973. Hasty
observations, but some exciting alternatives are posed. INTRODUCTORY.

Young, Marilyn Blatt, ed., *Women in China: Studies in Social
Change and Feminism.* **Ann Arbor, Center for Chinese Studies, Univ.
of Michigan, 1973.** Well-researched studies on Chinese women before
and after the Revolution. INTERMEDIATE.

Wolf, Margery, and Roxane Witke, eds., *Women in Chinese Society.* **Stanford Univ. Press, 1975.**

Hartman, Mary, and Lois W. Banner, eds., *Clio's Consciousness
Raised: New Perspectives on the History of Women.* **Harper & Row,
1974.** Papers from the first Berkshire Conference of Women Historians,
including work on sexuality, medicine, ladies and prostitutes, in England, Western Europe, and America. ADVANCED.

Rowbotham, Sheila, *Hidden From History: Rediscovering Women
in History from the Seventeenth Century to the Present.* **Pantheon
(hard cover), 1975.** Intelligent essay on women in English history since
the seventeenth century. INTERMEDIATE.

Mandel, William E., *Soviet Women.* **Doubleday, 1975.** Standard
source on women in Russia since the Revolution. INTERMEDIATE.

Scott, Hilda, *Does Socialism Liberate Women? Experience from
Eastern Europe.* **Beacon Press (hard cover), 1974.** Analysis of the
position of women in Eastern Europe since the Second World War.
INTERMEDIATE.

Bridenthal, Renate, and Claudia Koonz, eds., *Becoming Visible:
Women in European History.* **Houghton-Mifflin, 1976.** Useful collection of essays.

CONTEMPORARY STATUS OF WOMEN

General Anthologies

The following anthologies collect studies on most aspects of women's current status: work-force participation, domestic roles, socialization, literature, and psychology. Although there is some duplication, each contains vital information.

Gornick, Vivian, and Barbara K. Moran, *Women in Sexist Society.* **NAL, 1972.** INTRODUCTORY.

Malbin, Nora G., *Woman in a Man-Made World.* **Rand McNally, 1972.** INTERMEDIATE.

Lifton, Robert Jay, ed., *The Woman in America.* **Beacon, 1967.** INTERMEDIATE.

Morgan, Robin, ed., *Sisterhood is Powerful: An Anthology of Writings from the Women's Liberation Movement.* **Random House, 1970.** INTRODUCTORY.

Economic and Social Status of Women

Kreps, Juanita, *Sex in the Market Place: American Women at Work.* **Johns Hopkins Univ. Press, 1971.** Brief survey of women's distribution through the labor force. INTRODUCTORY.

Epstein, Cynthia F., *Woman's Place: Options and Limits in Professional Careers.* **Univ. of California Press, 1970.** Particularly good on women in the professions. INTRODUCTORY.

Ginzberg, Eli, ed., *Corporate Lib: Women's Challenge to Management.* **Johns Hopkins Univ. Press, 1973.** Women's assault on the upper regions of the business professions. INTERMEDIATE.

Kundsin, Ruth B., *Women and Success: The Anatomy of Achievement.* **Morrow (hard cover), 1974.** Helpful collection of social-science literature on the subject, with testimony from successful women. INTERMEDIATE.

Politics and Law

Amundsen, Kirsten, *The Silenced Majority: Women and American Democracy.* **Prentice-Hall, 1971.** Careful examination of women's participation in American politics and limited access to seats of power. INTRODUCTORY.

Chamberlin, Hope, *A Minority of Members: Women in the United States Congress 1917–1972.* **Praeger, 1973.** INTRODUCTORY.

Tolchin, Martin, and Susan Tolchin, *Clout: Woman Power and Politics.* **Coward (hard cover), 1974.** Examines current attempts on the part of women to make their way into the political establishment. INTRODUCTORY.

Kanowitz, Leo, *Women and the Law: The Unfinished Revolution.* Univ. of New Mexico Press, 1969. Describes the current inequities in women's legal status and the process of legal change, including Equal Opportunity legislation and the Equal Rights Amendment. INTERMEDIATE.

Ross, Susan C., *The Rights of Women.* Manual available from the American Civil Liberties Union (ACLU); comprehensive. ADVANCED.

Housewives and Mothers

Lopata, Helena Z., *Occupation Housewife.* Oxford Univ. Press, 1972. Valuable survey data and intriguing quotations; lacking in critical assessment. INTERMEDIATE.

Friedan, Betty, *The Feminine Mystique.* Dell, 1975. In addition to its impact on the revival of the women's movement, this bestseller offers a good cultural history of postwar domesticity. INTRODUCTORY.

Bernard, Jessie, *The Future of Marriage.* Bantam, 1973. An appeal for the reform of marriage to assure equal rewards and burdens to husbands and wives; includes summary of sociological data on the differential benefits of marriage to men and to women. INTERMEDIATE.

Steinfels, Margaret, *Who's Minding the Children? The History and Politics of Day Care in America.* Simon & Schuster, 1974. A history of the day care movement since the Second World War and description of its current operation, prospects, and implications for the future. INTERMEDIATE.

Oakley, Ann, *Women's Work: A History of the House Wife.* Pantheon, 1975. With considerable attention to the current dimensions of this role. INTRODUCTORY.

Rich, Adrienne, *Of Woman Born: Motherhood as Experience and Institution.* Bantam, 1977. Pioneering and provocative analysis of a central facet of womanhood. INTERMEDIATE.

Komarovsky, Mirra, *Dilemmas of Masculinity: A Study of College Youth.* Norton, 1966. Describes young male responses to changing sex roles and their expectations of prospective wives.

Medicine, Health and Sexuality

Much of this literature is polemical; justly angry, it supplies information and evidence of outrage rather than academic treatment.

Boston Women's Health Book Collective, *Our Bodies Ourselves.* Simon & Schuster, 1973. This manual for women can also be read as a document on the concerns and approaches of women's liberation as they relate to health, contraception, pregnancy. INTRODUCTORY.

Chesler, Phyllis, *Women and Madness.* Avon, 1973. Polemical analysis of treatment of women by psychiatrists and mental institutions. INTERMEDIATE.

Brownmiller, Susan, *Against Our Will: Men, Women and Rape.* Bantam, 1976. A history of rape and analysis of its meaning for the relations of the sexes. INTERMEDIATE.

Belliveau, Fred, and Lin Richter, *Understanding Human Sexual Inadequacy.* Bantam, 1970. Explains the findings of Masters and Johnson, with great significance for women. INTERMEDIATE.

Millett, Kate, *The Prostitution Papers.* Avon, 1973. Accounts of experiences of New York prostitutes. INTERMEDIATE.

Abbott, Sidney, and Barbara Love, *Sappho Was a Right On Woman: A Liberated View of Lesbianism.* Stein & Day, 1973. A standard introductory source.

In Church and Education

Daly, Mary, *Beyond God the Father: Toward a Philosophy of Women's Liberation.* Beacon, 1974. The theological and institutional oppression of women by established churches is explored in depth. INTERMEDIATE.

Ruether, Rosemary R., *Religion and Sexism.* Simon & Schuster, 1974. Images of women in Christian and Jewish literature. INTRODUCTORY.

Frazier, Nancy and Myra Sadker, *Sexism in School and Society.* Harper & Row, 1973. Account and implications of the inculcation of sex roles and stereotypes in the schools, with suggestions for change. INTRODUCTORY.

Bernard, Jessie, *Academic Women.* Pennsylvania State Univ. Press (hard cover), 1964. Women in colleges and universities. ADVANCED.

Change Magazine, ed., *Women on Campus: The Unfinished Liberation.* Change Magazine Publications (New Rochelle, N. Y.), 1975. A collection of 22 essays reporting on the current movement among women to attain equality as professionals in higher education; introduction by Elizabeth Janeway.

Varieties of Contemporary Female Experience (Class and Race)

Komarovsky, Mirra, *Blue Collar Marriage.* Random House, 1964. Thorough and sensitive sociological case study of the distinctive family attitudes and patterns of white Protestant working-class women. INTERMEDIATE.

Rainwater, Lee, *Workingman's Wife.* Oceana (hard cover), 1959. Focused on market research, but some valuable data can be retrieved from this context. INTERMEDIATE.

Cade, Toni, *The Black Woman.* NAL, 1970. Black women speak of their struggle. INTRODUCTORY.

Ladner, Joyce, *Tomorrow's Tomorrow.* Doubleday, 1972. Includes interviews with adolescent Black women in the ghetto; very revealing. INTERMEDIATE.

Seifer, Nancy, *Nobody Speaks for Me: Self-Portraits of American Working-Class Women.* Simon & Schuster, 1977. INTRODUCTORY.

Staples, Robert, *The Black Woman in America: Sex, Marriage and the Family.* Nelson-Hall (hard cover), 1973. Surveys major historical and sociological issues, including the myth of Black matriarchy. INTRODUCTORY.

Stack, Carol, *All Our Kin: Strategies for Survival in a Black Community.* Harper & Row, 1975. Describes the domestic networks of a black neighborhood and presents a very useful concept for women's studies. INTERMEDIATE.

Kahn, Kathy, *Hillbilly Women.* Doubleday (hard cover), 1973. Personal accounts of the experience and values of rural poor women. INTERMEDIATE.

Young, Michael, and Peter Willmott, *Family and Kinship in East London.* Penguin, 1962. Fine description of the distinct pattern of womanhood in a working-class neighborhood. INTERMEDIATE.

BIBLIOGRAPHIC AIDS AND ONGOING SOURCES

Jacobs, Sue-Ellen, *Women in Perspective, A Guide for Cross-Cultural Studies.* Univ. of Ill. Press, 1974.

Soltow, Martha Jane, Carolyn Force, and Murray Massre, *Women in American Labor History.* School of Labor and Industrial Relations, Michigan State Univ.

Women Studies Abstracts, P.O. Box 1, Rush, NY 14543. This reference tool provides an index of many Women's Studies articles now appearing in journals and periodicals relating to a wide range of academic disciplines.

The Guide to Female Studies. Issued annually from the Feminist Press, Box 334, Old Westbury, NY 11568.

Female Studies I–VI, Clearinghouse of Women's Studies, The Feminist Press, Box 334, Old Westbury, NY 11568.

Robinson, Lora H., *Women's Studies: Courses and Programs for Higher Education.* American Association for Higher Education, 1973. See the book's bibliography.

Periodicals Devoted to Women's Studies

Feminist Studies, University of Maryland, College Park, MA 20742.

Women's Studies Newsletter, Feminist Press, Box 334, Old Westbury, NY 11568.

Frontiers, Women's Studies Program, Hillside Court, #104, University of Colorado, Boulder, CO 80302.

Signs, Univ. of Chicago Press, 5801 S. Ellis Avenue, Chicago, IL 60630.

Women's Studies: An Interdisciplinary Journal, Gordon and Breach Science Publications, Inc., One Park Ave., New York, NY 10016.

Quest, A Feminist Journal, 1909 Que Street, N.W., Washington, DC 20009.

Sex Roles: A Journal of Research, Plenum Publishing Corp., 227 West 17th Street, New York, NY 10011.

Camera Obscura: A Journal of Feminism and Film Theory, P.O. Box 4517, Berkeley, CA 94704.

The Social Sciences

Chapter Nine

ANTHROPOLOGY
"... the study of
human nature and possibilities"

Editorial Advisors:
Michelle and Renato Rosaldo
Department of Anthropology
Stanford University

INTRODUCTION

Anthropology means "the study of man"—that is, the study of human nature and its possibilities on the basis of comparative research. Traditionally, anthropology is divided into four subfields: sociocultural anthropology, which focuses on the customs and organization of living human groups; linguistics, which is the comparative study of human language; archaeology, which is the study of human history on the basis of material remains of past cultures; and physical anthropology, which is the study of the physical characteristics of the species *Homo sapiens* in different environments and in contrast to nonhuman primates.

Because anthropology is most widely known for providing us with knowledge of other and, in particular, simpler or "more primitive" human cultures, the focus of this section is on sociocultural anthropology (although some linguistic material is mentioned). This sociocultural subfield is generally called "social anthropology" by the British and "cultural anthropology" by Americans.

Sociocultural anthropologists are concerned with advancing our understanding of the human situation—who we are and what we can be—from a comparative and historical perspective. Their work is based on descriptions (generally referred to as *ethnographies*) of the social life and customs of diverse human groups. It is probably fair to say that most anthropologists recognize three basic levels of analysis in the study of human groups.

The first is social structure—the patterns (how people organize their relationships to one another), and the principles (economic relations, kinship, community values) that underlie these patterns. Another is culture—the customs, ideas, and symbols (everything from religious practices to ornaments, from values to knowledge about and conceptions of the natural and social worlds) which determine how people ordinarily act and "make sense" of their actions, Finally there is personality—the typical motivations and dispositions of individuals, as these are developed from their experience of a particular society and culture throughout their lives.

While many anthropologists do not deal with materials on all three levels, most recognize that significant aspects of each vary from one human group to another; they further assume that the three are always mutually determinant or interlinked. Traditionally, anthropologists take one of three stances towards their material:

CROSS-CULTURAL   Societies around the world may be compared in order to establish human universals (for example, all societies manifest some form of the incest taboo) or to demonstrate lawful correlations among, particular societal characteristics (for example, between technological development and forms of social organization, or between child-rearing practices and religious beliefs). Alternatively, cross-cultural theorists may highlight human differences, to alert us to the unique and peculiar features of our own society or of other societies when compared to most human societies. From such a perspective, the American belief that husbands and wives should be best friends whose allegiance to one another surpasses their allegiance to parents or co-workers is as peculiar as the belief (held in parts of Indonesia and the Philippines) that headhunting promotes the fertility of women and of crops.

HISTORICAL AND COMPARATIVE   This approach focuses on characteristics of groups that are historically related, on the assumption that they represent diverse realizations of a common heritage. When we know what several groups have in common, their differences are more precisely understood. Scholars in this tradition may, for example, focus on similarities and differences in the myths or kinship ideologies of South American societies; they may examine differences in what Christianity, Buddhism, or Islam, means to peasants or to traders, to urban elites or to agricultural villagers, in an attempt to specify relationships between religious ideology and social class. Work under this rubric also includes the attempt to relate social life in a village or local community to the economic and political organization of the states, colonies, or nations of which they are a part.

INTENSIVE CASE STUDY   The approach here is ethnographic, an attempt to provide a holistic account of the life of a particular group of people, one in which social life, economics politics, beliefs, motivations and so on, are all interlinked. These case studies provide in-depth knowledge of other societies. In showing the coherence and intelligibility of the practices of people elsewhere and translating their customs into terms which can make sense to the investigator and his audience, ethnography resembles the work of the literary critic—both translate, or interpret, someone else's thought and practice. Just as the literary critic is informed by familiarity with world literature, so the ethnographer who describes the life of a particular community is informed by a knowledge of the range of human cultures previously described.

Anthropologists obtain their data in both the library and "the field." As field workers, they participate in the life of the communities they study and describe. Their methods include those of most other social scientists—quantitative surveys, psychological tests, formal interviews, and historical investigation. But anthropological approaches tend to be distinctive in several important respects: in using participant observation as a primary tool of field work; in stressing culture—that is, the distinctive ideas and orientations of groups of people in diverse situations; in being committed to holistic description; in assuming that no one way of life is more natural or better than any other; and finally, in being self-conscious about the problems of translating other people's customs into academic prose.

HISTORY OF THEORY

Modern anthropology arose with the development of museums in England and America during the latter half of the nineteenth century. The fact that the discipline was housed in museums colored much of the thinking about past human development. Anthropologists in the evolutionary or cultural-historical schools of thought, for example, developed, as if for display cases, theories of how all paths of human development culminated in Western European civilization.

Evolutionists, inspired by French Enlightenment social theory and Darwin, hypothesized that human societies had passed through earlier stages (more "primitive," "savage," or "barbaric") in their ascent to civilization. By relegating much of the non-Western world to a lower rung on the evolutionary ladder, they avoided serious confrontation with the "otherness" and alternatives posed by peoples whom they were meeting face-to-face in their colonial and imperial ventures.

Cultural historians, following their German predecessors and inspired by zoological classifications, took the world as the only natural unit of classification and attempted to trace the origins and dissemination of such human inventions as writing, pottery, and tools. Debates centered on "single origin" versus "independent invention"—that is, whether traits diffused from a single origin point to other cultures or were invented in a number of places independent of one another. At issue were assumptions about human creativity and about the factors that made different cultures more or less likely to borrow or reject traits from other cultures.

From 1890 to 1914 anthropological studies of "primitive" societies caught the attention of Emile Durkheim and Sigmund Freud. British social anthropology was to be deeply influenced by the French sociology of Durkheim, while American cultural anthropology was to be shaped by Freud's psychoanalytic theory. The French school viewed society as a system of functionally interdependent parts. Both it and British social anthropology tended to be concerned with norms and institutions, with social morphology and enduring structures, and with the functions of institutions in keeping the larger social system working smoothly. In American cultural anthropology, psychoanalytic influences led to concern with the relation of individual personality and larger cultural patterns, with the relation of early childhood socialization and dominant cultural themes, and with such concepts as ethos, world view, national character, and basic personality. This divergence still holds between British and American anthropology.

During the same period anthropology developed its characteristic method, that of intensive and systematic field work. Until that time reports from travelers and missionaries had all too often provided the data for sweeping speculative theories, ranging from the evolutionism of Sir Edward Tylor to the broadly comparative studies of James Frazer. Their theories were only as good as the facts, and their facts were poorly understood and taken out of cultural context. Franz Boas in America and Bronislaw Malinowski in England were the first consciously to develop field work as a necessary part of an anthropologist's training. They stressed the importance of knowing the native language and actually witnessing events in another culture, as well as interviewing the participants to determine their understanding of their culture. The emergence of the field-work tradition revolutionized the empirical basis of anthropological theory. At the same time anthropologists found themselves working, if not hand in hand with, at least physically under the jurisdiction of government and colonial officials. Their material was at times relevant to the American Bureau of Indian Affairs or British policies of "indirect rule."

From 1920 to 1940 the British developed their structural-functional methods and produced an admirable series of ethnographic monographs by E. E. Evans-Pritchard and Meyer Fortes, among others. American anthropology proved more adventurous and rode off in all directions: its major interest was in the notion of "cultural relativism," the idea that every culture is a unique configuration of elements and must be understood from within, on its own terms. This was closely linked to the idea that human beings, whatever their genetic composition, have the same capacity for thought. For example, anthropologists held that a New Englander born and raised among the Booga Booga would act and speak like a member of that culture, and that the reverse would, of course, be true as well. Margaret Mead asked what we ourselves can learn from the study of other cultures. She returned from field work in Samoa to tell Americans that adolescent turmoil was produced by culture and not by biology. Ruth Benedict also popularized the notion of relativism with her *Patterns of Culture*.

After 1945 the British increased their production of fine ethnographies, while Americans frequently concentrated on particular institutions requiring familiarity with other, neighboring academic disciplines (such as religion, political science, law, economics, and psychology). There has also been a return to nineteenth-century concerns, with neo-evolutionism (White, Sahlins, Service) and comparative studies based either on the "World Ethnographic Sample" initiated by G. P. Murdock or the more sophisticated method of "controlled comparison" among a small number of societies understood more fully. Other recent work stresses that cultures are historical products and have to be understood in terms of the past and of larger processes of the societies and world around them.

THEORETICAL AREAS OF CONTEMPORARY ANTHROPOLOGY

The sections below correspond to the subsections under the rubric of "Theoretical Areas" in the following bibliography. They are thus designed both to give an overall view of the field today and to introduce the readings listed.

Evolution

In this area, research is directed toward the question of how we came to be what we are. Most anthropologists explicitly or implicitly adhere to a ranking of societies in terms of socioeconomic complexity. Such ranking ranges from the "band societies" of hunter-gatherers through "tribal societies" using hoe agriculture and peasant societies, or "agricultural states," to contemporary industrial society. Societies on each level are known to share certain characteristics (for example, hunter-gatherers tend to be egalitarian), but anthropologists differ in the importance they attach to such facts. Some, committed to "cultural relativism," underemphasize the typology because of its possible implication that some one kind of social group is more primitive than, and so deficient in relation to, another. Others claim that we can learn from the study of contemporary hunter-gatherers, for example, a good deal about the "origins" of more complex societies and consequently come to understand the factors that promote societal development everywhere and to see the bases of such elements as social stratification and religious secularism in the modern world.

The evolutionary questions that preoccupied earlier anthropologists—who tended, for example, to equate the belief systems of tribal communities with the thought of children—have been rejected. Rather than opposing our own "scientific" civilization to all others, contemporary anthropologists use evolutionary schemata to ask such questions as: How is increasing complexity in the division of labor related to the development of social classes and forms of economic exploitation? What kinds of societies have codified legal systems? How does women's status change as economies develop and women are increasingly defined as wives and mothers rather than as producers? How do the belief systems of tribalists differ from those of peasants?

Related to but different from the evolutionary approach is one that emphasizes history and insists that no society that can be observed today is a pristine exemplification of something "primitive." All societies have histories, all have been affected by relations with other groups, and, it is overwhelmingly clear, the colonial expansion of the West has indelibly affected even the simplest communities observable at this time. Such a realization encourages the study of societal development from the point of view of specific historical contingencies that operate in a particular place or time, rather than of universally operative evolutionary sequences.

Social Organization

The study of social forms in the early twentieth century was an attempt to discover the anatomy, morphology, and structure of society. For Alfred Radcliffe-Brown, "social structure" referred to the enduring form of society through the generations. The structure was made up of social relations, of the rights and duties giving jural form to the relations between persons in particular statuses, such as father and son or doctor and patient. It was assumed that social structure varied less than culture. Hence anthropology could be conceived as the comparative study of the finite number of organizing principles of societies. Among the central concerns of social structure were kinship and descent—a person's circle of relatives and the transmission of status and commodities from one generation to the next. This was because the special province of anthropology was then taken to be small-scale rural societies, where kith, kin and lineage were often crucially important.

Contemporary studies have departed from analyses like Radcliffe-Brown's in a number of directions. Rather than viewing social structure as an invariable anatomy, as solid as bone, scholars now view it as a set of categories, an idiom of discourse or way of speaking about social relations. Structure in this sense concentrates on how categories are used, their flexibility and manipulability in labeling relations, groups, and events. Far from seeing social structure as timeless, studies now focus on its temporal processes and its reproduction as it is passed from generation to generation. Key concepts here are the life cycle, domestic cycle, regular phases of long-term political processes, and the irreversible movements of history.

Systems of Meaning

The concern in this area of contemporary anthropology is with making sense of our own ideas or those of others, with showing how cultures are shaped by particular social systems, and with understanding the ways in which ideas and actions are interlinked. Earlier anthropologists cared more for the "origins" of "customs" than for questions of the coherence or intelligibility of particular ways of life. But scholars in the past 40 years have applied sophisticated social theories, developed in the nineteenth century, in their attempt to make sense of foreign systems of belief. Particularly important among those theories were Durkheim's discussion of the way in which religious systems reflect the organization of society and Max Weber's stress on the importance of ideological factors in influencing people to act in certain ways (in particular, the importance of Protestantism as an ideology that encouraged certain kinds of activities on the part of early capitalists).

One outgrowth of the Durkheim tradition, for example, was Malinowski's claim that myths do not reflect real history but rather serve as "charters" that help to rationalize particular forms of organization and power alignments in a society (by claiming that these were given by the gods). Also linked to Durkheim (through his contemporary, A. Van Gennep) are approaches to rituals of initiation which focus on the fact that such rituals mark a change in status, from child to adult. Many characteristics of these rituals—like their use of violence and of symbols suggesting chaos and disorder—are explained by reference to the fact that the "child" who would become an "adult" is, in some sense, neither. He or she is a disorderly being, a person out of place, until incorporated into the new status. Weber was the most influential figure for such writers as Clifford Geertz, who has tried to interpret the pragmatic orientations of Indonesians by reference to their religious ideas and their conceptions of themselves and their society.

The classic work in systems of meaning consists of a number of anthropological descriptions of religion, some focussing on traditional religion (Evans-Pritchard, Lienhardt, Stanner, Nadel, Kluckhohn, Spiro), others on messianic cults which seem to emerge in times of radical social change (Worsley, Jorgenson, Burridge, Jarvie, Hobsbaum). "Structuralism"—an approach that stresses the principles of analogical thought by which a particular system of ideas is ordered—grows out of the Durkheimian tradition and is associated with the writings of such social theorists as Marcel Mauss, R. Hertz, and Van Gennep and with the linguist Roman Jakobson. Its best-known contemporary proponent, Claude Levi-Strauss, has stimulated exciting work by Mary Douglas, V. Turner, Edmund Leach, Rodney Needham, T. Turner, and Nancy Munn. More holistic, and closer to Weber's stress on the relationship between ideas and motivations, is the work of Geertz and D. M. Schneider. Finally, a linguistic approach to the study of systems of meaning that stresses the ways in which people in particular cultures categorize the people and things of their world is called "ethnoscience." Leading figures include Frake, Harold Conklin, Floyd Lounsbury, and Ward Goodenough.

Linguistics

Linguistic anthropologists ask what can be learned about a culture by studying its language. Answers have been of two kinds. First, by studying relationships among languages (the extent to which their vocabularies appear to derive from a common base), it is possible to make hypotheses about the historical relationships of speakers. Historical linguistics, in which such hypotheses are made, is a field unto itself. Two of its key anthropological representatives are Edward Sapir and Joseph Greenberg.

The second kind of answer refers to the fact that people who learn to speak other languages tend to feel that their experience of another culture is intimately bound up with their knowledge of its language; it claims that the thoughts and understandings characteristic of a cultural community become accessible only through acquaintance with its native speech. The idea that language and culture are intimately related, that they shape one another, is associated, on a theoretical level, with the names of Benjamin Whorf and Sapir.

On a practical level, these same ideas are manifest in the view that anthropological field work should involve learning and documenting native languages, a view first voiced by Boas and Malinowski. Interest in the relationship between language and culture is reflected in the careful attention Evans-Pritchard gives to the translation of Nuer religious concepts. It has led to a wide range of studies concerning such questions as: What is the relation between classificatory systems in a language (for example, different ways of categorizing colors) and modes of perception? Why do classificatory systems differ? Why do people use different styles (such as religious language) or modes of communication (drum language, for instance) in different contexts? Ethnoscience, mentioned above, represents one approach to these questions.

More recently, sociolinguists have claimed that the relationship between language and culture is not so much one of a correlation between categories and perception as between habits or styles of speaking and forms of social life; key writers in this school are Dell Hymes, John Gumperz and William Labov.

Critical Theory

While newer theory is always critical of its antecedents, recent work in radical anthropology and critical theory represents a departure from past work insofar as the latter claimed to be value-neutral, apolitical, and theoretical rather than applied. Though much of earlier anthropology was "applied," it saw capitalist-sponsored development as inevitable and emphasized "helping them progress" and using agencies for modernization in local communities. Rather than "knowing what's best for the natives," present anthropologists of radical persuasion view themselves as people with the skills necessary to work on problems initiated and formulated by indigenous communities. In addition, there is a growing recognition that the nature of our own society needs examination, and urban and American studies have renewed emphasis. We need to study ourselves and "study up," paying attention to urban elites as well as peasants in the hinterlands and hunters in the forests.

Anthropology has always been an advocate of the "underdog" and has done much to combat racism, yet critical theory sees the anthropological enterprise as having been inextricably linked to colonialism and imperialism. Insofar as radical anthropologists believe the discipline cannot be apolitical, they have chosen to be self-consciously and explicitly political. This perspective leads to seeing small-scale rural societies (so-called primitive societies) in a larger framework, especially in terms of capitalist and imperialist penetration into the third world. While previous theory in anthropology drew from Durkheim and Freud, and later from Weber, these recent efforts to reinvent anthropology have led to a much more sophisticated and widespread use of Marx.

BIBLIOGRAPHY

NOTE   The sections of this bibliography generally correspond to the sections of the introductory essay. Within each section of readings, the books are ordered in a recommended sequence for study. Works available in paperback editions were chosen whenever feasible. INTRODUCTORY at the end of an entry indicates a work on the introductory college level; INTERMEDIATE designates a work on a more advanced level (approximately intermediate).

GENERAL AND HISTORICAL

Kluckhohn, C., *Mirror for Man.* McGraw-Hill, 1949. Introduction to American anthropology; includes the four subfields of cultural anthropology, linguistics, archaeology, and physical anthropology. INTRODUCTORY.

Lienhardt, G., *Social Anthropology.* Oxford Univ. Press, 1967. Introduction to British social anthropology. INTRODUCTORY.

Hays, H. R., *From Ape to Angel: An Informal History of Social Anthropology.* Putnam, 1964. Gives a fine sense of the history of anthropology; at times careless, but always lively and readable. INTRODUCTORY.

Levi-Strauss, C., *Tristes-Tropiques,* tr. John Weightman and Doreen Weightman. Atheneum, 1974. A romantic story of field work as intellectual quest; a way into Levi-Strauss's structuralism as well as his reflections on wider goals of the field. INTERMEDIATE.

Harris, M., *The Rise of Anthropological Theory: A History of Theories of Culture.* Crowell (hard cover), 1968. Controversial view by American cultural materialist; American cultural anthropology stood on its head. INTERMEDIATE.

Wagley, C., ed., "Leaders of Modern Anthropology" (series). Columbia Univ. Press. Individual volumes in this series present some fine biographies of American cultural anthropologists, with major essays by the anthropologist treated; especially good are **Murphy, R., *Robert Lowie (1972),*** and **Mead, M., *Ruth Benedict* (1974).**

Kroeber, A., *Anthropology: Culture Patterns and Processes.* Harcourt Brace Jovanovich, 1963. An example of the American school of culture history; comprehensive. INTERMEDIATE.

Evans-Pritchard, E. E., *Social Anthropology and Other Essays.* Macmillan (Free Press), 1964. On different topics of general interest; lucid yet subtle presentation of problems by a leading British social anthropologist. INTRODUCTORY.

CLASSICAL SOCIAL THEORY FOR BACKGROUND— DURKHEIM, FREUD, WEBER, MARX

Durkheim, Emile, *The Elementary Forms of the Religious Life.* **Macmillan (Free Press), 1954.** A study of Australian aboriginal religion; stresses integrative functions of religion for society. INTERMEDIATE.

Freud, Sigmund, *Totem and Taboo.* **Norton, 1952.** Uses material from Australian aboriginal societies; its theory of primal parracide is not taken seriously today. INTERMEDIATE.

Freud, S., *Group Psychology and the Analysis of the Ego.* **Norton, 1959.** May be read alongside Durkheim for complementary understandings of crowd phenomena and group processes. INTERMEDIATE.

Weber, M., *From Max Weber: Essays in Sociology.* **tr. H. Gerth and C. W. Mills. Oxford Univ. Press, 1946.** A fine selection of essays with biographical introduction; essays give the gist of Weber's theory and are a good introduction to it. INTERMEDIATE.

Weber, M., *The Protestant Ethic and the Spirit of Capitalism.* **Scribner's, 1930.** A well-known historical study; especially influential for Geertz. INTERMEDIATE.

Marx, K., and F. Engels, *The German Ideology; Part 1 and Selections from Parts 2 and 3,* **ed. C. J. Arthur. International Pub. Co., 1970.** For studies of alienation, and place of ideology. INTERMEDIATE.

Marx, K., *Capital,* **3 vols. (Vol. 1,** *Process of Capitalist Production;* **Vol. 2,** *Process of Circulation of Capital;* **Vol. 3,** *Process of Capitalist Production as a Whole),* **ed. F. Engels. International Pub. Co., 1967.** Represents background for the study of the French structural-Marxists; only a few of their works have been translated into English, but they are influencing American anthropology. INTERMEDIATE.

SOURCES FOR BROAD BACKGROUND AND ONGOING DEVELOPMENTS

Reviews, Handbooks

NOTE The following titles generally represent difficult reading, but they are valuable as sources of up-to-date summaries of the field.

Sills, D. E., ed., *The International Encyclopedia of the Social Sciences,* **17 vols. Macmillan, 1968.** Well indexed; essays are readable, concise, sophisticated; usually written by the leading figure in the field.

Current Anthropology, Univ. of Chicago Press. A journal that often carries review articles written less to cover subfields of anthropology than to focus on developing areas of the field; articles include some of the best material available on ethics and colonialism, with responses from a wide range of scholars throughout the world.

Siegel, B. J. ed., *Biennial Review of Anthropology* (Stanford Univ. Press); Siegel, B. J., *et al.*, eds. *Annual Review of Anthropology* (Annual Reviews, Palo Alto, CA). Unusually high caliber; summarize recent literature in the four subfields of anthropology.

Honigmann, John J., ed., *Handbook of Social and Cultural Anthropology*. Rand McNally (hard cover), 1973. A fine collection of articles by leading scholars reviewing all four subfields.

Collections

"A. S. A. Monographs" (series), Association of Social Anthropologists. Barnes & Noble (U. S. distributor). A series issued by the Association of Social Anthropologists of the British Commonwealth; includes papers of unusually high quality growing out of yearly conferences, ranging from religion to urban anthropology. INTERMEDIATE.

"American Museum Sourcebooks in Anthropology" (series of volumes), P. Bohannan, general ed. Doubleday (Anchor Press). High-quality collections of essays already published in journals. INTERMEDIATE.

Comparative Studies; Methodology

Moore, F. W., ed., *Readings in Cross-Cultural Methodology*. Human Relations Area File Press, 1966. A readable collection with some classic and more recent papers on comparative method; well rounded. INTRODUCTION.

Epstein, A. L., ed., *The Craft of Social Anthropology*. Barnes & Noble, 1967. Essays on field methods for intensive study of one society; reflects the British approach. INTERMEDIATE.

Middleton, J., *Study of the Lugbara: Expectation and Paradox in Anthropological Research*. Holt Rinehart & Winston, 1970. An account of intensive field research. INTRODUCTORY.

Whiting, J., *A Field Guide to the Study of Socialization*. Wiley, 1966. (out of print). Instructions on how to study socialization; actually used in a field study organized by the Whitings.

Whiting, J., *Child Training and Personality: A Cross-Cultural Study*. Yale Univ. Press, 1953. An illustration of work using cross-cultural files. INTERMEDIATE.

Murdock, G. P., *Social Structure*. Macmillan (Free Press), 1965. Early use of cross-cultural files by the originator of this technique; very tedious. INTERMEDIATE.

Naroll, R., and R. Cohen, eds., *A Handbook of Method in Cultural Anthropology*. Columbia Univ. Press, 1973. Highly technical account of methodology in anthropology; some papers are of high caliber. INTERMEDIATE.

CLASSIC WORKS IN AMERICAN CULTURAL ANTHROPOLOGY FOR BACKGROUND

Benedict, R., *Patterns of Culture*. Houghton Mifflin, 1961. An early and influential statement on cultural relativism; opposes Apollonian and Dionysian cultural configurations. INTRODUCTORY.

Sapir, E., ed., *Language, Culture, and Personality: Essays in the Memory of Edward Sapir*. Univ. of Utah Press, 1960. Many of these beautifully written essays still stand as unsurpassed statements of conceptual problems in language and culture and personality. INTRODUCTORY.

Hallowell, A. I., *Culture and Experience*. Univ. of Pennsylvania Press, 1974. In the tradition of Sapir, but with more emphasis on culture and personality and on use of psychological tests for getting at work view and ethos. INTRODUCTORY.

Redfield, R., *The Little Community, Bound with Peasant Society and Culture*. Univ. of Chicago Press, 1960. Vivid essay on a number of perspectives from which a single community might be studied; all holistic and humanistic. INTRODUCTORY.

Kluckhohn, C., *Culture and Behavior: Collected Essays of Clyde Kluckhohn*, ed. R. Kluckhohn. Macmillan (Free Press), 1962. A collection of essays on a wide range of topics. INTRODUCTORY.

Lee, D., *Freedom and Culture*. Prentice-Hall, 1959. Sensitive essays on different cultures from an extreme relativist position; exciting reading. INTRODUCTORY.

Mead, M., *Coming of Age in Samoa*. Morrow, 1971 (also Dell, 1967). Directed toward an American audience concerned with problems of adolescent turmoil. INTRODUCTORY.

Mead, M., *Sex and Temperament in Three Primitive Societies*. Morrow, 1963. Directed toward an American audience concerned with the personality characteristics universally linked with sex and the male/female differences that are culture-specific. INTRODUCTORY.

Du Bois, C. A., *The People of Alor: A Social-Psychological Study of an East Indian Island*. Harper & Row, 1960. An early field study of culture and personality in an Indonesian island community through the use of life histories and psychological tests. INTERMEDIATE.

Kluckhohn, C., *Navaho Witchcraft*. Beacon, 1962. Psychodynamic study of Navaho witchcraft. INTRODUCTORY.

Boas, F., *Race, Language, and Culture*. Macmillan (Free Press), 1966. Collected essays of Boas, many of which now seem like common sense; most leading thinkers in American cultural theory were students of Boas. INTERMEDIATE.

Kroeber, A. L., and C. Kluckhohn, *Culture: A Critical Review of Concepts and Definitions*. Peabody Museum, Cambridge, Mass.,

(hard cover), 1952. An encyclopedic inventory of definitions of culture, showing how diverse they have been and how they have become less cosmic and more modest in recent trends. INTRODUCTORY.

THEORETICAL AREAS OF CONTEMPORARY ANTHROPOLOGY

Evolution

Steward, J. H., *Theory of Culture Change: The Methodology of Multilinear Evolution.* Univ. of Illinois Press, 1972. Uses notion of adaptation; a readable account. INTRODUCTORY.

Fried, M., *The Evolution of Political Society: An Evolutionary View.* Random House, 1968. A general framework, within which Fried traces the development of political systems. INTERMEDIATE.

Sahlins, M., and E. Service, *Evolution and Culture.* Univ. of Michigan Press (hard cover), 1960. General theoretical statements on mechanisms underlying evolution. INTERMEDIATE.

Vayda, A. P., ed., *Environment and Cultural Behavior: Ecological Studies in Cultural Anthropology.* Doubleday (Natural History), 1969. Essays representing recent work on adaptation and ecology; this work underlies most contemporary evolutionary theory and is used in much recent ethnography.

Service, E., *Hunters.* Prentice-Hall, 1966. On a level of evolution. INTRODUCTORY.

De Vore, I., and R. Lee, eds., *Man the Hunter.* Aldine, 1968. A collection of papers on recent hunter-gatherer studies.

Sahlins, M., *Tribesmen.* Prentice-Hall, 1968. On an evolutionary level. INTRODUCTORY.

Wolf, E., *Peasants.* Prentice-Hall, 1966. On an evolutionary level. INTRODUCTORY.

Social Organization

Fox, R., *Kinship and Marriage.* Penguin, 1968. Well-written introduction to a complex subject; lively and lucid. INTRODUCTORY.

Park, G., *The Idea of Social Structure.* Doubleday, 1974. A lively introduction to the topic, at once clear and on a high level of sophistication. INTERMEDIATE.

Leach, E., *Rethinking Anthropology.* Humanities, 1971. Essays on topics in social anthropology, British; influenced by Levi-Strauss and against Radcliffe-Brown; technical but lively.

Levi-Strauss, C., *The Elementary Structures of Kinship.* ed. R. Needham. Beacon, 1969. Wide-ranging, on incest and many other topics, to show the formal properties and consequences of rare marriage rules. Slow-going but stimulating.

Bailey, F. G., *Stratagems and Spoils: A Social Anthropology of Politics.* **Schocken, 1973.** Puts the decision-making actor in the middle of things.

Graburn, N. H., ed., *Readings in Kinship and Social Structure.* **Harper & Row, 1971.** A well-balanced collection of essays.

Systems of Meaning—
Works Treating More than One Culture

Geertz, C., ed., *The Interpretation of Cultures.* **Basic Books (hard cover), 1973.** Outstanding collection of essays formerly widely scattered; stimulating, beautifully written. INTERMEDIATE.

Evans-Pritchard, E. E., *Theories of Primitive Religion.* **Oxford Univ. Press, 1965.** Clear introduction to the topic; a review of earlier theories from a British point of view. INTRODUCTION.

Lessa, W. A., and E. Z. Vogt, eds., *Reader in Comparative Religion: An Anthropological Approach.* **Harper & Row, 1972.** Well-chosen collection of articles, intended to give a survey of the best past and present work in the field; a classic reader now in its third edition. INTRODUCTORY.

Beidelman, T., *W. Robertson Smith and the Sociological Study of Religion.* **Univ. of Chicago Press, 1974.** Biography that is also implicitly a concise statement of what the sociological study of religion should be; British. INTRODUCTORY.

Malinowski, B., *Magic, Science and Religion and Other Essays.* **Doubleday, 1954.** Classic essays on the nature of myth and the difference between magic and science. INTRODUCTORY.

Levi-Strauss, C., *Structural Anthropology.* **Basic Books, 1963.** A collection of essays on structural method, ranging from social organization to religion. INTERMEDIATE.

Levi-Strauss, C., *Totemism.* **Beacon, 1963.** Treats earlier theories of totemism; serves as an introduction to *The Savage Mind.* INTERMEDIATE.

Levi-Strauss, C., *The Savage Mind.* **Univ. of Chicago Press, 1966.** A comprehensive statement on the problems of "primitive mentality." INTERMEDIATE.

Douglas, M., *Purity and Danger.* **Penguin, 1970.** Concerns ideas of purity and pollution and the ways in which these are bound up in people's ways of ordering their social worlds. INTERMEDIATE.

Turner, V., *The Forest of Symbols: Aspects of Ndembu Ritual.* **Cornell Univ. Press, 1967.** A collection of essays on method in study of symbols as well as empirical studies of Ndembu religion in Africa. INTERMEDIATE.

Spencer, R. F., ed., *Forms of Symbolic Action.* Univ. of Washington Press, 1970. Papers by T. Turner and N. Munn are especially recommended from this collection. INTERMEDIATE.

Jakobson, R., and M. Halle, *Fundamentals of Language,* 2nd ed. Humanities, 1971. Gives an understanding of one source of Levi-Strauss' structuralism. INTERMEDIATE.

Van Gennep, A., *Rites of Passage,* tr. M. B. Vizendon and G. L. Caffee, Univ. of Chicago Press, 1960. Classic formulation of the structure of rituals surrounding crises in the life cycle—birth, initiation, marriage, death. INTERMEDIATE.

Mauss, M., *Gift: Forms & Functions of Exchange in Archaic Societies.* Norton, 1967. Statement from the French sociological school that shaped Levi-Strauss's work; Mauss is Durkheim's nephew. INTERMEDIATE.

Schneider, D. M., *American Kinship: A Cultural Account.* Prentice-Hall, 1968. Analyzes family relationships from the anthropological viewpoint. INTRODUCTORY.

Middleton, J., ed., *Myth and Cosmos: Readings in Mythology and Symbolism.* Doubleday, 1967. Essays on myths of the creation of the universe. INTRODUCTORY.

Systems of Meaning— Monographs on Religions in Individual Cultures

NOTE Monographs are the basic accounts against which anthropological theory is tested; they attempt at once to be holistic, descriptive, and theoretically informed. Though descriptive detail may be burdensome, concepts are rarely too difficult for the introductory level. The Holt, Rinehart & Winston series is written for undergraduate use, but other monographs should be sampled at the introductory level as well.

Evans-Pritchard, E. E., *Nuer Religion.* Oxford Univ. Press, 1956. Focuses on the problem of translation of key cultural concepts; a British point of view. INTRODUCTORY.

Evans-Pritchard, E. E., *Magic, Witchcraft, Oracles and Magic Among the Azande.* Oxford Univ. Press (hard cover), 1937. A study to show that, once certain presuppositions are granted, magic is an intelligible system of thought—a position opposed to the concept of primitive mentality. INTRODUCTORY.

Lienhardt, G., *Divinity and Experience: The Religion of the Dinka.* Oxford Univ. Press, 1961. By a student of Evans-Pritchard; fine work. INTRODUCTORY.

Stanner, W. E. H., "On Aboriginal Religion." *Oceania* (journal published by Univ. of Sydney, New South Wales, Australia). A study of Australian aboriginal religion; up-dates a well-known study by Durkheim. INTERMEDIATE.

Worsely, P., ***The Trumpet Shall Sound: A Study of Cargo Cults in Melanesia.*** **Schocken, 1968.** About cargo cults in New Guinea. INTRODUCTORY.

Burridge, Kenelm, ***Mambu: A Study of Melanesian Cargo Movements and Their Social Ideological Background.*** **Harper & Row (out of print), 1960.** More demanding work on cargo cults in New Guinea. INTERMEDIATE.

Jarvie, I. C., ***The Revolution in Anthropology.*** **Regnery, 1969.** On the logic of explanation related to cargo cults.

Hobsbawm, E. J., ***Primitive Rebels.*** **Norton, 1965.** Treats millenarian and other social movements inspired by prophecies of the world's end. INTRODUCTORY.

Jorgenson, Joseph G., ***The Sun Dance Religion: Power to the Powerless.*** **Univ. of Chicago Press, 1974.** On a movement among Native Americans. INTRODUCTORY.

Nadel, S. F., ***Nupe Religion: Traditional Beliefs and the Influence of Islam in a West African Chiefdom.*** **Schocken (hard cover), 1970.** On an African religion. INTERMEDIATE.

Geertz, C., ***The Religion of Java.*** **Macmillan (Free Press), 1960.** In the Weberian tradition. INTRODUCTORY.

Spiro, M., ed., ***Burmese Supernaturalism.*** **Prentice-Hall, 1967.** Culture and personality as influenced by old beliefs in a modern society. INTRODUCTORY.

Linguistics—
General Analyses

Greenberg, J., ***Anthropological Linguistics: An Introduction.*** **Random House, 1968.** A good recent statement.

Sapir, E., ***Language: An Introduction to the Study of Speech.*** **Harcourt Brace Jovanovich, 1955.** An older statement. INTRODUCTORY.

Whorf, B., ***Language, Thought, Reality: Selected Writings of Benjamin Lee Whorf,*** **ed. J. B. Carroll. MIT Press, 1956.** Has to be read with caution; an extreme statement that stimulated much research. INTRODUCTORY.

Burling, R., Man's Many Voices. Holt, Rinehart & Winston (hard cover), 1970. A clear and enticing review of anthropological linguistics, with special emphasis on the "language and culture" question. INTRODUCTORY.

Linguistics—Collections

NOTE The following titles include articles by Frake, Conklin, and others in linguistic anthropology mentioned in the section introduction.

Hymes, D., ed., *Language in Culture and Society.* **Harper & Row (hard cover), 1964.** One of the best general collections of articles on the place of language in cultural and social life. INTRODUCTORY.

Gumperz, J., and D. Hymes, ed., *Directions in Sociolinguistics: The Ethnography of Communication.* **Holt, Rinehart & Winston, 1972.** Fairly technical; includes several classic articles that underlie recent sociolinguistic research. INTRODUCTORY.

Giglioli, P., ed., *Language and Social Context.* **Penguin, 1972.** Readable articles on sociolinguistic topics. INTERMEDIATE.

Critical Theory

Deloria, V., Jr., *Custer Died for Your Sins.* **Avon, 1970.** An account of American history from a Native American point of view, with criticism of the work of anthropologists. INTRODUCTORY.

Hymes, D., ed., *Reinventing Anthropology.* **Random House, 1973.** A collection of radical and politically motivated essays, concerned largely with applications of anthropology in the interest of oppressed groups. INTRODUCTORY.

Asad, T., ed., *Anthropology and the Colonial Encounter.* **Humanities, 1974.** Essays on the impact of imperialism on native populations, with special emphasis on the role of anthropologists. INTERMEDIATE.

Rosaldo, M. Z., and L. Lamphere, *Woman, Culture and Society.* **Stanford Univ. Press, 1974.** Essays bringing a feminist perspective to bear on anthropology. INTERMEDIATE.

ETHNOGRAPHIES—
A SELECTION FOR FURTHER READING

NOTE See introductory note for previous section, "Systems of Meaning—Monographs on Religions in Individual Cultures."

Bateson, G., *Naven.* **Stanford Univ. Press, 1958.** A classic account of a New Guinea society, discussing sex roles in terms of social, cultural and personal dimensions, with special emphasis on ritual. INTERMEDIATE.

Beidelman, T. O., *The Kaguru: A Matrilineal People of East Africa.* **Holt, Rinehart & Winston, 1971.** A clear, readable, and theoretically suggestive description of a matrilineal people of East Africa; combines historical and structural perspectives. INTRODUCTORY.

Campbell, J. K., *Family and Patronage: A Study of Institutions and Moral Values in a Greek Mountain Community.* Oxford Univ. Press, **1973.** A complex but brilliant description of kinship, economics, and ideology among Greek pastoralists. INTERMEDIATE.

Cancian, F., *Economics and Prestige in a Maya Community: The Religious Cargo System of Zinacatan.* **Stanford Univ. Press, 1965.** An account of the relationship between participation in a religious system, economic success, and the achievement of social recognition in southern Mexico. INTERMEDIATE.

Chagnon, N. A., *The Yanomomo: The Fierce People.* **Holt, Rinehart & Winston, 1968.** A readable, vivid account of life with a South American group that places a high value on expressions of violence. INTRODUCTORY.

Drake, S. C., and H. R. Cayton, *Black Metropolis,* **2 vols., Harcourt Brace Jovanovich, 1970.** A holistic description touching social class, aspirations, values among Blacks in a small town in the South. INTRODUCTORY.

Dumont, L., *Homo Hierarchicus: The Caste System and Its Implications,* tr. from French, Mark Sainbury. **Univ. of Chicago Press, 1974.** Important theoretical contribution on India, contrasting conceptions of person and society in a caste-based society to the ideology of the West. INTERMEDIATE.

Evans-Pritchard, E. E., *The Nuer: A Description of the Modes of Livelihood and Political Institutions of a Nilotic People.* **Oxford Univ. Press, 1969.** A description of a Nilotic society, *The Nuer* is probably one of the best monographs ever written; its account of segmentary lineage organization provides a basis for most subsequent work on African social organization and kinship; it also treats ideas of time and relations between social life and ecology. INTRODUCTORY.

Firth, R., *We, The Tikopia.* **Beacon, 1963.** A classic, rich and detailed description of kinship and social life in a Polynesian community. INTRODUCTORY.

Fortes, M., *Analysis of the Social Structure of a Trans-Volta Tribe,* **2 parts:** *Pt. 1: Dynamics of Clanship Among the Tallensi; Pt. 2: Web of Kinship Among the Tallensi.* **Humanities, 1967.** Dense but worthwhile account of kinship dynamics and their political implications among a West African group. INTERMEDIATE.

Fortune, R. F., *Sorcerers of Dobu.* **Dutton, 1963.** A readable, suggestive description of kinship and religion on a Melanesian island, where mistrust and fear of witchcraft are common elements of daily social life. INTERMEDIATE.

Goodenough, W. H., *Property, Kin and Community on Truk.* **Shoe String (hard cover), 1967.** This account of a Micronesian society is especially important for its use of a formal and explicit methodology. INTERMEDIATE.

Kiefer, T., *The Tausug: Violence and Law in a Philippine Moslem Society*. Holt, Rinehart & Winston (hard cover), 1972. This account of Philippine Muslims, their social organization and their feuds, is a good example of the description of societies with bilateral kinship systems. INTRODUCTORY.

Liebow, E., *Tally's Corner*. Little, Brown, 1967. Perceptive, sympathetic portrayal of street-corner society among urban Black men. INTRODUCTORY.

Lowie, R. H., *The Crow Indians*. Holt, Rinehart & Winston, 1956. A classic, readable ethnography on a Native American society of the Great Plains. INTERMEDIATE.

Malinowski, B., *Argonauts of the Western Pacific*. Dutton, 1922. Malinowski's vivid description of the Trobriands is a classic of functionalist ethnography; it concerns a ritualized exchange network among a set of Melanesian islands. INTERMEDIATE.

Maybury-Lewis, D., *Akwe-Shavante Society*. Oxford Univ. Press, 1974. Probably the outstanding "structuralist" ethnography, this book integrates material concerning topics as diverse as kinship, childrearing, factionalism, ritual, and sex roles into a problematic but readable and challenging interpretation of "oppositional structures" at work in a South American society. INTERMEDIATE.

Oliver, D. L., *Solomon Island Society*. Beacon, 1955. A rich and methodologically suggestive description of a Melanesian society.

Ortiz, A., *The Tewa World: Space, Time, Being, and Becoming in a Pueblo Society*. Univ. of Chicago Press, 1972. Thoughtful and original structuralist account of the beliefs and cosmology of a Pueblo Indian community. INTRODUCTORY.

Rappaport, R., *Pigs for the Ancestors: Ritual in the Ecology of New Guinea People*. Yale Univ. Press, 1968. A fine example of a study within the tradition of cultural evolution; shows how "adaptation" becomes the key concept in an intensive field study of a single society. INTERMEDIATE.

Redfield, R., *A Village that Chose Progess: Chan Kom Revisited*. Univ. of Chicago Press, 1962. A description by an American anthropologist of a Yucatec Mayan community; the work is particularly important because it is written as a reflection on an earlier book about the same community by the same author; here he examines ways in which the community has changed. INTERMEDIATE.

Turnbull, C. M., *The Forest People*. Simon & Schuster, 1968. A warm, loving description of the Mbuti Pygmies, hunter-gatherers in southern Africa; the book touches economics, religion, relations to neighboring tribes, and most dramatically, the attitudes of Pygmies towards the forest. INTRODUCTORY.

Warner, W. L., *The Family of God: Symbolic Study of Christian*

Life in America. **Yale Univ. Press, 1961.** The religion, community life, and values of a small New England town, as these were exemplified in the community's bicentennial celebration, provide the basis of this rich work of symbolic analysis. INTERMEDIATE.

Wilson, M., ***Good Company.*** **Beacon, 1963.** A classic, highly read-able description of a fascinating form of village organization—in which groups of age mates, rather than kinsmen, provide the core of a village—and its implications in social life and belief among a southern African group, the Nyakyusa. INTERMEDIATE.

Wylie, L. W., ***Village in the Vaucluse,*** **3rd ed. Harvard Univ. Press, 1974.** A highly readable, vivid description of the life of peasants in France. INTRODUCTORY.

Chapter Ten

ECONOMICS:
"... the physical needs and wants of people"

Editorial Advisor:
Rosalind S. Seneca
Department of Economics
Columbia University

INTRODUCTION

Price rises, poverty, opportunities "to get ahead," recessions, wars, pollution, mass starvation: all these involve the workings of economic systems—systems for meeting (or not meeting) the physical needs and wants of people. Economics is the study of those systems and the theories by which they do (or should) operate. Everyone of us acts daily on the basis of some sense of economic understanding—in our work, our family life, our buying and selling, our political life and voting, our career planning. But a deeper understanding of one decisive dimension of life and death in the modern world cannot be achieved without fairly extensive knowledge of economics.

It is often said that economics began as a distinct field of study in 1776 (by coincidence, the same year as the birth of the United States). That was the year in which the first comprehensive treatise in economics was published: *An Inquiry into the Nature and Causes of the Wealth of Nations* by a Scottish philosopher, Adam Smith. However, Smith's work was certainly not the first attempt to explain the complexities of the economic world through the use of abstract reasoning and conceptual models. Before and since, writers on economic questions have typically developed theories to explain the particular economic problems of their time. Economic theories have changed as countries have developed economically, politically, and socially. Long before Smith, for example, Aristotle was concerned with monopoly in ancient Greece and with what determines the "just" price of commodities (questions still with us, it seems). The "scholastic" philosophers of the Church in Medieval Europe also wrote on the just price and condemned the charging of interest on loans as the sin of usury.

Adam Smith's contribution was to show how the economic system (in the European tradition of private property and trading customs) is organized through a system of prices. (His analysis led to the development over a century later of the now familiar "law of supply and demand.") He also explained the role of the division of labor and specialization in the workings of the market mechanism, and he developed ideas of efficiency as a prime economic goal. He saw efficiency as a goal to be reached under government policies characterized by a name we still hear today—laissez-faire; he apparently acquired this term in conversations with French "physiocrats" in the 1760s. Reflecting other influences of his time, he wrote his book largely to argue that Britain would be enriched by fostering free trade rather than by then favored policies of protective tariffs—called "mercantilism"; such policies were making Spain comparatively impoverished despite the influx of gold from the Americas.

Among other early eminences in the field was David Ricardo. Viewing the English economy before the repeal of the Corn Laws and observing the high rents earned by landowners when corn was scarce, he developed a theory to explain the distribution of income among wages, profits, and rent. A contemporary of Ricardo's, Thomas Malthus, reacted to the population explosion of the early 1800s by predicting periods of mass starvation. Shocked contemporaries began calling economics "the dismal science"—a phrase used to this day by critics who would rather not face unwelcome alternatives discerned by economists. But current prospects for famines on an unprecedented scale have recently revived interest in Malthusian theories.

Karl Marx, although known as a political philosopher, was also an economist. His explosive ideas have their roots partly in the Ricardian model of income distribution. Marx explained the role of capital in industrial society and developed a theory of value and interest. He also introduced dynamics into his theoretical model of the capitalist economic system through his explanation of the cyclical movements in income, prices, and employment—the cycles of prosperity and depression, boom and bust.

Non-Marxian economic theory today is now divided (sometimes rather artificially) into "macro" and "micro" economics. Macroeconomics is based heavily on the work of John Maynard Keynes. His enormously influential work, *General Theory of Employment, Interest and Money*, appeared in 1936, in the midst of the Great Depression. It explained how high levels of unemployment would persist in the absence of sufficient aggregate demand and prescribed massive government spending as the cure. Today macroeconomics deals with the relationships between aggregate economic variables—such as total consumption, total investment, total savings, total income, and employment—and the overall price level—features of the national economy viewed as a whole.

Microeconomics grew out of the work of the neoclassical economists—John Stuart Mill, Jeremy Bentham, Alfred Marshall, Leon Walras—and in the 1930s was reformulated by John R. Hicks. Fundamental to it are the facts that all societies are constrained by the scarcity of resources—that they must develop mechanisms for choosing which commodities to produce, which combinations of scarce inputs to use in producing commodities, and how the scarce commodities shall be distributed among consumers. Microeconomics explains how individual economic units make related choices of their own. For example, the theory of consumer behavior describes the decision-making process of a single consumer who wishes to maximize the satisfaction he derives from his income, how he chooses which goods to buy; in this way it explains the characteristics of individual demand and market demand for commodities. The theory of the firm accounts for the ways in which an individual firm chooses which inputs to buy, how much output to produce, what price to set—in other words, it explains the characteristics of the firm's supply and market supply of commodities. The theory of production underlying the theory of the firm is also important because of its links to growth (capital theory) and income distribution.

Moreover, microeconomics deals with the interaction between economic units through the market—for example, how supply and demand determine relative prices and quantities of commodities exchanged and how this in turn affects factors of production.

Microeconomics also includes welfare economics (see "Public Finance and Welfare Economics," below).

MAJOR FIELDS OF RESEARCH INTEREST

Modern economic research is carried on in the following major fields of interest.

Money and Banking

Research concerning money and banking is based on modern macroeconomic models but is specifically directed toward the role of money and financial instruments in advanced industrial economies. It considers the relationship between money and interest and covers the development of the banking system, the working of the Federal Reserve banks (the United States central bank), and their links to the commercial banking system. The field also deals with monetary policy as a means by which the government can influence prices, income, and employment by controlling the money supply.

International Trade

International-trade economics has two parts. Analysis of the "real" phenomena underlying trade flows asks such questions as, "What are the factors causing countries to trade? What commodities will be traded? At what price will they be traded? What will the effects of trade be on income, employment, and prices in the domestic economy?" It also includes discussion of tariff policy. Analysis of the monetary relationships between nations seeks to explain foreign exchange markets, balance of payments adjustments, and the financial ramifications on the domestic economy. Discussions of exchange rate policy overlap with the money-and-banking field.

The Economics of Growth and Development

This area investigates the causes underlying the sustained economic growth experienced by advanced industrial countries. What, historically, have been the economic, social and political factors which have caused rapid increases in factor productivity in some countries and not in others? Research emphasizes the nature and role of capital, introducing time explicitly into economic models. Abstract models have been developed by Harrod and Domar, Joan Robinson, Paul Samuelson, and Robert M. Solow to explain the dynamic interaction between economic variables, such as growth rates of saving, investment, consumption, income, and population. These theories are difficult and require the use of mathematics.

The field of economic development is concerned with currently less advanced nations and analyzes the particular problems associated with raising living standards in these areas. Much country-specific knowledge of historical development and current institutions is required.

Economic History

Very closely allied with the economics of growth is the field of economic history, since the aim is not simply to describe historical economic phenomena but also to explain them. A very hot topic nowadays is the economics of slavery; one major dispute concerns the economic viability of the slavery in the Southern states. Statistical techniques for estimating historical relationships (called "cliometrics") have been introduced into this field (see below, "Econometrics").

Comparative Systems and the Economics of Planned Economies

Economic theory, as taught in Western Europe and America, assumes an institutional framework based on private ownership of land, labor and capital, and the free participation of individuals in the economic activity of the marketplace. Many socialist countries have rejected what they perceive to be the inequities of private enterprise and have adopted economic planning as society's main choice mechanism. The USSR is the prototype of a centrally planned economy where, in theory at least, all decisions about production and distribution are made by the Central Planning Board and passed down to individual firms as commands through the planning hierarchy. Movements to experiment with decentralized planning systems within the socialist framework have taken place in, for example, Hungary, Poland, and Yugoslavia.

The field of planning in economics covers an extensive literature in the theory of planning (much of which is highly mathematical) and the planning experiences of different countries. In the latter area, much country-specific knowledge is required for useful research.

Public Finance and Welfare Economics

Even though the United States is characterized as a free-enterprise economy, the government sector accounts for as much as 25 percent of Gross National Product. Expenditure and tax policy is the major part of public finance. Specialists in the field of public finance inquire into the reasons for the growth of the government sector, analyze the governmental decision-making process, and estimate the impact of governmental decisions on the rest of the economy.

Much of this literature is closely tied in with the field of welfare economics, a branch of economic theory which attempts to define a set of normative economic goals that economists can use in evaluating whether or not economic policies have improved social welfare. The meaning of economic efficiency is explored. The literature of welfare economics is mathematical and tied to philosophy.

Within this framework, public-finance researchers evaluate public expenditure programs on a micro level (cost-benefit analysis), fiscal policies on a macro level, and different tax systems on both levels.

Industrial Organization

The study of industrial organization, based on recent developments in microeconomics and the theory of the firm, investigates the behavior of modern firms and recent changes in the structure of markets. Typical questions are, "What determines the price, output and investment behavior of a large, multidivision firm, where there is separation of ownership and control? How do imperfectly competitive markets function? What should government policy be toward monopoly and restrictive practices?" This last question leads to the extensive literature on the antitrust laws—their meaning as well as their legal and economic impact on the economy.

A subfield deals with direct government regulation of public utilities and their pricing and investment policies; it ties in closely with the public-finance literature.

Labor Economics

Labor economics covers the workings of the labor market— determination of the supply and demand for labor, the organization and impact of labor unions, and effects of such government policies as the minimum-wage laws. It draws mainly on microeconomic theory, but new approaches which link microeconomics more closely to macroeconomics are being developed here (see below).

Econometrics and Forecasting

Many economic variables are subject to measurement (such as income, output, employment, the price level). Most advanced countries collect detailed statistics (especially those on Gross National Product and national income accounting) that can be used by economists to test the hypotheses they derive from their theoretical models. In all of the above fields the testing of hypotheses using real-world data has become an extremely important part of modern research. But since the economist cannot conduct controlled experiments on his subjects (consumers, firms, and the like), a special branch of statistical estimation has been developed to deal with the problem of interdependence between economic variables. Understanding these methods requires a knowledge of statistical inference, calculus, and matrix algebra. (Some introductory books not requiring advanced mathematics are noted in the bibliography).

One important use of econometric methods is in the development of econometric models for forecasting. It is possible to characterize macroeconomic relationships in functional form, estimate the functions using real-world data, and make predictions about the future course of the economy. These forecasts are used extensively for making economic policy.

Mathematical Economics

This area spans the whole field of economics, being concerned with the expression of economic ideas in mathematical form. In particular, growth and planning models require the use of advanced mathematics.

Future Directions

A major concern of ongoing research is the analysis and explanation of the current inflationary trend and the failure of prices to respond rapidly to a decline in aggregate demand. The traditional fiscal and monetary policies no longer appear to be so useful in dealing with the peculiar combination of economic problems (energy crisis, inflation, unemployment) facing contemporary society. Attempts are being made to provide more detailed links between microeconomics and macroeconomics (as in labor economics). There is renewed interest in the functioning of institutions and the recognition that it is becoming more difficult to produce *general* economic theories. Particularly hot topics are energy policy and environmental economics.

A group of economists, called radical, discard much of the received micro and macro theory outlined above and are attempting new approaches, usually with Marxist overtones.

SUGGESTIONS ON HOW TO PROCEED

Economics today encompasses a large set of general theoretical principles and techniques of considerable power. These can be studied in different stages and at different levels. College students pursuing a major in Economics build up ability to deal with economic theory by confronting common principles many times and developing familiarity with them. In addition, each field of research in economics has its own theory and wide range of applications and problems. Such an enormous literature has grown in economics that the student will usually select several fields in which to specialize and will perhaps take up to three courses in each.

The bibliography that follows has been designed to help readers learn economics on their own in a similar progression. It opens with some books giving an introduction to economics in general. Sections on microeconomics and macroeconomics come next. Each lists more advanced books as a further introduction to the theoretical literature. You should be able to save much time if you choose a couple of the good introductory or intermediate texts indicated and go through them systematically. Next, sections on the main fields of economics research today are presented, among which to choose according to your interests.

To provide access to some original work, the sections on each field often list collections of many good recent articles in books of readings (with particularly important articles noted). These can help you in much the same way as professors' lectures would.

Sections usually open with one or two useful texts to serve as an introduction to the special theory in the field. Books that survey the field and often have comprehensive bibliographies at the end follow the texts as leads into higher-level discussion.

BIBLIOGRAPHY

INTRODUCTION TO ECONOMIC IDEAS—
BOOKS FOR GENERAL READERS

Heilbroner, Robert L., *The Making of Economic Society,* 4th ed. Prentice-Hall, 1972. Lucid and readable introduction to economic ideas.

Heilbroner, Robert L., *The Worldly Philosophers: The Lives, Times and Ideas of the Great Economic Thinkers,* rev. ed. Simon & Schuster, 1972. Heilbroner at his able best. Easy reading, complicated ideas but very clearly presented.

Friedman, Milton, *Capitalism and Freedom.* Univ. of Chicago Press, 1962. The leader of the Chicago school of economists sets forth his case for "laissez faire."

Baran, Paul A., and Paul M. Sweezy, *Monopoly Capital: An Essay on the American Economic and Social Order.* Monthly Review, 1968. A modern Marxist view of the world.

Galbraith, John Kenneth, *The New Industrial State.* Houghton

Mifflin, 1972. Controversial analysis of modern industrial organization; argues that advanced technology determines economic relationships.

Friedman, Milton, "The Methodology of Positive Economics," in his *Essays in Positive Economics,* pp. 3–43. Univ of Chicago Press, 1953.

Samuelson, Paul A., *Economics.* McGraw-Hill, 1973. The most famous of a large number of introductory textbooks. Contains a complete survey of the field. Much of the exposition is excellent; some is unnecessarily complicated. Text comes in a package including student manual and book of readings; all very useful.

Robinson, Joan, and John Eatwell, *An Introduction to Modern Economics.* McGraw-Hill (London), 1973. An answer to Samuelson (above). The authors present a nonneoclassical introduction to economic theory free of the biases they perceive in Samuelson's work. A very interesting book indeed, but a beginning student might find it very hard, even though it professes to be an introduction.

Robinson, Joan, *Economic Philosophy.* Penguin (London), 1970. Lucid and revealing clarification of the assumptions behind economic theory.

MICROECONOMICS

Haveman, Robert H., and Kenyon Knopf, *The Market System,* 2nd ed. Wiley, 1970. Excellent introduction to microeconomic theory.

Dorfman, Robert, *Price System.* Prentice-Hall, 1964. Also recommended as an introduction.

Stigler, George J., *Theory of Price,* 3rd ed. Macmillan (hard cover), 1966. One of the classics among many good intermediate texts.

Ferguson, Charles E., *Microeconomic Theory,* 3rd ed., Irwin (hard cover), 1972. Another classic intermediate text. A detailed, rigorous treatment.

Mansfield, Edwin, *Microeconomics: Theory and Applications* (intermediate text); *Microeconomic Problems* (casebook); *Microeconomics: Selected Readings.* Norton, 1970, 1971. These three works, designed to be used together, constitute a very helpful package, in which the emphasis throughout is on applications and problem solving. Readers may find this approach a more stimulating way of learning what are otherwise a rather dry set of principles. Included in the combined works are both major theoretical contributions and applications of theoretical concepts as well as empirical research.

Henderson, J. M. and R. E. Quandt, *Microeconomic Theory: A Mathematical Approach,* 2nd ed. McGraw-Hill, 1971. Clear and systematic. Requires knowledge of calculus. ADVANCED.

Hicks, John R., *Value and Capital: An Inquiry into Some Funda-*

mental Principles of Economic Theory, 2nd ed. Oxford Univ. Press (hard cover), 1946. The original formulation of modern micro-economic theory, including important discussions of partial and general equilibrium. Difficult, but certainly within the capability of an advanced undergraduate.

MACROECONOMICS

Heilbroner, Robert L., *Understanding Macroeconomics,* 4th ed. Prentice-Hall, 1972. An unusually readable introduction.

Schultze, Charles L., *National Income Analysis,* 3rd ed. Prentice-Hall, 1971. An introduction useful because of emphases differing somewhat from the work above.

Ackley, Gardner, *Macroeconomic Theory.* Macmillan (hard cover), 1961. Though old, this intermediate text is very thorough and readable and more sensible than some of the modern texts.

Shapiro, Edward, *Macroeconomic Analysis,* 3rd ed. Harcourt Brace Jovanovich (hard cover), 1974. Solid, thorough.

Evans, Michael K., *Macroeconomic Activity: Theory, Fore-Casting and Control.* Harper & Row (hard cover), 1969. An econometric approach. Surveys recent theoretical and empirical research. Very well written. For the advanced student with a working knowledge of econometrics (see "Econometrics and Forecasting," below).

Okun, Arthur M., ed., *Battle Against Unemployment,* rev. ed. Norton, 1972. A set of readings at the introductory-intermediate level on fiscal policy, monetary policy, and inflation. Spans all views.

U.S. Department of Commerce, *Survey of Current Business.* Published monthly. Contains data (national income statistics, price indices, and the like) and articles on the current state of the economy. Annual subscription, $48.30, but available in libraries.

Keynes, John M., *General Theory of Employment, Interest and Money.* Harcourt Brace Jovanovich, 1965. The book which changed society and affected the lives of millions. Difficult but manageable, and very exciting to read.

Klein, Lawrence R., *The Keynesian Revolution.* Macmillan (London), 1967. An early, extremely clear exposition of the Keynesian model, introducing the policy and forecasting implications. Should be read in conjunction with Keynes' *General Theory.*

Matthews, Robert C., *The Trade Cycle.* Cambridge Univ. Press (hard cover), 1959. The causes of economic fluctuations. An early classic. Lucid, extremely useful. INTERMEDIATE.

Gordon, R. A., "How Obsolete is the Business Cycle?" *The Public Interest,* Fall, 1970.

MONEY AND BANKING

Duesenberry, James, *Money and Credit: Impact and Control,* 3rd ed. Prentice-Hall (hard cover), 1972. Useful, clear introduction.

The Federal Reserve System: Purposes and Functions. "The Fed's" own explanation of how it does monetary policy. Very useful. Available from the System's Board of Governors, Washington, DC 20551.

Rousseas, Stephen, *Monetary Theory.* Knopf (hard cover), 1971. Advanced undergraduate. Excellent treatment of the Keynesian/Friedman controversy. Covers most important modern issues.

Smith, Warren L. and Ronald L. Teigen, ed., *Readings in Money, National Income and Stabilization Policy,* 3rd ed. Irwin, 1974. See especially two articles by Warren Smith: "A Graphical Exposition of the Complete Keynesian System" and "The Instruments of General Monetary Control." Many other important readings at an introductory-intermediate level.

Articles

Here are some useful articles on the development of monetary concepts.

Park, Y., *Some Current Issues on the Transmission Process of Monetary Policy,* International Monetary Fund, March, 1972.

Humphrey, T., "Evolution of the Concept of the Demand for Money" (Dec., 1973), "The Quantity Theory of Money, Its Historical Evolution and Role in Policy Debates" (May-June, 1974), **Monthly Review, Federal Reserve Bank of Richmond,** Box 27622, Richmond, VA 23261.

INTERNATIONAL ECONOMICS

Kenen, Peter B., *International Economics,* 2nd ed. Prentice-Hall, 1967. A useful introduction.

Sodersten, Bo, *International Economics.* Harper & Row (hard cover), 1970. Good introduction with differing emphases.

Aliber, Robert, *The International Money Game.* Basic, 1973. Covers only monetary issues and does not deal with the theory of comparative advantage. INTRODUCTORY.

Ingram, James, *International Economic Problems,* 2nd ed. Wiley, 1970. Excellent introduction to modern issues of policy, for example toward developing nations and the European common market.

Bhagwati, J. V., "The Pure Theory of International Trade: A Survey." *American Economic Association Surveys,* Vol. II. The Association, 1970.

ECONOMICS OF GROWTH AND DEVELOPMENT

Solow, Robert M., *Growth Theory: An Exposition.* **Oxford Univ. Press, 1970.** Lucid introduction to the neoclassical growth model. Requires calculus.

Solow, Robert M., *Capital Theory and the Rate of Return.* **Rand McNally, 1964.** Three important lectures in neoclassical growth theory, advanced treatment.

Hahn, F. H. and R. C. Matthews, *The Theory of Economic Growth–A Survey.* **American Economic Association Review Articles, Vol. 2.** Well-known, useful survey and evaluation of neoclassical and nonneoclassical approaches to growth. Includes helpful discussion of technical progress. ADVANCED, but not so advanced that you cannot get something useful out of it.

Robinson, Joan, *The Accumulation of Capital,* **2nd ed. St. Martin (hard cover), 1969.** An important work. The development of post-Keynesian growth theory. Long and difficult, but worth attempting to read at least some of it.

Gill, Richard T., *Economic Development: Past and Present,* **3rd ed. Prentice-Hall, 1973.** Introduction to the theory and issues regarding underdeveloped countries.

Ward, Barbara, and P. T. Bauer, *Two Views on Aid to Underdeveloped Countries.* **Transatlantic, 1967.** An introduction to economic aid for developing nations.

Miller, Herman P., *Rich Man, Poor Man.* **Apollo, 1971.** Another useful introduction to aid for national development.

Chenery, Hollis B., "Comparative Advantage and Development Policy," *American Economic Association Surveys,* **Vol. II. The Association, 1970.** Knowledge of international trade theory required. Comprehensive review of the different approaches to development. AD-VANCED.

Myrdal, Gunnar, *Economic Theory and Underdeveloped Regions.* **Harper & Row, 1971.** Early classic. ADVANCED.

Rostow, W. W., *The Stages of Economic Growth,* **2nd ed. Cambridge Univ. Press, 1971.** Famous but much criticized analysis of the process of growth; of interest in economic history as well as in economic theory.

ECONOMIC HISTORY

Fogel, Robert W., and Stanley L. Engerman, ed., *Reinterpretation of American Economic History.* **Harper & Row, 1971.** Modern approach. Comprehensive.

Rostow, W. W., *The Stages of Economic Growth,* **2nd ed. Cam-**

bridge Univ. Press, 1971. See preceding section, "Economics of Growth and Development."

Fogel, Robert W., and Stanley L. Engerman. *Time on the Cross,* 2 vols. Little, Brown, 1974. Explosive book. A new look at the economics of American Negro slavery. Uses modern econometric methods to estimate historical relationships.

Deane, Phyllis, and W. A. Cole, *British Economic Growth, 1688–1959: Trends and Structure,* 2nd ed. Cambridge Univ. Press, 1969. Detailed; analyzes causes of the Industrial Revolution and subsequent trends. Important as a model of how economic historians proceed. Contains an enormous amount of factual information.

COMPARATIVE ECONOMIC SYSTEMS AND THE ECONOMICS OF PLANNED ECONOMIES

Kohler, Heinz, *Welfare and Planning: An Analysis of Capitalism vs. Socialism.* Krieger, 1966. Excellent introduction. Includes discussion of the great price debate, input-output, linear programming.

Nove, Alec, *The Soviet Economy; An Introduction,* 2nd ed. Praeger, 1969. Classic, comprehensive treatment. INTERMEDIATE.

Goldman, Marshall, I., ed., *Comparative Economic Systems: A Reader,* 2nd ed. Random House, 1970. Excellent, comprehensive. Includes sections on the theory of planning, capitalism, socialism, and communism, and readings on individual countries.

PUBLIC FINANCE AND WELFARE ECONOMICS

Eckstein, Otto, *Public Finance,* 3rd ed. Prentice-Hall, 1973. Useful introduction.

Musgrave, R. A., *The Theory of Public Finance: A Study in Public Economy.* McGraw-Hill (hard cover), 1959. The classic treatment. Comprehensive, clear. INTERMEDIATE-ADVANCED.

Phelps, Edmund S., ed., *Private Wants and Public Needs,* rev. ed. Norton, 1965. Useful book of readings on the size and scope of government expenditure.

DeGraaf, Johannes, *Theoretical Welfare Economics.* Cambridge Univ. Press, 1957. Famous exposition of modern theory. ADVANCED.

Bator, F. M., "The Simple Analytics of Welfare Maximization," in David Kamerschen, ed., *Readings in Microeconomics.* Wiley, 1969. Clear, geometrical exposition of the meaning of Pareto optimality and welfare. INTERMEDIATE-ADVANCED. Originally published in *American Economic Review,* March, 1957.

Mishan, E. J., *A Survey of Welfare Economics, 1939–1959.* American Economic Association, Surveys of Economic Theory, Vol. I, 1965. Early but extremely useful.

Prest, A. R., and R. Turvey, *Cost Benefit Analysis—A Survey.* American Economic Association Surveys Vol. III, 1972. Useful. Includes discussion of investment criteria, social rate of discount, and measurement problems.

Haveman, Robert H. and Julius Margolis, eds., *Public Expenditures and Policy Analysis,* rev. ed. Rand McNally, 1970. Excellent book of readings covering wide range of topics. See particularly articles by Steiner, Davis and Kamien, and Haveman.

INDUSTRIAL ORGANIZATION

Caves, Richard, *American Industry: Structure, Conduct and Performance,* 3rd ed. Prentice-Hall, 1972. Useful if rather brief introduction to modern issues. Requires minimal knowledge of microeconomics. Includes some discussion of antitrust.

Scherer, F. M., *Industrial Market Structure and Economic Performance.* Rand McNally (hard cover), 1971. Advanced, detailed presentation of current theory, with particular emphasis on pricing problems. Also includes excellent reviews of the empirical literature.

Asch, Peter, *Economic Theory and the Antitrust Dilemma.* Wiley (hard cover), 1970. Lucid presentation of the problem of antitrust. Includes good review of relevant microtheory, summary of important antitrust cases, and objective evaluation of theory and policy. INTERMEDIATE.

Mansfield, Edwin, ed., *Monopoly Power and Economic Performance.* Norton, 1974. Readings emphasizing policy issues. Spans all views. INTRODUCTORY-INTERMEDIATE.

Needham, D., ed., *Readings in the Economics of Industrial Organization.* Holt, Rinehart & Winston, 1970. Advanced readings in theory and empirical research.

Stelzer, Irwin M., *Selected Antitrust Cases: Landmark Decisions.* Irwin, 1972. Excerpts from the transcripts of important cases, with brief summaries of the issues.

MacAvoy, Paul W., *Crisis of the Regulatory Commissions.* Norton, 1970. Readings on problems of regulation. Includes articles by Baumol, Posner. INTRODUCTORY-INTERMEDIATE.

Kahn, A. E., *Economics of Regulation.* 2 vols. Wiley (hard cover), 1970, 1971. Comprehensive treatment of theory and policy issues. Covers all the literature. Very clear. ADVANCED.

LABOR ECONOMICS

Rees, A., The *Economics of Work and Pay.* Harper & Row (hard cover), 1973. Useful introduction.

Perlman, Richard, *The Economics of Education: Conceptual Problems and Policy Issues.* McGraw-Hill, 1973. Modern approach.

Rees, Albert, *The Economics of Trade Unions.* Univ. of Chicago Press (hard cover), 1962. Excellent introduction.

ECONOMETRICS AND FORECASTING

Klein, Lawrence R., *Introduction to Econometrics.* Prentice-Hall (hard cover), 1962. Excellent, lucid, intuitive approach.

Johnston, John, *Econometric Methods,* 2nd ed. McGraw-Hill (hard cover), 1972. A solid introduction.

Goldberger, Arthur S., *Econometric Theory.* Wiley (hard cover), 1964. ADVANCED treatment.

Zellner, Arnold, ed., *Readings in Economic Statistics and Econometrics.* Little, Brown, 1968. See particularly the article by Daniel Suits, "Forecasting and Analysis with an Econometric Model."

MATHEMATICAL ECONOMICS

Allen, Roy G., *Mathematical Analysis for Economists,* rev. ed. St. Martin, 1962. Excellent introduction. Goes from the rudiments to the calculus of variations.

Baumol, William J., *Economic Dynamics,* 3rd ed. Macmillan (hard cover), 1970. Includes description of Marxian growth model, Harrod growth model, uncertainty, differential equations. Much recommended.

Samuelson, Paul A., *Foundations of Economic Analysis.* Atheneum, 1965. Famous original formulation of modern economic microtheory with full discussion of equilibrium. ADVANCED.

FUTURE DIRECTIONS, MISCELLANEOUS READINGS

Brookings Institution (Washington, D. C.), *Brookings Papers on Economic Activity.* Excellent, up-to-date analysis of the current state of the economy; issued quarterly. Much emphasis recently on inflation and unemployment.

Okun, Arthur M., *Equality and Efficiency: The Big Trade-Off.* The Brookings Institution, 1975. Realistic discussion of the modern economic dilemma.

Scoville, James G., *Perspectives on Poverty and Income Distribution.* Heath, 1971. Book of readings.

Chamberlain, Neil W., ed., *Contemporary Economic Issues.* Irwin, 1973. See particularly: W. R. Thompson, "The Economic Base of Urban Problems"; Mary Jean Bowman's famous article, "Poverty in an

Affluent Society"; William Vickrey's "Current Issues in Transportation"; and Richard Easterlin's "Population."

Crocker, Thomas D., and A. J. Rogers, III, *Environmental Economics.* **Holt, Rinehart & Winston, 1971**

Seneca, Joseph J., and Michael K. Taussig, *Environmental Economics.* **Prentice-Hall (hard cover), 1974.** A more extensive treatment.

Olson, Mancur, and Hans H. Landsberg, eds., *The No-Growth Society.* **Norton, 1973.** Collected articles on the costs and consequences of rapid economic growth.

Arrow, Kenneth J., *The Limits of Organization.* **Norton, 1974.** A new look at the underpinnings of economic life by a Nobel Laureate in economics.

Balinky, Alexander, *Marx's Economics: Origin and Development.* **Heath, 1970.** An introduction to the views of today's radical economists. Lucid clarification, objective and fair. Much recommended.

Gurley, John G., "The State of Political Economy," *American Economic Review,* **May, 1971.** A radical critique of mainstream economics.

Mermelstein, David, ed., *Economics: Mainstream Readings and Radical Critiques.* **Random House, 1970.** Excellent, comprehensive; deals with both domestic and international issues.

Chapter Eleven

HISTORY— AMERICAN

". . . patterns of culture
and the reactions of individuals
to historical situations"

Editorial Advisor:
James Shenton
Department of History
Columbia University

INTRODUCTION

It may be an exaggeration to say that those who do not know history are doomed to relive it, but not knowing history, particularly the history of your own country, *does* make it more difficult to have any real perspective on contemporary events. The horror Americans feel about the number of assassinations and assassination threats in the last decade is not diminished by a historical perspective. The fact that three of the seven presidents elected between 1864 and 1901 were murdered does not make the assassination of John Kennedy seem somehow more acceptable or expected, but a comparison of the Civil War period with events of the 1960s and early 1970s may give us some insight into the reasons for assassinations.

Clearly idiosyncratic factors are involved; the pathologies of assassins and would-be assassins cannot be subsumed under a single clinical heading. Yet there are striking parallels between the two widely separated periods in American history. Both were marked by widespread social and political disturbances during which it was (and is) possible for an individual to feel that the only way to make a statement against the "system" was (and is) to kill the person who embodied it—whether the president or a presidential hopeful.

To know something about the history of violence in America—or the history of racism, to take another example—is to avoid jumping to conclusions about how much better things were in the good old days and to gain insight into the complex relationship between patterns of culture and the reactions of specific individuals to specific historical situations. Until quite recently historians were primarily concerned with major public events—wars, elections, economic disasters—but increasingly they have broadened their inquiries to write what is often referred to as "history from the bottom up." Using new methodologies and source materials, they have sought to discover the relationship between the anonymous lives of very average people and the major developments that characterized the life of the nation as a whole.

Women's history illustrates this trend in historiography (as the chapter on Women's Studies reflects). This new field has been developed in response to the growing awareness that American history traditionally has been the history of white males.

The growing field of Black American (or Afro-American) history represents another significant manifestation of this tendency to rethink history from the bottom up (as the following chapter indicates). Its emergence has in turn led to active development of many other varieties of ethnic history. Significant work is now being done in the history of Irish-Americans, Italian-Americans, Chinese-Americans, and Hispanic-Americans, as well as Native Americans. Together these developments have broadened the framework in which American history is understood.

Work in history today has broadened its methodology as well as scope, often drawing on methods developed in other scholarly disciplines. The analysis that marks much current research provides a striking example of use of new techniques to document the life of people who lived anonymous lives. "Cliometry," as some term it, employs statistical methods of the sort used by sociologists or economists to shed light on important questions concerning life in the past epochs. Was slavery profitable in the ante-bellum South? Just how much economic mobility was there at the end of the nineteenth century?

Recently a group of New Left historians has brought a Marxist viewpoint to historical interpretation. (A number of such works are included in the following bibliography.) These historians seek to push against or "correct" the interpretations of the majority of their colleagues who have, at least up until the last decade, represented the consensus school or viewpoint. To put the contrast most simply, consensus historians generally feel that American society has been characterized by an underlying harmony of interests that outweigh conflicts and stresses. Current New Left histories, like the Progressive histories earlier in the century, have instead emphasized the divisions in American society and the overriding importance of economic issues. Analysis along these latter lines has in turn fueled the growing interest in history of the ordinary people.

As college History majors advance from the freshman through the senior year, they are often expected to do their own research as well as to be able to analyze the merits of conflicting interpretations. Students often begin their study of American history with a one-year (or two-year) introductory course or sequence of courses covering the Colonial period to the present, although it is not uncommon for students to plunge into work in a particular period, preferring to focus first on the craft of producing defensible interpretations rather than trying to swallow more than three centuries of American experience in one gulp. Those majoring in History almost invariably come to concentrate on discrete periods or topics and take such courses as nineteenth-century intellectual history, United States foreign relations in the twentieth century, or labor history during the Civil War.

The following bibliography represents an attempt to give a comprehensive introduction to American history. It has been designed to identify works covering the full range of studies typically pursued by college majors today. If you are strongly interested in all of American history, you may want to work through the bibliography in chronological order. This procedure should make it easier for you to understand studies of later periods, which often assume knowledge of earlier events. Moreover, through chronological study you can trace developments step by step and come to see the roots of the present in the past.

An alternative approach can concentrate on any one aspect of American history that most interests you. The bibliography offers a way to begin if you want to concentrate on a single period or group of people of America's past. No college major is asked to become familiar with nearly as many books as the bibliography lists. What will be expected is fair knowledge of many of the books given as "introductory" and rather detailed knowledge of "advanced" books in several periods (or a roughly equivalent number on some aspect of history—for example, economic or ethnic history—over a substantial time span.)

Sustained study in the books listed should take you to a point at which you will begin to know what you want to study next. In almost every work there are extensive bibliographies. In time you should be able to draw on these to make up your own reading lists for pursuing those questions most important to you. Ideally you will reach a point where secondary sources will not be enough and you will want to go on to read the original materials for yourself.

Some of the greatest histories of our country have been written by amateurs, people never formally trained. Henry Adams, for example, graduated from college but developed an interest in history on his own. His multivolume study of the Jefferson and Madison administrations is a classic, indeed a monumental, work. Francis Parkman was another amateur who produced histories of enduring significance. More recently Allan Nevins and Bruce Catton have kept up this tradition.

An Englishman, a man now virtually unknown who had never gone beyond secondary school, spent all of his time after retirement pursuing an intense interest in the Iroquois Indians. He produced a two-million-word handwritten manuscript on every conceivable aspect of Iroquois life, having visited Canada and upstate New York for research and located archival materials in England. The manuscript is now being readied for publication as a two-volume, definitive work on the Iroquois. In sum, although professional training is available and valuable, history is still a field where the serious student is not barred from the pleasures of the scholar. Indeed, the line between the two is constantly being crossed by those who move beyond reading others' interpretations to try to discover their own.

BIBLIOGRAPHY

Books are listed in the order of their recommended sequence for reading and study. Those given first in a section are generally more comprehensive, more easily understood, or primary in order of historical time among the books grouped in the section. If you are strongly interested in specific topics (indicated by subheadings), remember to consult the works listed in the "Advanced" as well as the "Introductory" sections under each subheading.

Subheadings that indicate major historical periods are intended as general guides rather than rigid categories. Books listed under them may treat events extending somewhat beyond the period indicated.

COLONIAL DEVELOPMENT

Introductory

Notestein, Wallace, *The English People on the Eve of Colonization, 1603–1630.* Harper & Row, 1954. An account based on a life-time of research in the English background of colonization; an example of what accomplished scholarship can discover about a brief span of history.

Andrews, Charles M., *The Colonial Period of American History.* Yale Univ. Press (hard cover), 1934. A balanced, short background treatment of Colonial history that is widely respected.

Ver Steeg, Clarence L., *The Formative Years, 1607–1763.* Hill & Wang, 1964. Readable and sensible, portrays the Colonial period.

Wright, Louis B., ed., *The Atlantic Frontier: Colonial American Civilization, 1607–1763.* Cornell Univ. Press, 1963. Focuses on the social, intellectual, and cultural history of the Colonies; lively, easy to read.

Advanced

Boorstin, Daniel J., *The Americans: The Colonial Experience.* Random House, 1958. Examines the structure of colonial society in order to convey a sense of the Colonial Americans as a people; a major, challenging treatment of Colonial social history.

Craven, Wesley Frank, *The Colonies in Transition, 1660–1761.* Harper & Row, 1968. Colonial history during the period of salutary neglect by Britain.

COLONIAL FIGURES

Introductory

Crane, Verner W., *Benjamin Franklin and a Rising People.* Little, Brown, 1954. A short, perceptive analysis of Franklin's career and its relationship to the shaping of the American character.

Advanced

Miller, Perry, *Jonathan Edwards.* **Greenwood (hard cover), 1973.** Provocatively interprets the career of the great Puritan divine and his role in the Great Awakening.

Knollenberg, Bernhard, *George Washington: The Virginia Period.* **Duke Univ. Press (hard cover), 1964.** Depicts the revolutionary and presidential career of the "father of his country."

Murdock, Kenneth B., *Increase Mather, the Foremost American Puritan.* **Russell & Russell (hard cover), 1966.** More than a biography, this work deals with the main currents of change in Puritanism.

Bailyn, Bernard, *The Ordeal of Thomas Hutchinson.* **Harvard Univ. Press (hard cover), 1974.** Portrait of an American Tory that won a National Book Award.

COLONIAL POLITICS

Introductory

Dargo, George, *Roots of the Republic: A New Perspective on Early American Constitutionalism.* **Praeger, 1974.** Analyzes the development of systems of constitutional government throughout the American colonies.

Rossiter, Clinton L., *Seedtime of the Republic: The Origin of the American Tradition of Political Liberty.* **Harcourt Brace Jovanovich (hard cover), 1953.** Concentrates on the major constitutional conflicts that arose between Britain and the colonies.

Advanced

Larabee, Leonard W., *Royal Government in America.* **Yale Univ. Press (hard cover), 1934.** Treats the development and nature of the royal government of the Colonies; very thorough.

Bailyn, Bernard, *The Origins of American Politics.* **Random House, 1970.** A penetrating interpretation of colonial political life; generally conservative in viewpoint, it presents illuminating analyses of political tracts of the time.

Lynd, Staughton, *Intellectual Origins of American Radicalism.* **Random House, 1969.** A New Left analysis of the coming and course of the American Revolution.

COLONIAL ECONOMY AND SOCIETY

Introductory

Bridenbaugh, Carl, *Myths and Realities; Societies of the Colonial South*. Atheneum, 1963. A series of succinct essays that demolish a number of myths about the colonial South.

Bruchey, Stuart, *The Roots of American Economic Growth, 1607–1861: An Essay in Social Causation*. Harper & Row, 1968. Very short; outlines the beginnings of America's eventual economic might in such enterprises as mercantile trade, staple crop production, and early stages of the factory system.

Henretta, James A., *The Evolution of American Society, 1700–1815*. Heath, 1973. Synthesizes the findings of extensive recent scholarship on the shaping of American society.

Advanced

Bushman, Richard L., *From Puritan to Yankee: Character and the Social Order in Connecticut*. Norton, 1970. A detailed analysis of life in Colonial Connecticut, sensitively depicts social and cultural change.

Demos, John, *A Little Commonwealth: Family Life in Plymouth Colony*. Oxford Univ. Press, 1971. In method, a model of what such a study should be. For a fuller treatment of attitudes toward women, see E. S. Morgan's work, below.

Main, Jackson T., *The Social Structure of Revolutionary America*. Princeton Univ. Press, 1965. Documents the distribution of property and status in America during the Revolutionary period.

Schafer, Joseph, *The Social History of American Agriculture*. Da Capo (hard cover), 1970. An old but still useful account of the interaction of society and the agricultural ethos.

Bailyn, Bernard, *The New England Merchants in the Seventeenth Century*. Peter Smith (hard cover), 1955. Analyzes the process of the accumulation of wealth in the first half of the colonial period.

Morris, Richard B., *Government and Labor in Early America*. Gannon (hard cover), 1970. Reports in detail on the history of labor in colonial America.

Bridenbaugh, Carl, *Cities in the Wilderness*. Oxford Univ. Press (hard cover), 1971. Discusses the important question of urban conditions and growth in the Colonial period.

Morgan, Edmund S., *Puritan Family; Religion and Domestic Relations in Seventeenth Century New England*. Harper & Row, 1966. Examines Colonial family structure; a pioneering study.

Vaughan, Alden, *New England Frontier.* Little, Brown (hard cover), **1965.** Delineates the interaction of Puritan and Indian culture; fascinating.

COLONIAL RELIGION

Introductory

Miller, Perry, *Errand Into the Wilderness.* Harvard Univ. Press (hard cover), **1956.** A series of extraordinary essays that provides, among other things, an introduction to the nature of colonial religious ideas.

Advanced

Bridenbaugh, Carl, *Mitre and Sceptre: Transatlantic Faiths, Ideas, Personalities, and Politics, 1689–1775.* Oxford Univ. Press (hard cover), **1967.** Traces the complex interaction between religion and politics.

Heimert, Alan, *Religion and the American Mind from the Great Awakening to the Revolution.* Harvard Univ. Press (hard cover), **1966.** Analyzes the relationship of changing religious ideas to the coming of the Revolution; comprehensive and judicious.

Willison, George, *Saints and Strangers.* Reynal & Hitchcock (hard cover), **1945.** An amusing and informative account of Pilgrim life and mores.

THE AMERICAN REVOLUTION

Introductory

Gipson, Lawrence Henry, *The Coming of the Revolution 1763–1775.* Harper & Row (hard cover), **1954.** Emphasizes the British interpretation in recounting the events that led to the Revolution; an impressive, one-volume synopsis of a fourteen-volume work on the subject. Miller's *Origins of the American Revolution* in the "Advanced" subsection relates these same events as viewed by Americans.

Morgan, Edmund S., *The Birth of the Republic, 1763–1789.* Univ. of Chicago Press, **1956.** A finely balanced and brief account of the Revolutionary period.

Advanced

Morgan, Edmund S., and Helen W. Morgan, *The Stamp Crisis: Prologue to a Revolution.* Macmillan, **1963.** Reports in detail on a major conflict that led toward Revolution.

Bailyn, Bernard, *The Ideological Origins of the American Revolu-*

tion. **Harvard Univ. Press, 1967.** A short, densely developed analysis of the ideas that underscored the Revolution.

Maier, Pauline, *From Resistance to Revolution: Colonial Radicals and the Development of American Opposition to Britain, 1765–1776.* **Random House, 1972.** Relates the story of the steady escalation of violence that finally climaxed in Revolution.

Nelson, William H., *The American Tory.* **Beacon, 1961.** Briefly but thoroughly treats those who opposed the Revolution.

Douglass, Elisha P., *Rebels and Democrats: The Struggle for Equal Political Rights and Majority Rule During the American Revolution.* **Quadrangle, 1965.** Analyzes how the Revolution advanced the cause of democracy.

Miller, John C., *Origins of the American Revolution.* **Stanford Univ. Press, 1959.** Treats in detail the background of the events leading up to the Revolution from the American viewpoint.

Miller, John C., *Triumph of Freedom, 1775–1783.* **Little, Brown, 1948** (out of print). Reports on the Revolutionary War; very readable.

Jameson, J. Franklin, *The American Revolution Considered as a Social Movement.* **Princeton Univ. Press, 1940.** Draws on social-science techniques to analyze how the Revolution changed American society.

Morris, Richard B., *The American Revolution Reconsidered.* **Harper & Row, 1968.** A highly readable analysis of the long-term effects of the Revolution by a leading historian.

Alden, John R., *The American Revolution, Seventeen Seventy-Five to Seventeen Eighty-Three.* **Harper & Row, 1954.** Emphasizes military history in presenting a narrative account of the Revolution.

THE CONSTITUTION AND FEDERALISM

Introductory

Levy, Leonard W., ed., *Judgments: Essays on American Constitutional History.* **Quadrangle (hard cover), 1972.** Provides a good introduction to recent findings on the formation of the Federal Constitution; represents an effort to reexamine all aspects of the background of the Constitutional Convention.

Montrose, Lynn, *The Reluctant Rebels: The Story of the Continental Congress, 1774–1789.* **Harper & Row (hard cover), 1950.** A detailed narrative of the period of the Continental Congress that explains why the colonists decided to establish the American Republic.

Miller, John C., *The Federalist Era, 1789–1801.* **Harper & Row, 1960.** Readable yet thorough coverage of every aspect of the Federalist period in the light of recent scholarship.

Advanced

Lipset, Seymour Martin, *The First New Nation: The United States in Historical and Comparative Perspective.* Doubleday, 1963. An engrossing, interdisciplinary analysis of the nation's founding; written by a sociologist, it represents an example of history from the sociological viewpoint.

Hofstadter, Richard, *The Idea of a Party System: The Rise of Legitimate Opposition in the U. S., 1780–1840.* Univ. of California Press, 1969. Traces the development of the system of American political parties from the end of the Revolution to the Civil War.

White, Leonard D., *The Federalists.* Macmillan (hard cover), 1948. Awarded a Pulitzer Prize in history; recounts the founding (in 1792) and early history of the administrative departments (those headed by cabinet members) of the federal government. It and three succeeding volumes in the series (see sections below) constitute a monumental administrative history.

Wood, Gordon S., *The Creation of the American Republic, 1776–1787.* Norton, 1972. Analyzes the revolutionary ideology that informed the shaping of the political institutions of the new republic.

THE JEFFERSONIANS

Introductory

Smelser, Marshall, *The Democratic Republic, 1801–1815.* Harper & Row, 1968. An easily read introduction to the Jeffersonian period.

Hofstadter, Richard, *The American Political Tradition and the Men Who Made It.* Knopf, 1948. Colorful and penetrating portrayals of the nation's major leaders from the founding fathers to Franklin Delano Roosevelt.

Advanced

White, Leonard D., *The Jeffersonians: A Study in Administrative History, 1801–1829.* Macmillan (hard cover), 1951. The second volume in White's extensive administrative history of the federal government.

Chambers, William N., *Political Parties in a New Nation: The American Experience 1776–1809.* Oxford Univ. Press, 1963. Describes the origins of America's political parties.

Nock, Albert Jay, *Jefferson.* Hill & Wang, 1960. An ascerbic, iconoclastic depiction of the third president that finds fault with Jefferson for emphasizing words over deeds; absorbing in style and thesis.

Pratt, Julius W., *Expansionists of 1812.* Peter Smith (hard cover), 1949. Brisk and brief account of the causes of the War of 1812.

Warren, Charles, *The Supreme Court in United States History,* Vol. I: *1789–1835.* Little, Brown (hard cover), 1960. Analysis of how the Court first secured its present great powers is of particular interest in this widely respected three-volume study.

Sisson, Daniel, *The American Revolution of Eighteen Hundred.* Knopf (hard cover), 1974. Argues that the election of Jefferson launched the United States on its experiment in democracy.

THE ERA OF TRANSITION

Introductory

Dangerfield, George, *Awakening of American Nationalism, 1815–1828.* Harper & Row, 1965. Treats a period of confidence for the new nation, the "Era of Good Feeling"; brief.

Snyder, Charles S., *Development of Southern Sectionalism, 1819–1848.* Louisiana State Univ. Press (hard cover), 1948. A good introduction to Southern history in the first half of the 1800s.

Nye, Russell B., *The Cultural Life of the New Nation, 1767–1830.* Harper & Row, 1960. Describes with gusto the cultural attitudes that dominated a young America.

Advanced

Livermore, Shaw, Jr., *The Twilight of Federalism: The Disintegration of the Federalist Party 1815–1830.* Gordian (hard cover), 1962. Tells in brief compass how one of America's first major political parties came to an end.

Bemis, Samuel F., *John Quincy Adams and the Foundations of American Foreign Policy.* Norton, 1973. A major biography and a key treatment of the essentials of American foreign policy.

Perkins, Dexter, *A History of the Monroe Doctrine.* Little, Brown, 1963. Old but still illuminating.

JACKSONIAN DEMOCRACY

Introductory

Schlesinger, Arthur, Jr., *The Age of Jackson.* Little, Brown, 1954. A controversial account of Jacksonian Democracy that sees Jackson as a precursor of Franklin D. Roosevelt and the New Deal; emphasizes the importance of the Eastern worker to the shaping of Jacksonianism.

Van Deusen, Glyndon G., *The Jacksonian Era, 1828–1848.* Harper & Row, 1959. A stodgy but solid narrative introduction to the Jacksonian Era.

Advanced

Benson, Lee, *The Concept of Jacksonian Democracy: New York as a Test Case.* Princeton Univ. Press, 1961. Interprets Jacksonian democracy in New York as something other than the equalitarian movement it is often assumed to be.

White, Leonard D., *The Jacksonians: A Study in Administrative History, 1829–1861.* Macmillan (hard cover), 1954. The third volume in White's administrative history of the federal government.

Meyers, Marvin, *The Jacksonian Persuasion: Politics and Belief.* Stanford Univ. Press, 1957. A series of provocative essays analyzing the complexities of Jacksonian belief.

Freehling, William W., *Prelude to Civil War: The Nullification Controversy in South Carolina, 1816–1836.* Harper & Row, 1968. Explains the doctrine of nullification and its peculiar appeal to South Carolina.

Hammond, Bray, *Banks and Politics in America from the Revolution to the Civil War.* Princeton Univ. Press, 1957. A massive and challenging interpretation of the interaction of politics and finance capitalism in ante-bellum America.

THE NATION OF SECTIONS

Introductory

Singletary, Otis, *The Mexican War.* Univ. of Chicago Press, 1960. Summarizes the events that eventually led to the annexation of lands from Texas to California.

Advanced

De Voto, Bernard, *The Year of Decision: 1846.* Houghton Mifflin, 1961. An irreverent, lively account of the Mexican War and the Polk administration.

Mark, Frederick, *Manifest Destiny: Mission in American History.* Random House, 1963. Introductory treatment of the ideology of American expansion.

Graebner, Norman A., *Empire on the Pacific: A Study in American Continental Expansion.* Ronald Press (hard cover), 1955. Analyzes the complex forces behind American expansion to the Pacific coast.

Smith, Henry Nash, *Virgin Land.* Harvard Univ. Press, 1970. An imaginative analysis of American land policies from the Revolution to the New Deal.

Foner, Eric, *Free Men, Free Labor and Free Soil.* Oxford Univ. Press, 1971. Traces the ideological roots of the Republican Party.

Hamilton, Holman, *Prologue to Conflict: The Crisis and Compromise of 1850.* **Norton, 1966.** Relates in brief a near-outbreak of civil war over the slavery expansion issue.

THE STRIDENT GIANT

Introductory

Gates, Paul W., *The Farmer's Age: Agriculture 1815–1860.* **Harper & Row, 1968.** Reports in detail on agricultural development in the ante-bellum period.

North, Douglass C., *The Economic Growth of the United States, 1790–1860.* **Norton, 1966.** Analyzes the factors underlying American economic development before the Civil War; a short volume.

Taylor, George R., *The Transportation Revolution, 1815–1860.* **Harper & Row, 1968.** Treats road, canal, and rail development in the pre-Civil War period, as well as factory and labor development.

Billington, Ray, *Westward Expansion: History of the American Frontier,* **4th ed. Macmillan (hard cover), 1974.** The story of America's westward expansion in the 1800s told in comprehensive detail.

Advanced

Handlin, Oscar, *Boston's Immigrants.* **Atheneum, 1968.** Analyzes the experiences of Irish immigrants who came to the United States from 1840 to 1860.

Stampp, Kenneth, *The Peculiar Institution.* **Knopf (hard cover), 1956.** Depicts American slavery; unusually informative.

Genovese, Eugene, *Roll, Jordan, Roll: The World the Slaves Made.* **Pantheon (hard cover), 1974, Random House (paper), 1976.** An extensive analysis of slavery's effects on the shaping of slave consciousness before the Civil War.

Litwack, Leon F., *North of Slavery: The Negro in the Free States, 1790–1860.* **Univ. of Chicago Press, 1961.** Graphically describes northern racism and segregation before 1860.

ANTE-BELLUM WINDS OF DOCTRINE

Introductory

Commager, Henry S., *Era of Reform, 1830–1860.* **Van Nostrand Reinhold, 1960.** On a period of surprisingly widespread and far-reaching reform agitation; succinct analysis.

Tyler, Alice F., *Freedom's Ferment: Phases of American Social History from the Revolution to the Outbreak of the Civil War.* **Harper**

& Row, 1962. More extensive treatment of pre-Civil War reform movements.

Sorin, Gerald, *Abolitionism*. Praeger, 1972. Short but thorough account of abolitionist reform.

Advanced

Billington, Ray A., *The Protestant Crusade*. Quadrangle, 1964. A detailed treatment of nativism and Know-Nothingism before the Civil War.

Smith, Timothy L., *Revivalism and Social Reform: American Protestantism on the Eve of the Civil War*. Harper & Row, 1957. Reports on the interaction of Protestantism and reform agitation in the pre-Civil War years.

Duberman, Martin, ed., *The Antislavery Vanguard: New Essays on the Abolitionists*. Princeton Univ. Press, 1965. Essays on many aspects of abolitionist reform.

A NATION DIVIDED

Introductory

Nevins, Allan, *Ordeal of the Union, 1847–57*, 2 vols., and *The Emergence of Lincoln, 1857–1861*, 2 vols. Scribner's, 1947. Two works that treat the coming of the Civil War in extensive detail.

Advanced

Nichols, Roy F., *The Disruption of the American Democracy*. Macmillan (Free Press), 1967. A Pulitzer Prize-winning account of the collapse of the Buchanan administration on the eve of the Civil War.

Craven, Avery, *The Coming of the Civil War*, 2nd ed. Univ. of Chicago Press, 1957. A lively account which sees the approach of the Civil War as the outcome of needless agitation.

Fehrenbacker, Don E., *Prelude to Greatness: Lincoln in the 1850s*. Stanford Univ. Press, 1970. Delightful essays recounting Lincoln's rise to prominence.

Potter, David M., *Lincoln and His Party in the Secession Crisis*. Yale Univ. Press, 1942. Analyzes the role of Lincoln and the Republicans in the final steps leading to war.

Stampp, Kenneth M., *And the War Came: The North and the Secession Crisis, 1860–1861*. Reports on the Northern attitudes toward the crisis.

THE CIVIL WAR

Introductory

Nevins, Allan, *The War for the Union, 1861–63,* 2 vols. Scribner's (hard cover), 1960. Extraordinarily detailed history of the Civil War.

Randall, J. G., and David Donald, *The Civil War and Reconstruction,* 2nd ed. Little, Brown (hard cover), 1973. An able summary.

Advanced

Wilson, Edmund, *Patriotic Gore: Studies in the Literature of the American Civil War.* Oxford Univ. Press, 1966. Ironic review of writings on the Civil War by a leading literary critic.

Andreano, Ralph, ed., *The Economic Impact of the American Civil War.* Shenkman, 1967. Essays on the war's economic consequences.

Catton, Bruce, *Mister Lincoln's Army* (1962); *Glory Road: The Bloody Route from Fredericksburg to Gettysburg* (1952); *A Stillness at Appomattox* (1953). Doubleday (hard cover). A series of three books that presents a gripping and colorful narrative account of the Army of the Potomac.

Randall, J. G., *Lincoln, The President,* 4 vols. Peter Smith (hard cover), 1945. A magisterial biography of the Civil War president.

Eaton, Clement, *History of the Southern Confederacy.* Macmillan (Free Press), 1965. Traces the rise and fall of the Confederate States of America.

Barney, William L., *Flawed Victory; A New Perspective on the Civil War.* Praeger, 1975. A short interpretation of the Civil War emphasizing its failure to solve the racial problem.

Frederickson, George M., *The Inner Civil War: Northern Intellectuals and the Crisis of the Union.* Harper & Row, 1968. Analyzes the response of Northern intellectuals to the psychic damage wrought by the Civil War.

RECONSTRUCTION

Introductory

Franklin, John Hope, *Reconstruction: After the Civil War.* See Black American History bibliography.

Stampp, Kenneth, *The Era of Reconstruction, 1865–1877.* See Black American History bibliography.

Woodward, Vann, *Origins of the New South: 1877–1913.* See Black American History bibliography.

Advanced

Du Bois, W. E. B., *Black Reconstruction in America, 1860–1880.* **Atheneum, 1969.** A leading account of the role of Black Americans in Reconstruction.

Unger, Irwin, *The Greenback Era: A Social and Political History of American Finance, 1865 to 1879.* **Princeton Univ. Press, 1964.** The Pulitzer Prize-winning account of fiscal and political developments of the Reconstruction era.

Williamson, Joel, *After Slavery: The Negro in South Carolina Reconstruction, 1861–1877.* **Univ. of North Carolina Press, 1969.** Sheds light on Reconstruction in the first state that seceded from the Union.

Rose, Willie Lee, *Rehearsal for Reconstruction: A Historical and Contemporary Reader.* **Random House, 1964.** Reports on the Port Royal experiment, which offered a way to secure the economic freedom of slaves liberated by the Civil War.

Wharton, Vernon Lane, *The Negro in Mississippi, 1865–1890.* **Harper & Row, 1965.** Portrays the role of Blacks in Mississippi before segregation was imposed.

Brock, W. R., *An American Crisis: Congress and Reconstruction.* **Harper & Row, 1963.** Trenchant analysis of Reconstruction by a leading British historian.

McKitrick, Eric, *Andrew Johnson and Reconstruction.* **Univ. of Chicago Press, 1960.** Interprets Andrew Johnson's part in Reconstruction and presents a challenging defense of his position.

Montgomery, David, *Beyond Equality; Labor and the Radical Republicans.* **Random House, 1972.** Full of insights into the attitudes of the Radical Republicans and the abandonment of their program of Radical Reconstruction.

McPherson, James M., *The Struggle for Equality: Abolitionists and the Negro in the Civil War and Reconstruction.* **Princeton Univ. Press, 1964.** A massive study of the role of abolitionists before, during, and after the Civil War.

THE GILDED AGE

Introductory

Garraty, John A., *The New Commonwealth 1877–1890.* **Harper & Row, 1968.** Describes the country's enormous industrial development following the Civil War.

Cochran, T. C., and W. Miller, *The Age of Enterprise: A Social History of America.* **Harper & Row, 1968.** Summarizes the background of American industrialization.

Advanced

Josephson, Matthew, *The Robber Barons*. Harcourt Brace Jovano-vich, 1962. A lively and often comic (though indignant) treatment of the ruthless tycoons who were the early builders of America's great corporations.

Morgan, Howard Wayne, *The Gilded Age: A Reappraisal*. Brown Book, 1970. Essays assessing constructive achievements and destruc-tive exploitation by big business, 1870–1896.

Josephson, Matthew, *The Politicos*. Harcourt Brace Jovanovich, 1964. Treats late-nineteenth-century politics and those who profited by corruption.

White, Leonard D., *The Republican Era, 1869–1901*. Macmillan (Free Press), 1965. The fourth and final volume in Wmvte e administra-tive history.

Hoogenboom, Ari, *Outlawing the Spoils: A History of the Civil Service Reform Movement, 1865–1883*. Univ. of Illinois Press, 1968. Portrays the reform efforts that culminated in introduction of the fed-eral civil service.

Hofstadter, Richard, *Social Darwinism in American Thought*. Beacon, 1955. Traces the application in American government and business policy of such ideas as "the survival of the fittest" drawn from Darwin's theory of evolution.

Ginger, Ray, *Altgeld's America: The Lincoln Ideal Vs. Changing Realities*. Watts, 1965. Analyzes the social dislocations that wracked a rapidly industrializing and urbanizing America at the end of the nineteenth century.

THE GREAT PLAINS

Introductory

Faulkner, Harold U., *Politics, Reform and Expansion, 1890–1900*. Harper & Row, 1959. A sensible treatment of the final decade of the nineteenth century.

Shannon, Fred A., *The Farmer's Last Frontier*. Holt, Rinehart & Winston (hard cover), 1945 (out of print). Narrative of the conquest of the Great Plains.

Webb, Walter P., *The Great Plains*. Grosset & Dunlap, 1957. The standard work on the complex process by which the West was settled.

Robbins, Roy M., *Our Landed Heritage: The Public Domain, 1776–1936*. Univ. of Nebraska Press, 1962. A detailed account of land policy.

Advanced

Glad, Paul W., *McKinley, Bryan and the People.* **Lippincott, 1964.** Reports on the defeat of the Populist movement by big-business interests in the election of 1896.

Hicks, John D., *The Populist Revolt: A History of the Farmers' Alliance and the People's Party.* **Univ. of Nebraska Press, 1961.** An old but sound account of Populism.

Pollack, Norman, *The Populist Response to Industrial America.* **Norton, 1966.** An analysis of the Populist movement which emphasizes the creative potential it held for a more democratic society.

INDUSTRY, IMMIGRANTS AND THE CITY

Introductory

Weibe, Robert H., *The Search for Order, 1877–1920.* **Hill & Wang, 1967.** Delineates the impact of industrial dislocation on the United States.

Hays, Samuel P., *The Response to Industrialism, 1885–1914.* **Univ. of Chicago Press, 1957.** A brief and lively account of industrialization.

Handlin, Oscar, *The Uprooted.* **Grosset & Dunlap, 1957.** The Pulitzer Prize-winning account of the immigrant experience.

Advanced

Hingham, John, *Strangers in the Land.* **Atheneum, 1963.** An examination of American nativism (prejudice against those perceived to be less "American").

Thernstrom, Stephen, *Poverty and Progress: Social Mobility in a Nineteenth Century City.* **Atheneum, 1969.** Documents how members of various groups rose and fell in social position in Newburyport, Mass; refutes the ahistoricism of sociology.

Schlesinger, Arthur M., Jr., *The Rise of the City, 1878–1898.* **Watts, 1971.** Analyzes the impact of urbanization on the United States.

THE DILEMMA OF RACE

Introductory

Woodward, C. Vann, *The Strange Career of Jim Crow.* See Black American History bibliography.

LaFeber, Walter, *The New Empire: An Interpretation of American Expansion, 1860–1898.* **Cornell Univ. Press, 1963.** A striking analysis of American empire-building before the Spanish-American War including campaigns against the American Indians.

Advanced

Lewinson, Paul, *Race, Class, and Party: A History of Negro Suffrage and White Politics in the South.* Atheneum (hard cover), 1932. Analyzes the interaction of race and class in the development of political control in the South.

Brown, Dee, *Bury My Heart at Wounded Knee.* Bantam, 1972. Eloquently recounts the tragic last stand of the Plains Indians.

Saxton, Alexander, *The Indispensable Enemy: Labor and the Anti-Chinese Movement in California.* Univ. of California Press (hard cover), 1971. Reports on American actions against Oriental immigrants.

Logan, Rayford W., *The Betrayal of the Negro: From Rutherford B. Hayes to Woodrow Wilson.* Macmillan, 1965. Portrays in detail the devastation wreaked on Black Americans by segregation.

Pratt, Julius W., *Expansionists of 1898: The Acquisition of Hawaii and the Spanish Islands.* Quadrangle, 1964. Treats the Spanish-American War in the Pacific, analyzing expansionism overseas at the end of the nineteenth century.

PROGRESSIVISM

Introductory

Hofstadter, Richard, *The Age of Reform: From Bryan to F. D. R.* Knopf (hard cover), 1955. The Pulitzer Prize analysis of Progressivism and its precursors.

Mowry, George E., *The Era of Theodore Roosevelt: 1900 to 1912.* Harper & Row, 1958. Progressivism under Theodore Roosevelt; thorough yet easily read.

Link, Arthur S., *Woodrow Wilson and the Progressive Era, 1910–1917.* Harper & Row, 1954. An engrossing introduction to the role of Woodrow Wilson in Progressivism.

Advanced

May, Henry F., *The End of American Innocence: A Study of the First Years of Our Own Time, 1912–1917.* Watts, 1964. Explains the decline of American confidence in Progressive reform.

Blum, John, *The Republican Roosevelt.* Atheneum, 1962. A short and lively account of the career of Theodore Roosevelt.

Kolko, Gabriel, *The Triumph of Conservatism.* Quadrangle, 1967. Interprets Progressive reform as essentially a series of conservative accommodations designed to preclude more radical reforms.

**Shannon, David, *The Socialist Party of America: A History.* Quad-

rangle, 1967. Reports on the political party that at the start of this century seemed destined to become a major party.

Bremner, Robert, *From the Depths: The Discovery of Poverty in the United States.* New York Univ. Press, 1956. A study of the growing awareness of poverty in America at the turn of the century.

Kennedy, David M., ed., *Progressivism: The Critical Issues.* Little, Brown, 1971. Essays analyzing the key issues that confronted the Progressives.

FOREIGN POLICY IN THE PROGRESSIVE ERA

Introductory

Williams, William A., *The Tragedy of American Diplomacy.* Dell, 1972. A provocative New Left analysis of American foreign policy in this century.

Advanced

Osgood, R. E., *Ideals and Self-Interest in America's Foreign Relations.* Univ. of Chicago Press, 1963. Delineates complex issues; thoughtful.

Beale, Howard K., *Theodore Roosevelt and the Rise of America to World Power.* Macmillan, 1966. A tough-minded analysis of Roosevelt's foreign policy.

Smith, Daniel M., *American Intervention, 1917.* Portrays the background of America's entry into the First World War.

Levin, N. Gordon, *Woodrow Wilson and World Politics: America's Response to War and Revolution.* Oxford Univ. Press, 1970. Critically analyzes Wilson's peace proposals and ultimate failure at Versailles.

Cooper, John Milton, *The Vanity of Power.* Greenwood (hard cover), 1969. Reports on the opposition to America's entry into the First World War.

Bailey, Thomas A., *Woodrow Wilson and the Lost Peace.* Watts, 1963. Wilson and the Treaty of Versailles from a sympathetic viewpoint.

THE TEMPESTUOUS TWENTIES

Introductory

Allen, Frederick Lewis, *Only Yesterday.* Harper & Row, 1957. A delightful reminiscence that deals with the 1920s perceptively but irreverently.

Carter, Paul, *The Twenties in America.* T. Y. Crowell, 1968. Interpretive account treating the period as a national identity crisis.

Leuchtenberg, William E., *Perils of Prosperity: 1914–1932.* Univ. of Chicago Press, 1958. A lively account of America from Progressivism to Depression.

Advanced

Murray, Robert K., Red Scare: *A Study in National Hysteria, 1919–1920.* McGraw-Hill, 1964. Analyzes anti-Communism in the 1920s.

Sinclair, Andrew, *Era of Excess: A Social History of the Prohibition Movement.* Harper & Row, 1962. An account of the Prohibition years, when alcohol was banned.

Bernstein, Irving, *The Lean Years: A History of the American Worker, 1920–1933.* Houghton Mifflin, 1972. Depicts the plight of labor in the 1920s.

Galbraith, John Kenneth, *The Great Crash, 1929.* Houghton Mifflin, 1972. A description by a liberal economist of the collapse of the American economy and the coming of the Great Depression.

Chambers, Clarke A., *Seedtime for Reform: American Social Service and Social Action, 1918–1933.* Univ. of Michigan Press, 1967. Argues that many of the New Deal reforms of the 1930s had their origin in the social work of the 1920s.

Jackson, Kenneth T., *The Ku Klux Klan in the City, 1915–1930.* Oxford Univ. Press, 1967. Narrative account of the Ku Klux Klan in the 1920s that emphasizes its strong urban roots, particularly in the North.

Burner, David, *Politics of Provincialism: The Democratic Party in Transition, 1918–1932.* Knopf (hard cover), 1968. Traces the character and consequences of the rift between urban ethnic and native rural groups in the Democratic Party during the 1920s.

Ellis, L. Ethan, *Republican Foreign Policy 1921–1933.* Rutgers Univ. Press, 1968. Narrative summary; neutral in viewpoint.

Wilson, Joan Hoff, *American Business and Foreign Policy, 1920–1933.* Beacon, 1973. A New Left treatment of an expanding American capitalism and its influence on foreign policy in the 1920s.

THE GREAT DEPRESSION AND THE NEW DEAL

Introductory

Leuchtenberg, William E., *Franklin D. Roosevelt and the New Deal, 1932–1940.* Harper & Row (hard cover), 1963. Brief analysis of the New Deal; vivid reading.

Bernstein, Irving, *Turbulent Years; A History of the American Worker, 1933–1941.* Houghton Mifflin, 1971. Recounts in colorful detail the vicissitudes of labor.

Advanced

Schlesinger, Arthur M., Jr., *The Age of Roosevelt,* Vol. 2: *The Coming of the New Deal.* Houghton Mifflin (hard cover), 1959. A detailed study of the opening stages of Franklin D. Roosevelt's New Deal; reads like a novel.

Burns, James McGregor, *Roosevelt: The Lion and the Fox.* Harcourt Brace Jovanovich, 1963. A widely respected biography.

Hawley, Ellis W., *The New Deal and the Problem of Monopoly.* Princeton Univ. Press, 1969. Analyzes changing aspects of New Deal economic policy.

Romasco, Albert U., *The Poverty of Abundance: Hoover, the Nation, the Depression.* Oxford Univ. Press, 1968. A sympathetically critical investigation of Hoover's efforts to resolve the Depression.

Patterson, James T., *Congressional Conservatism and the New Deal: The Growth of the Conservative Coalition in Congress, 1933–1939.* Univ. Press of Kentucky, 1967. Treats the conservative coalition that brought an end to further domestic reformism.

Williams, T. Harry, *Huey Long.* Bantam, 1970. A colorful account of a Southern demagogue; characterizes him as a spokesman for populist reforms.

Graham, Otis L., Jr., *Encore for Reform: The Old Progressives and the New Deal.* Oxford Univ. Press, 1967. Traces the role of Progressives in shaping New Deal reforms.

DIPLOMACY IN THE 1930s AND THE SECOND WORLD WAR

Introductory

Buchanan, A. Russel, *The United States and World War Two,* 2 vols. Harper & Row (hard cover), 1964. A comprehensive analysis of the American participation in the Second World War.

Smith, Gaddis, *American Diplomacy During the Second World War: 1941–1945.* Wiley, 1965. A general but critical account of American foreign policy during the war period that emphasizes the absence of well-defined strategy during the Second World War.

Morison, Samuel Eliot, *Strategy and Compromise.* Little, Brown, 1958. Highly readable commentary on American naval and military strategy during the Second World War.

Wiltz, John E., *From Isolation to War, 1931–1941.* Crowell, 1968.

Summarizes American foreign policy from the Japanese invasion of Manchuria to the bombing of Pearl Harbor.

Divine, Robert, *Roosevelt and World War II*. Penguin, 1970. Traces F. D. R.'s changing attitudes and policies during the war.

Advanced

Langer, William L., and S. Everett Gleason, *The Challenge to Isolation: The World Crisis of 1937–1940 and American Foreign Policy*, 2 vols. Peter Smith (hard cover), 1972. Recounts America's entrance into the Second World War in absorbing detail.

Feis, Herbert, *Churchill-Roosevelt-Stalin: The War They Waged and the Peace They Sought*, 2nd ed. Princeton Univ. Press, 1967. A major study of American diplomacy during the Second World War.

Jonas, Manfred, *Isolationism in America, 1935–1941*. Cornell Univ. Press, 1969. Analyzes the forces that opposed American involvement in the Second World War.

Russett, Bruce M., *No Clear and Present Danger: A Skeptical View of the United States Entry into World War II*. Harper & Row, 1972. Provocatively argues that American involvement in the Second World War was unnecessary.

Ferrell, Robert H., *American Diplomacy in the Great Depression: Hoover-Stimson Foreign Policy, 1929–1933*. Norton, 1970. A general account of Hoover's foreign policy.

AMERICA AS A WORLD POWER AFTER THE SECOND WORLD WAR

Introductory

Graebner, Norman, *Cold War Diplomacy, 1945–1960*. Van Nostrand Reinhold, 1962. Reports on the confrontation of the United States and Communism after the war.

Gaddis, John Lewis, *The United States and the Origins of the Cold War, 1941–1947*. Columbia Univ. Press, 1972. A careful balancing of traditional and revisionist accounts of the origins of the Cold War that focuses on the extent of American responsibility for the confrontation between East and West.

Advanced

Horwitz, David, *The Free World Colossus*. Hill & Wang, 1971. A New Left analysis of American foreign policy after the Second World War.

Reischauer, Edwin, *The United States and Japan*, 3rd ed. Viking,

1962. Characterizes American-Japanese relations in a balanced perspective.

Gardner, Lloyd, *Architects of Illusion: Men and Ideas in American Foreign Policy, 1941–1949.* **Watts, 1972.** Succinctly describes the major figures who shaped American foreign policy from 1941 to 1948; a New Left viewpoint.

Alperovitz, Gar, *Atomic Diplomacy.* **Simon & Schuster, 1965.** A controversial account of the decision to drop the atom bomb; it contends the primary motive was to intimidate the Soviet Union.

Freeland, Richard M., *The Truman Doctrine and the Origins of McCarthyism: Foreign Policy, Domestic Politics, and Internal Security, 1946–1948.* **Schocken, 1974.** Traces the origins of the Red-baiting of the early 1950s to the Truman administration's use of a Russian menace to justify American assumption of the defense of Greece and Turkey.

Spanier, John W., *The Truman-McCarthy Controversy and the Korean War.* **Norton, 1965.** An account of the Korean War that explains its disruptive effects on domestic politics.

TECHNOLOGY TRIUMPHANT

Introductory

Potter, David M., *People of Plenty: Economic Abundance and the American Character.* **Univ. of Chicago Press, 1954.** Affluence after the Second World War.

Goldman, Eric F., *Crucial Decade and After: America 1945–1960* **Random House, 1960.** A lively account of the postwar period.

Advanced

Lasch, Christopher, *The New Radicalism in America.* **Random House, 1965.** Analyzes modern American dissent, mainly as epitomized by young radicals emerging in the 1960s.

Harrington, Michael, *The Other America.* **Penguin, 1962.** A widely influential study of poverty and its victims.

Gottman, Jean, *Megalopolis: The Urbanized Northeastern Seaboard of the United States.* **M.I.T. Press, 1964.** Presents extensive data on large-scale urban development.

Kolko, Gabriel, *Wealth and Power in America; An Analysis of Social Class: Income Distribution.* **Praeger, 1962.** An irreverent study of the unbalanced distribution of wealth in America.

Hofstadter, Richard, *The Paranoid Style in American Politics and Other Essays.* **Random House, 1965.** Analyzes the background of the McCarthy era and the Red scare that it spawned.

Schlesinger, Arthur M., Jr., *A Thousand Days.* **Fawcett, 1971.** Portrays the brief promise of the Kennedy administration.

IN BLACK AMERICA—1909 TO THE PRESENT

Introductory

Franklin, John Hope, *From Slavery to Freedom: A History of American Negroes.* See Black American History bibliography.

Logan, Rayford, *The Negro in the United States: A Brief History.* **Peter Smith (hard cover), 1957.** Short but thorough; especially good on recent decades.

Advanced

Broderick, Francis, *W. E. B. DuBois: Negro Leader in a Time of Crisis.* See Black American History bibliography.

Frazier, E. Franklin, *Black Bourgeoisie: The Rise of a New Middle Class in the United States.* See Black American History bibliography.

Zinn, Howard, *The Southern Mystique.* **Knopf (hard cover), 1964.** Treats dominant views of the present-day South.

Cleaver, Eldridge, *Soul On Ice.* See Black American History bibliography.

Kerner, Otto, chmn., *Report of the National Advisory Commission on Civil Disorders.* **Dutton (hard cover), 1968.** Federally sponsored study with extensive analyses of violence in American cities, particularly in riots in Black ghettoes during the 1960s.

Chapter Twelve

HISTORY—
BLACK AMERICAN
". . . to correct large
and long-standing omissions"

Editorial Advisor:
James Shenton
Department of History
Columbia University

INTRODUCTION

The rapid rise of Black American History as a college major and research specialty began with the civil-rights movement of the late 1950s and 1960s. Certainly distinguished work in the history of Black Americans had been done before; but the fast-changing consciousness of Americans in those years brought with it an explosion in the numbers of new courses and scholarly studies.

Many of the country's liberal-arts colleges now offer course work in Black American History. More than 200 colleges have still more comprehensive Black Studies programs, according to a recent estimate. Such Afro-American Studies programs, as they are also often called, include study in literature and the arts as well as in history and the social sciences.

Work in Black History has begun to correct large and long-standing omissions in the historiography of the United States. Blacks have played vital roles in almost all periods of the nation's past and figured crucially in the issues over which our one civil war was fought. But ingrained social prejudice, guilt, and timidity have together prevented adequate treatment of Black Americans in college history studies until recent years.

During the 1960s Black American History was often felt to be a subject that could be taught best (or solely) by Black scholars and that was essential primarily (or solely) for Black students. Today, however, these feelings have been substantially modified in the light of a growing sense that no Americans seriously interested in the history of their country can afford to be ignorant about the Black experience.

One of the finest recent interpretations of the slave experience was written by a white of Italian origin—*Roll, Jordan, Roll* by Eugene

Genovese. Readers may come away from Genovese's book unconvinced that the theses he argues are entirely demonstrated, but the idea that his ethnicity has prevented him from significant insight would be hard to take too seriously.

Afro-American History has in turn led to substantial new work in the history of other ethnic groups in America that goes far beyond speculations about the ways and extent of assimilation or "Americanization." Ethnic historians sometimes find that particular groups in the United States have not only shaped our nation's history, but have continued to have a significant impact on the countries from which they came. The history of modern Ireland, for example, is difficult to understand unless it is realized that the Irish long relied on the Irish-American community as a kind of sanctuary in struggling against what they saw as the imperial power of England.

In using this chapter's bibliography on Black American History, you can proceed in either of the two ways suggested in the introduction to the previous chapter on American History. This bibliography, like the preceding one, is presented chronologically. Studying the books in order should familiarize you with that fundamental part of the nation's past that the field represents. But if some period or aspect of Black American life particularly interests you, you can turn directly to those more specialized works. Bibliographies in almost all the books can guide you to still other sources of information. If you do start working through the bibliography systematically, you will soon discover areas that are badly in need of further scholarly work. Until very recently scholars have not understood the role of the free Blacks in the slavery era, the full contributions of Blacks in the abolitionist movement, or the nature of the experience of Blacks in military service. But much work remains to be done. There is as yet not even the beginnings of a comprehensive history of segregation, one that presents definitive interpretations as well as factual knowledge. No truly thorough studies have been made of even such an explosive subject as lynching. Almost the only coverage of the subject is the short book written by Walter White more than four decades ago.

You may, accordingly, wonder whether in time you might complete some part of the missing record. Interested amateurs have long produced works of prime importance in history. The depth and persistence of your own interest can be the key factor in leading you to become one of these contributors to the sum of our understandings, or alternatively, might lead you as a first step to explore degree programs for which you may qualify.

You will learn as you study on your own in Black History that the field (though not the bibliography) includes historical works that espouse or reflect pro-segregationist views. Many older books on the Reconstruction period, for instance, were written as a means of justifying segregationist practices. Such works now represent primary sources for historians interested in tracing the development of social attitudes, but they should not be mistaken for substantial histories in themselves. W. E. B. DuBois has treated this subject in his *Black Reconstruction*, where he devotes a chapter to "The Propaganda of

History." It might be a very good place to begin your studies in the field.

BIBLIOGRAPHY

Books are listed in the order of their recommended sequence for reading and study. Those given first in a section are generally more comprehensive, more easily understood, or primary in order of historical time among the books grouped in the section. If you are strongly interested in specific topics (indicated by subheadings), remember to consult the works listed in the "Advanced" as well as the "Introductory" sections under each subheading.

Subheadings that indicate major historical periods are intended as general guides rather than rigid categories. Books listed under them may treat events extending somewhat beyond the period indicated.

BROAD SURVEYS—
AFRICAN ORIGINS TO PRESENT

Introductory

Foner, Eric, ed., *America's Black Past.* **Harper & Row, 1971.** An anthology of essays by historical scholars on key aspects of the Black experience in America.

Advanced

Franklin, John Hope, *From Slavery to Freedom.* **Random House (Vintage), 1969.** A long and demanding college textbook, but one of the very few volumes that relates the total experience of Black Americans within a coherent structure; includes an extensive bibliography.

Aptheker, Herbert, ed., *A Documentary History of the Negro People in the United States,* **Vol. I:** *From Colonial Times through the Civil War;* **Vol. II:** *From the Reconstruction Years to the Founding of the National Association for the Advancement of Colored People 1910.* **Citadel, 1964.** Texts of actual documents that significantly shaped or reported on the history of Black Americans.

Foner, Philip S., ed., *The Voice of Black America: Major Speeches by Negroes in the United States, 1797–1871.* **Simon and Schuster, 1972.** Presents a wealth of previously neglected major addresses by Black Americans.

Huggins, Nathan, I., *Black Odyssey: The Afro-American Ordeal in Slavery.* **Pantheon, 1977.**

THE AFRICAN ORIGINS

Introductory

Oliver, Roland and J. D. Fage, *A Short History of Africa,* rev. ed. Penguin, 1966. A concise general history of sub-Saharan Africa.

Advanced

Oliver, Roland, *Middle Age of African History*. Oxford Univ. Press, 1967. Treats in considerable detail the situation in sub-Saharan African societies when the slave trade opened.

Herskovits, Melville J., *The Myth of the Negro Past*. Beacon, 1958. Describes major stereotypes which Americans still hold about African societies and culture of the past, contrasting these beliefs with the historical facts.

THE SLAVE TRADE

Introductory

Curtin, Philip, *The Atlantic Slave Trade: a Census*. Univ. of Wisconsin Press, 1969. Documents the dimensions of the slave trade. Introductory chapter and conclusions can be readily understood; the other chapters are generally technical and difficult.

Davidson, Basil, *Black Mother: The Years of the African Slave Trade*. Little, Brown, 1961. Unusually readable account, dealing in large part with the conditions in Africa which led some blacks to sell others into slavery.

Du Bois, W. E. B., *The Suppression of the African Slave Trade to the United States of America 1638–1870*. Schocken, 1969. An account, by one of the most famous Black American scholar-editors of the first half of this century, of the effort to end the slave trade to the United States.

Advanced

Williams, Eric, *Capitalism and Slavery*. Putnam, 1966. Eric Williams, a prime minister of Trinidad-Tobago and one of the most distinguished Black historians, writes on the interaction of slavery and developing capitalism; he argues the controversial thesis that the slave trade provided the major source of capital accumulation which made possible the development of modern capitalism in Europe and the United States.

COMPARATIVE SLAVERY

Introductory

Foner, Laura, and Eugene D. Genovese, eds., *Slavery in the New World: A Reader in Comparative History.* **Prentice-Hall, 1974.** A scholarly collection of essays that provides a comparative analysis of slavery in various parts of the Americas; also appropriate for reading as an advanced work.

Advanced

Degler, Carl N., *Neither Black Nor White: Slavery and Race Relations in Brazil and the United States.* **Macmillan, 1971.** A comparative study emphasizing Brazilian society, in which social status decreases with gradations of darkening skin color rather than being polarized between black and white as in the United States.

Tannenbaum, Frank, *Slave and Citizen.* **Random House, 1946.** Presents a regionwide study of the history of slavery in the American South, the Caribbean Basin, and such adjacent areas as Northeastern Brazil.

Klein, Herbert, *Slavery in the Americas.* **Watts, 1972.** Contrasts slavery in Cuba and Virginia.

THE PROBLEM OF SLAVERY AND RACISM

Advanced

Davis, David B., *The Problem of Slavery in Western Culture.* **Cornell Univ. Press, 1966.** Reports on the long historical development of slavery in European and Western Hemisphere countries from antiquity (Greece and Rome) to the nineteenth century.

Davis, David B., *The Problem of Slavery in the Age of Revolution, 1770–1823.* **Cornell Univ. Press (hard cover), 1975.** Examines the impact of the American and French revolutions on slavery.

Jordan, Winthrop, *White over Black.* **Penguin, 1969.** Explores the general origins and development of Anglo-Saxon racism.

THE INTRODUCTION OF SLAVERY
INTO THE UNITED STATES

Advanced

Tate, Thad W., *The Negro in Eighteenth Century Williamsburg.* **Univ. Press of Virginia, 1965.** An account of slavery in a Southern Colonial capital.

Greene, Lorenzo, *The Negro in Colonial New England.* **Atheneum,**

1968. The standard work on Black Americans in Colonial New England.

McManus, Edgar J., *A History of Negro Slavery in New York,* **Syracuse Univ. Press, 1966.** Treats Black slavery during the Colonial period in New York; thorough.

Wood, Peter H., *Black Majority: Negroes in Colonial South Carolina from 1670 through the Stono Rebellion.* **Knopf (hard cover), 1974.** Analyzes slavery and Black rebellion in Colonial South Carolina.

Mullin, Gerald W., *Flight and Rebellion: Slave Resistance in Eighteenth-Century Virginia.* **Oxford Univ. Press, 1974.** Reports on the turbulent Colonial history of slavery and acculturation of the Blacks in Virginia.

THE AMERICAN REVOLUTION AND THE BLACK

Introductory

Quarles, Benjamin, *The Negro in the American Revolution.* **Norton, 1973.** A detailed account by a well-known Black American historian of the role of Blacks in winning American independence.

Advanced

Zilversmit, Arthur, *The First Emancipation: Abolition of Slavery in the North.* **Univ. of Chicago Press, 1971.** Recounts how slavery was ended in the North.

Lynd, Staughton, *Class Conflict, Slavery, and the United States Constitution: Ten Essays.* **Bobbs-Merrill, 1967.** An account of the framing of the Constitution presented from a controversial New Left viewpoint; lively.

McColley, Robert, *Slavery and Jeffersonian Virginia.* **Univ. of Illinois Press, 1973.** Traces the impact of the Revolutionary War on slavery in Virginia.

PLANTATION SLAVERY

Introductory

Phillips, Ulrich B., *American Negro Slavery.* **Louisiana State Univ. Press, 1966.** Treats slavery as an integral part of a unique Southern way of life.

Stampp, Kenneth M., *The Peculiar Institution: Slavery in the Ante-Bellum South.* **Random House, 1956.** Emphasizes the economic dimensions of slavery in its general description of slavery as an institution.

Olmsted, Frederic Law, *The Cotton Kingdom,* ed. David F. Hawke, abridged ed. Bobbs-Merrill, 1971. A report of long-enduring interest on every aspect of antebellum Southern life, written in the 1860s by a leading American landscape architect and writer.

Weinstein, Allan, and Frank O. Gatell, eds., *American Negro Slavery: A Modern Reader.* Oxford Univ. Press, 1973. Essays presenting the findings of recent scholarship on many aspects of slavery.

Advanced

Genovese, Eugene D., *Roll, Jordan, Roll: The World the Slaves Made.* Pantheon (hard cover), 1974; Random House (paper), 1976. Analyzes slavery from the perspective of its victims largely on the basis of little-known documentary writings of the time (often by slaves themselves); brilliant.

Genovese, Eugene D., *The World the Slaveholders Made: Two Essays in Interpretation.* Random House, 1971. Should be read along with *Roll, Jordan, Roll* (above), since it draws on similar source material to portray the white slaveholders.

Fogel, Robert William, and Stanley L. Engerman, *Time On the Cross,* 2 vols. Little, Brown, 1974. A controversial account that is a thoroughgoing quantitative analysis of the economics of slavery on plantations; is widely regarded as a pioneering work in cliometry—historical analysis through statistical methods. (In ancient mythology, Clio is the muse of history.)

Sydnor, Charles, *Slavery in Mississippi.* Lousiana State Univ. Press, 1966. A detailed treatment of slavery on the state level.

Bancroft, Frederic, *Slave Trading in the Old South.* Ungar, 1970. The standard work on the slave trade in the antebellum South by a leading historian of the mid-nineteenth century.

Wade, Richard C., *Slavery in the Cities: The South, 1820–1860.* Oxford Univ. Press, 1967. Describes urban slavery in the era of plantation slavery; also a useful source for the study of slave rebellions.

Starobin, Robert, *Industrial Slavery in the Old South.* Oxford Univ. Press, 1971. Examines the neglected subject of slaves who worked in factories and businesses.

Elkins, Stanley, *Slavery: A Problem in American Institutional and Intellectual Life.* Univ. of Chicago Press, 1968. Analyzes contradictions in American positions for and against slavery.

Lane, Ann J., ed., *The Debate Over Slavery: Stanley Elkins and His Critics.* Univ. of Illinois Press, 1971. A detailed report on the extensive debate aroused by the book by Elkins (above).

Woodman, Harold D., *King Cotton and His Retainers: Financing and Marketing the Cotton Crop of the South 1800–1925.* Univ. Press

of Kentucky, 1968. Describes the complex economic system that developed around cotton; a thorough examination.

Conrad, Alfred, and J. H. Meyer, *The Economics of Slavery and Other Studies in Economic History.* **Aldine, 1964.** Presents a strong argument to support the profitability of slavery.

Cash, W. J., *The Mind of the South.* **Random House, 1941.** An analysis of the impact of slavery on white Southerners.

Osofsky, Gilber, ed., *Puttin' On Ole Massa: The Slave Narratives of Henry Bibb, William W. Brown and Solomon Northrup.* **Harper & Row, 1969.** Three accounts by slaves of the relationship between slave and master.

Foner, Philip S., ed., *Frederick Douglass: Selections.* **International, 1945.** The biography of a slave who became a leading Black Abolitionist, told in selections from his own writings; particularly illuminating in its account of slave life.

Botkin, Benjamin, *Lay My Burden Down.* **Univ. of Chicago Press, 1945.** Brings together a wide range of slave reminiscences.

Blassingame, John W., *The Slave Community: Plantation Life in the Ante-Bellum South.* **Oxford Univ. Press, 1973.** An account of plantation slave life in the pre-Civil War years; vivid.

Johnston, James Hugo, *Race Relations in Virginia & Miscegenation in the South 1776–1860.* **Univ. of Massachusetts Press, 1970.** Reports on the complex problem of intercourse between the races.

SLAVE REBELLIONS

Introductory

Aptheker, Herbert, *American Negro Slave Revolts.* **International, 1969.** A summary of the spontaneous rebellions of Black American slaves that broke out before the Civil War, including the famed ones led by Nat Turner and John Brown.

Foner, Eric, ed., *Nat Turner.* **Prentice-Hall, 1971.** Reports on the life of Nat Turner, who led one of the most significant slave rebellions; includes his complete confessions and traces Turner's legend as it came to be widely known among Blacks and Whites.

Advanced

Lofton, John, *Insurrection in South Carolina: The Turbulent World of Denmark Vesey.* **Kent State Univ. Press, 1964.** Treats the unsuccessful slave revolt led by Vesey, himself a former slave, in 1882.

Starobin, Robert S., ed., *Denmark Vesey: The Slave Conspiracy of*

1882. **Prentice-Hall, 1970.** Brings together the relevant data on Vesey's rebellion; thorough.

James, Cyril L., *Black Jacobins: Toussaint L'Ouverture and the San Domingo Revolution*. Random House, 1963. An account of the successful Haitian revolution, which profoundly influenced white American fears of slave insurrections.

Wade, Richard, *Slavery in the Cities: The South, 1820–1860*. Oxford Univ. Press, 1967. An account arguing that the fear of slave insurrections was central to the conduct of slavery in the Southern cities.

THE FREE BLACK

Introductory

Bracey, John H., Jr., August Meier, and Elliott Rudwick, *Free Blacks in America: 1800–1860*. Wadsworth, 1971. Relates the history of those Black Americans who were not in bondage during the period of slavery; comprehensive.

Ruchames, Louis, ed., *Racial Thought in America: A Documentary History*. Grosset & Dunlap, 1969. Original source material that makes vivid reading; of interest particularly for the documentary sections providing insights into the treatment of free Blacks.

Advanced

Litwack, Leon F., *North of Slavery: The Negro in the Free States 1790–1860*. Univ. of Chicago Press, 1961. The standard work on the free Black of the North.

Franklin, John H., *Free Negro in North Carolina, 1790–1860*. Norton, 1971. A report on the problems faced by free Blacks in the South.

BLACK ABOLITIONISM

Introductory

Sorin, Gerald, *Abolitionism: A New Perspective*. Praeger, 1972. Summarizes and analyzes differing historical interpretations of abolitionism.

Douglass, Frederick, *The Life and Times of Frederick Douglass: The Complete Autobiography*. Macmillan, 1962. A former slave and a leading American abolitionist tells his own life story, including events that led to his becoming an advisor to President Lincoln and the U.S. minister to Haiti.

Advanced

Quarles, Benjamin, *Black Abolitionist.* Oxford Univ. Press, 1969. Summarizes the work of all the major Black abolitionists.

Quarles, Benjamin, *Blacks on John Brown.* Univ. of Illinois Press (hard cover), 1972. A report on a complex area of militant abolitionism.

Aptheker, Herbert, ed., *One Continual Cry: David Walker's Appeal to the Colored Citizens of the World 1829–1830.* Humanities, 1965. Edited writings of a leading militant Black abolitionist.

Bell, Howard, H., *The Negro Convention Movement, 1830–1861.* Arno, 1969. Treats an often neglected aspect of Black abolitionist agitation.

Gara, Larry, *The Liberty Line: The Legend of the Underground Railroad.* Univ. Press of Kentucky, 1967. A study of the people who secretly helped runaway slaves escape to the North.

Staudenraus, Philip J., *The African Colonization Movement 1816–1865.* Columbia Univ. Press, 1961. The standard work on the movement to transport free Blacks from the United States and settle them in Africa through the American Colonization Society; this effort led to the formation of an African nation, Liberia.

Bell, Howard H., ed., *Search for a Place: Black Separation and Africa.* Univ. of Michigan Press, 1971. Presents the writings of two Black Americans who became African colonists through the movement to return Blacks to Africa.

Duberman, Martin, *The Antislavery Vanguard.* Princeton Univ. Press, 1965. Treats every aspect of antislavery and civil rights efforts up to the contemporary period.

Berwanger, Eugene H., *The Frontier Against Slavery: Western Anti-Negro Prejudice and the Slavery Extension Controversy.* Univ. of Illinois Press, 1967. Reports in detail on the prevalent antislavery but racist sentiment of the western frontier.

THE CIVIL WAR

Introductory

Quarles, Benjamin, *The Negro in the Civil War.* Little, Brown, 1969. An account of the many roles played by Black Americans in the great conflict that led to emancipation.

Quarles, Benjamin, *Abraham Lincoln and the Negro.* Oxford Univ. Press, 1962. Analyzes Lincoln's evolving and often self-agonizing positions with respect to Black Americans.

Foner, Jack, *Blacks and the Military in American History: A New Perspective.* Praeger, 1974. Documents the previously ignored but significant roles played by Black Americans in the armed services.

Franklin, John Hope, ed., *The Emancipation Proclamation.* **Doubleday, 1963.** A brief examination, setting the historical context for the proclamation that freed the slaves.

Advanced

Cornish, Dudley, *The Sable Arm: Negro Troops in the Union Army 1861–1865.* **Norton, 1966.** A detailed report of the Black role in the Union Army throughout the Civil War.

McPherson, James, ed., *The Negro's Civil War: How American Negroes Felt and Acted.* **Random House, 1965.** A vivid anthology that brings together key documents of first-hand Black experience during the Civil War.

Wiley, Bell I., *Southern Negroes, 1861–1865.* **Yale Univ. Press, 1965.** A general account tracing the wartime disintegration of slavery.

Brewer, James H., *The Confederate Negro: Virginia's Craftsmen and Military Laborers, 1861–1865.* **Duke Univ. Press (hard cover), 1969.** Reports in detail on the role of some Black slaves in contributing to Confederate resistance.

Voegeli, V. Jacques, *Free But Not Equal: The Midwest and the Negro During the Civil War.* **Univ. of Chicago Press, 1970.** An analysis of the situation faced by newly freed Blacks in the Midwest.

Wagandt, C. L., *The Mighty Revolution: Negro Emancipation in Maryland 1862–1864.* **Johns Hopkins Univ. Press (hard cover), 1964.** An interesting account of emancipation in a border state not covered by the Emancipation Proclamation.

Higginson, Thomas Wentworth, *Army Life in a Black Regiment.* **Macmillan, 1962.** A portrayal made vivid by first-hand details.

RECONSTRUCTION

Introductory

Franklin, John Hope, *Reconstruction After the Civil War.* **Univ. of Chicago Press, 1961.** A treatment of the period of beginning freedom for the former slaves and of the turbulent reunion of the North and the South.

Cruden, Robert, *The Negro in Reconstruction.* **Prentice-Hall, 1969.** A balanced portrayal of the lives of Black Americans after the Civil War.

Bennett, Lerone, Jr., *Black Power U.S.A.: The Human Side of Reconstruction, 1867–1877.* **Johnson, 1967.** A popular account of the

Black struggle for political and economic independence during Reconstruction.

Advanced

Du Bois, W. E. B., *Black Reconstruction in America: 1860–1880.* **Atheneum, 1969.** A study by a major Black historian; first issued in 1935, it significantly affected the interpretation of Reconstruction.

Wilson, Theodore, *The Black Codes of the South.* **Univ. of Alabama Press (hard cover), 1966.** A summary report on the severely restrictive state laws enacted after the Civil War defining the status of the former slaves.

Rose, Willie Lee, ed., *Rehearsal for Reconstruction: The Port Royal Experiment.* **Bobbs-Merrill, 1964.** A suggestive collection of source documents on a neglected phase of Reconstruction.

Wood, Forrest G., *Black Scare: The Racist Response to Emancipation and Reconstruction.* **Univ. of California Press, 1968.** An easily read account of how Northerners responded to Reconstruction.

Nash, Gary B., and Richard Weiss, eds., *The Great Fear: Race in the Mind of America.* **Holt, Rinehart & Winston, 1970.** Provides comprehensive material on racist behavior toward Blacks.

Williamson, Joel, *After Slavery: The Negro in South Carolina During Reconstruction 1861–1877.* **Univ. of North Carolina Press, 1969.** A substantial study of the freedman.

Wharton, Vernon Lane, *The Negro in Mississippi; 1865–1890.* **Harper & Row, 1942.** A study of Black Americans in the decades after the Civil War; provides insights extending beyond Mississippi itself.

Singletary, Otis A., *Negro Militia and Reconstruction.* **McGraw-Hill, 1957.** A very brief account, but one that is helpful to an understanding of Southern white fears during the Reconstruction.

Uya, Okon Edet, *From Slavery to Public Service: Robert Smalls, 1839–1915.* **Oxford Univ. Press, 1971.** Tells of a fascinating Black leader in South Carolina.

Harris, William C., and John R. Lynch, eds., *The Facts of Reconstruction.* **Bobbs-Merrill, 1970.** A first-hand account by a Black participant in Reconstruction.

Bentley, George R., *A History of the Freedmen's Bureau.* **Octagon, 1970.** A thorough examination of the history of the federal bureau that, in 1866–1869, acted to aid and protect the newly freed slaves in the South.

Trelease, Allen W., *White Terror: The Ku Klux Klan Conspiracy and Southern Reconstruction.* **Harper & Row, 1971.** Reports on the violent methods used by the Ku Klux Klan to help end Reconstruction.

THE RISE OF SEGREGATION

Introductory

Woodward, C. Vann, *Origins of the New South, 1877–1913.* Louisiana State Univ. Press, 1972. An analysis of the post-Reconstruction period that traces the rise of segregation especially in connection with industrial and professional segments of the urban South.

Weinstein, Allen, and Frank Otto Gatell, eds., *The Segregation Era 1863–1954: A Modern Reader.* Oxford Univ. Press, 1970. An anthology of chapter-length excerpts on the Black as "separate but equal" in American society.

Bullock, Henry, *A History of Negro Education in the South: From 1619 to the Present.* Praeger, 1970. Reports on the limited opportunities in education for the Southern Black throughout the nation's history.

Advanced

Woodward, C. Vann, ed., *The Strange Career of Jim Crow.* Oxford Univ. Press, 1966. Analyzes the origins and long-continued practices of Black segregation in the South, popularly referred to as "Jim Crow."

Wynes, Charles, ed., *The Negro in the South since 1865.* Harper & Row, 1968. Scholarly essays about Blacks in the South through the segregation period.

Newby, I. A., *The Development of Segregationist Thought.* Dorsey, 1972. Provides insight into white thought on segregation.

Newby, I. A., *Jim Crow's Defense: Anti-Negro Thought in America, 1900–1930.* Louisiana State Univ. Press, 1965. A thorough survey.

Logan, Rayford, *The Betrayal of the Negro: From Rutherford B. Hayes to Woodrow Wilson.* Macmillan, 1965. A general account tracing the end of Black participation in southern politics and the rise of segregation.

Tindall, George B., *South Carolina Negroes, 1877–1900.* Louisiana State Univ. Press, 1966. Reports on the growth of segregation at the state level.

Wynes, Charles E., *Race Relations in Virginia, 1870–1902.* Rowman & Littlefield, 1971. A report on the development of segregation in the upper South.

Bond, Horace Mann, *Negro Education in Alabama: A Study in Cotton and Steel.* Atheneum, 1969. Analyzes the growth of segregation as it was developed in the schools.

Harlan, Louis R., *Separate and Unequal: Public School Campaigns and Racism in the Southern Seaboard States 1901–1915.*

Atheneum, 1968. A study of the development of school segregation in a number of states.

Leckie, William H., *The Buffalo Soldiers: A Narrative of the Negro Cavalry in the West.* **Univ. of Oklahoma Press (hard cover), 1970.** Tells the story of the Black Americans who served in the U.S. Cavalry during the settlement of the far West; fascinating.

Durham, Philip and Everett Jones, *Negro Cowboys.* **Dodd, Mead (hard cover), 1965.** A little-known but illuminating aspect of the Black experience.

PROGRESSIVISM AND THE BLACK

Introductory

Meier, August, *Negro Thought in America: Racial Ideologies in the Age of Booker T. Washington 1880–1915.* **Univ. of Michigan Press, 1963.** Traces the improvement in Black American rights during the Progressive era, outlining both the ideologies that favored integration—those of Booker T. Washington, for example—and the thinking of Black separatists.

Du Bois, W. E. B., *The Souls of Black Folk.* **Fawcett World Library, 1970.** States the viewpoint and hopes of Black Americans in the era of Progressivism.

Advanced

Harlan, Louis R., *Booker T. Washington: The Making of a Black Leader.* **Oxford Univ. Press (hard cover), 1972.** A comprehensive biography of a famed Black educator and lecturer who, in 1881, organized the Tuskegee Institute as a school where Blacks could gain self-respect and financial independence through industrial training.

Washington, Booker T., *Up From Slavery.* **Dodd, Mead, 1972.** Booker T. Washington's autobiography.

Broderick, Francis, *W. E. B. Du Bois: Propagandist of the Negro Protest.* **Atheneum, 1968.** A study of an impassioned exponent for the full equality of the Black in America.

Du Bois, W. E. B., *Autobiography of W. E. Burghardt Du Bois: A Soliloquy on Viewing My Life From the Last Decade of Its First Century,* **ed. Herbert Aptheker. International, 1968.** Dubois's autobiography; important for a full understanding of this Black leader.

Kellogg, Charles Flint, *NAACP: A History of the National Association for the Advancement of Colored People.* **Johns Hopkins Univ. Press, 1967.** Reports on a pioneering organization dedicated to winning full equality for Black Americans.

Rudwick, Elliott M., *Race Riot at East St. Louis, July 2, 1917.*

Atheneum, 1972. Analyzes the violence directed toward the Black in a typical major race riot.

White, Walter, *Rope and Faggot: A Biography of Judge Lynch.* Arno, 1969. A scathing report on lynching (first issued in 1929) by a nationally known leader of the NAACP.

THE FIRST MIGRATION NORTH

Introductory

Foner, Philip, *Organized Labor and the Black Worker, 1619–1973.* Praeger (hard cover), 1973. A summary of the relations between Black Americans and organized labor throughout American History.

Advanced

Spero, Sterling D., and Abram Harris, *The Black Worker: The Negro and the Labor Movement.* Atheneum, 1968. A collection of essays by scholars on the unequal treatment of Blacks by the labor movement in America.

Osofsky, Gilbert, *Harlem: The Making of a Ghetto, 1890–1930.* Harper & Row, 1966. An engrossing account of how a segregated Black neighborhood was formed in a Northern city.

Spear, Allan, *Black Chicago: The Making of a Negro Ghetto 1890–1920.* Univ. of Chicago Press, 1969. Reports in depth on the growth of the Black ghetto in Chicago.

Kennedy, Louise V., *The Negro Peasant Turns Cityward.* McGraw-Hill, 1930. An account tracing the first major migration of Blacks northward in the early decades of this century.

Johnson, James Weldon, *Black Manhattan.* Atheneum, 1968. A major work on the Harlem Renaissance in artistic and cultural life.

Jackson, Kenneth T., *The Ku Klux Klan in the City,* ed. Richard C. Wade. Oxford Univ. Press, 1967. Reports on anti-Black sentiment in cities of the Northern United States during the 1920s.

GARVEYISM

Advanced

Redkey, Edwin S., *Black Exodus: Black Nationalist and Back-to-Africa Movements, 1890–1910.* Yale Univ. Press, 1969. Provides useful background for understanding the Garvey movement.

Cronon, E. David, *Black Moses: The Story of Marcus Garvey and the Universal Negro Improvement Association.* Univ. of Wisconsin Press, 1969. Reports on the efforts of Garvey, the best-known separatist leader of the 1920s, to form a state in Africa settled by Black Americans.

THE HARLEM RENAISSANCE

Introductory

Huggins, Nathan Irvin. *Harlem Renaissance.* **Oxford Univ. Press, 1973.** Outlines the major trends of the cultural rebirth of the 1920s in the Black community which came to be known as the Harlem Renaissance.

Locke, Alain, ed, *The New Negro: An Interpretation.* **Atheneum, 1968.** A documentary collection on Black American art, literature, and music from 1915 to 1925.

Advanced

Emanuel, John A., and Theodore Gross, eds., *Dark Symphony: Literature in America.* **Macmillan (Free Press), 1968.** An anthology that provides an introduction to Harlem Renaissance writers.

THE NEW DEAL AND THE BLACK

Introductory

Sternsher, Bernard, ed., *The Negro in Depressions and War: Prelude to Revolution.* **Watts, 1969.** Reports the extremely difficult conditions of Black American life during the 1930s and 1940s, before the Black civil rights movement that began in the 1950s.

Advanced

Carter, Dan T., *Scottsboro: A Tragedy of the American South.* **Oxford Univ. Press, 1971.** A report on a widely celebrated trial of the 1930s that provides revealing insights into Southern Black life in that period.

Myrdal, Gunnar, *An American Dilemma: The Negro Problem and Modern Democracy.* **Harper & Row, 1962.** A landmark work by a Swedish sociologist, analyzing the American race problem from the outside.

Cruse, Harold, *The Crisis of the Negro Intellectual.* **Morrow, 1967.** Tells of a Black's relationship with the Communist Party.

Dollard, John, *Caste and Class in a Southern Town.* **Doubleday, 1957.** A study of life in a small Southern town.

Conrad, David Eugene, *The Forgotten Farmers: The Story of Sharecroppers in the New Deal.* **Univ. of Illinois Press, 1965.** A study of the collapse of the system of tenant farming in the South.

Rosengarten, Theodore, *All God's Dangers: The Life of Nate Shaw.* **Knopf (hard cover), 1974.** An edited transcript of the reminiscences of an aged Black American who had broken out of sharecropping in Alabama in the 1930s and successfully resisted many efforts by his white neighbors to destroy his independence in farming and in spirit.

WORLD WAR II

Introductory

Lee, Ulysses G., *The Employment of Negro Troops.* **U. S. Govt. Printing Office, 1966.** Reports in detail on the organization of a segregated Army in World War II.

Advanced

Garfinkel, Herbert, *When Negroes March.* **Atheneum, 1969.** An account of the 1940–1942 March on Washington Movement; striking, rich in detail.

CIVIL RIGHTS

Introductory

Muse, Benjamin, *The American Negro Revolution: From Nonviolence to Black Power, 1963–1967.* **Citadel, 1970.** Traces the evolution of the Civil Rights movement from nonviolence to Black Militance.

Lewis, David L., *King: A Critical Biography.* **Praeger, 1970.** Outlines Martin Luther King's career, a major part of which involved his leadership of the nonviolent civil rights movement for which he was awarded the Nobel Prize for Peace.

Lynch, Hollis, ed., *The Black Urban Condition.* **Crowell, 1973.** Explores the ramifications of the vast Black migration into cities.

Miller, Loren, *The Petitioners: The Story of the Supreme Court and the Negro.* **Pantheon (hard cover), 1966.** A readily understood survey of the Court's role in advancing civil rights since 1954.

Advanced

Krislow, Samuel, *The Negro in Federal Employment: The Quest for Equal Opportunity.* **Univ. of Minnesota Press (hard cover), 1967.** Reports on Blacks in the federal civil service; thorough.

Zinn, Howard, *SNCC: The New Abolitionists.* **Beacon, 1965.** Deals with the development of the 1960s Black militants by focusing on one of their leading organizations.

Bartley, Norman V., *The Rise of Massive Resistance: Race and Politics in the South During the 1950s.* **Louisiana State Univ. Press, 1969.** An account of the rise of the Black civil rights movement led most notably by Martin Luther King.

Silberman, Charles, *Crisis in Black and White.* Random House, **1964.** A suggestive analysis of the developing civil rights crisis of the 1960s.

BLACK MILITANCY

Introductory

Malcolm X, *Autobiography of Malcolm X.* Ballantine, **1973.** The life story of one of the most influential and electrifying Black militants of the 1950s and early 1960s who played a major role in shifting the civil rights movement from the nonviolence of King to credos of Black Power.

Cleaver, Eldridge, *Soul on Ice.* Dell, **1970.** Autobiographical and analytic essays written by a California leader of the militant Black Panther movement while he was in jail during the 1960s; the essays are widely admired for literary skills and power as well as content.

Advanced

Barbour, Floyd, ed., *The Black Power Revolt.* Macmillan, **1969.** A study of how Black Power supplanted the civil rights movement.

Wright, Nathan, *Black Power and Urban Unrest.* Hawthorn, **1967.** A report that treats the relationship of Black militance to urban protest and riot in such cities as Newark, Los Angeles, and Chicago.

Lincoln, C. Eric, *The Black Muslims in America.* Beacon, **1973.** Describes the character and influence of the Mohammedan religious movement among contemporary Black Americans.

THE BLACK NOW

Introductory

Clark, Kenneth, *Dark Ghetto: Dilemmas of Social Power.* Harper & Row, **1965.** An analysis of the conditions of ghetto life today by a famed Black psychologist whose testimony played a pivotal part in the U. S. Supreme Court Decision of 1954 on school desegregation.

Frazier, E. Franklin, *Black Bourgeoisie: The Rise of a New Middle Class in the U. S.* Macmillan, **1962.** A sociological analysis tracing the rise of the Black middle class into the 1960s, reporting on actual economic conditions and social status and on the values held by this group of Black Americans.

Frazier, E. Franklin, *The Negro Church in America.* Schocken, **1973.** A brief work delineating the religious life of the Black by one of America's leading Black sociologists.

Advanced

Feinman, Louis A., *Negroes and Jobs: A Book of Readings.* Univ. of Michigan Press, 1968. A work that treats the long-standing problem of Black unemployment.

Kardiner, Abram, and Lionel Ovesey, *The Mark of Oppression: Explorations in Personality of the American Negro.* World, 1964. A psychological study of the effects of discrimination on Blacks.

Grier, William H., and Price M. Cobbs, *Black Rage.* Bantam, 1969. A psychiatric analysis exploring the dimensions of the emotional conflicts and desperation of the Black man in America.

Chapter Thirteen

POLITICAL SCIENCE
*". . . what human beings should make
of their common life together"*

Editorial Advisor:
Mary L. Shanley
Department of Political Science
Vassar College

INTRODUCTION

Politics affects everyone. Politics determines not only who gets elected
to public office, but also what taxes each of us pays, what services we
are entitled to, whether our laws are enacted and enforced fairly, and so
on almost indefinitely. The study of politics is therefore concerned
with those human interactions that influence the quality of our common life.

Often people talk of the "politics" of a fraternity or sorority rush
week, of the decisions taken by a church or business organization, or
even of family deliberations. These activities are political insofar as
they involve the discussion of disputed values or priorities in the
process of allocating the goods that the group has at its disposal.
Usually, however, the study of politics is confined to the decisions of
government (be it a town, state, national, or international body), while
fraternities and families are "political" by analogy to the activity of the
state. Decisions of state or governmental institutions differ from decisions made by other groups both because they affect a broader range of
people and also because they are authoritative: they are backed by the
power of the political, legal, and police or military forces of the government. Politics involves the attempt by the community or its representatives to resolve conflict that grows from different interests and
values held by members of the political community.

Since it deals with the concerns of our common life, the academic
field of Political Science covers a great deal of ground. One way of
dividing the field is by geographical unit. American politics includes
the study of American national, state, and municipal governments and
laws; comparative politics focuses on the governing process in coun-

tries other than the United States; international politics deals with the relations among nations, the formation and execution of foreign policy, and the operation of such international organizations as the United Nations.

These divisions based on geography dominated the field of political science at its inception in the late nineteenth and early twentieth centuries, when the focus of study was primarily on differences in national political systems. With time, however, new areas of study have arisen, many of which cut across these traditional categories.

Some political scientists are interested in the political behavior of individuals rather than in the organization of institutions and therefore study the economic, social, and psychological determinants of political behavior in whatever context it appears. Others have undertaken the challenge not simply of analyzing political systems as they are today, but also of explaining the process of political change, development, disintegration, and revolution. Looking beyond formal or constitutionally sanctioned aspects of government, still others study the impact on government of political parties, factions, and interest groups which are not part of the formal governmental system. Studies by all these types of political scientists use data from a variety of countries and cultures in order to try to reach conclusions that will be valid for a number of national settings.

The rise of the civil rights, New Left, and other political movements of the 1960s encouraged the development of policy-oriented studies by American political scientists. An understanding of contemporary issues such as ecology, poverty, urban development and urban deterioration, ethnic politics, and women's liberation is clearly necessary for those who want to think deeply about factors that will affect the quality of the common life that people will lead in years to come.

It is impossible to study any of these subjects, however, without raising profound questions of value. The study of politics involves not only gathering reliable information about the actual functioning of different governments and societies, but also asks, "What kinds of governments *ought to* exist, and what kinds of policies *should* they pursue?" Here the works of the great political philosophers become central to the study of politics. Plato's *Republic*, St. Augustine's *City of God*, Machiavelli's *The Prince*, and Marx's *Capital* pose profound questions concerning the basis and ends of people's common life.

Nevertheless it is a mistake to approach the classic works of political theory thinking that they will contain the final and absolute answers to these questions. *The Republic* attempts to answer the question, "What is justice?" but many have disagreed violently with Plato's answer. *The Prince* asks, "What constitutes the proper exercise of political power?" but Machiavelli's analysis has outraged many people through the centuries. *Capital* and the *Communist Manifesto* contain Marx's thoughts on the forces that determine the course of history, but Marx by no means converted the world. Such contemporary theorists as Herbert Marcuse, Hannah Arendt, and John Rawls continue to raise these and other questions and to share their own profound insights into the human political condition. Reading their works is a way of entering into a dialogue with these philosophers and of learning how to ask and respond to such questions oneself.

The study of politics also raises questions of epistemology (how we know certain things to be true) and methodology (how we can best find out whatever it is we want to know). Any empirical study that attempts to gather information and organize it into useful knowledge must ask what material is relevant to its project and why, must make decisions about how much quantitative material can be obtained and how much of it will be useful, and must decide how much of the human behavior it is dealing with is subject to scientific analysis. These issues arise whether the study is of American voting behavior, African tribal organization, collectivization in China, or parliamentary politics in Italy. Political science attempts to discover those laws of human behavior which have a bearing on the authoritative allocation of values in society. One of the questions that political scientists must continuously pose for themselves, therefore, is whether such "laws" are in fact discoverable, and if so, how they may best be discovered.

The political theorist no less than the empirical researcher faces epistemological questions. How does anyone know what is the right, or the just, or the good thing for society or the individual? Is it possible to arrive at truth concerning such matters, or only to hold subjective opinions about them? Does what is "just" change with time, or is it a constant and unchanging value? In addition to attempting to illuminate the values by which the policy will conduct its collective life, the political theorist must question the basis of those values.

The study of politics aims at an accurate description and understanding of political phenomena that affect all people in almost every aspect of their daily lives. More than that, it tries to discern what is common to the myriad of different kinds of political activities in which people engage that makes those activities all "political." Finally, it attempts to determine what human beings should make of their common life together and what values they should espouse and pursue. It is a rich, rewarding and vital area of study.

The following bibliography is divided into five sections. "American Government" includes books on the institutions of American government (the presidency, the congress, and the courts), and on electoral behavior, political behavior, and political socialization in the United States. "Comparative Government" lists general works on comparative politics, on the methodology of comparative politics, on political development and modernization, and on comparative political structures and processes. "International Relations" includes books on international politics, on the formation of U. S. foreign policy, and on international organizations and international law. "Political Theory" lists some of the classic texts of political philosophers past and contemporary and suggests a few useful interpretive essays. "Political Analysis and Methodology" includes works that discuss the epistemological and methodological questions raised by the study of politics. In addition, a list of the leading journals of political science is appended to the bibliography; they are an excellent guide to the most recent work in the field.

BIBLIOGRAPHY

NOTE   Mary L. Shanley thanks her colleagues in the Department of Political Science at Vassar College for their suggestions for this bibliography.

AMERICAN GOVERNMENT

General Books

Dahl, Robert A., *Preface to Democratic Theory.* Univ. of Chicago Press, 1956. A thought-provoking discussion of the premises of the American democratic system.

Dolbeare, Kenneth, and Murray J. Edelman, *American Politics: Policies, Power, and Change,* 2nd ed. Heath, 1974. An introductory text.

Dye, Thomas R., and L. Harmon Ziegler, Jr., *The Irony of Democracy,* 3rd ed. Duxbury, 1975. An introduction to American politics which examines the role of elites in the American political system.

Schattschneider, Elmer E., *The Semi-Sovereign People: A Realist's View of Democracy in America.* Holt, Rinehart & Winston, 1961. A stimulating consideration of the extent to which a people can achieve self-government.

The Executive

Barber, James D., *The Presidential Character: Predicting Performance in the White House.* Prentice-Hall, 1973. Applies psychological insight to the study of presidential character and performance. INTERMEDIATE.

Cronin, Thomas, *The State of the Presidency.* Little, Brown, 1975. An evaluation of the contemporary presidency. INTERMEDIATE.

Kennedy, Robert F., *Thirteen Days: A Memoir of the Cuban Missile Crisis,* ed. Richard Neustadt and Graham Allison. Norton, 1971. A participant's account of the Cuban Missile Crisis from the U. S. point of view; an inside view of Presidential decision-making. INTRODUCTORY.

Neustadt, Richard, Presidential Power: *The Politics of Leadership.* Wiley, 1960. Using case studies of controversial decisions by modern presidents, Neustadt argues the thesis that presidential power is the power to persuade others to do what you want them to do. INTRODUCTORY-INTERMEDIATE.

Polsby, Nelson W., and Aaron Wildavsky, *Presidential Elections: Strategies of American Electoral Politics.* Scribner's, 1972. A study of the strategic considerations in presidential campaigns. INTERMEDIATE.

Strum, Philippa, *Presidential Power and American Democracy.* Goodyear, 1971. Argues persuasively that the presidency has accumulated too much power for the well-being of the nation. Chapters on Vietnam. INTRODUCTORY.

White, Theodore H., *The Making of the President: 1960;* NAL, 1967. *The Making of the President: 1964;* NAL, 1966. *The Making of the President: 1968;* Atheneum (hard cover) 1969. *The Making of the President: 1972;* Bantam, 1973. Narrative case studies of presidential election campaigns of the major parties.

Wildavsky, Aaron, *The Politics of the Budgetary Process.* Little, Brown, 1974. A readable and informative book on the federal bureaucracy. INTRODUCTORY-INTERMEDIATE.

Wills, Gary, *Nixon Agonistes: The Crisis of the Self-Made Man.* NAL, 1971. Analyzes the Nixon character and American political behavior; written before Watergate.

The Congress

Bibby, John, and Roger Davidson, *On Capitol Hill: Studies in the Legislative Process.* Holt, Rinehart & Winston, 1972. An introduction to the American legislative process.

Dexter, Lewis A., *The Sociology and Politics of Congress.* Rand McNally, 1969. An introduction to congress which brings sociological insight to bear on the actions and interactions of the legislators.

Green, Mark *et al., Who Runs Congress?* Bantam, 1972. A journalistic account of Capitol Hill lobbying and lobbyists, with a concluding chapter on citizens' lobbying. INTRODUCTORY.

Harris, Richard, *Decision.* Ballantine, 1971. A case study of the struggle inside and outside the senate to defeat President Nixon's nomination of G. Harrold Carswell to the Supreme Court. INTRODUCTORY-INTERMEDIATE.

Mayhew, David, Congress: *The Electoral Connection.* Yale Univ. Press, 1974. Studies congressional behavior as a response to electoral exigencies. INTERMEDIATE.

Polsby, Nelson, *Congress and the Presidency.* Prentice-Hall, 1971. A short book on congress, the presidency, and the relations between them. Contains a summary of the budgetary process. INTRODUCTORY.

Weaver, Warren, *Both Your Houses: The Truth About Congress.* Praeger, 1973. A critical look at congress. INTRODUCTORY-INTERMEDIATE.

Wolfinger, Raymond E., *Readings on Congress.* Prentice-Hall, 1971. A collection of articles on the congress. INTERMEDIATE.

The Courts

Abraham, Henry J., *The Judiciary: The Supreme Court in the Governmental Process,* 3rd ed. Allyn & Bacon, 1973. An introduction to the Supreme Court as part of the larger political system.

Bickel, Alexander, *The Supreme Court and the Idea of Progress.* **Harper & Row, 1970.** Analyzes and evaluates the performance of the Warren Court, often critically. INTERMEDIATE.

Eisenstein, James. *Politics and the Legal Process.* **Harper & Row, 1973.** A book on the functioning of the courts (both federal and state) in the political system. INTRODUCTORY.

Jacob, Herbert, *Justice in America.* **Little, Brown, 1972.** Politically oriented analysis of the American system of courts, federal and state. Discusses lawyers and their organizations, trials, negotiations, and juries; also treats bail and prosecution.

Lewis, Anthony, *Gideon's Trumpet.* **Random House, 1964.** A case study of a Supreme Court decision. Exciting legal drama. INTRODUCTORY.

McCloskey, Robert G., *The American Supreme Court.* **Univ. of Chicago Press, 1960.** A historical interpretation, through a study of major cases, of the Supreme Court's part in constructing the U. S. Constitution. An overview of constitutional and social history. Contains a bibliographic essay. INTRODUCTORY-INTERMEDIATE.

Elections, Political Behavior, and Political Socialization

Campbell, Angus, *et al., The American Voter: An Abridgement.* **Wiley, 1966.** Classic study of who votes in the United States, and why. INTERMEDIATE.

Greenstein, Fred, *Children and Politics,* rev. ed. **Yale Univ. Press, 1970.** A study of the political socialization and attitudes of American elementary-school children. INTERMEDIATE.

Jaros, Dean, *Socialization to Politics.* **Praeger, 1973.** Somewhat technical introduction to the concept and literature of political socialization. Focuses on family, school, and peer group influences. Outlines methodological problems. INTERMEDIATE.

Nimmo, Dan, *The Political Persuaders: The Techniques of Modern Election Campaigns.* **Prentice-Hall, 1970.** A realistic examination of the techniques of modern election campaigns in the United States. Suggests that modern campaign technology may threaten our democratic system.

Pomper, Gerald, *Voters' Choice: Varieties of American Electoral Behavior.* **Dodd-Mead, 1975.** Up-to-date study of the behavior of the American electorate.

Scammon, Richard, and Ben Wattenberg, *The Real Majority: How the Silent Center of the American Electorate Chooses its President.* **Coward, McCann, 1970.** Examines the demography of the American electorate, assessing the strategy of presidential candidates in the 1960s and 1970s. Uses statistics and quantitative material. INTERMEDIATE.

Wolfinger, Raymond, ed., *Readings in Political Behavior.* Prentice-Hall, 1970. A collection of articles on political behavior. INTRODUCTORY-INTERMEDIATE.

Public Policy

NOTE The following chapters should be consulted for areas dealing with public policy matters of importance to political science. American History and Black American History: poverty and ethnic politics; Economics: public finance and welfare economics; Environmental Studies, Economics: ecology. Women's Studies: women's rights.

COMPARATIVE GOVERNMENT

Survey Texts

Almond, Gabriel *et al.*, eds., *Comparative Politics Today: A World View.* Little, Brown, 1974. A collection of essays on comparative politics.

Beer, Samuel *et al., Patterns of Government: The Major Political Systems of Europe, 3rd ed.* Random House (hard cover), 1973. Studies of Britain, France, Germany, and the Soviet Union, with an introductory chapter on modern political development. Sections available as separate paperbacks. INTRODUCTORY.

Carter, Gwendolyn, *Major Foreign Powers.* Harcourt Brace Jovanovich, 1972. An introductory text. Certain sections (France, United Kingdom, Soviet Union) available as separate paperbacks. INTRODUCTORY.

Comparative Method

Bill, James A., and Robert Hardbrave, *Comparative Politics: The Quest for Theory.* Merrill, 1973. Presents and analyzes the basic concepts and approaches used in the study of comparative politics. Provides a critical guide to the literature in an extensive bibliography. INTERMEDIATE.

Deutsch, Karl, *et al., The Nerves of Government: Models of Political Communication and Control.* Macmillan (Free Press), 1963. Because Deutsch sees political systems as steering and manipulating human behavior, he applies the insights of cybernetics to the study of politics. ADVANCED.

Holt, Robert, and John Turner, eds., *The Methodology of Comparative Political Research.* Macmillan (Free Press), 1970. A collection of eight papers reflecting on methodological problems of comparative research. ADVANCED.

Political Development and Modernization

Black, Cyril, *The Dynamics of Modernization: A Study in Comparative History.* Harper & Row, 1968. A provocative book by a historian who views modernization on a continuum from ancient past to the future in an effort to describe the dynamics of social change. INTERMEDIATE/ADVANCED.

Enloe, Cynthia H., *Ethnic Conflict and Political Development: An Analytic Study.* Little, Brown, 1973. Uses 57 different cases of ethnic conflict to try to break away from the bias toward regarding the nation-state as the fundamental political unit. Analyzes the role of ethnic minorities in political life and development. INTERMEDIATE.

Finkle, Jason L., and Richard W. Gable, *Political Development and Social Change,* 2nd ed. Wiley, 1971. A collection of 45 readings which seeks to provide a conceptual framework for understanding political development and its relationship to other social and economic transformations. ADVANCED.

Huntington, Samuel, *Political Order in Changing Societies.* Yale Univ. Press, 1968. A discussion of political development which deals both with "modernizing nations" and with the United States and Europe in order to explain the process of modernization. INTERMEDIATE.

Rustow, Dankwart A., *A World of Nations: Problems of Political Modernization.* Brookings Institution, 1967. Examines the political problems of modernizing nations. Studies the relative appeals of communism and democracy to these nations.

Political Structures and Processes

Almond, Gabriel, and Sidney Verba, *The Civic Culture: Political Attitudes and Democracy in Five Countries.* Princeton Univ. Press, 1963. Describes basic political attitudes in Britain, the United States, Germany, Italy, and Mexico. Data are drawn from surveys, and the book contains a discussion of cross-national application of survey research methods. INTERMEDIATE.

Brzezinski, Zbigniew, and Samuel Huntington, *Political Power: USA/USSR.* Viking, 1965. Compares the political systems of the United States and the Soviet Union, describing their strengths and weaknesses, and their similarities as well as their differences. INTRODUCTORY.

Crozier, Michael, *The Bureaucratic Phenomenon.* Univ. of Chicago Press, 1967. A sociologist's views of bureaucratic functioning, based primarily on studies done in France but drawing on other works as well. Shows how organizational patterns are related to cultural features. INTERMEDIATE.

Ehrmann, Henry W., ed., *Interest Groups on Four Continents.* Univ. of Pittsburgh Press, 1958. Discusses the role, organization, and operation of interest groups in Australia, Finland, France, Germany, Great Britain, Japan, Sweden, the United States, and Yugoslavia; also contains a general discussion of pressure groups and the formation of public policy. INTERMEDIATE.

Gurr, Ted Robert, *Why Men Rebel*. Princeton Univ. Press, 1970. Explores the individual and social sources of violence in politics— psychological, socioeconomic, and political. INTERMEDIATE-ADVANCED.

Huntington, Samuel, and Clement Moore, eds., *Authoritarian Politics in Modern Society: The Dynamics of Established One-Party Systems*. Basic, 1970. A collection of articles on one-party political systems which analyze the growth of such systems and their stability or instability. INTERMEDIATE-ADVANCED.

Janowitz, Morris, *The Military in the Political Development of the New Nations: An Essay in Comparative Analysis*. Univ. of Chicago Press, 1963. A comparative analysis of the role of the armed forces in the political development of the so-called new nations, focusing on the potentials and limitations of the military for political leadership. INTERMEDIATE.

Kornberg, Allen, ed., *Legislatures in Comparative Perspective*. MacKay, 1973. A comparison of the legislative systems of different nations.

Lipset, Seymour Martin, *Political Man: The Social Bases of Politics*. Doubleday, 1960. Analyzes how social systems support (or undermine) democratic institutions and behavior and how people are led to participate in political life. INTERMEDIATE.

INTERNATIONAL RELATIONS

General Books

Aron, Raymond, *Peace and War: A Theory of International Relations*, tr. Richard Howard and Annette Baker Fox. Doubleday, 1966. Addresses the question of whether peaceful coexistence without mutual annihilation will be possible for today's nation-states; a theoretical work. INTERMEDIATE-ADVANCED.

Brodie, Bernard, *War and Politics*. Macmillan, 1974. A consideration of why human beings go to war. A historical section contains chapters on the Second World War, Korea, and Vietnam; a theoretical section examines theories about the causes of war.

Keohane, Robert, and Joseph S. Nye, Jr., eds., *Transnational Relations and World Politics*. Harvard Univ. Press, 1972. A collection of papers which studies international relations of nongovernmental groups: scientists, foundations, labor groups, churches, revolutionary organizations. INTERMEDIATE.

Knorr, Klaus, and Sidney Verba, eds., *The International System:*

Theoretical Essays. Princeton Univ. Press, 1961. A collection of readings on theories about the international system. INTERMEDIATE.

Lijphart, Arend, ed., *World Politics: The Writings of Theorists and Practitioners, Ancient and Modern,* 2nd ed. Allyn & Bacon, 1971. A consideration of important issues in international relations (nationalism, war, collective security, balance of power, and the like) through the writings of such political theorists as Plato, Machiavelli, Lenin, and Dag Hammarskjold. INTRODUCTORY-INTERMEDIATE.

McLellan, D. S., et al., *Theory and Practice of International Relations.* Prentice-Hall, 1970. A compilation of writings by leading students of international affairs, including psychologists, sociologists, and anthropologists. INTRODUCTORY-INTERMEDIATE.

Morgenthau, Hans, *Politics Among Nations: The Struggle for Power and Peace,* 5th ed. Knopf, 1974. First published in 1948 and revised since then, this is a classic study of the role of power in international politics.

Pfaltzgraff, Robert, ed., *Politics and the International System,* 2nd ed. Lippincott, 1972.

Shelling, Thomas, *Strategy of Conflict.* Oxford Univ. Press, 1963. A pioneering, clearly written book on game theory and the study of international politics. INTRODUCTORY-INTERMEDIATE.

Stoessinger, John, *The Might of Nations,* 3rd ed. Random House, 1969. Studies the international struggle for power, emphasizing the role of the United Nations in international relations. INTRODUCTORY.

Formation of United States Foreign Policy

Allison, Graham, *Essence of Decision: Explaining the Cuban Missle Crisis.* Little, Brown, 1971. Uses the Cuban Missile Crisis as a case study to analyze how political scientists study foreign policy decision-making. ADVANCED.

Bliss, Howard, and M. Glen Johnson, *Beyond the Water's Edge: America's Foreign Policy.* Lippincott, 1975. A study of United States foreign policy-making, and a good introduction to the literature. INTRODUCTORY.

Brown, Seyom, *The Faces of Power: Constancy and Change in United States Foreign Policy From Truman to Johnson.* Columbia Univ. Press, 1968. A history based on security and balance of power themes. Interesting for students of the Cold War. INTERMEDIATE.

Kolko, Joyce, and Gabriel Kolko, *The Limits of Power: The World and United States Foreign Policy.* Harper & Row, 1972. A major reevaluation of the Cold War which focuses on the role played by United States economic interests in postwar power politics.

Kulski, W. W., *International Politics in a Revolutionary Age,* 2nd

rev. ed. Lippincott, 1968. A clear description of the problems and policy alternatives in contemporary international affairs. INTRODUCTORY.

Rosenau, James, ed., *International Politics and Foreign Policy: A Reader in Research and Theory.* Macmillan (Free Press), 1969. Collects a great many leading articles on comparative politics. Particularly strong on the theory and research techniques of the study of comparative politics. INTERMEDIATE.

Tucker, Robert W., *The Radical Left and American Foreign Policy.* Johns Hopkins Univ. Press, 1971. A provocative evaluation of the arguments of the radical left which both praises and criticizes a Marxian analysis of United States foreign policy. INTERMEDIATE.

Wallace, William, *Foreign Policy and the Political Process.* Macmillan, 1971. A discussion of the nature of foreign policy, containing a summary of the literature.

International Organization and International Law

Brierly, James L., *The Law of Nations: An Introduction to the International Law of Peace,* 6th ed. Oxford Univ. Press, 1963.

Clark, Grenville, and Louis Sohn, *Introduction to World Peace Through World Law.* World Without War Publishers, 1973. A study of international law and the possibilities of peaceful settlement of international disputes through a legal system. INTRODUCTORY-INTERMEDIATE.

Claude, Inis, *The Changing United Nations.* Random House, 1967. INTRODUCTORY-INTERMEDIATE.

Claude, Inis, *Swords into Plowshares: The Problems and Progress of International Organization,* 4th ed. Random House, 1971.

Haas, Ernst B., *Beyond the Nation State: Functionalism and International Organization.* Stanford Univ. Press, 1964. Studies international integration and assesses particularly the contribution of the International Labor Organization to international integration. INTERMEDIATE.

Henkin, Louis, *How Nations Behave,* Praeger, 1968. A study of the way international law influences the behavior and relations of nation states. INTRODUCTORY.

Kelsen, Hans, *Principles of International Law,* 2nd ed. Holt, Rinehart & Winston, 1966.

Stoessinger, John, *The United Nations and the Superpowers: United States-Soviet Interaction at the United Nations.* Random House, 1966. Studies the effect of United States-Russian struggle in the United Nations on international affairs and on the UN's strength. INTERMEDIATE.

POLITICAL THEORY

NOTE The works of major Western political theorists are given below, with the dates of their authors' lives and of their original publication. These books examine the philosophical questions raised by human social and political life. They discuss the nature of the common good; the need for authority; the problem of justice in society; and the meaning of such concepts as equality, liberty, and rights and obligation. These books are both of historical interest and important to the understanding of the enduring problems of politics.

Classic Works (arranged chronologically)

Thucydides (c.460–c.400 B.C.), *The Peloponnesian War* (c.431–402 B.C.), tr. E. Crawley, intro. J. H. Finley, Jr. Modern Library (College Editions), 1951.

Bloom, Allan, tr., *The Republic of Plato (Plato,* c.428–347 B.C.; The Republic, c.388–366 B.C.). Basic, 1971.

Aristotle (384–322 B.C.), *The Politics* (c.336–322 B.C.), tr. Ernest Baker. Oxford Univ. Press, 1946.

St. Augustine (354–430), *City of God* (c. 413–426), ed. and intro. V. J. Bourke. Doubleday, 1950.

Aquinas, St. Thomas (1224–1274), *The Political Ideas of St. Thomas Aquinas* (c.1260–1272), ed. and intro. Dino Bigongiari. Hafner, 1953.

Machiavelli, Niccolo (1469–1527), *The Prince* (1512–1513), tr. G. Bull. Penguin, 1961.

Machiavelli, Niccolo (1469–1527), *The Discourses* (1513–1517), ed. B. Crick. Penguin, 1971.

Hobbes, Thomas (1588–1679), *Leviathan: On the Matter, Forme and Power of a Commonwealth Ecclesiastical and Civil* (1651), ed. M. Oakeshott. Collier-Macmillan, 1968.

Locke, John (1632–1704), *Two Treatises of Government* (1690), ed. P. Laslett. Cambridge Univ. Press, 1960.

Rousseau, Jean-Jacques (1712–1778), *The Social Contract (1762) and Discourse on the Origin of Inequality* (1755), ed. L. Crocker. Pocket, 1971.

Rousseau, Jean-Jacques (1712–1778), *Two Discourses* (I: 1750; II: 1755), ed. R. Masters. St. Martin's, 1964.

Hamilton, Alexander, James Madison, and John Jay, *The Federalist Papers* (1787–1788), ed. Clinton Rossiter. NAL, 1961.

Hegel, G. W. F. (1770–1831), *Reason in History* (1837), tr. Robert S. Hartman, Bobbs-Merrill, 1953.

Mill, John Stuart (1806–1873), *On Liberty* (1859), ed. Currin V. Shields. Bobbs-Merrill, 1956.

Tucker, Robert C., ed., *The Marx-Engels Reader* (Karl Marx, 1818–1883; Friedrich Engels 1820–1895). Norton, 1972.

Nietzsche, Friedrich (1844–1900), *The Use and Abuse of History* (1874), tr. Adrian Collins. Bobbs-Merrill, 1957.

Arendt, Hannah, *One-Dimensional Man.* Beacon, 1964.

Rawls, John, *A Theory of Justice.* Harvard Univ. Press, 1971.

Nozick, Robert, *Anarchy, The State, and Utopia.* Basic, 1974.

Interpretive Essays

Friedrich, Carl J., *An Introduction to Political Theory.* Harper & Row, 1967. Twelve lectures on great political theorists and problems in political theory. INTRODUCTORY.

Hartz, Louis, *The Liberal Tradition in America: An Interpretation of American Political Thought Since the Revolution.* Harcourt Brace Jovanovich, 1962. An introduction to the specifically American contribution to Anglo-American liberal theory. INTERMEDIATE.

Kateb, George, *Political Theory: Its Nature and Uses.* St. Martin's, 1968. Examines the kinds of questions which political theorists ask and shows what makes them so compelling. INTRODUCTORY.

Raphael, D. D., *Problems of Political Philosophy.* Praeger, 1971. Introduces the problems of political theory. INTRODUCTORY.

Sabine, George, *A History of Political Theory.* Holt, Rinehart & Winston, (hard cover), 1973. A thorough history of the great political thinkers from Plato to the twentieth century. INTERMEDIATE.

Strauss, Leo, and Joseph Cropsey, eds., *History of Political Philosophy.* Rand McNally, 1963. A series of articles about the major Western political thinkers. Bibliographies included. INTERMEDIATE.

Tinder, Glenn, *Political Thinking: The Perennial Questions.* Little, Brown, 1970. A thematic introduction to the issues of political philosophy. INTRODUCTORY.

Wolin, Sheldon, *Politics and Vision: Continuity and Innovation in Western Political Thought.* Little, Brown (hard cover), 1960. Interpretive essays about political theorists and about the political assumptions and views of their eras. INTERMEDIATE-ADVANCED.

POLITICAL ANALYSIS AND METHODOLOGY

Dahl, Robert A., and Deane E. Neubauer, *Readings in Modern Political Analysis.* Prentice-Hall, 1968. A short introduction to the methodology of political science. INTRODUCTORY.

Daston, David, *A Framework for Political Analysis.* **Prentice-Hall, 1965.** A theoretical work on the methodology of political science. ADVANCED.

Eulau, Heinz, *The Behavioral Persuasion in Politics.* **Random, 1963.** A discussion of the tenets and methodology of behavioral political science. INTERMEDIATE-ADVANCED.

Graham, George J., and George W. Carey, eds., *The Post-Behavioral Era: Perspectives on Political Science.* **McKay, 1972.**

Gurr, Ted R., *Politmetrics: An Introduction to Quantitative Macropolitics.* **Prentice-Hall, 1972.** A theoretical work on the quantitative aspects of the study of politics. ADVANCED.

Winch, Peter, *The Idea of a Social Science and Its Relation to Philosophy.* **Humanities, 1970.** A short book on the philosophical assumptions of social science research and on their validity. Readable and concise. INTERMEDIATE.

JOURNALS

American Journal of Political Science **(continues Midwest Journal of Political Science, 1957–1973).** Wayne State Univ. Press, Detroit, MI 48202.

American Political Science Review. American Political Science Association, 1527 New Hampshire Ave., N. W., Washington, DC 20036.

Journal of Politics. Southern Political Science Assn. Peabody Hall, University of Florida, Gainesville, FL 32601.

Philosophy and Public Affairs. Princeton Univ. Press, Princeton, NJ 08540.

Political Theory. Sage Publications, Beverly Hills, CA.

Polity. Northeastern Political Science Association, Univ. of Massachusetts Press, Amherst, MA 01002.

Social Science Quarterly. Southwestern Social Science Association, University of Texas, Austin, TX 78712.

Western Political Quarterly. University of Utah, Salt Lake City, Institute of Government, Salt Lake City, UT 84112.

Chapter Fourteen

PSYCHOLOGY

*". . . who we are and
why we act the way we do"*

Editorial Advisor:
Susan Carey
Department of Psychology
Massachusetts Institute of Technology

INTRODUCTION

Psychology is not an integrated field. Psychologists do not agree on what the important problems are, much less on how to solve them. Different views are reflected in different academic disciplines within psychology. An odd consequence of this diversity is that what appears to be a single topic, such as schizophrenia, will be dealt with very differently by each of the disciplines.

One introductory text that makes a deliberate effort to counter this trend by cutting across as many academic disciplines within psychology as possible when looking at specific topics is Roger Brown and Richard Herrnstein, *Psychology*, Little, Brown (hard cover), 1975. This work organizes its chapters around topics of interest to everyone— layman and professional alike. It is strongly recommended that you obtain your own copy; buy it or get it from your local library. References to the book's various chapters have been included in the bibliography whenever they are relevant to a particular question within a traditional discipline.

Psychology, as a whole, has close connections with many fields of science, mathematics, and social science. Any study of behavior must intersect with biology; physiological psychology can be, and in many cases is, a branch of neurophysiology. The study of animal behavior belongs equally in the field of biology known as ethology. The boundary between social psychology, sociology, and anthropology is a blurry one. A professional psychologist must know a reasonable amount of statistics, and a student of psychology should know at least a little.

The sections below introduce the different disciplines of psychology. They generally correspond to the sections in the bibliography, where there are also extensive introductory notes in the sections and subsections.

PERSONALITY

Surely the study of personality is the layman's conception of what psychology is all about. A theory of personality should provide a way of describing who we are and how we differ from each other, how we got to be that way, what can go wrong, and what can be done about it. The dominant figure in personality theory is, of course, Sigmund Freud, whose influence in the twentieth century extends way beyond psychology itself.

The study of personality must begin with Freud because much of what has followed is either an extension of his work or a reaction against it. However, any major branch of psychology should, and does, have something to say about personality. Behaviorism, for instance, gives quite another account of people's motivation and actions than does the Freudian approach. Similarly, cognitive psychology, concerned with what we know and what we believe, certainly must contribute to a description of who we are and why we act the way we do.

PERCEPTION

Perception is the core of experimental psychology. This branch of psychology has the longest history, dating back to the time before psychology was a field separate from philosophy, with major advances made as long ago as Isaac Newton's studies of color vision. Much of the modern work in perception was done in the nineteenth century by such men as H. L. F. Helmholtz and Ewald Hering, geniuses whose work spanned medicine and philosophy. However, perception plays the role it does in modern psychology not because of its venerable history, but because of its successes. The study of perception, more than anything else, has shown the world that experimental psychology is possible— that is, that one can learn about the workings of the mind and brain by studying behavior.

The field of perception is tied to physiology on the one hand and to information-processing cognitive psychology on the other. One reason the list of readings given for this central area of psychology is so short is that large parts of the readings given for both physiological psychology and cognition also deal with perceptual processes.

At least three divisions can be made within the field of perception— sensory processes, psychophysics, and complex perceptual processes. Our sensations are usually divided into six modalities—vision, hearing, taste, olfaction (smell), touch, and kinaesthesia (the sense of body position). Psychologists and physiologists have discovered what types of receptors are responsible for each kind of sensation, what kind of stimuli affect each of them, where in the brain these impulses go, and how they are related to what we see, hear, smell, or feel.

Psychophysics is the science of quantitatively relating changes in the physical stimulus—increasing the amplitude of a sound, for example—to changes in the perception of the sound. What is the threshold below which the human ear cannot hear? What is the threshold above which a sound is painful? If you double the amplitude of a noise, will it sound twice as loud? (No.)

Brown and Herrnstein, Chapter 7, provides an introduction to psychophysics as well as to the two sense modalities of hearing and sight. In addition, this chapter introduces some complex perceptual phenomena in the two modalities. One example of a complex perceptual phenomenon is depth perception. Light, reflected from objects in the real world, is projected onto our retina, essentially a two-dimensional surface. How do we see things in depth? Bearing on this issue are visual illusions, experiments isolating various cues to depth, the famous Ames demonstrations, Julesz' work on binocular fusion, and the like. You should know about all these lines of research, and you will learn about them in the books listed in the bibliography to the section, "Perception."

PHYSIOLOGICAL PSYCHOLOGY

What is the relation between the brain and behavior? To answer this question, you must know about the brain and you must know about psychology. Physiological psychology, like developmental psychology, cuts across all other fields; the study of physiological psychology teaches the bases of learning, motivation, perception, memory, personality, action, and cognition.

Before these questions can be approached, some questions on basic neuroanatomy should be asked. What are the major structures in the brain? What connections do they have to each other? How are the central nervous system and peripheral nervous systems (sympathetic and parasympathetic) distinguished from each other? Some physiology of the nervous system should also be known. How are impulses propagated along a nerve cell? How are they transmitted from one neuron to another? With this background you will be ready to understand the literature on how various parts of the brain work in order to control hunger, movement, language, and so on.

There are several classes of techniques used in physiological psychology—lesions, electrophysiological recording, and stimulation. In the first technique part of the brain is removed and the effects of the lesion are studied. This technique is used in a controlled way with animals to assess the functions of certain parts of the brain. For example, a lesion in part of the hypothalamus causes a rat to overeat to the point that he may kill himself; a lesion in another part of the hypothalamus causes a rat to starve himself to death. Experiments with humans are out of the question of course, but nature (strokes) and accidents (such as gunshot wounds) cause lesions in people's brains, the effects of which are becoming more clearly understood. With both animals and people, reversible lesions can be caused by injecting a chemical into part of the brain to put it temporarily out of action without destroying it permanently. This technique is often done on people before certain neurosurgical operations.

In the second technique the electrical activity of the brain can be recorded. This can be performed with electrodes placed on the skull (for EEGs, or Evoked Potentials) or from electrodes placed inside the brain. The former technique can be used with humans, but electrodes are implanted only in the brains of animals. Particularly important are single-cell recordings—tiny electrodes put in the brain which pick up the activity of one neuron. It is then possible to study what causes this single neuron to fire.

In the third class of techniques small amounts of electrical (or chemical) stimulation can be delivered to parts of the brain, and the effects can be noted. Stimulation in one part of the brain may cause the animal to eat, in a second to move spastically, in another to seek to prolong the stimulation (that is, the animal will work hard to deliver tiny shocks to particular parts of the brain). This technique is sometimes used with humans in the course of neurosurgical procedures for epilepsy. Wilder Penfield has discovered that stimulation of some part of the brain can apparently cause a person to relive long-forgotten episodes from 20, 30, or 40 years earlier.

COGNITION

The study of cognition is the study of knowledge and thinking. The modern study of cognition is grounded in the metaphor of the mind as a computer. The topics covered are ordinary enough—memory, imagery, attention, pattern recognition (how do we recognize a certain set of lines as an "A"?), problem solving and thinking—but current theories covering these topics are subtle and difficult.

Cognitive psychology is a close relative of a burgeoning field within computer science, artificial intelligence. In research on artificial intelligence, computers are programed to mimic complex human actions such as talking, playing chess, or ordering from a menu. One difference between the field of artificial intelligence and cognitive psychology is that the workers in psychology are concerned with finding how people do what they do. What unconscious processes are involved? Of the various ways that a computer might represent some piece of knowledge in its memory, which one(s), if any, are analogous to the ways the human memory works?

Of central importance to cognitive psychology is the fact that mental processes take time—very little time, to be sure; special machines have therefore been developed to measure in thousandths of a second (milliseconds) and to present stimuli to subjects for very short periods. Inferences can be drawn from the patterns of reaction times, about underlying processes, usually processes that the individual is completely unaware of.

There are many other techniques used in experimentation in cognitive psychology, including the manipulation of the structure of material to be remembered to see whether efficiency of memory is affected. All of the techniques are designed to sort out different models of how knowledge is represented in our permanent memory or how incoming information is processed, starting with patterns of light on our eyes or

236   COLLEGE ON YOUR OWN

of sound on our inner ears to the recognition of objects and sentences, the extraction of their meaning, and finally, the formulation of appropriate plans of action.

SOCIAL PSYCHOLOGY

Social psychology studies the relationship between humans and society. How do the institutions and groupings of our larger culture affect who we are and what we do? The subfield of social psychology mirrors psychology in general; there are a huge number and variety of problems in its domain, and a range of complementary approaches to these problems.

Within psychology, social psychology is most closely related to personality theory. After all, one of the major social institutions is the family, and much of personality theory can be viewed as the study of the individual in relation to that institution. On the other side, social psychology blends into sociology and anthropology, sharing their interests in understanding social institutions in general. Finally, social psychology blends into ethology—the naturalistic study of animals in their interactions with each other.

It is difficult to separate different theoretical approaches from different methods of study and, in turn, from different choices of subject matter. For instance, an important social unit is the "group"—several people gathered together for a common purpose, whether to run a company, design a sewage system, or help each other in personal-political matters (a women's consciousness-raising group or a T-group). Are there regularities in the structure of all such groups, however diverse their purposes? Subject matter limits the methodological options: groups must be studied in naturalistic settings (real committees and associations) or under laboratory conditions designed to simulate real-life situations. Naturalistic observation is a method highly developed by the ethologists in their study of animals and is widely used by social psychologists. You will see other examples of the interconnections among subject matter, methodology, and theoretical approach as you work through the bibliography on social psychology.

LEARNING

The study of learning as an academic discipline within psychology has two separate branches. One branch has its roots in the work of Hermann Ebbinghaus, a German scholar who taught himself hundreds of lists of nonsense syllables and discovered many of the laws of rote learning. This tradition has blossomed into modern cognitive psychology. The other branch has its roots in the study of animal learning—classical conditioning (Pavlov) and operant conditioning (B. F. Skinner). This branch of animal learning, called behaviorism, doubles as one of the dominant influences in American psychology.

DEVELOPMENTAL PSYCHOLOGY

The study of development cannot be divorced from the rest of psychology. Any adult function can be studied developmentally. For instance, understanding the baby's increasing ability to see objects at various distances will help to settle issues about the mechanisms of depth perception in adults. Thus there is, and should be, a developmental aspect to each of the subfields of psychology—perception, cognition, social, personality, learning, and physiological. Since the main theories in Freudian personality theory are developmental the opening section of the bibliography ("Personality") could be seen as a subheading of "development."

Although any function can be studied developmentally, certain general questions about development can be asked, and these provide a basis for the field. One instance is provided by the issues of "stages of development." Freudians describe major stages of development—oral, anal, Oedipal, and the like—and relate adult personality to the faulty resolution of conflicts in each of them. According to Freudian theory, people can get fixated in an early stage or can regress to an earlier stage at moments of stress. Passage through the Freudian stages is inevitable, a result of the kinds of animals we are.

In cognitive psychology, the man with stature comparable to Freud's is Jean Piaget. Piaget posits four major stages of cognitive development—from the prelinguistic infant through prelogicality and a stage with a slightly different logic from that of the adult to adult logic. Piaget's notions of stages, however, is quite different from Freud's. He does not, for example, include either the notion of fixation or regression, nor does he believe that the last stage is necessarily reached by everyone. The most important difference between the two, however, is that Piaget is describing ways of thinking, the nature of concepts and knowledge, while Freud is describing personality development.

BIBLIOGRAPHY

NOTE The sections of this bibliography generally correspond to the sections of the introductory essay. Works available in paperback editions were chosen whenever feasible. The word INTRODUCTORY at the end of an entry indicates a work on the beginning college level; INTERMEDIATE, a work on the intermediate level; and ADVANCED, a work on the advanced level.

PERSONALITY

This section is divided into four parts: general theoretical perspectives, abnormal personalities, therapies, and the major methodologies in the study of personality. If, after you have browsed in many of these paperbacks and read the relevant sections in Brown and Herrnstein (see below), you decide you want to study personality further, the following book is recommended.

Maher, Brendan, A., *Principles of Psychopathology*. McGraw-Hill **(hard cover), 1966.** Grapples with the problems of evaluating the truth of various claims made in the field of personality.

Theoretical Approaches to the Study of Personality

Brown, Roger and Richard Herrnstein, *Psychology*. **Little, Brown (hard cover), 1975.** Ch. 11 summarizes four rather eccentrically chosen approaches. Sheldon's theory of body types is not taken seriously by very many people.

Freud and the Neo-Freudians

Erikson, Erik H., ed., *Childhood and Society*. **Norton, 1964.** Provides a readable account of Freudian "stages" of development and their role in fixing adult personality structures, and gives insight into argument from case histories and into Freudian therapies. The cross-cultural parts of the book are irrelevent as a general introduction and may be skipped. INTRODUCTORY.

Freud, Sigmund, *New Introductory Lectures on Psychoanalysis*, **ed. James Strachey. Norton, 1965.** Freud's own introduction, intended originally for medical students. It contains long sections on his theories of the unconscious, including his work on dreams. Read this slowly, a little at a time, and realize that the elaborate arguments in it were meant to convince doubters of what most people now take for granted. INTERMEDIATE.

There are many theorists who provided variants on Freud (Jung, Adler, Klein and others). Their books can be found in any paperback bookstore in the section on psychology, but they should not be read until you have some grasp of the original theory.

Existential and Actualization Theories

Brown and Herrnstein, *Psychology* **(above).** Ch. 4 provides an introduction to Maslow, one major figure in this school.

Other major figures include Carl Rogers, Rollo May, R. D. Laing and Victor Frankel, whose books can easily be found in paperback. Influenced by European phenomenology and existentialism, these writers emphasize "the present," "being" in it, fully experiencing it, and controlling it. This is in contrast to Freud's historical and deterministic approach.

Learning Theories of Personality

The section on behaviorism provides the theoretical background for the application of learning theory to personality, including the important behavior-modification therapies. The following are two good books on this subject.

Bandura, Albert and R. H. Walters, *Social Learning and Personality Development.* **Holt, Rinehart & Winston (hard cover), 1963.** INTERMEDIATE.

Dollard, John, and Neal E. Miller, *Personality and Psychotherapy: An Analysis in Terms of Learning, Thinking and Culture.* **McGraw-Hill, 1950.** INTERMEDIATE.

Cognitive Approaches

The section on cognitive psychology provides a general background. There are several cognitive theorists, a good example being George Kelly.

Maher, Brendan, ed., *Clinical Psychology and Personality: The Selected Papers of George Kelly.* **Krieger (hard cover), 1969.** ADVANCED.

Abnormal Psychology

There are two basic categories of abnormalities in personality—the neurosis and the psychosis.

Maher, Brendan A., *Principles of Psychopathology.* **McGraw-Hill (hard cover), 1966.** Deals extensively with both neurosis and psychosis.

Szasz, Thomas S., *The Myth of Mental Illness: Foundations of a Theory of Personal Conduct,* **rev. ed. Harper & Row, 1974.** Szasz argues that neuroses and perhaps psychoses are not diseases. INTRODUCTORY.

Neurosis

The first order of business includes definitions and catagorization of symptoms. Phobias, hysteria, anxiety, depression, psychosomatic disorders, and character disorders, are all part of the study of neurosis. Various theories about the causes and cures of neurosis depend upon the description and classification of these phenomena. Maher's text, above, deals extensively with neurosis.

Horney, Karen, *The Neurotic Personality of Our Time.* **Norton, 1937.** Provides an eloquent description of many different neurotic ways we all have of preventing ourselves from full self-realization. INTRODUCTORY.

Psychosis

By far the most extensive work has been done on schizophrenia. Topics in the study of schizophenia includes its possible biological basis (is it inherited? does a chemical in the blood cause it?), its exact characterization (do schizophrenics think differently or use language differently from normal people?), and its treatment (including new drug therapies).

Brown, and Herrnstein, *Psychology* (above). Ch. 13 is excellent.

Maher, *Principles* (above). Also deals with this topic.

Laing, R. D., *The Divided Self*. Penguin, 1965. A rather difficult but rewarding attempt to capture the essence of schizophrenia. INTERMEDIATE.

Psychotherapies

There are four basic types of psychotherapies—Freudian individual therapy and psychoanalysis, group therapies, family therapies, and behavior therapies.

Brown and Herrnstein, *Psychology* (above). Ch. 12 gives an introduction to all but family therapies.

The shelves of any section on psychology in a bookstore are lined with paperback books on therapy, including works by all the people mentioned in Ch. 12 of Brown and Herrnstein. These therapies, both individual and group, can all be related to Freudian and neo-Freudian conceptions. Therapies are appropriate to neuroses, not psychoses. Further, many people are concerned with the problem of how to tell whether therapy actually helps (see, for example, discussion of Eysenck in Brown and Herrnstein).

Family Therapies

The idea of family therapy is that since individual neuroses are part of a system, that whole system must be dealt with at once.

Laing, R. D., *Politics of the Family and Other Essays*. Random, 1972. This collection of essays illustrates the need for family therapy, although it does not provide a good account of the techniques. INTRODUCTORY.

Drug Therapies

The so-called miracle drugs are now being used in such profusion that they might count as a kind of therapy themselves. They are used in the treatment of both neuroses and psychoses.

Longo, V. G., *Neuropharmacology and Behavior*. Freeman, 1972. Includes historical, neurophysiological, and animal behavioral aspects of psychoactive drugs (including hallucinogens). INTRODUCTORY.

Behavior Therapies

Behavior therapies, such as Joseph Wolpe's, are based on the principles of classical conditioning, while others are based on the principles of Skinnerian conditioning.

Wolpe, Joseph, *Psychotherapy by Reciprocal Inhibition*. Stanford Univ. Press (hard cover), 1958. INTERMEDIATE.

The Methods of Personality Theory

Case Studies

One method, pioneered by Freud, is the study of individuals in full detail, with an attempt to understand them and thereby to discover principles that can be generalized to other individuals. Both normal and abnormal lives have been studied.

Brown and Herrnstein, *Psychology* (above). Ch. 11 presents Eugene O'Neill's account of his family in *A Long Day's Journey Into Night* as a case.

Erikson, Erik H., *Young Man Luther*. Norton, 1958. Case study of an individual. INTERMEDIATE.

Erikson, Erik H., *Gandi's Truth: On the Origins of Militant Nonviolence*. Norton, 1969. Another attempt at an individual case history. INTERMEDIATE.

White, Robert H., *Lives in Progress: A Study of the Natural Growth of Personality*, 3rd ed. Holt, Rinehart & Winston, 1975. Presents more ordinary normal people. INTERMEDIATE.

Freud, Sigmund, "Dora, An Analysis of a Case of Hysteria" (1908) in *Collected Papers of Sigmund Freud*, 5 vols., ed. Ernest Jones. Basic (hard cover), 1959. INTERMEDIATE.

Clinical and Projective Approaches

Rorschach Tests and other projective tests, such as McClelland's Achievement Motivation test are based on the assumption that what people see in an ambiguous picture reveals their personality in a consistently interpretable way. **Brown and Herrnstein, *Psychology*, (above).** (See Ch. 4).

Mischel, W., *Personality and Assessment*. Wiley (hard cover), 1968. Deals with these methods and the problems of validity of the methods. ADVANCED.

Trait and Factor Approaches

A third approach is based on long objective tests. Attempts are made to discover stable patterns of responses that correspond to personality types. An example is the Minnesota Multiphasic Test, which contains over 500 true-false questions. Patterns of responses are then factor-analyzed.

Brown and Herrnstein, *Psychology* (above). See Ch. 11 for an account of this methodology in the case of mental traits as opposed to personality traits.

Tyler, Leona E., *Psychology of Human Differences.* Prentice-Hall (hard cover), 1965. Covers both IQ and personality assessment. Do not buy it unless you are interested in these difficult and important methodological issues. ADVANCED.

PERCEPTION

It is in the area of psychology focused on perception where there is the most to learn before you can understand current research. You must learn about the nervous system and about 100 years of research, but the effort is worth it. There are only a few books in this section. If any particular problem comes up, these books can be your guide to where to go next.

Gregory, Richard L., *Eye and Brain: The Psychology of Seeing.* McGraw-Hill, 1973. A well-written, popular introduction to vision, with special emphasis on visual illusions. INTRODUCTORY.

Gregory, Richard L., *The Intelligent Eye.* McGraw-Hill, 1970. Deals with all the ways in which perceptual processes involve complex inferences about what we must be seeing. INTRODUCTORY.

Denes, Peter B., and Elliot N. Pinson, *Speech Chains: The Physics and Biology of Spoken Language.* Doubleday, 1973. Deals with the production and perception of speech, tracing elements from the articulatory system to specialized receptors in the brain. ADVANCED.

The two following books consist of reprints from *Scientific American*. This magazine is an excellent source of up-to-date research written in a competent but not overly technical way. These books are each courses in perception all by themselves. A study guide is available for Held and Whitman.

Held, Richard M., ed., *Image, Object and Illusion: Readings From Scientific American.* Freeman, 1974. INTERMEDIATE.

Held, Richard L., and Whitman Richards, eds., *Perception: Mechanisms and Models—Readings From Scientific American.* Freeman, 1972. INTERMEDIATE.

Geldard, Frank A., *Human Senses.* Wiley (hard cover), 1972. This is a reference book you can consult in a library if you are interested in learning about some sense modalities other than vision and hearing. The book concentrates on sensation, with relatively little on complex perceptual processes.

PHYSIOLOGICAL PSYCHOLOGY

Brown and Herrnstein, *Psychology* **(above).** Read Ch. 2 on the physiological bases of eating and hunger and Ch. 7 on the physiology of seeing and hearing.

There are several good readers and texts, and the collection from *Scientific American* (below) should be browsed through. These readings together with Thompson's introductions and Thompson's text, can be read as the core of a solid course in the topic. Before you commit yourself, read the relevant sections in Brown and Herrnstein and try to browse in the collections cited below. The three books on higher processes in humans (also identified below) can be read with no background before you commit yourself to doing physiological psychology on your own.

Thompson, Richard F., ed., *Introduction to Biopsychology.* **Albion, 1973.** INTRODUCTORY.

Collections of Readings

Thompson, Richard F., ed., *Physiological Psychology: Readings from Scientific American.* **Freeman, 1972.** INTERMEDIATE.

Pribram, Karl H., ed., *Brain and Behavior,* **4 vols.; Vol. 1,** *Moods, States and Mind* **(1969); Vol. 2,** *Perception and Action* **(1969); Vol. 3,** *Memory Mechanisms* **(1962); Vol. 4,** *Adaption* **(1962). Penguin.** ADVANCED.

Gross, C. G., and H. P. Zeigler, eds., *Readings in Physiological Psychology,* **3 vols.; Vol. 1,** *Neurophysiology/Sensory Processes;* **Vol. 2,** *Motivation;* **Vol. 3,** *Learning and Memory.* **Harper & Row (hard cover), 1969 (out of print).** ADVANCED.

Higher Human Processes

Gardner, Howard, *The Shattered Mind.* **Knopf (hard cover), 1974.** Well-written, absorbing account of the effects of strokes and other neurological diseases—including aphasias (loss of language due to lesions in the left hemispheres), amnesias (as in Korsakoff's syndrome, a disease some alchoholics get), and agnosias (the patient can see but cannot recognize what he sees). INTRODUCTORY.

Ornstein, Robert E., *Psychology of Consciousness.* **Viking (hard cover), 1973.** INTRODUCTORY.

Ornstein, Robert E., ed., *The Nature of Human Consciousness: A Book of Readings.* **Freeman, 1973.** Ornstein's two books build on the work of Sperry on the differences between the two hemispheres; they deal with biofeedback, mind-expanding drugs, and other higher human phenomena. INTERMEDIATE.

COGNITION

This section is divided into five parts: an introduction to the computer metaphor, information processing, problem solving, the structure of knowledge, and language.

The Computer Metaphor

Simon, Herbert A., *Sciences of the Artificial.* M.I.T. Press, 1969. Presents many of the concepts shared by researchers in artificial intelligence and cognitive psychology. INTRODUCTORY.

Miller, George A., *et al., Plans and the Structure of Behavior.* Holt, Rinehart & Winston, 1960. A classic. Three psychologists introduce the computer metaphor, explicity contrasting this approach to that of the behaviorists. INTERMEDIATE.

Information Processing

The computer metaphor calls for an information-processing approach at all levels of cognition, but this has been most fully developed in models of attention, sensory storage (very short-term memories which prolong the visual or auditory input), and short-term memory.

Norman, Donald A., *Memory and Attention: An Introduction to Human Information Processing.* Wiley, 1969. Collection of excerpts from original important papers, with a commentary tying the material together. INTRODUCTORY.

Posner, Michael I., *Cognition: An Introduction.* Scott, Foresman, 1974. Covers some of the same ground as Norman's work but places much more emphasis on the crucial concept of "representation." INTERMEDIATE.

Neisser, Ulric, *Cognitive Psychology.* Prentice-Hall (hard cover), 1967. Most complete introduction to cognitive psychology. Skip the sections on language; they are dated. ADVANCED.

Problem Solving

The traditional approach to problem solving in psychology dates back to the Gestalt psychologists. In modern times their insights have been carried further by artificial-intelligence investigators. Read Simon (above) before reading the following.

Wason, P. C., and P. N. Johnson, eds., *Thinking and Reasoning.* Penguin, 1968. A collection of reprints, including sections on the Gestalt tradition, plus selections on the question of whether thinking is logical. INTERMEDIATE.

Wickelgren, Wayne E., *How to Solve Problems: Elements of the*

Theory of Problems and Problem Solving. **Freeman, 1974.** The artificial-intelligence approach to problem solving is illustrated in the context of the student's solving a variety of problems. INTERMEDIATE.

Kohler, Wolfgang, *The Mentality of Apes,* **tr. Ella Winter. Routledge & Kegan Paul, 1973.** A classic. The Gestalt position on problem solving is developed in the context of chimpanzees. Kohler tries to show that chimps have moments of "insight" when they restructure the concepts. ADVANCED.

Bruner, Jerome S., *Beyond the Information Given: Studies in the Psychology of Knowing,* **ed. Jeremey M. Anglin. Norton, 1973.** A collection of works by Bruner, who has made important contributions to all areas of cognitive psychology. See especially Bruner's discussion of perception in the context of problem solving.

The Structure of Knowledge

How is long-term (permanent) memory organized? How do we store new things in it? How do we find things in it when we need to?

Bartlett, Frederic C., *Remembering: A Study in Experimental and Social Psychology.* **Cambridge Univ. Press, 1932.** A classic. Bartlett proposes that we have a schema for organizing new information and that recall is an active process consisting of reconstructing what must have been, rather than simply reading what was, from our long-term memory. INTRODUCTORY.

Collins, A., and M. R. Quillian, "Retrieval Time from Semantic Memory" in *Journal of Verbal Learning and Verbal Behavior,* **1969, Vol. 8, pp. 240–247.** A classic article, which attempts to discover the organization of knowledge in our heads. It takes its hypotheses about organization from the semantic network models in artificial intelligence. INTERMEDIATE.

Psycholinguistics

The production and understanding of language is really a special topic within information processing psychology. It differs from the rest, however, because linguists have given us a detailed account of language, so that we can ask very detailed questions about the "psychological reality" of the structures linguists have discovered.

Brown and Herrnstein, *Psychology* **(above).** Ch. 9 provides an introduction to the study of language, including its development and recent experiments in teaching chimpanzees to talk.

Green, Judith, *Psycholinguistics: Chomsky and Psychology.* **Penguin, 1972.** Gives a full account of Noam Chomsky's theory of grammar and of attempts to base models of language behavior on generative transformational grammar. INTERMEDIATE.

Winograd, Terry, "Understanding Natural Language" in *Cognitive*

Psychology, Vol. 3, No. 1 (1972). The whole journal is devoted to one long article. Winograd's work provides the best example of the artificial-intelligence approach to language processing. ADVANCED.

Fodor, J. et. al., Psycholinguistics. McGraw-Hill (hard cover), 1974. If you are seriously interested in psycholinguistics, this is the book you should work through. ADVANCED.

SOCIAL PSYCHOLOGY

Within social psychology there is a wide range of experimental procedures—from the highly naturalistic to laboratory simulations. At the naturalistic end of the continuum, real-life situations are set up to observe people's behavior, these people have no idea that they are part of an experiment.

Brown and Herrnstein, *Psychology* (above). For example, a car is abandoned on an expressway. Movies are taken of people stripping it and then destroying it—a real-life incident which just happens to be part of a study. Or, a more contrived experiment: people come into a laboratory for what they think is one purpose when, in fact, their behavior is being observed in terms of some social variables. Finally, there is the overt experiment; for example, subjects are asked to pretend they are bargaining, and game-playing strategies are studied.

A nonexperimental method employed by social psychologists is the survey. Patterns of answers are related to such variables as sex, occupation, degree of education, and geographic location. The large polls, such as the Gallup Poll, are well-known examples.

Finally, another nonexperimental method is the in-depth interview. An excellent example is:

Terkel, Studs, *Working: People Talk About What They Do All Day and How They Feel About What They Do.* Pantheon (hard cover), 1974; Avon (paper), 1975. Terkel interviews people from a wide range of professions—from housewives to prostitutes to teachers to factory workers to doctors. These interviews shed light on the common problems in work; alienation, commitment, and control over one's own life.

You will meet all types of studies in the bibliography below. It has been rather arbitrarily divided into two sections—one of theoretical options and one of special, illustrative topics.

Theoretical Approaches to Social Psychology

Consistency, Dissonance, Balance, and Congruity Theories

These theories represent major cognitive approaches to social psychology. The topics of beliefs, attitudes, and prejudices are dealt with in terms of systems that minimize conflict among different beliefs. A major portion of the work within this class of theories concerns the ways of dealing with inevitable conflicts.

Brown, Roger, *Social Psychology*. **Macmillan (Free Press; hard cover), 1965.** Contains a first-rate chapter on consistency and congruity theories. INTRODUCTORY.

Festinger, Leon, *Conflict, Decision and Dissonance*. **Stanford Univ. Press (hard cover), 1964.** Festinger is the originator of the theory of "cognitive dissonance," which concerns the workings of emotional factors in consequences of making choices.

Gestalt and Field Theory

Another class of cognitive approaches, Gestalt and Field Theory, emphasize that man is part of a system which has laws of its own.

Lewin, Kurt, *Field Theory in Social Psychology*. **Harper & Row (hard cover), 1951, (out of print).** A classic statement of Gestalt principles applied to social psychology, this book should be looked at near the end of your studies of social psychology. It is historically important.

Social Comparison Theories

These theories give central importance to the question of how individuals see themselves in reference to others in society. What do they see as their role in various situations? What groups do they identify with?

Goffman, Erving, *The Presentation of Self in Everyday Life*. **Doubleday, 1959.** INTERMEDIATE.

Goffman, Erving, *Interaction Ritual: Essays on Face-to-Face Behavior*. **Doubleday, 1967.** INTERMEDIATE.

Goffman's books are almost novelistic; he is an observer and describer, seeing things that most of us keep out of consciousness. Any serious student of social psychology will want to read one or more of his many works.

Depth Psychology—Psychoanalytic Approaches

See "Personality" and "Developmental Psychology (Social and Personality Development)" sections.

Learning Theory

See "Learning" section.

Animal Social Behavior

Both laboratory studies and naturalistic field studies of social behavior in animals are made in the hope of discovering universal laws of social behavior.

Brown and Herrnstein, *Psychology* **(above).** Ch. 5.

Brown, Roger, *Social Psychology* **(above).** This book contains an excellent chapter, "The Social Behavior of Animals." INTRODUCTORY.

Harlow, H. F., and K. Harlow, "Social Deprivation in Monkeys" in *Scientific American,* **November, 1962.** A classic article on the effects of depriving infant monkeys of their mother. INTRODUCTORY.

Wilson, E. O., *Sociobiology.* **Belknap (Harvard Univ. Press; hard cover), 1975.** Very expensive; get it from the library. Encyclopedic in scope, bringing together all the work on social behavior of animals into a new theory. You will find references to all the relevant ethological work. If you are interested in the question of whether the laws which determine social behavior among animals also apply to humans, give this book a try. ADVANCED.

Special Topics in Social Psychology

Group Behavior

There is a natural division of this area of social psychology into the study of small groups—such as T-groups, encounter groups, committees, seminars—and the study of the behavior of large groups, such as mass movements and mobs.

Small Groups

Mills, Theodore M., *The Sociology of Small Groups.* **Prentice-Hall, 1972.** Describes the basic phenomena observed in the study of ongoing groups and presents a theoretical framework under which they can be subsumed. INTRODUCTORY.

Bales, R. F., *Personality and Interpersonal Behavior.* **Holt, Rinehart & Winston (hard cover), 1970.** Is much more extensively based on experimental data than is Mills' text. Bales presents case studies of small groups. INTERMEDIATE.

Collective Behavior

Festinger, Leon, *et al., When Prophecy Fails: A Social and Psychological Study of a Modern Group that Predicted the Destruction of the World.* **Harper & Row, 1956.** People involved in a religious movement who believe in and are prepared for the end of the world by a given date are studied for their reaction to the failure of that millenial prophecy. This study is important for its place in the development of Festinger's theory of cognitive dissonance. INTERMEDIATE.

Interpersonal Communication

Within this large topic are included such questions as how relative status affects interpersonal interactions, how our expectancies of each other are communicated, and how they affect us and how we project ourselves to others.

Brown and Herrnstein, *Psychology* **(above).** See Ch. 5 for some comments on status.

Garfinkel, Harold, *Studies in Ethnomethodology.* **Prentice-Hall (hard cover), 1967.** As is true for Goffman's work, any serious student of social psychology should be familiar with Garfinkel's writings; they are difficult but extremely important. He has developed techniques for discovering the nonlinguistic rules of interpersonal interaction by trying to test their limits; he deliberately breaks these rules and then studies people's reactions.

Rosenthal, R., and K. Jacobson, *Pygmalion in the Classroom: Teacher Expectations and Pupil's Intellectual Ability.* **Holt, Rinehart & Winston, 1968.** A classic study of how teachers' expectations that certain students would surge ahead intellectually led to increased achievement score for these students. INTERMEDIATE.

Rapoport, Anatol, and Albert M. Chammah, *Prisoner's Dilemma.* **Univ. of Michigan Press (hard cover), 1970.** Presents an extremely experimental and mathematical approach to interpersonal communication—in this case, in the context of strategies of cooperation and competition in certain games. ADVANCED.

Social Motivation

See "Learning" and "Physiological Psychology" sections.

Brown and Herrnstein, *Psychology* **(above).** See Chs. 4 and 5, which deal with topics in social motivation—stress and aggression, achievement motivation, and self-actualization.

Persuasion and Conformity

What leads one person to stand up against the crowd? How did the Nazis get normal people to allow, even participate in, genocide? Why are people prone to prejudice? Why is propaganda effective? These are some topics within this speciality of social psychology.

Brown and Herrnstein, *Psychology* **(above).** Ch. 6.

Bell, Daniel, *The End of Ideology: On the Exhaustion of Political Ideas in the Fifties.* **Macmillan (Free Press), 1960.** A classic, if somewhat dated, study of ideological change.

Zimbardo, Philip G., and Ebbe B. Ebbesen, *Influencing Attitudes and Changing Behavior,* **ed. Charles A. Kiesler. Addison-Wesley, 1969.** A more modern study on attitudes and attitude change.

Allport, Gordon W., *The Nature of Prejudice,* **abr. ed. Doubleday, 1958.** A classic.

LEARNING

Perhaps the best brief statement available anywhere today of current issues in learning theory is in

Brown and Herrnstein, *Psychology* **(above).** Chs. 1, 2, 3 relate learning to instinct, motivation, and memory.

There are many applications of behaviorism—behavior modification, behavior therapies, and programed instruction (within education) are just a few. The readings suggested below provide the background necessary for understanding these applications.

Rachlin, Howard, *Introduction to Modern Behaviorism.* **Freeman, 1970.** Extends the introductory material in Brown and Herrnstein. It provides a synthesis of modern behavioristic theory. INTERMEDIATE.

Bolles, Robert C., *Learning Theory.* **Holt, Rinehart & Winston (hard cover), 1975.** Differing radically from Rachlin, it is organized around the contributions of several of the major figures in the history of animal learning—Pavlov, Watson, Hull, Guthrie, Thorndike, and Skinner. Thus it provides a historical perspective useful in following the current literature. INTRODUCTORY.

Skinner, B. F., *Walden Two.* **Macmillan, 1960.** This is a novel. Skinner shows the application of his theory to one vision of society. INTRODUCTORY.

Skinner, B. F., *The Behavior of Organisms: An Experimental Analysis.* **Prentice-Hall, 1966.** A major statement of Skinner's theory and its implications for many different problems within psychology. ADVANCED.

DEVELOPMENTAL PSYCHOLOGY

Corresponding to the intellectual giants of the fields, there are two major divisions in developmental psychology. The first is cognitive and perceptual development; the second, personality and social development.

Cognitive and Perceptual Development

The methodology in perceptual development derives from the parent fields. Experimental and observational work describes the behavior of individual children or groups of children. Piaget's famous work on infancy was based entirely on observations and informal experiments with his own three children. Because development is a dynamic process, it should be studied over time, and this introduces special methodological problems. There are two basic ways of charting changes over time—longitudinal studies and cross-sectional studies. In the former, a single child or a group of children are observed repeatedly at varying intervals, to note the developmental process within the individual. In the latter, behavior of different groups of children at different ages is studied, and it is assumed that the younger children's performance reflects an earlier stage in the same line of development shown in the older children's performance. Examples of both kinds of studies are given in the following readings.

Your task is to become familiar with the work of Piaget, but this is no easy job. Piaget and his collaborators have written hundreds of volumes, and each is difficult going. Read the following as a general introduction.

Ginsburg, Herbert, and Silvia Opper, eds., *Piaget's Theory of Intellectual Development: An Introduction.* **Prentice-Hall, 1969.** While oversimplifying, this text provides a clear statement of an overview from which to proceed. Introductory.

Piaget, Jean, *Six Psychological Studies.* **Random House, 1968.** One of Piaget's own attempts to give an introduction to his work. It is richer, more interesting, than Ginsburg and Opper, but it is so selective that it provides no overview. Start on this one if you do not like secondary sources.

Flavell, John H., *The Developmental Psychology of Jean Piaget.* **Van Nostrand Reinhold, 1973.** Can be treated as a reference once you read the introductory work for Piaget. It remains the most comprehensive secondary source on Piaget's work.

This section on cognitive and perceptual development is divided into four parts: infancy, early childhood, late childhood, and special topics.

Infancy

Piaget, Jean, *The Construction of Reality in the Child.* **Ballantine, 1954.** Advanced.

Piaget, Jean, *The Origins of Intelligence in Children.* **Norton, 1963.** Advanced.

Any original work by Piaget is difficult to read. The two above books develop Piaget's characterization of the six phases within the sensorimotor stage (birth to age two). He also presents his famous work on "object permanence"—claiming that young infants do not realize that objects continue to exist when they are out of sight. Ginsberg and Opper provide an adequate account of this material.

Bower, T. G. R., *Development in Infancy.* **Freeman, 1974.** An excellent account of perceptual and cognitive development in infancy, this book also offers experimental evidence against Piaget's theories of object permanence.

Early Childhood

Ages two to ten span two of Piaget's stages. The first, preoperational (up to about age six), characterizes the child as egocentric (cannot take the point of view of others), nonlogical, self-contradictory, and concrete in his thinking. The second, concrete operational (up to about age ten), is the first stage of logic. The child can handle relations and classification but not more complex and abstract logical operations, these will develop in the early teens. Ginsburg and Opper give a good account of Piaget's views of these stages.

Bryant, P., *Perception and Understanding in Young Children.* Basic, 1974. Presents an experimental approach to cognitive development. Bryant questions Piaget's interpretations of his transitivity experiments (preoperational children, being nonlogical, cannot solve problems of the sort, "The red ball is heavier than the white ball; the white ball is heavier than the green ball—which is heavier, the red or the green?"). He also questions Piaget's interpretations of his famous conservation experiments (a preoperational child will judge that the quantity of water has increased if it has been poured into a thinner glass). INTRODUCTORY.

Vygotsky, Lev S., *Thought and Language,* tr. Eugenia Hanfmann and Gertrude Vakar. M. I. T. Press, 1962. A classic account of the nature of children's concepts, of the function of the young child's talking to himself or herself, and of the relationship between thought and language during development. ADVANCED.

Late Childhood

In this stage adult logical thought is developed. Ginsberg and Opper provide an adequate account of this stage.

Inhelder, Baerbel, and Jean Piaget, *The Growth of Logical Thinking: From Childhood to Adolescence.* Basic, 1958. The most relevant book from Piaget's laboratories themselves. ADVANCED.

Special Topics—Language Development

Brown and Herrnstein, *Psychology* (above). Ch. 9.

McNeill, David, *Acquisition of Language: The Study of Developmental Psycholinguistics.* Harper & Row, 1972. A good introduction, although a bit out of date. INTERMEDIATE.

Special Topics—IQ

A non-Piagetian approach to intelligence. Do IQ tests measure intelligence? Are differences in IQ between people due to genetic or environmental factors?

Brown and Herrnstein, *Psychology* (above). Ch. 10.

Block, N., and J. Dworkin, eds., *The IQ Controversy: Critical Readings.* Pantheon, 1976. The best collection of articles critical of the original Jensen and Herrnstein work on IQ, heritability, social class, and race differences. Especially useful in Block and Dworkin's own article, "IQ, Heritability and Inequality," where the psychometric concepts are criticized from a philosophical point of view. ADVANCED.

Special Topics—Piaget's Concepts

Much of Piaget's work has traced the development of centrally important concepts and bodies of knowledge. Thus there are books on space, time, geometry, perception, number, causality, and others. Any good paperback psychology section will have several of these. The following are suggested.

Piaget, Jean, *The Child's Conception of Number*. Norton, 1965. Puts Piaget's work on seriation and conservation in quite a different light than simply as indications of concrete operations. Bryant's book (see "Early Childhood" section) offers an alternative view on the development of the concept of number. ADVANCED.

Piaget, Jean, *The Moral Judgment of the Child*. Macmillan (Free Press), 1932. This early work of Piaget's is more accessible than is the later one (above). See also Brown and Herrnstein, *Psychology*, Ch. 5, for a presentation of Kohlberg's neo-Piagetian work on moral development. INTERMEDIATE.

Social and Personality Development

The whole section on personality is relevant to social and personality development. Freudian theory is, among other things, a theory of development. Therefore, only selected special topics are included here.

Moral Development

Kohlberg and Piaget are interested in moral reasoning, but equally important is the question of moral behavior. How do children come to control their own behavior and to decide for themselves what they should or should not do? In Freudian theory, this process is related to the development of the superego. Social psychologists discuss socialization—the process by which children take on the values of their society.

Brown, Roger, *Social Psychology*. Macmillan (Free Press; hard cover), 1965. The chapter "The Acquisition of Morality" is an exposition of Freud's theory of the development of the superego, contrasting this approach to moral development with Piaget's. You should look at this book in a college library. INTRODUCTION.

Birth Order

Sampson, E. E., "The Study of Ordinal Position: Antecedents and Outcome" in *Progress in Experimental Personality Research*, 5 vols., ed. B. Maher. Academic Press (hard cover), 1964–1972. Deals with personality differences among children as a function of whether they were born first, second, third, and so on, in their family. The work is a good example of the experimental approach to the study of personality. The whole set of books in this series is worth browsing through in a library.

Attachment and Maternal Deprivation

How does the infant become attached to his or her mother (father, caretaker) and what are the long-term consequences, if any, of the lack of a normal attachment to a mother in infancy?

Ainsworth, M. D. S., "Object Relations, Dependency and Attachment: A Theoretical Review of the Infant-Mother Relationship" in *Child Development*, 1969 (journal).

Bowlby, John, *Attachment*. Basic (hard cover), 1969.

Sex-Typing and Sex Role Identification

(See also "Women's Studies".)

How do boys come to act like boys and girls like girls? The following are the authoritative sources on this issue, as on sex difference in general.

Maccoby, Eleanor, and Carol N. Jacklin, *The Psychology of Sex Differences*. Stanford Univ. Press (hard cover), 1974. Advanced.

Money, John, and A. Anke, *Man and Woman, Boy and Girl*. NAL, 1974. Deals with the biological determinants of sex-linked behavior, presenting various types of hermaphrodism and androgeny (having characteristics of both sexes). Intermediate.

Adolescence

Included under the rubric "adolescence" is work as varied as the "identity crisis" and studies of delinquent gangs. The following are only two representative analyses.

Erikson, Erik H., *Identity: Youth and Crisis*. Norton, 1968. Intermediate.

Kenniston, Kenneth, *The Uncommitted: Alienated Youth in American Society*. Dell, 1967. Deals with the early 1960s. Consider whether Kenniston's picture still holds true for the 1970s. Intermediate.

Cross-Cultural Perspectives

There are many variants on the question, "Do the vast differences among cultures affect thought (perception, personality, and so on)?" Alternatively, it can be asked how basic psychological facts constrain cultural variation. Both kinds of questions have been posed by psychologists and anthropologists. The four titles included here provide a mere scratch on the surface; if these questions interest you, you should look into social anthropology.

Cole, Michael, and Sylvia Scribner, *Culture and Thought: A Psychological Introduction*. Wiley, 1974. A review of the work on cognitive and perceptual differences among peoples from different cultures. Representative topics: the Whorfian hypothesis (the claim that the structure of a language determines how its speakers perceive the world and how they think); cultural differences in basic thought processes (the authors examine the claim that some non-Western peoples do not think "logically"). INTRODUCTORY.

Erikson, Erik H., *Childhood and Society* (above). A classic introduction to Erikson's Freudian theory of the life cycle put in a cross-cultural perspective. INTRODUCTORY.

Price-Williams, D. R., ed., *Cross-Cultural Studies*. Penguin (Modern Psychology Readings), 1969. Includes research on cognitive development, perception, and personality. In particular, it provides a source for Whiting's work relating cultural institutions such as initiation rites to Freudian interpretations of early child care. ADVANCED.

Hsu, Francis L., ed., *Psychological Anthropology*. Schenkman, 1972. Entirely concerned with personality and culture (socialization, projective tests, mental illness, and so on). ADVANCED.

Chapter Fifteen

SOCIOLOGY
". . . a systematic attempt to
understand social behavior and society"

Editorial Advisor:
Charlotte Weissberg
Department of Sociology
Brandeis University

INTRODUCTION

As a systematic attempt to understand social behavior and society, the field of sociology is a modern endeavor. Philosophers of classical antiquity and medieval feudalism did develop significant analyses of the relationships between social arrangements and desirable social ends; but their systems of thought were invariably motivated by ethical rather than scientific concerns—defining personal virtue, the just state, the good society.

Sociology as now conceived really begins only with the rise of modern capitalism and, more specifically, industrialism in nineteenth-century Europe. During that period social structures that most people believed to be immutable and of divine origin seemed to change almost overnight. The stability of peasant agrarianism in the countryside and the guild system in the cities was undermined. Rapid urbanization created unforeseen social developments, affected in large part by the emergence of a wage-earning proletariat. The penetration of all social life by market relationships led to the disruption of centuries-old standards of social ranking based on birth, title, and favor. They were replaced increasingly by market-determined systems of distributing power and prestige. Above all, these changes brought untold misery and massive social upheaval to great numbers of people.

Sociology began when some men of thought, concerned with these cataclysmic changes, turned to the task of understanding their new social world. The example provided by contemporary natural science, with its methods of gathering information and predicting events, encouraged these nineteenth-century figures to try to create a "science" of society.

Sociology was thus born in the midst of social chaos, with the massive social problems caused by industrialization as the prime interest of its originators. In England, Jeremy Bentham and John Stuart Mill wrote early speculative works on the sociology of economic life. They called the new field of these works "political economy," and it later developed into the modern social science of economics. Thomas Malthus, another Englishman, formulated as an "iron law" the theory holding that human populations multiplied until limited by famine or other mass disaster. His reflections on the biological underpinnings of society began the science of demography (study of the factors involved in population growth, decline, distribution, and fertility).

In France, Henri de St. Simon and Alexis de Tocqueville explored the relationships between the division of labor and social structures. They also investigated the ties between social stratification (the ways in which people and groups are hierarchically organized in societies), and order and change in society. Their countryman, August Compte, was an ambitious—perhaps overly ambitious—intellectual, who believed that he could construct a science of everything and in the attempt gave sociology its name. Compte focused on the nature and historical development of those culturally shared values which underlie social solidarity.

German writers, in particular Karl Marx and Friedrich Engels, set out a variety of important hypotheses. Their theories concerned the interaction among economy, society, and politics; social conflict; the relation of society to ideas and values; and the centrality of social classes as historical actors.

THE EUROPEAN CLASSICS

The questions asked by these early social thinkers continued to preoccupy their intellectual successors in the late nineteenth and early twentieth centuries. It is in this period that sociology as we know it today was established. No more important work stems from this period than that of Max Weber and Emile Durkheim.

German sociologists were more strongly influenced by Marx than were those of other nations. Max Weber was one who came to prominence at the turn of the century as a worthy sociological successor to Marx as well as opponent of Marx's theories. Like Marx, Weber was preoccupied with questions of vast historical change—in particular, those raised by the transition from feudalism to capitalism in the West. Much of his work was devoted to analyzing the advent of capitalism in the Western world and contrasting it with non-Western societies that had clung to traditional ways.

In his magnificent work, Weber focused on the relationships between the "ethos" of specific societies and social groups (for example, that system of religious or, later, secular values which seemed to have consequences in practical day-to-day life to provide meaning for groups of people and to set directions for social action). He was struck by the propensity of some social groups to modernize while others remained traditional. In contrast to Marx, who saw economic behavior and class conflict as motors of social life and change, Weber posited a

COLLEGE ON YOUR OWN

more complicated network of social causality which, while far from eliminating economic factors, recognized the influence of charismatic leadership and the action-orienting implications of shared values in creating or preventing social change.

Weber stressed the fundamental importance of the rise of "instrumental rationality" as embodied in the procedures used in the natural sciences, in European systems of accounting and law, and in the use of calculations to attain maximum efficiency in various spheres of business. Important concomitants of this rationality were hierarchically organized bureaucracies, where each office and function was carefully defined and coordinated and individual worth was based on merit—ability to do the job well—and not on birth, fortune, or tradition. For him these represented the most salient features of modern societies. Unlike the Marxists, Weber believed rationality and bureaucracy to be of greater salience in understanding in the modern world than social class and modes of production.

Weber also modified the Marxian understanding of political life by questioning the explanatory utility of the concept of social class and introducing the new concept of "status group" as a major political and social category. He introduced new lucidity into social research by elaborating the comparative-historical methodology that had already been developed, by stressing the necessity of investigating the frameworks of meaning with which social actors invested their behavior in different societies at different historical times (such as the concept that religious beliefs were organized differently and had different consequences in practical daily behavior in different times and places), and, finally, by elaborating the notion of "ideal type"—a means of ordering generalizations derived from data in order to provide an illuminating model for comparison with reality.

The other giant of early-twentieth-century sociology, Emile Durkheim, made contributions of a very different sort. Durkheim was concerned less with problems of change and history than with the relationships between individuals and social beliefs. To Durkheim society was an entity that stood above and logically preceded the individual lives of its members—a totality much greater than the sum of its parts, one that could be studied and measured in itself. Durkheim's organic metaphor for social life implied that the primary purpose of each part of society is to perform a vital function for society as a whole. This concept laid the foundations for contemporary functionalism in sociological theory.

The nature and origins of social solidarity—the integrative life-blood of the social organism—were Durkheim's central interest. He was preoccupied generally with the problems that industrial capitalism seemed to pose for solidarity and social order. But Durkheim comforted himself with the vision that ultimately "organic" solidarity (based on the interdependence of a complex division of labor) would solidly integrate modern societies. Such integration would replace the "mechanical" solidarity of traditional societies (based on social likeness, interchangeability of individuals, and a low level of economic diversity). Durkheim's notion of the organic integration of modern societies led him to study social problems—for example suicide—as key examples or symptoms of the failure or incompleteness of the bonds of solidarity.

Weber and Durkheim have come to us as the acknowledged masters of early European sociology, and their influence has lasted to the present (as will become clear in the discussion of modern American social thought). Their European contemporaries are also worth noting, however. Followers of the Marxian tradition, concerned with the late arrival of the proletarian revolution, worked in their chosen realm of "political economy" to update Marx's own work. They contributed particularly to an understanding of European capitalism as it outgrew its earlier stages and passed toward maturity, one marked essentially by imperialism, according to Rosa Luxemburg and Lenin. Unfortunately, and ironically, the aftereffects of the first socialist revolution in the Soviet Union—in the form of Stalinism—rendered creative development in the Marxian tradition quite difficult from the late 1920s onward.

Karl Mannheim, following in the footsteps of Max Weber, made important contributions to the sociology of knowledge and culture and to the study of the relationships between social structures (political organization, economic organization, occupational organization, and the like) and ideas (art, political ideology, literature). The study of so-called primitive cultures by English and French anthropologists, although often motivated by the political concerns of imperial domination, further developed the theoretical bases of functionalism first set out by Durkheim. These anthropologists searched for the role that various rituals, customs, and values play in a given culture.

Finally, the political upheavals during and after the First World War (the Russian Revolution, the failure of revolution in Germany, the rise of Fascism) prompted important, if often pessimistic, developments in the sociology of politics. The works of Vilfredo Pareto, Gaetano Mosca, and Roberto Michels all cast serious doubts on the practical possibilities for democracy. Each of these writers, in his own (often conservative) way, suggested that major social organizations and the state itself were foreordained to be dominated by elites who decided the fate of the powerless "masses."

THE FIRST STAGE OF AMERICAN SOCIOLOGY

American sociology, developing at about the same time that Weber and Durkheim were producing their seminal work, took a much different course. Here, too, the concerns of sociology tended to coincide with the nature and problems of the society that it attempted to understand.

American society experienced the transition to modern capitalism in ways basically different from the European experience. In the United States liberal individualism reigned unchallenged as a system of values for understanding the social world; this was in contrast to the situation in Europe, where liberalism was in constant conflict with various forms of conservatism on its right and socialism on its left. Vast national resources and a substantial internal market cushioned the shocks of great economic changes. Americans did not think as readily in terms of social class as did Europeans. This tendency, combined with the peculiar American phenomenon of a largely immigrant labor force, made it natural for American sociologists to see the problems of industrialization in terms of acculturation, community development, and ethnicity. Most Europeans, while focusing on the same general issues, were inclined instead to see the central problem in terms of the economy and its relation to social and political life. As it emerged, American sociology was therefore much more pragmatic (both in the common sense of the word and in the sense conveyed by the then-dominant American philosophical school of Pragmatism). It was also more oriented toward social problems than its European counterpart.

These new American departures were typified by the work of the Chicago School of sociologists, which included Robert Park, W. I. Thomas, William F. Ogburn, Ernest W. Burgess, and other scholars at the University of Chicago. Situated in a city where vast social changes of the early 1900s were highly visible, the Chicago School was first and foremost concerned with the assimilation, accommodation, and adjustment of newcomers to the city and with the nature of the city that these newcomers were transforming. Beginning with few assumptions (except, perhaps, for a desire to see these new social elements integrated into American society with as little turmoil as possible), the Chicago sociologists tried to map out the social geography, ecology, and probable development of the new multiethnic American city. A direct outcome of their approach was the American tradition of "community studies" which represents one of the most original of all the contributions of American sociology to the discipline. The tendency is seen at its best in Robert and Helen Lynd's *Middletown* studies of depression-ridden Muncie, Indiana.

American sociology also demonstrated a remarkable inventiveness in the realm of research methods. European sociologists, preoccupied with the broad sweep of historical change and conflict, had been prone to use historical and comparative methods of inquiry. Americans, by contrast, tended to have an ahistorical perspective and a concommitant commitment to finding solutions to social problems that could be transformed into actual social policy. The Americans thus frequently preferred to go directly into the field rather than to the library for research. Techniques for observation as a participant (in which the sociologist integrated himself into the setting to be investigated and then gathered data) was one important American innovation in research methods. Another was the use of statistical calculations in the processing of data gathered by surveys of attitudes and behavior.

Finally, sociology in America tended to reflect basic interests in social relations, individual attitudes, and ways that people adapt to the environment, while also largely free of *a priori* notions about the influence of social structures. American sociologists were accordingly interested in the psychology of interactions between individuals and between individuals and social institutions, as well as in the development of personality as a complex "product" of natural and social-environmental factors. Such interests were evidenced notably in the work of C. H. Cooley and George Herbert Mead, the founder of the symbolic interactionist school, who began a long American tradition of sociological social psychology. Work of this kind stands in stark contrast to European treatments of similar problems, which tended to keep separate the study of social questions and individual personality.

THE TRIUMPH OF AMERICAN SOCIOLOGY

American sociology reached its fullest development after the Second World War. In the two decades after 1945 American society seemed to go from strength to strength. Economic prosperity, social stability, and political success in the world of the Cold War led Americans in general to believe that they had solved most of the outstanding questions of industrialism—a belief shared and propagated by American sociologists. In the new perspective of the "Great American Celebration" (a term coined by C. Wright Mills, one of the few dissenters from this new consensus), the United States had become the "vanguard" of advanced Western societies—a model that the rest were destined to follow, an industrial society that had surmounted all of the difficulties of the transition to modernity and was fast moving toward "postindustrial" abundance and rationality. This new America no longer needed to worry about assimilating immigrants, creating new communities, or defusing industrial conflict. It was no accident, then, that a new and vastly more optimistic sociology emerged.

The keystone of Cold War American sociology was a body of high sociological theory, in large part the creation of the Harvard sociologist Talcott Parsons (although Robert Merton, George Homans, and many others contributed as well). Judiciously combining Weber's historical and social action perspectives with Durkheim's organic metaphor and functionalism, Parsons developed an original and elaborate theory of social systems that soon came to be labeled "structural-functionalism."

According to this theory all societies or parts of a society had certain basic needs that must be met in order for them to survive. These needs were fulfilled by the functioning of identifiable social structures. Any given society was a complex of many different structures of this kind, interrelated in such a way as to allow the society as a whole to carry on. These structures included the economy, the polity, the family, and other institutions designed to socialize individuals, create and maintain values, and so on. Individuals, as social beings, were composites of various roles that they played within their social structures. For example, a person might have diverse roles as a family member, an employee, and a citizen of the community. Each role provided a set of obligations, duties, and expectations for behavior determined by the commonly held values and "norms" embodied in that area of social life. Thus individuals, socially speaking, were "bundles of roles." Shared values integrated specific social structures and ensured the coherence of the social whole. Because the role players shared the same values with others, their social actions would usually be harmonious.

To the structural-functionalist, social change occurs when factors entering into the functioning of a social structure cause peoples' values and their roles to come into conflict. Such conflict results when actors' understanding of their social context clashes with the actions they feel obliged to carry out. For example, as more women began to work in the United States, the roles of mother, wife, and job holder tended to come into conflict, creating what has been called "role strain." Such strain, in Parsons' theory, leads to a process in which either roles are redefined or values are changed until a new equilibrium of values and roles is established. In the same example, it is increasingly acceptable in America for middle-class mothers to leave young children in the care of others in order to work and for husbands and wives to redefine the division of labor in the family, thus reducing role strain.

A process of change of this sort occurring in one social structure, such as the economy, would in all likelihood cause adaptive changes in related social structures, such as the family and the polity. The process would ultimately cause gradual change of the whole society. The general thrust of historical change, "modernization," is toward ever greater social complexity—the subdivision of social structures and roles into ever more dense networks through a process of "structural differentiation." (This process represents Parsons' refinement of Weber's notion of the spread of instrumental rationality.)

Parsons provided American sociology with an intricate theoretical map of social life. This map could, on the one hand, be applied in principle to the analysis of any society at any stage of development. On the other, it could serve as a guide for analyzing any part of a given society and its relationships with other parts. Implicit in Parsons' work, then, was a clear division of sociological labor: the theory could be "carved up" into smaller research areas. Moreover, Parsons' thought provided American sociologists with the kind of social map with which they could feel ideologically and politically comfortable. An important purpose was served by its stress on causal complexity, its deep Durkheimian interest in integrative systems of shared values and social cohesion, and finally, its functionalist vision of societies (and social structures within societies) naturally seeking equilibria and therefore not in any fundamental conflict. Through such elements as these, Parsons' theory laid to rest, at least for a time, threatening Marxian notions—notions of the dominant causal power of economic life, the privileged status of classes as social actors, and the centrality of class conflict in change. To intellectuals in Cold War America, these features were welcome indeed.

Parsons' theory seemed to settle many of the issues left unresolved in European sociology. This was of great importance to American sociologists, primarily because it gave them a framework within which they might pursue work in their narrower subfields. The heyday of American sociology was, accordingly, not marked only by theoretical clarification. It was also characterized by the proliferation and development of a dense network of subfields, most of which involved the examination of just one social structure. One subfield that flourished on its own was the sociology of economic life, in which the work of such scholars as Neil Smelser, Wilbert Moore, and Amitai Etzioni depicted productive life as an organic subsystem seeking equilibrium within itself, rather than a system of conflict based on exploitation and domination, as in the Marxian formulation. The sociology of economic life also contributed to the more abstract study of the formal and informal workings of complex organizations (as well as to the sociology of the business firm, hospitals, educational institutions, prisons).

Other important work of the postwar period was done in political sociology, culminating in the virtual domination of the "pluralist" frame of reference for political analysis. Such analysis, in the studies of scholars including S. M. Lipset and Robert Dahl, construed democratic political life basically as the civil and peaceful conflict between collections of organized interest groups potentially equal in power, with their conflict tending toward political harmony.

Parsons himself was a major contributor to the sociology of small-group interactions (which sought to define the roles and implicit shared values of participants in small-group situations). He also added significantly to the related study of the sociology of the family, a subfield that was deeply concerned with the nature of the processes by which the young were socialized to share the values and norms of the broader society.

Parsons' model opened up new possibilities for studying social development comparatively. Americans found this field particularly captivating in an era of Cold War and decolonialization. The study of the behavior of the socially disoriented and the marginal, as social actors living in situations of role and value strain, was further developed in the sociology of deviance and the systematic examination of collective behavior (as in jobs, crowds, or riots) and social protest movements.

Liberated from the Marxian and Weberian notions of social class, many American sociologists turned to their own studies of social ranking and stratification. In these studies they stressed variables of income, education, occupation, and life style in efforts to explain ways in which people are differentiated and to measure social mobility.

The list of still other subfields that prospered in the post-1945 period might be extended much further indeed. Suffice it to say that the sociologies of religion, law, medicine, sex roles, urban and community studies, and many other areas could easily be discussed in detail. Moreover, theoretical innovations, not only in sociology, but also in psychology gave new life to the long-standing American tradition of sociological social psychology.

Parsons' synthesis provided more than a theoretical umbrella under which subfields could develop in a coherent, related way. It provided incentives for new methodological departures. It followed from the theory that social structures, social action, roles, and development and change in values could all be measured and subjected to rigorous empirical research. The subdivision of sociological inquiry meant that critical variables could be isolated and identified from data by means of statistical tests. The relationships *between* social subsystems, thus empirically investigated, were also often quantified through new techniques of mathematical modeling (borrowed from economic theory, in large part) and "systems analysis."

A high level of sophistication was reached in elaborate survey research techniques (usually involving the dissemination of carefully constructed questionnaires to a random sample of the population in question, often in search of data about individual attitudes). These techniques became very familiar to the public in political polls and election forecasting.

The possibilities opened by electronic computers for massive data processing further accelerated advances in research methods. Since data gathering on a large scale and electronic data processing were both very expensive, this period also saw the emergence of large-scale centers for social research, where studies were carried on by bureaucratically organized teams. Work at such centers was frequently funded by government agencies and large private foundations.

All of these trends tended to reshape the nature of careers in sociology. Theoretical agreement and methodological competence in these new research strategies became the key to professional certification. "Softer" methods of research, such as the participant observation of the Chicago School and the historical-comparative techniques of many Europeans, fell into great disrepute. Becoming affiliated with or creating well-funded research "empires" guaranteed the sociologist prestige and, often, professional productivity.

THE GREAT AMERICAN CELEBRATION IN QUESTION

Just at the point in history when American sociology was becoming dominant around the world, the social underpinnings of the entire field began to shake. By the late 1960s the Keynesian certainties of American economic life were losing their power to convince. Blacks and students were protesting in the streets in ways that profoundly altered political life. Conflicts related to social class multiplied in almost all advanced societies. In the light of these developments and the successes of social revolutionary movements in the non-Western world, the cold and calm certainties of Parsons' synthesis were called into serious question.

Beginning in earnest in the late 1960s and continuing to the present, sociology in America plunged into confusion. A creative movement of neo-Marxian political and economic sociology emerged to cast great doubt on the confident political pluralism of the 1950s and 1960s; it initiated what may well turn out to be major breakthroughs in the sociology of international relations through a process of reexamining and refining earlier Marxian notions of imperialism.

In another current movement major new works appeared in the Weberian historical perspective. Sociologists involved in both these movements asked once again, and in a deeply convincing way, many of the basic questions of earlier European sociology—questions about the causal importance of economic life, the role of social classes and class conflict, and the imperial destiny of advanced capitalism societies.

From quite another direction a new school of sociologists based on the earlier philosophical works of European phenomenologists (Husserl, Heidegger, Merleau-Ponty, Alfred Schutz) began a quiet attack on the epistemological foundations of all American "grand theory" and its research methods.

In general, dissatisfaction was rife with Parsons' synthesis and much of the work of American sociology since the second World War. At present it is too early to know what the results of this new heterodoxy and questioning will be for the evolution of sociology. For the moment, however, it is clear that the conclusions of the earlier American synthesis in sociology no longer hold their previous sway.

The following bibliography presents basic works in this sustained effort to understand human society. They span the range of studies typically covered by undergraduate majors in the field today.

BIBLIOGRAPHY

THE FOUNDERS AND THE CLASSICS

Aron, Raymond, *Main Currents in Sociological Thought*, 2 vols. Doubleday, 1968, 1970. Good brief essays on all the early "greats."

The following three books present the central writings of the founders of Marxism. These works pose many of the basic questions that were to preoccupy sociology for a century or more.

Marx, Karl, and Friedrich Engels, *Selected Works of Marx and Engels. International*, 1968. See especially The Communist Manifesto; The Eighteenth Brumaire of Louis Bonaparte; Socialism, Utopian and Scientific; The Origin of the Family, Private Property and the State.

Marx, Karl, and Friedrich Engels, *The German Ideology, Part I and Selections from Parts II and III*, ed. C. J. Arthur. International, 1970.

Marx, Karl, *Capital*, vol. 1. International, 1967.

De Toqueville, Alexis, *The Old Regime and the French Revolution*, Doubleday, 1955; *Democracy in America*, 2 vols., ed. Andrew Hacker, tr. Henry Reeve, Pocket Books, 1971. Empirically based reflections on the relationship between social structure, social history and change.

Durkheim, Emile, *Sucide* (1951), *The Division of Labor in Society* (1947), Macmillan (Free Press). Key works of a thinker who has provided some of the most important inspirations of modern sociology. Early functionalism and concern with social solidarity mark Durkheim's writings.

Weber, Max, *The Protestant Ethic and the Spirit of Capitalism*. Scribner's, 1930. Excerpts from Weber's mammoth works on comparative sociology and the sociology of religion, stressing the vital change-orienting function of early Protestantism in the rise of modern Western society.

Weber, Max, *Theory of Economic and Social Organization,* tr. Talcott Parsons. Macmillan (Free Press), 1947. Weber's major sociological summation, although very difficult going.

Weber, Max, *From Max Weber,* tr. and ed. Hans Gerth and C. Wright Mills. Oxford Univ. Press, 1946. Extremely useful and explanatory selections from Weber, with enlightening introduction by the editors.

The following are works by two of the more important contemporaries of Weber in Germany, men concerned with many of the same things as Weber—social structure, change, the sociology of knowledge, and culture.

Simmel, Georg, *Conflict and the Web of Group Affiliations.* Macmillan (Free Press), 1955.

Wolff, Kurt H., tr., *The Sociology of Georg Simmel.* Macmillan (Free Press), 1950.

Mannheim, Karl, *Ideology and Utopia: An Introduction to the Sociology of Knowledge.* Harcourt Brace Jovanovich, 1955.

Mannheim, Karl, *Essays on the Sociology of Knowledge,* ed. Paul Kecskemeti. Oxford Univ. Press (hard cover), 1952.

The following two books are written by the major elite theorists in interwar political sociology.

Mosca, Gaetano, *The Ruling Class.* McGraw-Hill, 1939.

Michels, Robert, *Political Parties.* Dover, 1958.

Bottomore, Thomas, *Elites and Society.* Penguin, 1964. A useful essay on elite theory.

PRE-SECOND WORLD WAR AMERICAN SOCIOLOGY

Dewey, John, *The Public and Its Problems.* Swallow, 1960. A brief introduction to the philosophical underpinnings (Pragmatism) of Chicago sociology.

The following works represent a sampling of the more important documents of Chicago School sociology, dealing with such issues as immigration, the development of new multiethnic cities, community, assimilation, and so forth, along with methods and procedures for investigating such phenomena.

Thomas, William I., and Florian Znaniecki, *The Polish Peasant in Europe and America,* 2 vols. Octagon (hard cover), 1971.

Hawley, Amos H., *Human Ecology: A Theory of Community Structure.* Ronald (hard cover), 1950.

Park, Robert, *et al., The City.* Univ. of Chicago Press, 1968.

Sumner, William G., *Folkways: A Study of the Sociological Importance of Usages, Manners, Customs, Mores, and Morals,* Dover, 1959.

Park, Robert E., and Ernest W. Burgess, *Introduction to the Science of Sociology,* abridged ed., ed. Morris Janowitz. Univ. of Chicago Press, 1970.

Below are two American classics in sociological social psychology (Mead's book is the foundation of symbolic interactionism).

Cooley, Charles Horton, *Social Organization: A Study of the Larger Mind.* Schocken, 1962.

Mead, George Herbert, *Mind, Self and Society: From the Standpoint of a Social Behaviorist,* ed. Charles W. Morris. Univ. of Chicago Press, 1934.

Lynd, Helen M., and Robert S., *Middletown* (1959), *Middletown in Transition: A Study in Cultural Conflicts* (1963). Harcourt Brace Jovanovich. The Lynd's classic community studies of Muncie, Indiana, before and during the depression of the 1930s.

MODERN WORKS (POST-SECOND WORLD WAR)

These works represent the major statements of postwar American structural-functionalism. Parsons is a somewhat inaccessible author, *Societies* being the most approachable book. Much of modern American sociology follows from, or is carried on in the spirit of, these theoretical statements.

Parsons, Talcott, *Societies: Evolutionary and Comparative Perspectives.* Prentice-Hall, 1966.

Parsons, Talcott, *The Social System.* Macmillan (Free Press; hard cover), 1951.

Parsons, Talcott, and Edward Shils, eds., *Toward a General Theory of Action: Theoretical Foundations for the Social Sciences.* Harper & Row, 1951.

Merton, Robert K., *Social Theory and Social Structure.* Macmillan (Free Press; hard cover), 1968.

Merton, Robert K., *On Theoretical Sociology: Five Essays, Old and New.* Macmillan (Free Press), 1967.

Sociology of the Economy

The following are two Parsonian treatments of the economic sphere of society.

Moore, Wilbert E., *The Impact of Industry.* Prentice-Hall, 1965.

Smelser, Neil J., *The Sociology of Economic Life.* Prentice-Hall, 1963.

Here are two intelligent, classic works from the American tradition of industrial sociology.

Bendix, Reinhard, *Work and Authority in Industry: Ideologies of Management in the Course of Industrialization.* Univ. of California Press, 1974.

Kerr, Clark, *et al.*, *Industrialism and Industrial Man: The Problem of Labor and Management in Economic Growth.* Harvard Univ. Press (hard cover), 1960.

The works that follow contain sociological interpretations of the modern giant corporation from the perspective of 1950s American sociology.

Drucker, Peter, *The Concept of the Corporation,* rev. ed. John Day (hard cover), 1972.

Berle, Adolf A., and Gardiner C. Means, *The Modern Corporation and Private Property,* rev. ed. Harcourt Brace Jovanovich, 1969.

The books below represent four very good studies of the American blue-collar worker, his work and its satisfactions (or lack thereof), his attitudes and aspirations.

Walker, Charles, and Robert Guest, *Man on the Assembly Line.* Harvard Univ. Press (hard cover), 1952.

Chinoy, Ely, *Automobile Workers and the American Dream.* Beacon Press, 1965.

Blauner, Robert, *Alienation and Freedom: The Factory Worker and His Industry.* Univ. of Chicago Press, 1964.

Gouldner, Alvin W., *Wildcat Strike: A Study in Worker-Management Relationships.* Harper & Row, 1954.

Goldthorpe, John H., *et al.*, *The Affluent Worker: Industrial Attitudes, The Affluent Worker: Political Attitudes, The Affluent Worker in the Class Structure.* Cambridge Univ. Press, 1968. A three-volume report on an important study of well-off, blue-collar English automobile workers (their feelings about work, politics, and prosperity, and their life styles) which challenges many orthodox views on the "middle-classification" of modern industrial workers.

Here are two fine pieces of work, one French, the other American, on the work lives of clerical workers.

Crozier, Michel, *The World of the Office Worker.* Schocken, 1973.

Mills, C. Wright, *White Collar: American Middle Classes.* Oxford Univ. Press, 1956.

Blau, Peter, and Otis Dudley Duncan, *The American Occupational*

Structure. **Wiley (hard cover), 1967.** The definitive essay on the shape and trends of the modern American workforce.

Political Sociology

Bendix, Reinhard, and Seymour Martin Lipset, eds., *Class, Status and Power: A Reader in Social Stratification,* **rev. ed. Macmillan (Free Press; hard cover), 1966.** The American sociological establishment together in one volume tries to deal with and, ultimately, transcend the difficult issues raised in the classic European tradition of political sociology (Marxism, Weber's work, elite theory).

Lipset, Seymour Martin, *Political Man: Essays on the Sociology of Democracy.* **Doubleday, 1959.** A major summation of research in political sociology, plus a strong argument for American society as democracy embodied, from the vantage point of a sophisticated advocate of the pluralist theory of politics.

The three works that follow are further important statements of the pluralist position, with data, from the perspective of decision-making in politics.

Dahl, Robert A., *Preface to Democratic Theory.* **Univ. of Chicago Press, 1956.**

Dahl, Robert A., *Who Governs: Democracy and Power in an American City.* **Yale Univ. Press, 1961.**

Rose, Arnold M., *The Power Structure: Political Process in American Society.* **Oxford Univ. Press, 1967.**

Hunter, Floyd, *Community Power Structure.* **Univ. of North Carolina Press, 1969.** Important, and controversial addition to the community power study tradition in America.

The following two studies of voting behavior by political scientists are outstanding illustrations of the sophisticated use of survey research techniques by scholars in political science.

Campbell, Angus, *et. al, The American Voter: An Abridgement.* **Wiley, 1964.**

Key, V. O., and M. C. Cummings, Jr., *The Responsible Electorate: Rationality in Presidential Voting, 1936–1960.* **Random House, 1968.**

Almond, Gabriel A., and Sidney Verba, *The Civic Culture: Political Attitudes and Democracy in Five Nations.* **Little, Brown, 1965.** A cross-cultural survey research study, following Lipset to uncover the attitudinal underpinnings of pluralist democracy and introducing the concept of "political culture."

Kornhauser, William, *The Politics of Mass Society.* **Macmillan (Free Press; hard cover), 1959.** A dissenting and rather gloomy essay on the "massification" of modern politics and its implications for stability and change.

Class and Stratification

The two books that follow confirm that Warner is the originator of many uniquely American views on social ranking.

Warner, W. Lloyd, *Social Class in America: The Evaluation of Status.* Harper & Row, 1960.

Warner, W. Lloyd, and V. O. Low, *Yankee City,* abr. ed. Yale Univ. Press (hard cover), 1963.

Tumin, Melvin M., *Social Stratification: The Forms and Functions of Inequality,* rev. ed. Prentice-Hall, 1967. Provides an excellent and thorough summary of current American views on social stratification.

Lipset, Seymour Martin, and Reinhard Bendix, *Social Mobility in Industrial Society: A Study of Political Sociology.* Univ. of Cal. Press, 1959. At attempt to gather hard data cross-culturally about social mobility, the evidence leading to a conclusion that rates of mobility are pretty much the same in all industrial societies.

The following books are three European attempts to deal with the classic questions, "Was Marx wrong, and if so, why?"

Dahrendorf, Ralf, *Class and Class Conflict in Industrial Society.* Stanford Univ. Press, 1959.

Marshall, T. H., *Class, Citizenship and Social Development.* Greenwood (hard cover), 1973.

Bottomore, Thomas B., *Classes in Modern Society.* Random House, 1966.

The following works represent three American attempts to provide a negative answer to the question "Is Marx relevant?" and to portray a future in which capitalism is transcended by organizational society.

Bell, Daniel, *The End of Ideology: On the Exhaustion of Political Ideas in the Fifties.* Macmillan (Free Press), 1960.

Bell, Daniel, *The Coming of Post-Industrial Society: A Venture in Social Forecasting.* Basic (hard cover), 1973.

Galbraith, John K., *The New Industrial State,* rev. ed. Houghton Mifflin, 1972.

The four books below deal with ethnicity and racism and the cultural devastations of class distinctions in modern America.

Glazer, Nathan, and Daniel Patrick Moynihan, *Beyond the Melting Pot: The Negroes, Puerto Ricans, Jews, Italians, and Irish of New York City,* 2nd rev. ed. M.I.T. Press, 1970.

Myrdal, Gunnar, *An American Dilemma: The Negro Problem and American Democracy.* Harper & Row, 1962.

Clark, Kenneth B., *Dark Ghetto: Dilemmas of Social Power.* Harper & Row, 1965.

Sennet, Richard, and Jonathan Cobb, *The Hidden Injuries of Class.* Random House, 1972.

Sociology of Education

Anderson, C. Arnold, et. al., *Education, Economy and Society.* Macmillan (Free Press), 1967. A reader setting forth many of the concerns of modern American educational sociology.

The following are three good essays on the development and social history of mass public education in America.

Cremin, Lawrence A., *The Transformation of the School: Progressivism in American Education, 1876–1957.* Random House, 1961.

Katz, Michael B., *Class, Bureaucracy and Schools: The Illusion of Educational Change in America.* Praeger, 1971.

Greer, Colin, *The Great School Legend: A Revisionist Interpretation of American Public Education.* Viking, 1973.

The first book below is the famous "Coleman Report" on modern American education—one of the greatest of all survey research projects; the one following it is an intelligent review of the same issues ten years later.

Coleman, James S., *Equality of Educational Opportunity.* U. S. Department of Health, Education, and Welfare, 1966.

Jencks, Christopher, et al., *Inequality: A Reassessment of the Effect of Family and Schooling in America.* Harper & Row, 1973.

Two collections of good articles from educational sociologists, often from a critical and unorthodox standpoint, are given below.

Useem, Elizabeth and Michael, eds., *The Educational Establishment.* Prentice-Hall, 1974.

Wasserman, Miriam, ed., *Demystifying School: Writings and Experiences.* Praeger, 1974.

Small Groups, the Family, Social Psychology

The works that follow deal with the theory and methods of small group research as it emerged in the 1950s and 1960s:

Bales, Robert F., *Interaction Process Analysis: A Method for the Study of Small Groups,* Addison-Wesley (hard cover), 1950.

Homans, George C., *The Human Group.* Harcourt Brace Jovanovich (hard cover), 1950.

Bennis, Warren, and Philip Slater, *Microcosm: Structural, Psychological and Religious Evolution in Groups.* Wiley (hard cover), 1966.

The following three works discuss the family in Parsonian perspective, both in theory and cross-culturally.

Parsons, Talcott, and Robert F. Bales, *Family, Socialization and Interaction Process.* Macmillan (Free Press; hard cover), 1955.

Goode, William J., *World Revolution and Family Patterns.* Macmillan (Free Press), 1963.

Christenson, Harold T., *Handbook of Marriage and the Family.* Rand McNally (hard cover), 1964.

Komarovsky, Mirra, *Blue Collar Marriage.* Random House, 1964. A rare attempt to research the American working class family.

Hollingshead, A. A., *Elmstown's Youth.* Wiley, 1949. Classic field study of youth.

Erikson, Erik H., *Childhood and Society,* rev. ed. (1964), *Identity: Youth and Crisis* (1968), Norton. Attempts to join psychoanalytic theory and sociology to explain human development and growth.

Riesman, David, and Ruel Denney, *The Lonely Crowd: A Study of the Changing American Character,* abr. ed. Yale Univ. Press, 1969. An important essay about the effects of mass consumer-oriented America on people's identity and sense of themselves.

Goffman, Erving, *Presentation of Self in Everyday Life,* (1959), *Asylums: Essays on the Social Situation of Mental Patients and Other Inmates* (1961), Doubleday. Rejuvenation and extension of symbolic interactionism. *Asylums* deals with the effects of total institutions on personality.

McClelland, David C., *The Achieving Society.* Macmillan (Free Press), 1967. Controversial attempt to isolate the personality factors that underlie modern economic and social life.

Flacks, Richard, ed., *Conformity, Resistance and Self-Determination: The Individual and Authority.* Little, Brown, 1973. A series of essays dealing with the reasons for social conformity and rebellion.

Gornick, Vivian, and Barbara K. Moran, *Women in Sexist Society.* NAL, 1972. A series of articles on the sociology and social psychology of women in American society.

Complex Organizations

Three major works in modern American formal organization analysis are listed below.

Blau, Peter M., *Bureaucracy in Modern Society.* Random House, 1956.

Etzioni, Amitai, *A Comparative Analysis of Complex Organizations,* 2nd ed. Macmillan (Free Press), 1975.

Ellul, Jacques, *The Technological Society.* Random House, 1964. On the social meaning of advanced organizational societies.

Collective Behavior—Social Movements

The first two books below discuss mobs, riots, crowds, and revolutions from the perspective of structural-functional sociology.

Smelser, Neil J., *Theory of Collective Behavior.* Macmillan (Free Press), 1962.

Johnson, Chalmers, *Revolutionary Change.* Little, Brown, 1966.

Gurr, Ted Robert, *Why Men Rebel.* Princeton Univ. Press, 1970. Searches for the social-psychological roots of rebellions in aggressive behavioral reactions to frustration.

Adorno, Theodor W., *et al., The Authoritarian Personality.* Norton, 1969. Classic search for the social-psychological roots of Fascism and extremism.

Bell, Daniel, ed., *The Radical Right.* Doubleday, 1963. Explanations of the "New Right" in America from the major writers of the pluralist school in political sociology.

Below are two sociological and social psychological analyses of the student movements of the 1960s.

Flacks, Richard, *Youth and Social Change.* Rand McNally, 1971.

Keniston, Kenneth, *Young Radicals: Notes on Committed Youth.* Harcourt Brace Jovanovich, 1968.

Urban Studies

The following four works are particularly good and useful accounts of aspects of the urban environment from the "streets," to school, to the ethnic neighborhood.

Liebow, Elliot, *Tally's Corner.* Little, Brown, 1967.

Whyte, William F., *Street Corner Society: The Social Structure of an Italian Slum.* Univ. of Chicago Press, 1955.

Gans, Herbert J., *The Urban Villagers.* Macmillan (Free Press), 1962.

Schrag, Peter, *Village School Downtown.* Beacon, 1967.

Vidich, Arthur J., and Joseph Bensman, *Small Town in Mass Society: Class, Power and Religion in a Rural Community,* rev. ed. Princeton Univ. Press, 1968. Community studies in the difficult contemporary era.

Stein, Maurice R., *The Eclipse of Community: An Interpretation of American Studies.* Princeton Univ. Press, 1971. Why, with the collapse of older forms of community, community studies are difficult.

Walton, John and Donald E. Carns, eds., *Cities in Change: Studies on the Urban Condition.* Allyn & Bacon, 1973. Articles on a variety of topics—concepts and origins of cities, processes of urbanization, urban life styles and politics, and so on.

THE NEW CRITICS: A SAMPLING

Neo-Marxism

The following five books discuss advanced "monopoly" capitalism in its domestic political economy and its imperialist outward face.

Baran, Paul A., *The Political Economy of Growth.* Monthly Review, 1957.

Baran, Paul A., and Paul M. Sweezy, *Monopoly Capital: An Essay on the American Economic and Social Order.* Monthly Review, 1968.

Magdoff, Harry, *The Age of Imperialism.* Monthly Review, 1969.

Frank, Andre Gunder, *Capitalism and Underdevelopment in Latin America,* rev. ed. Monthly Review, 1969.

Amin, Samir, *Accumulation on a World Scale: A Critique of the Theory of Underdevelopment,* 2 vols., tr. (from the French) Brian Pearce. Monthly Review (hard cover), 1974.

Braverman, Harry, *Labor and Monopoly Capital: The Degradation of Work in the Twentieth Century.* Monthly Review (hard cover), 1974. Monopoly capital and the degradation of human work lives.

Some New Marxist political sociology of a high quality is contained in the books that follow.

O'Connor, James, *The Fiscal Crisis of the State.* St. Martin's, 1973.

Miliband, Ralph, *The State in Capitalist Society: An Analysis of the Western System of Power.* Basic (hard cover), 1969.

Adherents of Marx and Weber

The two books that follow are successful pleas for the return of historical-comparative methods:

Barrington, Moore, Jr., *The Social Origins of Dictatorship and Democracy.* Beacon, 1966.

Giddens, Anthony, *The Class Structure of the Advanced Societies.* Barnes & Noble (hard cover), 1973.

Marx and Freud

Marcuse, Herbert, *Eros and Civilization: A Philosophical Inquiry into Freud* **(1974),** *One Dimensional Man* **(1964), Beacon.** Interpretations of advanced capitalist societies from the viewpoint of the "Frankfurt School."

Elite Theory Revisited

Mills, C. Wright, *The Power Elite.* **Oxford Univ. Press, 1959.** The great "underground classic" from the 1950s, which intellectually inspired the New Left.

Domhoff, G. William, *Who Rules America?,* **Prentice-Hall, 1967;** *The Higher Circles: The Governing Class in America,* **Random House, 1971;** *Fat Cats and Democrats: The Role of the Big Rich in the Party of the Common Man,* **Prentice-Hall (hard cover), 1972.** Mill's less imaginative intellectual successor.

Phenomenology

Schütz, Alfred, *Collected Papers,* **3 vols., ed. Maurice Natanson. Humanities (hard cover), 1962–1966.** The fountainhead of modern sociological phenomenology.

The following two books mark the beginnings of an American phenomenological sociology.

Garfinkel, Harold, *Studies in Ethnomethodology.* **Prentice-Hall (hard cover), 1967.**

Cicourel, Aaron V., *Cognitive Sociology.* **Macmillan (Free Press), 1973.**

The Humanities

Chapter Sixteen

ART HISTORY
". . . a coherent and
rich language of forms"

Editorial Advisor:
Eugene Santomasso
Department of. Art
Brooklyn College
City University of New York

INTRODUCTION

The history of art reveals the contexts in which people have created objects and symbols expressive of themselves. The essence of art history is the human will to communicate by shaping matter into a coherent and rich language of forms. Matisse's paintings, Michelangelo's sculpture, Chartres cathedral, India's temple carvings, and Chinese bronzes indicate something of the vast range of the history of art.

Art history is linked with aesthetics, that branch of philosophical inquiry concerned with determining the nature of creativity and artistic experience. A succinct analysis of the major questions addressed by aestheticians from the time of the Greeks to the early twentieth century is contained in Ernst Cassirer's *An Essay on Man: An Introduction to a Philosophy of Human Culture* (Doubleday). Current topics of aesthetics are examined in Morris Philipson, ed., *Aesthetics Today* (see Bibliography). An issue basic to aesthetic theory is the relation between representation and interpretation, between the objective character of art as imitation (mimesis) of certain phenomena in the actual world and its subjective character as a product of artistic imagination and feeling. Philosophers, historians, and critics have stressed one or the other of these polar positions in an effort to define the nature of art and to distinguish it from language and science, the other symbolic processes whereby we formulate a conception of ourselves and of things and events as we know them. The study of art history inevitably deals with these questions. It affirms that art exceeds the actual world, imparting to visible, tangible, and audible phenomena a special order with its own inherent logic of form.

Developments parallel to those found in the history of art are commonly present in the religion, philosophy, literature, or music of a place, period, or culture. Relevant to particular areas of art history are the insights to be gained from specialized historical, sociological, or anthropological studies, from semiotics, and from those aspects of psychology that deal with modes of creativity and perception. Relationships also exist between the history of art and the history of photography and film. The implications of art history as humanistic discipline have been discussed by Erwin Panofsky in *Meaning in the Visual Arts* (see Bibliography). Other studies—such as Arnold Hauser's *The Social History of Art* (Vintage, 1963), Wylie Sypher's *Four Stages of Renaissance Style* (Doubleday, 1955) and *Rococo to Cubism in Art and Literature* (Vintage, 1963)—are noteworthy for their examination of ways in which the visual arts relate to a constellation of cultural phenomena.

Studies in Art history may focus on the material, technical characteristics and function of a work; on problems of style, dating, provenance, and authenticity; on biographical data; or on the intrinsic meaning of a work and its significance as a synthetic expression of a historical moment. These diversified concerns have given rise to several methods of approach which were formulated early in our century by art historians from Germanic countries and which have since become a central aspect of art-history scholarship.

The method of formal analysis and stylistic criticism, exemplified by Heinrich Wölfflin's studies, is concerned strictly with the expressive characteristics of a work and their effect upon the beholder. Underlying this concern is the aesthetic theory of *Einfühlung*, or empathy, postulated by Theodor Lipps, which deals with our psychological and physiological responses to forms. At the other extreme are those who have focused on iconography and iconology—Panofsky, for example—concentrating on describing the inherent content or meaning of a work. Iconography is devoted to deriving meaning from singular forms or motifs. Iconology deals with texts which help to interpret a work as a synthesis of certain images, stories, or allegories.

Other approaches to art history aim at a broad view of the formative processes of art. Central to these is the theory of *Kunstwollen*—that a supraindividual "will to form" typifies the art of a particular age or culture. Originally developed by the art historian Alois Riegl, this point of view counters the notion prevalent in the late nineteenth century that artistic developments are largely determined by material factors and techniques. The "will to form" of a particular period is understood to be an autonomous impulse, free of materialism. This impulse is manifest in fundamental conceptions of form common to all works of a given time and place. An extension of these ideas is the approach known as *Geistesgeschichte*, or the history of ideas, and exemplified by the studies of Max Dvorak. These studies judge works of art to be products either of a single prevailing outlook or of representative outlooks of their time.

Developed from the ideas of Riegl is a method of approach known as *Strukturforschung*, or "structural analysis," exemplified by the investigations of Guido von Kaschnitz-Weinberg. Consonant with the ideals of *Kunstwollen* and *Geistesgeschichte*, objects of art are analyzed not as projections of individuals so much as embodiments of whole periods or cultures. The purpose of structural analysis, however, is to derive from the forms of a work, without subjective preconceptions and independent of a literary tradition, a sense of those who created the work. According to structuralist methodology, which is indebted to Edmund Husserl's philosophy of phenomenology, the formal characteristics of a work are metaphoric expressions of human experiences and beliefs, which may be wholly comprehended through objective analysis. Unlike the stylistic analysis and criticism of Wölfflin, structuralism is interested, not in our responses to forms, but in patterns of thought and action embodied by those forms.

Special problems and situations in the history of art are addressed by each of the methods of approach just summarized. The early art-historical studies which best demonstrate these methodologies are among the "classics" of the field. Recent studies have begun to probe more deeply than those of the past into the impact of social forces on art. As a whole, the writings of art history testify that the unique vitality of a work of art is its ability to provoke new questions and interpretations.

Because the literature of the discipline is vast, the following bibliography is necessarily selective. It is designed to present works typical of those read and pondered by students majoring in art history at many colleges. Although a number of the standard resources of art history are identified, the emphasis is on recent general studies that are noteworthy for their comprehensiveness and freshness of approach. Further bibliographies in works among those listed can guide you to more specialized studies of schools or groups, specific movements, and individual artists.

For more detailed and up-to-date information, consult the various periodicals, the quarterlies, monthlies, and yearbooks published by institutions and scholarly societies in Europe and America. These works contain specialized articles based on the latest research in a given area. The standard library guide to such publications is the *Art Index, A Cumulative Author and Subject Index to a Selected List of Fine Art Periodicals and Museum Bulletins.*

The large body of bibliographical material is arranged chronologically except for the opening surveys, anthologies and theoretical works, and the closing documentary collections and reference works and series.

A number of books in hard covers are included because works with reasonably faithful reproductions on important periods are not always available in paperback.

The sequential listing represents one way in which to proceed, but it is not meant to be taken as inviolable. It would be equally effective to learn about art history by cutting across standard historical and cultural divisions and focusing on kinds of art works or broad themes, such as still life, the nude, portraiture, landscape, or religious architecture. If you can visit museums, try to go often to enrich your learning with the invaluable experience of original works themselves.

BIBLIOGRAPHY

This bibliography opens with sections on Surveys, Anthologies, and Theoretical Works that cross periods and cultures to give the reader broad perspectives in art history. Next come sections that trace the history of art in Europe and America in successive periods, followed by sections on the art of other cultures—India, China, Japan, Africa, Oceania, American Indian and Pre-Columbian American. Sources, Documents, Reference Works, and Series are given last.

SURVEYS

Gardner, Helen, *Art Through the Ages,* 6th ed., eds. Horst de Croix and Richard G. Tensey. Harcourt Brace Jovanovich (hard cover), 1975. Historical survey of Western art and architecture from paleolithic times to the present, with extensive maps, charts and plans. Short concluding section devoted to highlights of Oriental art and the tribal arts of North and South American Indians, of Africa, and of Oceania.

Janson, H. W., *History of Art,* rev. ed., Abrams (hard cover), 1969. General historical survey of Western art; brief concluding chapter on the meeting of East and West.

Dorra, Henri, *Art in Perspective: A Brief History.* Harcourt Brace Jovanovich, 1973. Introduction to art history based on a select number of monuments analyzed in depth and related to cultural trends.

Gombrich, E. A., *The Story of Art,* 12th ed. Phaidon, 1972. Succinct introduction to art history from Egypt to the era of the 1930s; final chapter on the changing contemporary scene.

Hartt, Frederick, *Art: Painting, Sculpture, Architecture,* 2 vols., Abrams, 1976. Comprehensive survey including recent discoveries and re-evaluations.

Elsen, Albert E., *Purposes of Art: An Introduction to the History and Appreciation of Art,* 3rd ed. Holt, Rinehart & Winston (hard cover), 1972. Thematic rather than chronological approach.

Fleming, William, *Arts and Ideas: New Brief Edition.* Holt, Rinehart & Winston, 1974. Chronological history of art related to literature and music; abridged from the author's *Arts and Ideas.*

Lee, Sherman, *A History of Far Eastern Art.* Prentice-Hall (hard cover), 1973. Only general survey on this broad subject.

Haftmann, Werner, *Painting in the Twentieth Century: A Pictorial Survey.* Praeger, 1965. Comprehensive survey with over 1000 illustrations.

ANTHOLOGIES

Spencer, Harold, ed., *Readings in Art History,* 2 vols. Scribner's, 1969. Modern writings on aspects of the history of art, ranging from problems of style, technique, iconography, and theories of art to social contexts in art from ancient Egypt to the present.

Kleinbauer, W. Eugene, ed., *Modern Perspectives in Western Art History: An Anthology of Twentieth-Century Writings on the Visual Arts.* Holt, Rinehart & Winston, 1971. A collection of 17 scholarly essays chosen for their metholology and accompanied by a lengthy discussion of approaches and schools of art-historical research.

Gilbert, Creighton, ed., *Renaissance Art.* Harper & Row, 1973. Collection of essays by modern historians.

Branner, Robert, ed., *Norton Critical Studies in Art History.* Norton, 1969. A selected group of writings about critical monuments in the history of art.

Philipson, Morris, ed., *Aesthetics Today.* Meridian, 1961. Writings by art historians, critics, philosophers, and social scientists with a view to presenting current issues and modes of thought in aesthetics.

THEORETICAL WORKS

Arnheim, Rudolf, *Art and Visual Perception: A Psychology of the Creative Eye.* Univ. of California Press (hard cover), 1954. Application of the theory of Gestalt psychology to determine the nature of expression in plastic and graphic arts.

Fiedler, Konrad, *On Judging Works of Visual Art.* Univ. of California Press (hard cover) 1949 (out of print). Pursues the idea that artistic activity must be understood and evaluated on its own terms and according to its own laws.

Focillon, Henri, *The Life of Forms in Art,* 2nd ed. Wittenborn, Schultz, 1948 (out of print). Investigation of the syntax of formal expression in relation to material, technique, and the artist's vision.

Gombrich, Ernst H., *Art and Illusion: A Study in the Psychology of Pictorial Presentation,* 2nd ed. Princeton Univ. Press, 1961. Psychological roots of artistic form. Visual art as a symbolic rendition or substitute for actual objects.

Kubler, George, *The Shape of Time: Remarks on the History of Things.* Yale Univ. Press, 1962. Structuralist approach to art as a system of formal relationships independent of meanings and the problems of duration and sequence raised by this view.

Panofsky, Erwin, *Meaning in the Visual Arts.* Doubleday, 1955. Essays by the leading exponent of the iconographical and iconological approach to art history.

Wölfflin, Heinrich, *Principles of Art History,* tr. M. D. Hottinger. **Dover, 1950.** An objective set of formal criteria used to analyze trends in Renaissance art.

Worringer, Wilhelm, *Abstraction and Empathy,* tr. Michael Bullock. **International Univ. Press, 1963.** Combines Riegl's notion of *Kunstwollen* with Lipps' empathy theory to examine the motivating psychology of naturalistic and abstract styles in Western and Eastern art.

PREHISTORY

The following two books are broad, well illustrated surveys.

Graziosi, Paolo, *Paleolithic Art.* **McGraw-Hill (hard cover), 1960 (out of print).**

Sandars, N. K., *Prehistoric Art in Europe.* **Penguin (hard cover), 1968 (out of print).**

Ucko, Peter J., and Andrée Rosenfeld, *Paleolithic Cave Art.* **McGraw-Hill, 1967.** Refutations of some standard misconceptions about the subject.

ANCIENT NEAR EAST

Groenwegen-Frankfort, H. A., and Bernard Ashmole, *Art of the Ancient World.* **Abrams (hard cover), 1971.** Survey of art and culture.

Strommenger, Eva (photography by Max Hirmer), *Five Thousand Years of the Art of Mesopotamia.* **Abrams (hard cover), 1964 (out of print).** Compendious survey with excellent plates.

Ceram, C. W., *Gods, Graves and Scholars: The Story of Archeology,* rev. ed. **Knopf (hard cover), 1967.** Stimulating discussions of past archeological finds.

Mellart, James, *Catal Hüyük: A Neolithic Town in Anatolia.* **McGraw-Hill (hard cover), 1967.** Lively account of the earliest example of a planned town.

EGYPT

The following two books are comprehensive surveys of Egyptian art.

Aldred, Cyril, *The Development of Ancient Egyptian Art from 3200 to 1315 B. C.* **Tiranti, 1952.**

Woldering, Irmgard, *Gods, Men, and Pharaohs: The Glory of Egyptian Art.* **Abrams (hard cover), 1967 (out of print).**

Lange, Kurt (photography by Max Hirmer), *Egypt: Architecture,*

Sculpture, Painting. Phaidon (hard cover), 1968. Concise survey with excellent illustrations.

THE AEGEAN

Marinatos, Spyridon (photography by Max Hirmer), *Crete and Mycenae.* Abrams (hard cover), 1960 (out of print). General survey with stress on pictorial coverage.

The following two books are specialized but readable studies, the first dealing with the Minoans, the second with Mycenaeans; both are concerned with interrelationships between these cultures.

Graham, J. W., *The Palaces of Crete.* Princeton Univ. Press, 1962.

Vermeule, Emily, *Greece in the Bronze Age.* Univ. of Chicago Press, 1972.

Boardman, John, *Pre-Classical: From Crete to Archaic Greece.* Penguin (hard cover), 1967 (out of print). Exposition on changes in Hellenic art from pre-Classical to Classical.

GREECE

MacKendrick, Paul, *The Greek Stones Speak.* NAL, 1962. History of archeological discoveries in Greece with extensive bibliography.

Brilliant, Richard, *Arts of the Ancient Greeks.* McGraw-Hill (hard cover), 1973. Broad survey aimed at the more advanced student.

Pollitt, J. J., *Art and Experience in Classical Greece.* Cambridge Univ. Press, 1972. Fresh introduction to the character of classical art in relation to Greek life and thought.

Richter, Gisela, *Handbook of Greek Art.* Phaidon, 1969. Standard guide to the subject.

Arias, Paolo (photography by Max Hirmer), *A History of 1000 Years of Greek Vase Painting.* Abrams (hard cover), 1963 (out of print). Comprehensive pictorial survey with good bibliography.

Robertson, Martin, *Greek Painting.* Skira (hard cover), 1959 (out of print). Brief pictorial survey in color.

Lullies, Reinhard, *Greek Sculpture*, rev. ed., Abrams, 1957. General introduction with excellent photos.

Richter, Gisela M., *Sculptors and Sculpture of the Greeks*, 4th ed. Yale Univ. Press (hard cover), 1970. Basic factual handbook on the subject.

Berve, Helmut, and Gottfried Gruben (photography by Max Hirmer), *Greek Temples, Theaters, and Shrines.* Abrams (hard cover), 1963 (out of print). Comprehensive pictorial survey with good bibliography.

Scully, Vincent J., *The Earth, the Temple and the Gods: Greek Sacred Architecture*, rev. ed. Praeger (hard cover), 1969. Provocative study of Greek temples, sanctuaries, and landscape, set in the context of Greek art and literature.

ETRUSCAN AND ROMAN ART

MacKendrick, Paul Lachlan, *The Mute Stones Speak: The Story of Archeology in Italy*. NAL, 1966. A history of archeological discoveries in Italy with extensive bibliography.

The two books which follow are standard introductions to the art and culture of the Etruscans.

Pallottino, M., *The Etruscans,* rev. ed. Indiana Univ. Press (hard cover), 1974.

Mansuelli, Guido, *The Art of Etruria and Early Rome* (Art of the World Series). Crown (hard cover), 1965.

Brilliant, Richard, *Roman Art: From the Republic to Constantine.* Praeger, 1974. Balanced insightful survey of Roman art and culture.

Hanfmann, George M. A., *Roman Art: A Modern Survey of the Art of Imperial Rome.* Norton, 1975. Unorthodox organization but rewarding introduction to the subject.

Maiuri, A., *Roman Painting*. Skira (hard cover), 1953 (out of print). Discussion of the most famous examples of Roman wall painting.

Dorigo, Wladimiro, *Late Roman Painting: A Study of Pictorial Records.* Praeger (hard cover), 1971. Pictorial art from 30 B.C. to 500 A.D. and the transformation of classical ideals.

Brown, Frank E., *Roman Architecture.* Braziller, 1961. Brief essay that captures the essense of Roman architecture.

MacDonald, William L., *The Architecture of the Roman Empire.* Yale Univ. Press (hard cover), 1965 (out of print). In-depth study of Roman imperial achievements.

EARLY CHRISTIAN AND BYZANTINE ART

Volbach, W. F. (photography by Max Hirmer), *Early Christian Art.* Abrams (hard cover), 1962 (out of print). Concise survey with informative notations and excellent plates.

Grabar, André, *Christian Iconography: A Study of Its Origins.* Princeton Univ. Press (hard cover), 1968. The creation of Early Christian images and their relationship to other forms of their day.

Mathew, Gervase, *Byzantine Aesthetics.* Harper & Row, 1971. Historical and cultural factors underlying Byzantine art.

Rice, David T., *The Art of Byzantium.* Thames and Hudson (hard cover), 1959 (out of print). Well-illustrated survey of broad scope.

Demus, Otto, *Byzantine Art and the West.* New York Univ. Press (hard cover), 1969. Ramifications of the Byzantine style.

MacDonald, William, *Early Christian and Byzantine Architecture.* Braziller, 1963. Brief essay that captures the essence of these styles.

EARLY MEDIEVAL ART

Kidson, Peter, *The Medieval World.* McGraw-Hill (hard cover), 1967 (out of print). Overview of the period from Pre-Romanesque to late Gothic.

Kitzinger, Ernst, *Early Medieval Art.* Indiana Univ. Press, 1964. Outstanding survey of Christian art from late antiquity to the Romanesque period, based on objects in the British Museum.

Beckwith, John, *Early Medieval Art.* Praeger, 1964. General survey beginning with Carolingian art, omitting the art of the Migrations and Hiberno-Saxon art.

Grabar, André, and Carl Nordenfalk, *Early Medieval Painting from the Fourth to the Eleventh Century: Mosaics and Mural Painting.* Skira (hard cover), 1957 (out of print). Thorough survey, in color.

ROMANESQUE ART

Swarzenski, Hanns, *Monuments of Romanesque Art.* Univ. of Chicago Press, 1974. Introduction to the period.

Evans, Joan, *Art in Medieval France, 987–1498.* Oxford Univ. Press (hard cover), 1969. Pithy survey of Romanesque art in France.

Focillon, Henri, *The Art of the West in the Middle Ages,* vol. 1: *Romanesque Art,* 2nd ed. Phaidon, 1969. Application of the author's theory of forms to Romanesque art.

Stoddard, Whitney S., *Art and Architecture in France* (original hard-cover title: *Monastery and Cathedral in Medieval France*). Harper & Row, 1972. Comprehensive treatment of medieval art and architecture from Romanesque through late Gothic in France.

Grabar, André, and Carl Nordenfalk, *Romanesque Painting from the Eleventh to the Thirteenth Century: Mural Painting.* Skira (hard cover), 1958 (out of print). Emphasis on manuscript illumination.

Anthony, Edgar W., *Romanesque Frescoes.* Greenwood (hard cover), 1951. General survey of wall painting.

Saalman, Howard, *Medieval Architecture* (Great Ages of World Architecture Series). Braziller, 1963. Brief, well-illustrated survey.

GOTHIC ART

The following four books are introductions to Gothic art and have good bibliographies.

Focillon, Henri, *The Art of the West in the Middle Ages,* Vol. 2: Gothic Art, 2nd ed. Phaidon, 1969.

Evans, Joan, *The Flowering of the Middle Ages*. McGraw-Hill (hard cover), 1966.

Stoddard, Whitney S., *Art and Architecture in France*. Harper & Row, 1972. See above, under "Romanesque Art."

Martindale, Andrew, *Gothic Art* (World of Art Series). Praeger, 1976.

Dvorak, Max, *Idealism and Naturalism in Gothic Art*. Univ. of Notre Dame Press, 1967. Art evaluated in terms of its spiritual climate and viewed as a physical expression of the religious philosophy of the age.

Gimpel, Jean, *The Cathedral Builders*. Grove Press (hard cover), 1961 (out of print). Lively discussion of the political, financial, and spiritual background of the age of cathedral building.

Branner, Robert, *Gothic Architecture* (Great Ages of World Architecture Series). Braziller, 1961. Lucid coverage of the whole European development of Gothic.

Male, Emile, *Gothic Image: Religious Art in France of the Thirteenth Century*. Harper & Row, 1973. Basic introduction to the iconography of the Middle Ages.

ITALIAN RENAISSANCE, 1200–1600

The following two books are detailed surveys of Italian Renaissance art with excellent bibliographies.

DeWald, E. T., *Italian Painting: 1200–1600*. Holt, Rinehart & Winston (hard cover), 1961.

Hartt, Frederick, *History of Italian Renaissance Art*. Prentice-Hall (hard cover), 1969.

The following two books are well-illustrated, basic resources on Italian Renaissance sculpture.

Pope-Hennessey, John, *An Introduction to Italian Sculpture,* 2nd ed., 3 vols. Phaidon (hard cover), 1970–1972.

Seymour, Charles, Jr., *Sculpture in Italy 1400–1500* (Pelican History of Art Series). Penguin, 1968.

Helton, Tinsley, ed., *The Renaissance: A Reconstruction of the Theories and Interpretations of the Age*. Peter Smith (hard cover),

1964. Important essays dealing with revisions of earlier views of the period.

Wittkower, Rudolf, *Architectural Principles in the Age of Humanism.* Norton, 1971. Central introduction to Renaissance theories of architectural proportion and their relation to harmonic ratios in music.

Murray, Peter, and Linda Murray, *The Art of the Renaissance.* Thames and Hudson (hard cover), 1974. Concise survey of the fifteenth-century Renaissance.

Decker, Heinrich, *The Renaissance in Italy: Architecture, Frescoes, Sculpture.* Viking (hard cover), 1969. Broad survey of the fifteenth-century Renaissance.

Lowry, Bates, *Renaissance Architecture* (Great Ages of World Architecture Series). Braziller, 1962. Brief and sound survey of fifteenth century architecture.

The following two books are concise surveys of sixteenth-century Renaissance art.

Murray, Linda, *The Late Renaissance and Mannerism* (World of Art Series). Praeger, 1967.

Murray, Linda, *The High Renaissance* (World of Art Series). Praeger, 1967.

Freedberg; Sydney J., *Painting of the High Renaissance in Rome and Florence,* 2 vols. Harper & Row, 1972. Basic scholarly study of the early sixteenth century.

Friedlander, Walter, *Mannerism and Anti-Mannerism in Italian Painting.* Schocken, 1965. Basic study of two major styles of painting in sixteenth-century Italy.

RENAISSANCE ART IN NORTHERN EUROPE

Huizinga, Johan, *The Waning of the Middle Ages.* Doubleday, 1956. Classic study of the fifteenth century in the North.

Benesch, Otto, *Art of the Renaissance in Northern Europe: Its Relation to the Contemporary Spiritual and Intellectual Movements.* Harvard Univ. Press (hard cover), 1947 (out of print). Concise study of the intellectual and historical background.

Cutler, Charles, *Northern Painting from Pucelle to Bruegel, the Fourteenth, Fifteenth and Sixteenth Centuries.* Holt, Rinehart & Winston, 1973. Comprehensive and well-illustrated survey much indebted to Panofsky's *Early Netherlandish Painting* (1953).

Benesch, Otto, *German Painting: Dürer to Holbein.* Skira (hard cover), 1966 (out of print). Concise survey of painting and graphic arts.

Müller, Theodor, *Sculpture in the Netherlands, Germany, France and Spain 1400–1500.* Penguin (hard cover), 1966. Pictorial survey.

BAROQUE ART, 1600–1800

NOTE Consult pertinent volumes in the Pelican History of Art Series (Penguin, hard cover) devoted to the art of this period in Italy, Belgium, Holland, Spain, Central Europe, France, and England.

The following five books are general introductory surveys of the international Baroque; they are well illustrated and have good bibliographies.

Kitson, Michael, *The Age of Baroque*. McGraw-Hill (hard cover), 1966 (out of print).

Bazin, Germain, *Baroque and Rococo Art*. Praeger, 1964.

Sewter, A. C., *Baroque and Rococo* (History of Art Series). Harcourt Brace Jovanovich, 1972.

Tapie, Victor L., *The Age of Grandeur: Baroque Art and Architecture*. Grove (hard cover), 1960 (out of print).

Held, Julius S., and Donald Posner, *Seventeenth and Eighteenth Century Art: Baroque Painting, Sculpture and Architecture*. Prentice Hall (hard cover), 1972.

Levey, Michael, *Rococo to Revolution* (World of Art Series). Praeger, 1966. Stimulating overview of the eighteenth century.

Haskell, Francis, *Patrons and Painters*. Chatto & Windus (hard cover), 1963. Study in the relations between Italian art and society in the Baroque age.

Waterhouse, Ellis K., *Italian Baroque Painting*, rev. ed. Phaidon, 1970. Well-illustrated survey.

Stechow, Wolfgang, *Dutch Landscape Painting of the Seventeenth Century*. Phaidon (hard cover), 1966 (out of print). Major survey of the field.

Millon, Henry A., *Baroque and Rococo Architecture*. Braziller, 1961. Brief introductions with excellent bibliography.

NINETEENTH CENTURY ART
IN EUROPE AND AMERICA

Brion, Marcel, *Art of the Romantic Era: Classicism, Romanticism, Realism*. Praeger, 1966. Well-illustrated survey.

Hofmann, Werner, *The Earthly Paradise: Art in the Nineteenth Century*. Braziller (hard cover), 1961 (out of print). Unique survey that stresses little-known and often bizarre works.

Leymarie, Jean, *French Painting, The Nineteenth Century*. Skira (hard cover), 1962 (out of print). General survey; well illustrated.

Cummings, F. J., R. Rosenblum, and A. Staley, *Romantic Art in*

Britain: Paintings and Drawings 1760–1860. **Falcon, 1968.** Concise, up-to-date discussion of British developments.

Novak, Barbara, *American Painting in the Nineteenth Century.* **Praeger, 1969.** Work of leading artists with reference to such themes as conceptualism and Transcendentalism.

Larkin, Oliver, *Art and Life in America,* **rev. ed. Holt, Rinehart & Winston (hard cover) 1960.** Background material on American developments.

Champa, Kermit S., *German Painting of the Nineteenth Century.* **Yale Univ. Art Gallery (hard cover), 1970 (out of print).** Informative introductory essay and catalogue to an exhibition of German paintings in German collections.

Licht, Fred, *Sculpture—Nineteenth and Twentieth Centuries.* **New York Graphic (hard cover), 1967 (out of print).** General introduction; well illustrated.

The following two books are basic surveys of Impressionism and Post-Impressionism.

Rewald, John, *The History of Impressionism.* **Museum of Modern Art (hard cover), 1973.**

Rewald, John, *Post Impressionism: From Van Gogh to Gauguin.* **Museum of Modern Art (hard cover), 1962.**

Kaufmann, Edgar, Jr., ed., *The Rise of an American Architecture.* **Praeger, 1970.** Four essays by leading scholars in the field on major aspects of nineteenth-century American architecture.

Pevsner, Nikolaus, *The Sources of Modern Architecture and Design* **(World of Art Series). Praeger, 1968.** The period c. 1850 to 1914 discussed in relation to the various arts; based on the same author's scholarly *Pioneers of Modern Design.*

Pierson, William H., Jr., *American Buildings and Their Architects: The Colonial and Neo-Classical Styles.* **Doubleday (hard cover), 1970.** Together with the author's forthcoming study of nineteenth-century architecture in America, this will constitute the first complete survey of American building traditions before 1900.

TWENTIETH CENTURY ART
IN EUROPE AND AMERICA

Arnason, H. H., *History of Modern Art: Painting, Sculpture, Architecture.* **Prentice-Hall (hard cover), 1969.** Extensive, balanced, and well-illustrated survey, with good bibliography.

Haftmann, Werner, *Painting in the Twentieth Century: A Pictorial Survey.* **Praeger, 1965.** Comprehensive survey with over 1000 illustrations.

Bowness, Alan, *Modern European Art* (History of Art Series). Harcourt Brace Jovanovich, 1972. Up-to-date survey of twentieth-century developments.

Sandler, Irving, *The Triumph of American Painting: A History of Abstract Expressionism*. Praeger, 1973. Account of individual movements and trends after the Second World War.

The following three books are the basic surveys of modern sculpture.

Ritchie, Andrew D., *Sculpture of the Twentieth Century*. Arno (hard cover), 1952.

Giedion-Welcker, C., *Contemporary Sculpture: An Evolution in Volume and Space*. Wittenborn (hard cover), 1955 (out of print).

Kultermann, Udo, *The New Sculpture: Environments and Assemblages*. Praeger (hard cover), 1968 (out of print).

The following six books are introductions to modern architecture.

Scully, Vincent, *American Architecture and Urbanism: A Historical Essay*. Praeger, 1969. Provocative, sweeping view of the architectural scene.

Scully, Vincent, *Modern Architecture*, rev. ed. Braziller, 1974. Unique essay, recently expanded, on the major developments of modern architecture from 1780 to the present.

Banham, Reyner, *Guide to Modern Architecture*. London Architectural Press (hard cover), 1962 (out of print). Detailed commentary on 33 buildings or complexes representative of major developments.

Jencks, Charles, *Modern Movements in Architecture*. Doubleday, 1973. Stimulating analysis and criticism of twentieth-century developments with excellent bibliographical references.

Jordy, William H., *American Buildings and Their Architects: Progressive and Academic Ideals at the Turn of the Twentieth Century*. Doubleday, 1972.

Jordy, William H., *American Buildings and Their Architects: The Impact of European Modernism in the Mid-Twentieth Century*. Doubleday, 1972.

INDIA

Zimmer, Heinrich, *Art of Indian Asia*, 2 vols., ed. Joseph Campbell, 2nd ed. Princeton Univ. Press (hard cover), 1960. Detailed compendium of Indian art.

Goetz, Hermann, *India: Five Thousand Years of Indian Art*. McGraw-Hill (hardcover), 1959 (out of print). General, well-illustrated survey.

Joseph Campbell, *Myths and Symbols in Indian Art and Civiliza-*

tion, ed. Heinrich Zimmer. Princeton Univ. Press, 1971. Introduction to the iconography of Indian Art.

Lannoy, Richard, *The Speaking Tree: A Study of Indian Culture and Society.* Oxford Univ. Press, 1974. Provides the basis for a refreshing new approach to Indian art.

CHINA

Akiyama, Terukazu, *et al., Arts of China,* Vol. 1: *Neolithic Cultures to the T'ang Dynasty,* tr. Mary Tragear (1968); Vol. 2: *Buddhist Cave Temples,* tr. Alexander Soper (1969). Kodansha (hard cover). Comprehensive; based on recent archeological findings.

Sullivan, Michael, *Arts of China: A Short History.* Univ. of California Press, 1974. Basic survey containing recent archeological material.

Cahill, James, *Chinese Painting.* Skira (hard cover), 1972 (out of print). Well-illustrated and balanced survey of the subject.

Rowley, George, *Principles of Chinese Painting,* rev. ed. Princeton Univ. Press, 1959. Broad discussion of techniques, aesthetics, and philosophy.

Wheatley, Paul, *Pivot of the Four Quarters: A Preliminary Inquiry into the Origins and Characters of the Ancient Chinese City.* Aldine (hard cover), 1971. History of the planning of Chinese cities.

JAPAN

The following two books are two excellent introductions to Japanese art.

Seiroku, Noma, *Arts of Japan,* 2 vols. Kodansha (hard cover), 1967. Translated from the Japanese.

Akiyama, Terukazu, *Japanese Painting.* Skira (hard cover), 1961.

Varley, H. Paul, *Japanese Culture: A Short History.* Praeger, 1973. Account of Japanese cultural history with references to major monuments.

Drexler, Arthur, *The Architecture of Japan.* (Museum of Modern Art Pub. in Repr. Series) Arno (hard cover), 1955. Basic introduction; well illustrated.

AFRICA

The following four books are outstanding introductions to African art.

Leuzinger, E., *The Art of Black Africa.* New York Graphic, 1972. Account of religious and cultural contexts of the separate traditions of African art, based on detailed examinations of over 600 works.

Delange, J., and M. Leiris, *The Art and Peoples of Black Africa.* **Dutton, 1974.** Documentary study of the genres and styles of art; the basis for a history of Black African art.

Laude, Jean, *Arts of Black Africa.* Univ. of California Press, 1971. Interesting philosophical approach to the material.

Thompson, Robert F., *African Art in Motion: Icon and Art.* Univ. of California Press, 1974.

Frazer, Douglas, ed., *The Faces of Primitive Art.* **Prentice-Hall (hard cover), 1966 (out of print).** Collection of essays on aspects of African culture.

The Museum of Primitive Art (New York), *Senufo Sculpture from West Africa* (by Robert Goldwater, Director), New York Graphic Society, 1964; *Sculpture of Northern Nigeria* (by Roy Sieber), University Publishers, 1961. Also: **Museum of Primitive Art** pamphlet containing important articles by Roy Sieber and Robert Thompson on the aesthetics of primitive art.

Goldwater, Robert, et al., *Art of Oceania, Africa and the Americas from the Museum of Primitive Art.* **Metropolitan Museum of Art, 1969.** Catalogue to an exhibition at the Metropolitan Museum of Art. Excellent introduction to each subject.

OCEANIC ART

The following three books are the best general surveys of Oceanic art:

Buhler, A., *et al., Art of the South Sea Islands* (Art of the World Library). Crown (hard cover), 1962.

Guiart, Jean, *The Arts of the South Pacific* (Arts of Mankind Series). Braziller (hard cover), 1963.

Smitz, Carl, *Oceanic Art: Myth, Man and Image in the South Seas.* Abrams (hard cover), 1970.

AMERICAN INDIAN AND PRE-COLUMBIAN ART

American Indian

Walker Art Center of the Minneapolis Institute of Arts, *American Indian Art: Form and Tradition,* Dutton, 1973. Catalogue for an exhibition; synthesis of entire field with excellent bibliography.

The following two books are outstanding introductions to American Indian art.

Inverarity, Robert B., *Art of the Northwest Coast Indians,* 2nd ed. Univ. of California Press, 1967.

Haberland, W., *The Art of North America* (Art of the World Series). Crown (hard cover), 1964 (out of print).

Pre-Columbian

Easby, Elizabeth K., and John F. Scott, *Before Cortes: Sculpture of Middle America*. Metropolitan Museum of Art, 1970. Catalogue for an exhibition; synthesis of entire field.

The following three books are introductory surveys of Pre-Columbian art:

Bushnell, Geoffrey H., *Ancient Arts of the Americas* (World of Art Series). Praeger, 1965.

Disselhoff, Hans-Dietrich, and Sigvala Linne, *Art of Ancient America*. Crown (hard cover), 1961.

Weaver, Muriel P., *The Aztecs, Maya and Their Predecessors: Archeology of MesoAmerica*. Academic (hard cover), 1972.

Helfritz, Hans, *Mexican Cities of the Gods: An Archeological Guide*. Praeger, 1970. Excellent handbook to the ancient sites; replete with plans, diagrams, and superb photographs.

SOURCES AND DOCUMENTS

Holt, Elizabeth G., ed., *A Documentary History of Art*, 3 vols. Doubleday, 1957–1958. Vols. 1 and 2 contain writings of artists, architects, clerics, and philosophers from the ninth through the eighteenth centuries. Vol. 3 covers writings of the nineteenth century, including those of critics and city planners.

Janson, H. W., ed., *Sources and Documents in the History of Art Series*, rev. ed. Abrams (hard cover), 1969. A 14-volume series containing writings by artists, historians, philosophers, and critics from the time of the Greeks to that of Post-Impressionism.

Chipp, Herschel B., ed., *Theories of Modern Art: A Source Book by Artists and Critics*. Univ. of California Press, 1968. Writings by artists and critics on modern art from Post-Impressionism to the mid-1960s.

Chambers, D. S. *Patrons and Artists in the Italian Renaissance*. Univ. of South Carolina Press, 1971. Anthology of Renaissance documents in translation illustrative of patronage and working practice of artists of the fifteenth century.

REFERENCE WORKS AND SERIES

NOTE Reference works and series are identified here primarily for readers to consult rather than obtain. They can probably be found in many large libraries.

Chamberlin, Mary W., *Guide to Art Reference Books*. American Library Association (hard cover), 1959 (out of print). Basic listing of research materials in art history.

Encyclopedia of World Art, **15 vols. McGraw-Hill (hard cover), 1959–1968.** A somewhat arbitrary gathering of articles on both broad topics and specialized subjects with a separate index volume.

The Pelican History of Art Series, **ed. Nikolaus Pevsner. Penguin (hard cover).** Some 50 volumes written by leading international scholars. With a few exceptions, single studies in this series have not been listed in the chronological sections of this bibliography because of space limitations.

The Library of Art History Series, **ed. H. W. Janson. Abrams (hard cover), 1971.** Five volumes devoted to major periods of western art: the Ancient World, the Middle Ages, the Renaissance, the Baroque, and the Modern World.

Art of the World Series, **various authors, no single editor, 40 vols. Crown (hard cover).** Exceptional introductions to the historical, sociological, and religious background of the periods and cultures of world art, both European and non-European.

Fleming, John, and Hugh Honour, eds., *Art in Context Series.* **Viking Press (hard cover), 1974.** A fifteen-volume series devoted to famous paintings and sculptures, each of which is evaluated in its own special stylistic, technical, literary, religious, social, or political context.

Great Ages of World Architecture Series. **Braziller.** A twelve-volume series devoted to Western and non-Western architecture.

Planning and Cities, **ed. George R. Collins. Braziller, 1969 to present.** A twelve-volume series on the evolution and planning of cities in a wide range of historical periods and cultural areas.

Chapter Seventeen

AMERICAN LITERATURE
". . . our native sense of life"

Editorial Advisor:
William Alexander
Department of English
University of Michigan

INTRODUCTION

American literature expresses our native sense of life as a people. It is our national conscience, our past come alive. To read it is to reexperience the familiar and half-recognized—to appreciate the enormous diversity and richness found in what is for all of us, in the end, a shared experience. The life and the landscape around us resound with the echoes of those who came before. Through American literature we can experience the rich variety of other lives, thereby deepening our own.

SUGGESTIONS ON HOW TO PROCEED

The following reading list is arranged historically for the sake of those who wish to study American literature in sequence, as it is often, but by no means always, studied in colleges. Other approaches are possible: you may wish to work with particular major authors taken from anywhere within the entire range, or work intensively within one period, or work with a single genre—the novel or short story, the narrative poem or personal essay.

As still another alternative, you can develop a sequence in comparative literature of your own by, for example, drawing on this section in connection with like works or periods in the English Literature section. Or you could carry out a broad program in American culture by combining your study of literature with readings in related works listed under American History or Women's Studies.

In short, pursue what is of most interest, challenge, and satisfaction to you personally. Do not feel that you should proceed from beginning to end of the reading list simply because it is there. Follow your bent, take your own approach; literary understanding at its best is an accomplishment gained in personal ways.

A few suggestions on your actual reading may be helpful. The experience of reading is partly a reflective process. During or after a first reading (or both), ask questions: What is happening? How it is happening? Why is this said in this particular way at this point? Similar questions are noted for many works in the reading list.

All along, try to increase your sensitivity to literature and your range and depth of knowledge, at the same time recognizing the importance and validity of your personal responses. If you can, work with others with whom you can talk over what you have read openly and intelligently.

GETTING YOUR BEARINGS IN THE FIELD

However you choose to proceed, you will have some sense of the overall terrain and landmarks in American literature if you know something about the major historical periods into which it is generally organized by scholars. Brief characterizations and approximate time-spans of these periods follow; the periods correspond to the groupings of the reading list.

Colonial (1607–1765)

The Colonial period begins as a time marked by religious purpose, by theological and political discussion; the style tends to be plain according to the dictates of Puritan dogma. Later the literature begins to broaden in focus, suggesting more sectarian and secular concerns and exhibiting refinements and adornments of style. Throughout the Colonial period there is a constant definition and redefinition of the New World and its relation to the Old, especially England.

Revolutionary and Early Federal (1765–1830)

During the following period literature reflects the Age of Reason, with humanitarianism, concern for the rights of man, arguments that unjust governments should be overthrown, dominating the important writings of the period. The original literature is mainly political—the writings of Jefferson, Paine, Hamilton and others. Nonpolitical literature of the time is usually derivative of English neoclassicism, sentimentalism, and early Romanticism.

Romantic (1820–1865)

One of the most difficult periods to define clearly, it is the age of early urbanization, industrialization, and westward expansion. Reform movements culminate in the antislavery cause. There is an increasing

COLLEGE ON YOUR OWN

trend toward egalitarianism and materialism. Literary nationalism and Romanticism lead to celebrations of the American landscape and of individualism, coupled with an essentially secular investigation of the nature of good and evil. There is more personal, more psychological writing. A distinctively American literature—one that is not derivative—emerges at this time.

Realistic (1865–1900)

This is the time of the rise of cities, the end of the frontier, a period of great materialism—"The Gilded Age," Mark Twain called it—a time of vast business growth and the beginnings of labor organization. The literature is marked by a concern for the objective presentation of everyday manners and concerns, first of the middle class, later of the lower economic and social classes. There is also an interest in regionalism, local color, dialects. Critical realism attacks the social, political, and economic ills of the time. Naturalism becomes a substantial movement by the 1890s; it is marked by philosophical determinism as well as a concern with the lower classes.

Early Twentieth Century (1900–1930)

The efforts of Americans in the Progressive era to organize society along lines of expert planning, using the nation's technological capacities, subside with the First World War and the resultant disillusionment with progressive rhetoric and human nature. The 1920s is the decade of business boom and the "jazz age," made famous by Fitzgerald. Literary realism and naturalism continue in this period, but so does popular romance. It is also the age of muckraking, the debunking of the small-town myth, and the beginning of Black awareness as reflected in the Harlem Renaissance of the 1920s. Literature becomes more cynical, less reformist after the First World War with satirical criticism of American "boobs" and "Babbitts." The "waste land" becomes a dominant symbol.

1930s to present

The literature of the 1930s is dominated by the Great Depression—though Faulkner, Wolfe, and O'Neill are notable exceptions. Emerging in this period is a literature of protest, proletarian literature, the drama of commitment, and a new emphasis on documentary expression. Post-Second World War literature is troubled and ironic in tone, often surreal and absurd in content, existential in outlook. It represents writing in revolt against Cold War ideals abroad and complacency at home. In the 1960s and 1970s, particularly, it focuses on social injustice but lacks the hopeful reformism of earlier periods. Contemporary writers create antiheroes, perplexed victims, and rebels.

RESEARCH METHODS
AND LEADING SCHOLAR-CRITICS

For supplementary or advanced study of the sort pursued by American Literature majors or graduate students at colleges, you may be interested in getting to know something of leading scholar-critics in the field and their research methods. A number of these figures are identified here; you can easily obtain their works in libraries and bookstores. They explain their research methods in presenting their analyses.

Major American literary historians who concern themselves with American Literature within its historical and cultural context include Daniel Aaron, Van Wyck Brooks, Richard Chase, Malcolm Cowley, Howard Mumford Jones, Alfred Kazin, F. O. Matthiessen, Perry Miller, V. L. Parrington, Roy Harvey Pearce, Robert E. Spiller, Lionel Trilling, Hyatt Wagoner, and Edmund Wilson.

Prominent critics who focus upon the nature of particular genres are Wayne Booth (fiction), R. S. Crane (poetry and other genres), Elder Olson (poetry and drama) and Robert Scholes (fiction).

"New" or formalist critics, who concentrate on the images and language of the literary work itself, include Richard Blackmur, Cleanth Brooks, Reuben Brower, T. S. Eliot, Richard Poirier, John Crowe Ransom, and Allen Tate.

Maud Bodkin (an Englishwoman), Kenneth Burke, and Northrop Frye (a Canadian) are outstanding theorists of archetypal criticism, while those who have investigated American Literature for its prominent metaphors, myths, and symbols include Richard Chase, Charles Feidelson, Leslie Fiedler, Daniel G. Hoffman, D. H. Lawrence, R. W. B. Lewis, Leo Marx, and Henry Nash Smith.

Psychoanalytic critics have concerned themselves with unconscious motivations in literary characters, in authors, and in readers; important work in this area has been done by Kenneth Burke, Frederick Crews, Frederick J. Hoffman, Norman Holland, Ernest Jones, Simon Lesser, Leslie Fiedler, Lionel Trilling, and Edmund Wilson.

Other authors have brought social, political, and economic perspectives to literary works, among them Daniel Aaron, Mortimer Adler, Albert Guerard, and Granville Hicks. Susan Sontag is an example of a challenging critic who moves with ease among a number of disciplines.

A good general history (up to 1948) is *A Literary History of the United States* by Robert E. Spiller et. al. For sensitive introductions to the reading of literature, *Understanding Poetry* and *Understanding Fiction,* both by Cleanth Brooks and Robert Penn Warren, should be helpful. Provocative books on the psychology of reading are Maud Bodkin's *Archetypal Patterns in Poetry.* Norman Holland's *The Dynamics of Literary Response,* and Simon Lesser's *Fiction and the Unconscious.*

BIBLIOGRAPHY

COLONIAL PERIOD (1607–1765)

Basic Readings

Miller, Perry, and Thomas H. Johnson, eds., *The American Puritans: A Sourcebook of Their Writings,* vols. I and II. Harper & Row, **1938.** Read especially Chs. I-III, VI-VII, and the introductions to all sections. Pay special attention to style, to organization of argument, to definitions of America, and to developing ideas of proper spiritual and political behavior in a religious colony.

Taylor, Edward (c. 1642–1729), *The Poems of Edward Taylor.* Yale Univ. Press, 1963. Meditative poetry; note development of attitude and tone from beginning to end of poems. Watch Taylor's choice of figures of speech.

Edwards, Jonathan (1703–58), *Jonathan Edwards: Basic Writings,* ed. Ola Winslow. NAL, 1962. The great religious awakening. Worth close reading to get at Edwards' understanding of the psychology of sin, free will, and grace. Think out his relation to the Puritan writers of the first generations.

Franklin, Benjamin (1706–90), *Autobiography and Selected Writings,* Dixon Wecter and Larzer Ziff, eds. Holt, Rinehart & Winston, 1949. Determine his points of contact and his points of departure, in style and thought, with Puritan writing. Read carefully to define the nature and range of his values, the reasons for his profound and continuing influence on his countrymen.

Further Readings

Miller, Perry, ed., *Roger Williams: His Contribution to the American Tradition.* Atheneum, 1962.

Mather, Cotton (1663–1728), *Selections from Cotton Mather,* ed. Kenneth B. Murdock. Hafner, 1960.

REVOLUTIONARY AND EARLY FEDERAL PERIOD (1765–1830)

Basic Readings

Cady, Edwin H., ed., *Literature of the Early Republic* 2nd ed. Holt, Rinehart & Winston, 1969. A good, varied collection of writing in this period. Watch for specifically American variations on, and use of, eighteenth-century neoclassicism, belief in reason, human rights.

Franklin, Benjamin. See above.

Further Readings

Jefferson, Thomas (1743–1826), *Notes on the State of Virginia* (1784–1785), ed. William Peden. Norton, 1972.

Brown, Charles Brockden (1771–1810), *Wieland, or the Transformation* (1789); *Together with the Memoirs of Carwin the Biloquist,* ed. F. L. Pattee. Harcourt Brace Jovanovich, 1969.

ROMANTIC PERIOD (1820–1865)

Basic Readings

Irving, Washington (1783–1859), *The Sketch Book* (1820). NAL, 1961. Attempt to define Irving's particular sensibility and style, his attitude toward the past, toward his fellow men of all classes, toward political matters. Worth comparing his handling of the supernatural, the spiritual, and the human condition with treatment by Brown, Poe, Hawthorne.

Cooper, James Fenimore (1789–1851), *The Prairie* (1827). NAL, 1964. Note how Cooper relates aristocracy and democracy as well as human, natural and spiritual law, and how he defines an ideal American nation. One of our great writers of romances, worth comparing with Poe **(Poe's *Narrative of A. Gordon Pym,* Hill & Wang, 1960)**, Hawthorne, and Melville for his fiction patterns, his resolutions, his values.

Poe, Edgar Allen (1809–1849), *The Portable Poe,* ed. Philip Stern. Viking, 1959. Be sure to read "The Poetic Principle" and "The Philosophy of Composition" as suggestive ways of thinking about the tales and poems. Consider to what end Poe is so concerned with burials alive, starvation, cannibalism, and other extreme and grotesque experiences.

Miller, Perry, ed., *The Transcendentalists: An Anthology.* Harvard Univ. Press, 1950. A good introduction to the general movement of which Emerson, Thoreau, Fuller, and others were part and to which so many other writers have in one way or another reacted.

Emerson, Ralph Waldo (1803–1882), *The Portable Emerson,* ed. Mark Van Doren. Viking, 1946. One of the seminal American thinkers; it is well worth your while getting his ideas and values down. Piece together the behavior he advocates and his definitions of education, of evil, and of man's relation to nature, to society, and to other individuals. Watch for the troubling of his general optimism.

Thoreau, Henry David (1817–1862), *The Portable Thoreau,* rev. ed., ed. Carl Bode. Viking, 1957. Among the very best American prose. *Walden* is especially worth *careful* reading; the book is rich in integrity, rhetoric, experience, it is a challenge to us to get to our own roots, to simplify, to be reborn—what does this mean, individually and politically?

Whitman, Walt (1819–1892), *Leaves of Grass and Selected Prose,* ed. John Kouwenhoven. Random House (Modern Library), 1950. Read the 1855 Preface and "A Backward Glance O'er Traveled Roads" as an introduction to Whitman's intentions. Then read the poems sequentially, tracing in them the effects of events in America and in his personal life on his style and on his attitudes and ideas on individualism, democracy, and religion. What relation has his style to his idea of America and of the reader? Read "Democratic Vistas" after you have read the Civil War poems.

Hawthorne, Nathaniel (1804–1864), *Selected Short Stories of Nathaniel Hawthorne,* ed. Alfred Kazin. Fawcett World Library, 1973. Excellent in themselves and serving to enlarge the reader's understanding of Hawthorne.

Hawthorne, Nathaniel, *The Scarlet Letter* (1850). Macmillan, 1962. Read carefully, watching for tensions in Hawthorne's attitude toward antisocial behavior, toward sin and guilt. Think of him as a psychological romancer.

Hawthorne, Nathaniel, *The Marble Faun* (1860). NAL, 1962. Same as above; also watch for new concerns when the older writer confronts the old world.

Melville, Herman (1819–1891), *Moby Dick* (1851), Macmillan, 1962. Worth considering in the context of the romance and in the context of transcendentalism. Watch Melville's handling of the problems of human dependency and of independence, of evil, and of finding a viable philosophical attitude toward existence.

Melville, Herman, *Pierre, or the Ambiguities* (1852). NAL, 1957. Fascinating for the complexity of Melville's mind, for his handling of the romance, for his continuing attempt to discover a nonmaterial pattern for living in material America, for his study of the growth of consciousness and his study of the nature of innocence and experience.

Melville, Herman, *Billy Budd, Sailor* [1924] *and Other Stories,* ed. H. Beaver. Penguin, 1968. "Hawthorne and His Mosses" (try to be sure to see this commentary on Hawthorne's *Mosses from an Old Manse* in a library; not in the Penguin collection) gives some excellent insight into Melville's own writing, while "Bartleby" is a chilling index of Melville in the post-*Pierre* period, "Billy Budd" an index to the concerns of the late Melville.

Further Readings

Simms, William Gilmore (1806–1870), *The Yemassee* (1835), ed. Joseph V. Ridgely. College and Univ. Press, 1964.

Fuller, Margaret (1810–1850), *Margaret Fuller, American Romantic,* ed. Perry Miller. Cornell Univ. Press, 1970.

Parkman, Francis (1823–1893), *The Oregon Trail* (1847). Airmont, 1964.

Prescott, William Hickling (1796–1859), *History of the Conquest of Mexico* (1843), abr. ed., ed. C. Harvey Gardiner. Univ. of Chicago Press, 1966.

Stowe, Harriet Beecher (1811–1896), *Uncle Tom's Cabin* (1852). Macmillan, 1962.

Longfellow, Henry Wadsworth (1807–1882), *Poems.* Dutton, 1972. For the works of other leading poets of this period, see such hard cover works in a local library as **Bryant, William Cullen, *Poetical Works of William Cullen Bryant,*** Appleton, 1913; Holmes, Oliver Wendell, *The Poetical Works of Oliver Wendell Holmes,* Houghton Mifflin, 1902; Lowell, James Russell, *Complete Poetical Works,* Houghton Mifflin, 1925; and **Whittier, John Greenleaf, *The Poetical Works of John Greenleaf Whittier,*** Houghton Mifflin, 1887.

REALISTIC PERIOD (1865–1900)

Basic Readings

Howells, William Dean (1837–1920), *A Modern Instance* (1882), ed. William M. Gibson. Houghton Mifflin, 1957. Realistic fiction. Watch for methods of shaping plot, character, environment, language, and narrative position. Work out the values Howells places in opposition to those that determine Bartley's behavior.

Twain, Mark (1835–1910), *The Portable Mark Twain,* ed. Bernard De Voto. Viking, 1955. Contains *The Adventures of Huckleberry Finn* (1884) and *The Mysterious Stranger* (1916), with some other selections. In *The Adventures of Huckleberry Finn,* consider the effect of Huck as narrative voice, define the nature and resonance of Twain's brand of humor, determine Twain's attitude toward "adventures" and romance, his conception of human nature. Read *The Mysterious Stranger.*

Twain, Mark, *A Connecticut Yankee in King Arthur's Court* (1889), ed. Justin Kaplan. Penguin, 1972. Think of it as a critique of late nineteenth-century American civilization and of the literature of romance.

James, Henry (1843–1916), *The Portrait of a Lady* (1881), ed. Leon Edel. Houghton Mifflin, 1956. Watch James's exploration of the natures and boundaries of freedom, his handling of the relation between innocence and experience, America and Europe. Worth comparing him as a psychological realist to Hawthorne as a psychological romancer.

James, Henry, *The Ambassadors* (1903), ed. S. P. Rosenbaum. Norton, 1964. Same as above, also consider James's particular narrative position, his stylistic refinements, and their effects on the reading experience.

James, Henry, *Selected Fiction,* ed. Leon Edel. Dutton, 1964. Read especially *Daisy Miller* (1879), *The Aspern Papers* (1888), "The Beast in the Jungle" (1903), and "The Art of Fiction."

Dickinson, Emily (1830–1886), *Final Harvest: Emily Dickinson's Poems,* ed. Thomas H. Johnson, Little, Brown, 1962. Consider the effect of Dickinson's tight verse (based on Protestant hymn rhythms) on her handling of her subjects. Watch for her definitions of the boundaries of self in relation to environment, other people, death, and God.

Jewett, Sarah Orne (1849–1909), *The Country of the Pointed Firs* [1896] *and Other Stories.* Doubleday, 1954. Jewett is possibly the best of our regional writers; her careful style is worth analysis for its precision and its sensitivity to nuance of landscape and character. Determine the ways her work transcends the locale it is so deeply imbedded in.

Chopin, Kate (1851–1904). *The Awakening* [1899] *and Other Stories,* ed. L. Leary, Holt, Rinehart & Winston, 1970. Look at Chopin's techniques for presenting character through mood, symbolism, narrative restraint, and the like. Worth comparing her works with *Madame Bovary* and later American books on provincial life, such as *Winesburg, Ohio, Spoon River Anthology, Cane, My Antonia* (see below for all).

Crane, Stephen (1871–1900), *The Red Badge of Courage* [1895] and Selected Prose and Poetry, 3rd ed., William M. Gibson. Holt, Rinehart & Winston, 1969. Impressionism; note how characters see their environment, how their environment is portrayed through their speech, through the manner in which Crane describes what they see. Consider how people shape and are shaped by their surroundings.

Norris, Frank (1870–1902), *McTeague* (1899), ed. Carvel Collins. Holt, Rinehart & Winston, 1950. Worth defining the relation among environment, heredity, and character, the freedom of human will. Compare with Howells, James, Crane, Adams, Dreiser.

Adams, Henry (1838–1918), *The Education of Henry Adams* (1918). Houghton Mifflin, 1961. Determine the dynamics of order and chaos, and follow closely Adams' study of the nature of political and personal power, his study of historical forces and the relation of an individual to them. Work out his ideas of education.

Further Readings

Garland, Hamlin (1860–1940), *Main-Traveled Roads* (1891). NAL, 1962.

Cable, George Washington (1844–1925), *The Grandissimes* (1880), Hill & Wang, 1957.

De Forest, John W. (1829–1906), *Miss Ravenel's Conversion from Secession to Loyalty* (1867). ed. Gordon S. Haight. Holt, Rinehart & Winston, 1955.

Alger, Horatio (1834–1899), *Ragged Dick and Mark the Match Boy* (1867). Macmillan, 1966.

EARLY TWENTIETH CENTURY PERIOD (1900–1930)

Basic Readings

Dreiser, Theodore (1871–1945), *Sister Carrie* **(1900), Holt, Rinehart & Winston, 1957.** Compare Howells the naturalist with Crane, Norris, Adams. Determine the extent to which responsibility can be fixed for what happens to Carrie and Hurstwood. Worth working out the particular vitality and power of Dreiser's unrefined prose.

Wharton, Edith (1862–1937), *The House of Mirth* **(1905). NAL, 1964.** Define the ambivalence of Lily's relation to her social peers and the nature of Wharton's relation to the same group; consider the nature of the perspective and the amount of depth with which she treats her subject.

Franklin, John H., ed., *Three Negro Classics.* **Avon, 1965. Contains James Weldon Johnson,** *Autobiography of an Ex-Colored Man,* **1912; Booker T. Washington,** *Up From Slavery,* **1901; W. E. B. Du Bois,** *The Souls of Black Folk,* **1903.** In Johnson's work, keep an eye on conflict of interests, values; note the attitude toward white culture as it manifests itself in description, in aspiration, and in choice of prose style; also examine Johnson's stance toward different strata and manifestations of Black culture. Compare with Chesnutt and Toomer (below). In reading *The Souls of Black Folk,* think through the various ways white oppression works upon the Black American and upon the white; consider Du Bois' opposition to Booker T. Washington, the alternatives he holds out to members of his race, and the methods, rhetorical and argumentative, by which he asserts them.

Cather, Willa (1873–1947), *My Antonia* **(1918). Houghton Mifflin, 1961.** Determine Cather's feeling about how twentieth-century Americans should relate to Antonia and the Western past. Consider the function of the rather episodic plot and the choice of a person such as Jim as narrator.

Anderson, Sherwood (1876–1941), *Winesburg, Ohio* **(1919), 2nd ed. Viking, 1960.** Read carefully to trace common motifs and purposes through the stories; consider what purpose George Willard and Anderson might have in writing about these grotesques. Compare the short-story form here to other stories, including those in *Cane.* Think of Winesburg in comparison with Zenith (*Babbitt*), with the environment of *The Awakening,* with *Spoon River,* Garland's West, and Toomer's North and South (all, below).

Frost, Robert (1874–1963) *Selected Poems.* **Holt, Rinehart & Winston, 1963.** Study the relation among Frost's voice, his subjects, and the traditional verse forms and rhythms he uses. Consider the nature of his humor, his concern with bounds, with man's relation to the surrounding woods. See if it helps to think of his poems as (in his terms) momentary stays against confusion.

Eliot, T. S. (1888–1965), *Collected Poems, 1909–1962.* **Harcourt Brace Jovanovich (hard cover), 1963.** Consider the function of Eliot's complexity, his reference to past cultures and works of art in poems about fragmented culture and spiritual sterility. The later poems repay careful reading in their consideration of material and spiritual time and their exploration of religious experience and possibility. For light on his work, it is worth reading also his *Selected Essays* (rev. ed., Harcourt Brace Jovanovich, hard cover, 1950).

Stevens, Wallace (1879–1955), *The Palm at the End of the Mind: Selected Poems and a Play,* **ed. Holly Stevens. Random House, 1972.** Think of the poems as serious, suggestive studies of the nature and importance of the poetic, the imaginative act. Watch the relations between imagination and reality, between stasis and change. Consider the function of extravagant imagery.

Pound, Ezra (1885–1972), *Selected Poems.* **New Directions, 1957.** Examine Pound's choice of models, verse forms, subjects, and stances to determine the culture and outlook this influential expatriate sets in opposition to the cultures and people he criticizes.

Williams, William Carlos (1883–1963), *Selected Poems.* **New Directions, 1969.** Worth comparing with, say, Dickinson for the precise use of both form and image to catch moments, feelings, the look of objects. Consider what is gained by Williams' particular liberation of poetry from traditional rhythms and meters.

Lewis, Sinclair (1885–1951), *Babbitt* **(1922). NAL, 1961.** Important to determine just what Lewis has under attack here and where—in his own style, in references, in specific characters—one can find standards to set against the America depicted.

Toomer, Jean, *Cane* **(1923). Harper & Row, 1969.** Worthwhile to tie the stories together through similar characters, situations, themes to get at the frustrations and problems Toomer feels in America in the 1920s and at the kinds of authenticity he advocates.

Fitzgerald, F. Scott (1896–1940), *The Great Gatsby* **(1925). Bantam, 1974.** Define the various dimensions of Gatsby's aspirations, the meaning Daisy has for him, and the reasons Nick respects him.

Hemingway, Ernest (1899–1961), *The Sun Also Rises* **(1926). Scribner's, 1926. Also** *Short Stories of Ernest Hemingway.* **Scribner's, 1938.** The fishing, the bullfighting, the not being a bitch: think of these as manifestations of valuable existence—in relation to oneself, in relation to others—in the postwar disillusionment. Compare with Eliot, Pound, Lewis, Toomer, Stevens, Fitzgerald. Consider Hemingway's celebrated style as a reflection of his outlook.

Faulkner, William (1897–1962), *The Sound and the Fury* **(1929). Random, 1966.** *Light in August* **(1932). Random, 1972.** *The Hamlet* **(1931). Random, 1940.** Attempt to determine: the effects of the southern past on the present, the nature of time and of guilt, the relation of the natural and the intellectual, the focus of responsibility for the condition of the Compsons and Joe Christmas and for the advent of the Snopeses. Consider Faulkner's attitude toward reality and knowledge as implied in the varying points of view and kinds of consciousness.

O'Neill, Eugene (1888–1953), *Three Plays.* Random, 1959, (Contains *Desire Under the Elms,* 1924; *Strange Interlude,* 1928; *Mourning Becomes Electra,* 1931). Watch for O'Neill's techniques of getting at subconscious motivations, impulses, and the like, in his characters, for his expressionist methods of getting at reality, for his search for the resilient powers in man.

O'Neill, Eugene, *Long Day's Journey Into Night.* Yale Univ. Press, 1956. Note the subtleties of O'Neill's attitude toward his own anguishing family past.

Crane, Hart (1899–1932), *Complete Poems and Selected Letters and Prose of Hart Crane,* ed. Brom Weber. Doubleday, 1966. Worth reading "The Bridge" in the context of Eliot's "The Waste Land." Work out the nature and ramifications of the vital American myth Crane is probing for and the relations of his own complex style to it.

Further Readings

James, William (1842–1910), *William James Reader,* rev. ed., ed. Gay Wilson Allen. Houghton Mifflin, 1972.

Chesnutt, Charles, (1858–1932), *The House Behind the Cedars* (1900). Macmillan, 1969.

Sinclair, Upton (1865–1946), *The Jungle* (1906). NAL, 1973.

Brooks, Van Wyck (1886–1963), *Van Wyck Brooks, The Early Years: A Selection from His Works,* 1908–1921, ed. Claire Sprague. Harper & Row, 1968.

Masters, Edgar Lee (1869–1950), *Spoon River Anthology* (1919). Macmillan, 1962.

Lardner, Ring (1885–1933), *Gullible's Travels, Etc.* (1917). Univ. of Chicago Press, 1965.

Mencken, Henry L. (1880–1956), *The Vintage Mencken,* ed. Alistair Cooke. Random, 1955.

1930s TO PRESENT

Basic Readings

Dos Passos, John (1896–   ), *USA* (1938). Houghton Mifflin, 1963. Consider how various styles and approaches—biographies, fiction, "camera eye," and newsreels—work together for effect. Trace the development of Dos Passos' political position, attitude, judgment through the three volumes.

Steinbeck, John (1902–1968), *Grapes of Wrath* **(1939). Bantam, 1970.** Determine the author's social-political stance against the natural and man-made injustices portrayed; articulate what he discovers in his study of common people. Compare both with Agee and the proletarian writers in Salzman and Wallenstein (below).

Salzman, Jack, and Barry Wallenstein, eds., *Years of Protest; A Collection of American Writers of the 1930s.* **Pegasus, 1967.** An anthology of Depression writing, covering a range of genres and attitudes.

Wolfe, Thomas (1900–1938), *Look Homeward Angel: A Story of the Buried Life* **(1929). Scribner's, 1929.** Think of this novel as a robust self-portrait and consider the ways the style and treatment of characters and environment tell the reader about Wolfe. Compare with other autobiographical writing—Agee, O'Neill's *Long Day's Journey into Night,* Henry Adams, Mailer, poems by Rich, Lowell, Ginsberg.

Agee, James (1909–1955), and Walker Evans (1903–1975), *Let Us Now Praise Famous Men* **(1941). Ballantine, 1974.** Take the preface seriously; test the book against it as an effort to get to a greatness of style and of attitude toward subject and self. Worth listening for what Agee has to say about journalism, art, sensitivity, communication, realism, individuals' relation to poverty. Compare to other portraits of the poor of the 1930s in Steinbeck, Dos Passos, Salzman and Wallenstein, Wright.

Wright, Richard (1908–1960), *Native Son* **(1940). Harper & Row, 1969.** Consider not only the causes and nature of Bigger's crime, but also the results, the "gains," for him. Worth looking at essays by **James Baldwin (in** *Notes of a Native Son,* **Bantam, 1971) and Ralph Ellison (in** *Shadow and Act,* **Random, 1972)** in reaction to *Native Son.*

Ellison, Ralph (1914–   ), *The Invisible Man* **(1952). Random, 1952.** Consider how and why a person becomes, or is, invisible; look for both positive and negative perspectives on the protagonist as this particular and somewhat representative Black American of a particular era seeks for identity.

Bellow, Saul (1915–   ), *Henderson, the Rain King* **(1959). Fawcett World Library, 1974.** Consider the author's exploring in depth the problem of alienation and inadequacy, self-determination, and self-knowledge in modern times.

Mailer, Norman (1923–   ), *An American Dream* **(c. 1965). Dell, 1970.** Mailer is one of the very best contemporary prose stylists. Give credit to his complex *self-awareness,* as both critic and victim of his American era; this helps greatly with his writing.

Mailer, Norman, *Armies of the Night* **(c. 1968). NAL, 1971.** Consider the author's own rhetorical strategies in contrast to those of *Time* and others he denigrates in the book.

Baldwin, James (1924–   ), *Another Country* **(1961). Dell, 1970.**

Trace the author's efforts to get deeper than sociopolitical answers to the deep racial enmity he captures—and do not stop short with the opinion that he finds the answer in sexuality, homosexuality. Baldwin is an excellent, important essayist, and the novel is well supplemented with his *Notes of a Native Son* (Bantam, 1971) and *The Fire Next Time* (Dell, 1970).

O'Connor, Flannery (1925–1964), *Everything that Rises Must Converge,* **Farrar, Straus & Giroux, 1965.** Note what O'Connor makes happen to everyday reality as a way of hinting and expressing hidden springs of behavior. Determine what kinds of revelations, or points, her grotesques bring out.

McCullers, Carson (1917–   ), *The Heart is a Lonely Hunter* **(1940). Bantam, 1970.** Think of this novel as a study of lonelinesses, of people's efforts to get out of their own loneliness and break down that of others.

Heller, Joseph (1923–   ), *Catch-22* **(c. 1961). Dell, 1973.** Return to Twain for contrast as an aid to defining Heller's particular sort of humor. Consider the kind of reality to which his surreality penetrates. Determine the significance of his deviation from the usual structure of a novel.

Miller, Arthur (1915–   ), *Death of a Salesman.* **Viking, 1949.** Worth working out the dynamics by which Miller shapes our identifications with and attitudes toward characters in the play. Determine the nature of the play's power: overwhelming pathos or the tragedy of a noble, flawed figure, or still a third possibility? To define Miller's indictment and his sympathies, compare with *Babbitt* and *An American Dream.*

Williams, Tennessee (1914–   ), *Cat on a Hot Tin Roof.* **NAL, 1955.** Work at Williams' method—and compare it with Miller's—of getting at the conscious and unconscious impulses and conflicts in character. Pay attention to his treatment of money, love. Determine the function in his work of the use of shock.

Albee, Edward (1928–   ), *American Dream* **[1959–60]** *and Zoo Story* **[1958]. NAL, 1961.** Study what Albee finds missing in American civilization and how he uses language to reveal his perception. You may compare him with Heller for different manners of working with the absurd.

Jones, LeRoi (Imamu Amiri Baraka) (1934–   ), *Dutchman and The Slave, Two Plays,* **Morrow, 1964;** *The Dead Lecturer,* **Grove, 1964.** Compare Jones/Baraka with Whitman, Williams, and Ginsberg as a poet working in nontraditional and free verse styles, but also consider his intense concern with the relation of black and white traditions and cultures and with racial enmities in his poems (though this only begins to be a concern in *The Dead Lecturer*) and plays.

Lowell, Robert (1917–1977), *Lord Weary's Castle* **[1946]** *and The*

Mills of the Kavanaughs [1951], Harcourt Brace Jovanovich, 1968; *Life Studies* [1959] *and For the Union Dead*, Farrar, Straus & Giroux, 1967. Throughout, follow Lowell's grappling with his New England past, his family past, his own past, with tradition and individuality: watch his concept of personal, spiritual, and social salvation develop; follow the careful and varying sorts of tightness of the poems.

Ginsberg, Allen (1926–   ), *Howl and Other Poems*, City Lights, 1956; *Kaddish and Other Poems, 1958–1960*, City Lights, 1967. Especially read "Howl," "Sunflower Sutra," "America," and "Kaddish." Analyze the working of Ginsberg's long-breathed, free verse in intensely emotional lines. Consider him as a prophetic poet who laments and denounces contemporary evil and advocates a specific road to salvation. Recognize the complex self-awareness, watch for the way it colors his criticism and affirmation.

Roethke, Theodore (1908–1963), *Collected Poems of Theodore Roethke*. Doubleday, 1975. Note Roethke's working out of relationships between the self and things—especially natural things—and between the spiritual and physical. Follow his reflections on, and his various approaches to, continuity and the life processes from birth to death.

Rich, Adrienne (1929–   ), *Poems Selected and New, 1950–1974*. Norton (hard cover), 1975. Think of Rich as a woman constantly probing—often out of deep personal experience—the nature of human relationships, of social and political ills, and of a maturity reached and held through confrontation with the confusions and pain of experience.

Further Readings

Farrell, James T. (1904–   ), *Young Lonigan*, Avon, 1932; if interested after this first volume, see *The Young Manhood of Studs Lonigan* (1934), Avon, 1973 (and the third volume in *Studs Lonigan*, Vanguard, hard cover, 1935).

Cowley, Malcolm (1898–   ), *Exile's Return: A Literary Odyssey of the 1920s* (1934). Viking, 1959.

Hammett, Dashiell (1894–1961), *The Thin Man* (1932). Random, 1972.

Warren, Robert Penn (1905–   ), *All the King's Men* (1946). Bantam, 1973.

Malamud, Bernard (1914–   ), *The Magic Barrel* (1958). Dell, 1970.

Barth, John (1930–   ), *Lost in the Fun House*. Bantam, 1969.

Vonnegut, Kurt (1922–   ), *Cat's Cradle*. Dell, 1974.

Kosinski, Jerzy (1933–   ), *The Painted Bird*. Bantam, 1972.

Gelber, Jack (1932–   ), *The Connection.* Grove, 1960.

Hellman, Lillian (1905–   ), *The Little Foxes* [1939] *and Another Part of the Forest* [1946], Viking, 1973.

Hellman, Lillian, *Pentimento, NAL,* 1974.

Kerouac, Jack (1922–   ), *On the Road.* Viking, 1957.

Malcolm X, (1925–1965), *The Autobiography of Malcolm X.* Grove, 1965.

Plath, Sylvia (1932–1963), *Ariel.* Harper & Row, 1968.

Welty, Eudora (1909–   ), *The Golden Apples.* Harcourt Brace Jovanovich, 1949. (Those interested may instead see her *Delta Wedding,* out of print but in libraries.)

Singer, Isaac Bashevis (1904–   ), *The Spinoza of Market Street.* Avon, 1966.

Gardner, John (1933–   ), *Nickel Mountain.* Knopf, 1973.

ANTHOLOGIES

Carruth, Hayden; ed., *The Voice That Is Great Within Us; American Poetry of the Twentieth Century.* Bantam, 1970. Wideranging anthology that supplements books by individual poets.

Bontemps, Arna, ed., *American Negro Poetry.* Hill & Wang, 1963.

Edwards, Lee R., and Arlyn Diamond, eds., *American Voices, American Women.* Avon, 1973. An anthology of prose fiction by women.

Ortega, Philip D., ed., *We Are Chicanos: An Anthology of Mexican-American Literature.* Pocket Books (Washington Square Press), 1973. Another good anthology, though with more history and sociology than literature, is: **Ludwig, Edward W., and James Santibanez,** *The Chicanos: Mexican-American Voices,* Penguin, 1971.

Witt, Shirley Hill, and Stan Steiner, eds., *The Way; An Anthology of American Indian Literature.* Random, 1973. Another good hard cover anthology is: **Turner, Frederick W., III, ed.,** *The Portable American Indian Reader,* Viking, 1974.

WORKS BY CRITICS

Chase, Richard, *The American Novel and Its Tradition.* Doubleday, 1957.

Feidelson, Charles, *Symbolism and American Literature.* Univ. of Chicago Press (hard cover), 1953.

Hoffman, Daniel, *Form and Fable in American Fiction.* Norton, 1973.

Lawrence, D. H., *Studies in Classic American Literature.* Viking, 1964.

Lewis, R. W. B., *The American Adam; Innocence, Tragedy and Tradition in the Nineteenth Century.* Univ. of Chicago Press, 1955.

Margolies, Edward, *Native Sons: A Critical Study of Twentieth-Century Negro American Authors.* Lippincott, 1969.

Trilling, Lionel, *The Liberal Imagination; Essays on Literature and Society.* Viking, 1974.

Marx, Leo, *The Machine in the Garden; Technology and the Pastoral Ideal in America.* Oxford Univ. Press, 1967.

Matthiessen, F. O., *American Renaissance; Art and Expression in the Age of Emerson and Whitman.* Oxford Univ. Press, 1968.

Smith, Henry Nash, *Virgin Land; The American West as Symbol and Myth.* Random House, 1957.

Waggoner, H. H., *American Poets.* Dell, 1970.

Chapter Eighteen

ENGLISH COMPOSITION/
CREATIVE WRITING
". . . clarity and expressive power"

Editorial Advisor:
Jesse H. McKnight III
Department of English
Kent State University

INTRODUCTION

"The difference between the right word and the nearly right word," Mark Twain once said, "is the difference between lightning and lightning-bug." His observation holds true, not just for well-chosen words, but for all elements of good writing. Being able to write with clarity and expressive power is invaluable, not only in college studies, but throughout life.

The bibliography in this section identifies books frequently used today to help students develop writing skills in freshman or advanced English Composition courses. Their coverage ranges from brief review of correct grammar and usage to the subtleties of organization, tone, and style. To develop your writing abilities, you need select only a few of these books for intensive study and practice. Notations are intended to help you pick those that best fit your interests and needs.

You may, for example, decide first to concentrate on writing better sentences; then proceed to work on paragraphs, short reports, or essays; and finally, to practice improved style. To structure such a sequence you can begin with Robert Scholes' *Elements of Writing,* go on to *Writing with a Purpose* by James M. McCrimmon (particularly the parts of it dealing with paragraphs), *The Five-Hundred Word Theme* by Lee J. Martin, Baker's *The Complete Stylist,* or Strunk and White's *The Elements of Style* and finally study Donald Davidson's *American Composition and Rhetoric* for help in bringing your expository writing to a high degree of polish.

As a natural extension of studies in English composition and literature, colleges also often offer courses in creative writing—the writing of short stories and novels, plays and poems. For readers who want to develop skill in producing works of their own in these literary forms,

314

the bibliography includes several books used in many colleges in connection with Creative Writing courses.

Practice in writing itself is the chief means by which students (as well as successful writers generally) learn to write well. Therefore these books should serve you in a secondary way, as sources of advice and helpful examples, while you concentrate on writing regularly and often, improving your skills in the light of what you learn for yourself as well as from friends and professionals. Winston Churchill, the leader of Britain in the Second World War, traced his mastery of English prose to a course that he took and failed twice as a schoolboy. By his third try, he found that he had somehow "got into my head the essential sense of rhythm and style of our language." There is no substitute for patient practice.

BIBLIOGRAPHY

ENGLISH COMPOSITION

Many books are listed below to give you a wide choice. It is probably best to select only a few for close study. The books are divided into subgroups to help you choose the ones that seem most appealing and best fitted to your particular needs.

Introductory—Books with Especially Useful Features

Symes, Ken L., *The Writer's Voice.* **Holt, Rinehart & Winston, 1973.** Presents and comments on examples to help clarify essential elements of good writing. Emphasis on preparatory steps and revision. Clear and convenient format.

Hogins, James Burl, *Probing Common Ground: Sources for Writing.* **Prentice-Hall, 1974.** Covers many facets of good writing and a wide range of types of writing. Practical and straightforward. Diverse and stimulating exercises.

Herzen, John, and D. W. Cummings, *Writing: Plans, Drafts and Revisions.* **Random, 1971.** Unusual in its detailed treatment of outlining and research, first drafts, rewriting, and editing.

Canavan, P. J. *Elements of College Reading and Writing.* **McGraw-Hill, 1971.** Especially strong in vocabulary building.

Scholes, Robert, and Carl H. Klaus, *Elements of Writing.* **Oxford Univ. Press, 1972.** Designed for the first few weeks of composition courses. Deals mainly with the sentence. Well-written, easily understandable examples.

Kytle, Ray, *Clear Thinking for Composition.* **Random, 1969.** Designed to help the writer become more precise and cogent in thought and in writing. Lively discussions, conversational tone.

Smith, William F., and Ramond D. Liedlich, *Rhetoric for Today.* Harcourt Brace Jovanovich, 1974. Two areas of strength: workbook exercises that can be detached and that directly relate to the text; focus on description and narration as important techniques of explanatory writing.

Allen, David L., and Jane C. Parks, *Essential Rhetoric.* **Houghton Mifflin, 1969.** Concise; isolates a few fundamental principles and presents them without confusing details.

Martin, Lee J., *The Five-Hundred Word Theme.* **Prentice-Hall, 1974.** Conveys with unusual clarity the skills needed to write any short communication of substance—an explanatory business or personal letter, a memorandum, or a brief report. Has proven especially helpful to students with little background in writing who want to learn how to frame an introduction, summarize a body of material, and state a conclusion.

McCrimmon, James M., *Writing with a Purpose.* **Houghton Mifflin (hard cover), 1972.** A well-rounded introduction to composition with effective explanations of outlining, forming sentences and paragraphs, and revising.

Tibbets, A. M., *The Strategies of Rhetoric.* **Scott, Foresman, 1969.** Particularly strong on building a sound argument. Tells how to use logic and other techniques for stating one's viewpoints persuasively.

Winkler, Anthony C., and Jo Ray McCuen, *Rhetoric Made Plain.* Harcourt Brace Jovanovich, 1974. Emphasis on writing clearly; includes chapters on writing for nonliterary fields such as the sciences and business.

La Casce, Steward, and Terry Belaney, *The Art of Persuasion.* Scribner's, 1972. Outlines the major kinds of appeal used in persuasive writing, among them effective use of illustrative quotations.

Levin, Gerald, *Styles for Writing.* Harcourt Brace Jovanovich, 1972. A guide to composition that encourages better prose style through systematic study of examples by great stylists of the language.

Introductory—Books with Different Emphases

Kerrigan, William J., *Writing to the Point: Six Basic Steps.* Harcourt Brace Jovanovich, 1974. Highly structured approach to writing; almost everything one needs in beginning to learn to write.

Perrin, Porter G., *The Writer's Guide.* **Scott, Foresman, 1965.** Concentrates on basic principles of effective writing and explains points of correct grammar as they bear on writing effectiveness.

Hardison, O. B., Jr., *Practical Rhetoric.* **Meredith, 1966.** Designed primarily to serve as a concise reference handbook.

Burhans, Clinton S., Jr., *The Would-Be Writer.* Xerox College (hard

cover), 1971. Approaches composition as a liberal art, not a mechanical skill. Helps the student discover his own style, rhythm, and form.

Ross, Donald H., *The Writing Performance.* **Lippincott, 1973.** Draws on what students already know, to enable them to discover the basic principles of composition through practice rather than learning a set of rules.

Williams, Barbara, *Twelve Steps to Better Exposition.* **Merill, 1968.** Highly systematic guide to writing essays; can also be used for reference.

Cowan, Gregory, and Elizabeth McPherson, *Plain English Please.* **Random, 1969.** Emphasizes clarity and outlines exercises and projects for attaining a clear style; down-to-earth tone.

Intermediate—Books with Especially Useful Features

Brooks, Cleanth, and Robert Penn Warren, *Modern Rhetoric.* **Harcourt Brace Jovanovich, 1972.** Thorough treatment of effective explanatory writing; emphasizes planning, logical construction, and redrafting.

Kane, Thomas S., and Leonard J. Poters, *A Practical Rhetoric of Expository Prose.* **Oxford Univ. Press (hard cover), 1966.** One of the most comprehensive guides to writing.

Baker, Sheridan, *The Complete Stylist.* **Crowell, 1972.** Extensive and practical. Itself a model of effective prose writing, it emphasizes argument as the quickest and clearest teacher of the principles of good writing.

Everett, Dumas, *An Auto-Instructional Text in Correct Writing.* **Heath, 1964.** A wealth of exercises and examples. Diagnostic and achievement tests.

Strunk, Willard, and E. B. White, *Elements of Style.* **Macmillan, 1972.** Perhaps the most widely read book on style. Concise; emphasizes simplicity.

Weathers, Winston, and Otis Winchester, *The Strategy of Style.* **McGraw-Hill, 1967.** The thesis here is that a variety of writing techniques must be cultivated by the student in order to do different kinds of writing while developing a distinctive style of his own.

Kytle, Ray. Concepts in Context: *Aspects of the Writer's Craft.* **Wiley, 1974.** Deductive, sequential explanations of important concepts for both student and professional writers.

Intermediate—Books of Readings

Watkens, Floyd C., and Karl F. Knight, eds., *Writer to Writer: Readings on the Craft of Writing.* **Houghton, Mifflin, 1966.** Essays on writing by famous authors.

Gaskins, James R., and Jack Suberman, eds., *A Language Reader for Writers*. Prentice-Hall, 1966. Essays designed to provide the writer with a better understanding of such areas as slang, standard English, and formal discourse.

Hakonis, Tom E., and James C. Wilcox, eds., *Forms of Rhetoric*, McGraw-Hill, 1969. Each essay in this collection fully treats the particular rhetorical principle it considers.

Intermediate—Books with Different Emphases

Kirschbaum, Leo, *Clear Writing*. World, 1950. A superior standard guide to composition.

Robinson, James E., *The Scope of Rhetoric*. Scott, Foresman, 1970. Designed as a rhetorical guide for the study of literature as well as composition. Takes a classical approach to rhetoric.

Snortum, Neil K., *Contemporary Rhetoric*. Prentice-Hall, 1967. Explains current usage in good English and argues against outmoded usages of the past.

Advanced

Davidson, Donald, *American Composition and Rhetoric*. Scribner's (hard cover), 1968. A rare item—a study of rhetoric for its own sake and not as a means of satisfying freshman English requirements. Written as much for the professional writer as for the college student. Detailed discussions, copious illustrations.

Elbow, Peter, *Writing Without Teachers*. Oxford Univ. Press, 1973. Designed especially for learning to write well on your own. Emphasizes that one must write frequently and that the first-draft process should be followed by editorial revisions.

Love, Glen A., and Michael Payne, *Contemporary Essays on Style*. Scott, Foresman, 1969. Collection of illuminating essays; one of the best of its kind.

Hall, Lawrence Sargeant, *How Thinking is Written*. Heath (hard cover), 1963. Views language as a function, not a convention. Treats grammar as a set of ordering principles with which to translate thought into language.

CREATIVE WRITING

Introductory

Andrews, Clarence A., *Writing: Growth Through Structure*. Macmillan (Free Press), 1972. Step-by-step approach to writing in general; designed to help develop initial skills in different forms of creative writing by focusing on their basic structures.

Baker, William D., and T. Benson Strandness, *The Experience of Writing.* **Prentice-Hall, 1958.** Presents examples of creative writing with explanations that are particularly helpful for beginning students.

Snipes, Wilson Currin, *Writer and Audience.* **Holt, Rinehart & Winston, 1970.** Guides the beginner in creative writing through a natural sequence: writing about oneself, writing about other people, and writing for an audience.

Morgan, Fred, *Here and Now.* **Harcourt Brace Jovanovich, 1970.** Advises how to use one's immediate experience in creative writing.

White, Edward M., ed., *The Writer's Control of Tone.* **Norton, 1970.** Explains one aspect of writing in detail through varied examples. Helps the creative writer choose and control tone.

Intermediate

Kuehl, John, ed., *Creative Writing and Rewriting.* **Appleton-Century-Crofts, 1967.** Presents rough drafts and publishes versions of stories by prominent authors with commentaries that point out key changes from draft to final version.

West, Ray B., Jr., *The Art of Writing Fiction.* **Crowell (hard cover), 1968.** Advice on many aspects of writing fiction, illustrated with examples; particularly strong on the short story.

Advanced

Brashers, Howard C., *Creative Writing.* **American Book (hard cover), 1968.** Defines and illustrates a wide range of techniques used by creative writers.

Loomis, Edward, *Creative Writing: The Art of Lying.* **Cummings (hard cover), 1971.** Stresses reshaping reality into art; includes helpful exercises.

Minot, Stephen, *Three Genres: The Writing of Fiction, Poetry, and Drama.* **Prentice-Hall (hard cover), 1965.** Gives special attention to methods used to produce these forms of creative writing; unusually good treatment of fiction.

Chapter Nineteen

ENGLISH LITERATURE
". . . a long and rich portrayal of life"

Editorial Advisor:
William Alexander
Department of English
University of Michigan

INTRODUCTION

English literature opens to us a long and rich portrayal of life by people who, in a profound sense of the slang phrase, talk the same language.

American and English literatures have long been almost one, springing from that same mother tongue; England's literary lights today are also ours, and ours theirs. And in national descent, American literature stemmed directly from the ancient English heritage. It is no wonder that our colleges almost universally offer studies in English literature.

General suggestions on how to proceed on your own with study in the great domain of English letters are essentially the same as those given in the introduction to the section on American Literature. Again, with English literature, feel free to pursue any order of study that fits your interest. You should not automatically advance in the time order in which readings are presented. Several books helpful to reading literature are identified at the end of the introduction to the American Literature section; they can be equally useful in providing background for works from Great Britain.

GETTING YOUR BEARINGS IN THE FIELD

However you choose to proceed, you will find it useful to know some prime features of the historical periods into which English literature is generally organized by scholars. Highlights and approximate time-spans of those periods follow; they parallel the groupings of the reading list.

Middle Ages
(to 1485; divided at 1066 into Old and Middle English periods)

Old English: small societies composed of families or groups of families; values of kinship, kingly behavior; Christianity being integrated with older values; concern with transiency of existence, fate; epic style. Middle English: close to popular audience; high point, late fourteenth century—*Piers Plowman, Sir Gawain and the Green Knight,* Chaucer; fifteenth century one of popular literature, ballads, mystery and morality plays, Malory's *Le Morte D'Arthur.*

Sixteenth Century (1485–1603)

New accessibility of literature with invention of printing. Onset of colonialism and trade. Beginning of Renaissance humanism (a turn to classical literature and concepts) holding a basic idea of order in which man is between angels and animals on the chain of being, partaking of qualities of both. Growing split between popular and court audiences. Age of Reformation, religious controversy, persecution, relative stability of Elizabethan age (1558–1603). High development of sonnet; beginning of great age of English drama; literature of 1590s shows signs of growing tension.

Seventeenth Century (1603–1660)

Relative social and conceptual stability of sixteenth century broken by beginnings of modern science, Puritan individualism, Puritan attacks on social and religious order, civil war—period of flux, tension, uncertainty, creativity. Continuation of great age of English drama. A high-water mark in poetry: complex, argumentative, sometimes extravagant metaphysical verse; developing neoclassical and more formal verse; Shakespearean and Miltonic blank verse. Some great metaphysical prose, but gradual triumph of plainer, more utilitarian style, thanks to Puritanism, science, and growing influence of bourgeois interests.

Restoration and Eighteenth Century (1660–1798)

Restoration: lax behavior at court, growth of middle-class values elsewhere; religious intolerance until 1689, thereafter slow gains for toleration; development (in reaction against excesses of previous era) toward conservative notions of order, classical restraint, good sense, reason. Early eighteenth century shows consolidation of these tendencies, plus optimistic view of man; sentimentalism and feeling leading to benevolent social action; growing prosperity. Great age of satire, of heroic couplet, concern for rules of literature, rise of new middle-class genre—the novel. Late eighteenth century (1740s on) brings increase in blank verse, new attitudes toward man, nature, and creativity are forerunners of the Romantic movement.

Romantic (1798–1832)

Conservative political reaction to revolutionary wars abroad. Laissez-faire economic policy during extremely rapid growth to industrial nation causing grim working conditions, strong class division, labor agitation. Literature is stimulated by revolutionary ideas, by a sense of human freedom and potential, and by interest in common settings and persons. Belief in creative inspiration, spontaneity, primacy of individual artist's imagination. Nature colored by the imagination and permeated by spiritual meaning. Fascination with the supernatural and satanic, with extreme experience. Beginning of artist's alienation from material and bourgeois society.

Victorian (1832–1901)

Gradual improvement of working-class condition; dominance on world economic and political scene; controversy of religionists with evolutionary scientists and "higher critics" of Bible. Tensions between hard-working, energetic, materialistic, progressive attitudes and sense of spiritual-personal thinness deriving from such attitudes; poetry especially reflective of this phenomenon. In poetry, attempts generally to discipline continuing Romantic impulse, increased sense of mission to society. Rise of realistic novel, concerned with middle- and lower-class lives and with accurate social and psychological detail. Decadence of 1890s.

Twentieth Century (from 1901)

Early years (including 1890s): reaction against Victorian respectability, optimism, materialism; controversy over imperialism (Boer Wars, Ireland). Beginning of great period of poetry: reaction against Romantic and Victorian emotionalism and style; turn to precise, complex, and ironic verse in touch with colloquial languages of the time. First World War caused great disillusionment: civilization "an old bitch gone in the teeth," a wasteland of sterile people, of lost and fragmented values. Reaction (with exceptions) in fiction against external realism, interest now in nature of human consciousness. Writers in 1930s turned left in reaction to fascism, Depression. After Second World War: strong influence of Continental cynicism toward man and civilization, of absurd and existential ideas and forms; drama especially vital and experimental.

LEADING SCHOLAR-CRITICS AND THEIR RESEARCH METHODS

If you want to pursue more advanced studies in English Literature, you may be interested in learning something of leading scholar-critics in English literature and their research methods. A number of these figures are identified here; you can easily obtain their works in libraries and bookstores. They explain their methods in presenting their analyses.

Many of these scholar-critics are not limited to any single type of approach. The categories here suggested should thus be taken as starting points, not as fixed boundaries.

Scholar-critics who concern themselves with English literature within particular historical contexts include M. H. Abrams, Walter Jackson Bate, F. W. Bateson, C. M. Bowra, Jerome Buckley, Douglas Bush, David Daiches, Richard Ellmann, Helen Gardner, Robert Langbaum, Harry Levin, C. S. Lewis, Louis Martz, Allardyce Nicoll, D. W. Robertson Jr., George Steiner, E. M. W. Tillyard, and Lionel Trilling. Some focus upon a period, some upon a specific writer, some upon a genre. Among these, Douglas Bush might be singled out as a proponent of an ethical, humanist criticism in the tradition of Matthew Arnold and others before him.

Formalist criticism (also called practical, analytic, "new"; criticism with its eye principally to the images and language of the work itself) received its impulse from T. E. Hulme, T. S. Eliot, and I. A. Richards (who is also interested in the nature of literary communication and the effect of literature upon a reader). In England William Empson extended this approach to a subtle investigation of types of ambiguity in literature. In the United States a number of critics are among its foremost practitioners and theorists: R. P. Blackmur, Kenneth Burke, Cleanth Brooks, John Crowe Ransom, Alan Tate, and W. K. Wimsatt. T. S. Eliot concerned himself with the traditions of English literature, as does F. R. Leavis, a practical critic with a crusading sense of the importance of the "best" literature to English society.

Prominent critics who focus upon the nature of particular genres are Wayne Booth and Robert Scholes (fiction), R. S. Crane (poetry and other genres), Elder Olson (poetry and drama), and Northrop Frye (all genres).

Psychoanalytic critics concern themselves with unconscious material in literary characters, in authors, and in readers; important work in this area has been done by Freud and Jung, by Maud Bodkin, Norman O. Brown, Kenneth Burke, Frederick J. Hoffman, Norman Holland, Ernest Jones, Ernst Kris, Simon Lesser, F. L. Lucas, Hanns Sachs, Lionel Trilling, and Edmund Wilson.

Major theorists of archetypal criticism, of symbol and myth in English literature, are Maud Bodkin, Kenneth Burke, Joseph Campbell, Francis Fergusson, Northrop Frye, Robert Graves, G. Wilson Knight, and Philip Wheelwright.

Prominent scholars of the history of ideas are Arthur Lovejoy (*The Great Chain of Being*) and Marjorie Nicolson. John Livingston Lowes' *Road to Xanadu* is a classic investigation of the sources of literary creation. Other authors have brought social, political, and economic perspectives to literary criticism; among them are Mortimer Adler, Christopher Caudwell, David Daiches, George Steiner, Raymond Williams, and Edmund Wilson.

Among good general histories of English literature, you may want to consult *A Literary History of England* (rev. ed., 1967), by Albert C.

Baugh and others, and *Critical History of English Literature* (second edition), David Daiches.

BIBLIOGRAPHY

MIDDLE AGES

Beowulf and Other Old English Poems (c. 1000 A.D.), tr. **Constance B. Hieatt. Odyssey, 1967.** Read *Beowulf, The Battle of Malden,* "The Dream of the Rood," "The Wanderer." In *Beowulf,* work out the nature of heroism, the nuances of kinship, the importance of duty, the significance of awards, of death, of fate, the ways the poem becomes Christian.

"Sir Gawain and the Green Knight" (1300s) in *The Pearl-Poet; His Complete Works,* tr. Margaret Williams. Random, 1970. Identify the assumptions challenged in this long Middle English poem; identify the specifically Christian lessons and the tone in which the whole is treated. Be aware of the range and complexity of attitude of the author. Readers interested in other Middle English works may also see "Pearl" in this volume, and: **Langland, William (1332?–1400), *Piers Ploughman* (1360–1399), tr. J. F. Goodridge, Penguin, 1959; Malory, Sir Thomas (–1471), *Le Morte D'Arthur,* (finished between 1469 and 1470; first printing 1485), 2 vols., ed. Janet Cowen, Penguin, 1969.**

Chaucer, Geoffrey (1340?–1400), "The Canterbury Tales" (c. 1387) and "Troilus and Cressida" (written between 1372 and 1386), in *The Works of Geoffrey Chaucer,* 2nd ed., ed. F. N. Robinson. Houghton Mifflin (hard cover), 1957. Determine the author's relation to his subjects, the nature and degree of his nearness-distance to his characters. In "Troilus and Cressida," define the Chaucerian irony. Read the *Tales* as revelations of the tellers and of their relations to other pilgrims and other tales. Watch for Chaucer's values, ideals, sense of hierarchy. A less expensive volume that also presents Chaucer's writing in untranslated but explained Middle English is *The Canterbury Tales: A Selection,* **ed. Donald R. Howard. NAL, 1969.**

Medieval and Tudor Drama, **ed. John Gassner. Bantam, 1963.** Read especially *The Second Shepherd's Play* and *Everyman* (1400s), and, for the sixteenth century, *Gorbodoc* (first production 1561). In *The Second Shepherd's Play,* note the interrelation of events: the movement from opening to closing; consider how a mystery play is meant to appeal to and affect its audience, and compare it on this basis to *Everyman,* the morality play. Find how the latter is allegorical method that can be experienced as relevant even now.

SIXTEENTH CENTURY

Anchor Anthology of Sixteenth Century Verse, **ed. Richard S. Sylvester. Doubleday, 1974.** Read especially poems by Wyatt, Surrey,

Sidney, Drayton, and Campion. Keep an eye on variations on the sonnet form, how they relate to changes in attitudes toward love, war, honor, death, and the like, especially in the sonnets of Shakespeare and songs and sonnets of Donne. See also Spenser's "Amoretti" in the following volume.

Spenser, Edmund (1552?–1599), *Edmund Spenser's Poetry,* **ed. Hugh Maclean. Norton, 1968.** Read "The Shepheardes Calendar," "Amoretti," "Epithalamion," and Books I, II, and VI and the Mutability cantos in *The Faerie Queene.* Spenser's use of pastoral for comment on aesthetic, social, and other matters is worth recognizing; it opens a tradition carried on throughout English poetry. Work out the relations between his love of down-to-earth realities and his morality and Neoplatonism. *The Faerie Queene* is a marvelous poem, though it requires an effort of adjustment from the twentieth century; find a way to enter its allegory. One good route is via **Hough, Graham,** *A Preface to The Faerie Queene.* **Norton, 1963.**

Marlowe, Christopher (1564–1593), *Marlowe: Five Plays,* **ed., Havelock Ellis. Hill & Wang, 1956.** Read *Tamburlaine the Great* (1590), Part 1 of *Dr. Faustus* (1604), and *The Jew of Malta* (1633). Compare *Tamburlaine* to *Gorboduc* to note the advance in blank verse and in moral complexity. Regard Marlowe's plays as studies in ambition and determine his attitudes toward the overreaching heroes, not only in their fates, but through the verse and words assigned them.

Shakespeare, William (1564–1616), *Romeo and Juliet* **(c. 1594),** *A Midsummer Night's Dream* **(c. 1594),** *Richard II* **(c. 1595),** *Henry IV* **(c. 1597),** *Henry V* **(c. 1598),** *As You Like It* **(c. 1599),** *Twelfth Night* **(c. 1599). Penguin (The Pelican Shakespeare series), 1961.** For guidance, see the introduction to each work.

Dekker, Thomas (1572?–1632?), *The Shoemaker's Holiday* **(1600), in** *Four Great Elizabethan Plays,* **Bantam, 1963; Heywood, John, (1497?–1580?),** *A Woman Killed with Kindness* **(1607), in** *Three Elizabethan Domestic Tragedies,* **ed. Sturgess, Penguin, 1970.** Dekker and Heywood, popular dramatists of the time, are worth comparing with Jonson and Shakespeare in terms of bite and depth, of likely audience, of skill at plot and characterization. Define their positive qualities.

SEVENTEENTH CENTURY

English Seventeenth Century Verse, **Vol. I, ed. Louis L. Martz, Norton, 1973; Vol. II, ed. Richard S. Sylvester, Norton, 1974.** Read especially Donne, Herbert, Herrick, Jonson, and Marvel.

Jonson, Ben (1573?–1637), *Three Plays,* **Vol. I (***Volpone* **[1607],** *Epicoene* **[first acted in 1609],** *The Alchemist* **[1612], ed. Brinsley Nicholson and Charles H. Herford. Hill & Wang, 1957.** Compare with comedies of Shakespeare to understand two basic comic stances. Study Jonson as opposed to romantic dramas, a realistic satirist with a keen sense of social values. Watch the unobtrusive way he builds values ironically into his prose and verse; compare his dramatic language with that of his other verse; read *Discoveries* with his poems and plays (in *English Prose 1600–1660*, below).

Tourneur, Cyril (1575?–1626), *The Revenger's Tragedy* (1607). In *Jacobean Drama: An Anthology*, Vol. II, ed. Richard C. Hairner. Norton, 1963.

Webster, John (1580?–1625?), *The White Devil* (1612). In *Jacobean Drama: An Anthology*, Vol. I, ed. Richard C. Hairner. Norton, 1963. *The Duchess of Malfi* (1623). In *Four Great Elizabethan Plays*. Bantam, 1963. Worth getting some idea of the tradition of revenge tragedy (includes *Hamlet*), which usually involves a malcontent figure who comments on and satirizes contemporary corruption. Pay attention to Tourneur's and Webster's variations on the tradition. Note Tourneur's ability to accent key themes with rich, sometimes extravagant language. Note Webster's greater realism of character, his interest in the victims of revenge.

Middleton, Thomas (1570?–1627), *The Changeling* (1653). In *Jacobean Drama: An Anthology*, Vol. II, ed. Richard C. Hairner. Norton, 1963. Note the degree and nature of psychological realism, the keen sense of Beatrice's growing and partially willed involvement with DeFlores. Be aware of the function of the asides for characterization, for atmosphere, for view of human situation.

Ford, John (1586?– after 1638), *Tis Pity She's a Whore* (1633). In *Three Plays by John Ford*. Penguin, 1970. Ford is often seen as one of most decadent of late Jacobean dramatists, worth comparing with Webster and Tourneur, Beaumont and Fletcher, for exploitation of emotion, degree of meaning and depth, relation to social values.

Shakespeare, William (1564–1616), *The Merchant of Venice* (c. 1596), *Julius Caesar* (c. 1599), *Hamlet* (c. 1600), *Troilus and Cressida* (c. 1601), *Measure for Measure* (c. 1604), *Othello* (c. 1604), *King Lear* (c. 1605), *Macbeth* (c. 1605), *Anthony and Cleopatra* (c. 1606), *Coriolanus* (c. 1607), *The Winter's Tale* (c. 1610), *The Tempest* (c. 1611). Penguin (The Pelican Shakespeare series), 1961.

Milton, John (1608–1674), *The Complete Poetry of John Milton*, rev. ed., ed. John T. Shawcross. Doubleday, 1971. *Selected Prose of John Milton*, ed. C. A. Patrides. Penguin, 1974. Be sure to read, "L'Allegro," "Il Penseroso," "Lycidas," "Comus," "Paradise Lost," "Samson Agonistes," and the prose "Areopagitica." Watch through the poems Milton's development and elevation of English blank verse. Compare his style and diction to that of the metaphysicals, of the Cavalier poets, of Dryden. What attitudes toward poetry, politics, religion, life, accompany such verse?

***English Prose 1600–1660*, ed. Victor Harris and I. Husain. Holt, Rinehart & Winston, 1965.** Basic readings: selections from Bacon,

Browne, Donne, Jonson. Further readings: selections from Burton, Hobbes, Taylor.

RESTORATION AND EIGHTEENTH CENTURY

Basic Readings

Dryden, John (1631–1700), *Selected Works,* 2nd ed. Holt, Rinehart & Winston, 1971. Read "Annus Mirabilis," "Absalom and Achitophel," "Mac Flecknoe," "To the Memory of Mr. Oldham," "Alexander's Feast," "An Essay of Dramatic Poesy," and "The Dramatic Poetry of the Last Age." (In the work cited or in **Poetry and Prose of John Dryden, ed., D. N. Smith. Oxford Univ. Press, 1925.**) Dryden's couplets worth careful study as the first refined use of this neoclassical form, especially for satiric purposes; compare them with Pope's. Valuable to read his criticism along with his poetry.

Defoe, Daniel (1660–1731), *Moll Flanders* (1722). NAL, 1962. Possible to think of Moll in relation to the new middle class in England. Work out relation between Defoe and his first-person narrator and define his brand of realism, his combination of individual and type in Moll.

Pope, Alexander (1688–1744), *Poetry and Prose of Alexander Pope,* ed. Aubrey Williams. Houghton Mifflin, 1969. Read especially "Essay on Criticism," "Windsor Forest," "The Rape of the Lock," "Epistle to Martha Blount," "Elegy to the Memory of an Unfortunate Lady," "Essay on Man," "An Epistle to Dr. Arbuthnot," and Book IV of "The Dunciad." Think of Pope as a social poet, very much concerned with manners, traditions, values of his time. Read the "Essay on Criticism" as an introduction to Augustan thoughts on poetry; define the standards of art and behavior against which he tests his age. Determine what Pope means by nature and the rules. His rich and subtle use of the limited form of the heroic couplet repays analysis. Discover his strengths, his tricks, his underlying depths as a satirist and analyst of contemporary manners and the human condition.

Swift, Jonathan (1667–1745), *Gulliver's Travels* [1726] *and Other Writings,* ed. Ricardo Quintana. Modern Library, 1958. Also read "The Battle of the Books" (1704), "An Argument Against Abolishing Christianity" (1708), "A Modest Proposal" (1729), "A Letter to the Whole People of Ireland," and the poems. It is essential to grasp Swift's vision of human nature; in this context it is worth comparing his work with Pope's "Essay on Man" and the writings of Samuel Johnson. Analyze Swift's prose in relation to that of the metaphysicals, get at the kinds of depth his clarity can achieve. Work out the progression of *Gulliver's Travels,* the growth, if any, of Gulliver, the problem of whether Gulliver himself is a target of satire in the end.

Richardson, Samuel (1689–1761), *Pamela* **(1740). Norton, 1958.** Work out Pamela's motivation and Richardson's values, whether it is right to say that Pamela's morality is only a device to attain respectability, or whether Richardson goes beyond that theme. Fielding's book (below) was written as an answer to Richardson's.

Fielding, Henry (1707–1754), *Joseph Andrews* **(1742). Harper & Row, 1966.** Consider how Adams and "Fielding" (the narrator) function as characters in the book, the dimensions they bring to it. Worth comparing the comical and satirical outlook here to the comedies of Jonson and Shakespeare.

Johnson, Samuel (1709–1784), *Rasselas (1759), Poems, and Selected Prose.* **Holt, Rinehart & Winston, 1971.** Read *Rasselas*, "The Vanity of Human Wishes" (1749), the preface to Shakespeare, and the lives of Milton, Cowley, Dryden, Pope, Gray, Savage. The human condition as something much to be endured and little to be enjoyed: consider how Johnson works with and out of his basic pessimism; determine the pressures against which he seeks stability and order. Define his notions of reason and imagination; watch his testing of the neoclassical "rules" against his own and general experience. One of the great critics and personalities.

English Prose and Poetry, 1660–1800, **ed. R. Brady and Martin Price. Holt, Rinehart & Winston, 1961.** For guidance, see introductions.

Further Readings

Bunyan, John (1628–1688), *Pilgrim's Progess* **(1678–1684). Dutton, 1972.**

Six Restoration Plays (The Country Wife, **produced in 1675,** *The Man of Mode,* **produced in 1676,** *All for Love,* **1678,** *The Way of the World,* **produced in 1700,** *Venice Preserv'd,* **produced in 1682,** *The Beaux' Stratagem,* **produced in 1707). ed. John H. Wilson. Houghton Mifflin, 1959.**

Eighteenth Century Plays **(plays by Steele, Rowe, and Lillo and** *The Beggar's Opera,* **produced in 1728,** *The School for Scandal,* **produced in 1777,** *She Stoops to Conquer,* **produced in 1773), ed. John Hampden. Dutton, 1961.**

Boswell, James (1740–1795), *The Life of Samuel Johnson* **(1791) abr. ed., ed. Frank Brady. NAL, 1968.**

Sterne, Laurence (1713–1768), *Memoirs of Mr. Laurence Sterne, The Life and Opinions of Tristram Shandy, A Sentimental Journey, Selected Sermons and Letters.* **Harvard Univ. Press, 1970.** Read *Tristram Shandy.*

Radcliffe, Ann (1764–1823), *The Mysteries of Udolpho* **[1794]***; A Romance Interspersed with Some Pieces of Poetry.* **Oxford Univ. Press, 1970.**

Goldsmith, Oliver (1728–1774), *The Vicar of Wakefield* (1766). Dutton, 1972.

Smollett, Tobias (1721–1771), *Expedition of Humphrey Clinker.* Dutton, 1972.

ROMANTIC

Bloom, Harold, ed., *English Romantic Poetry.* Vol. 1 (Blake, Wordsworth, Coleridge and others); Vol. 2 (Byron, Shelley, Keats, and others). Doubleday, 1963. In this work, read selections as indicated in the following six entries.

Blake (1757–1827). Begin with *Songs of Innocence and Experience,* move on to *Book of Thel* and *The Marriage of Heaven and Hell,* then to the visionary works if you wish. Work out the results of the fall from innocence and the relations between excess and wisdom, energy and control, and so on. Even the simplest poems are worth lingering over to feel out the moods, the resonance of the images.

Wordsworth (1770–1850). With the poems, read the "Preface to the *Lyrical Ballads.*" Study especially "Tintern Abbey" and the selections from "The Prelude" to work out the poet's ideas on human growth, on recollection, on nature as a resource, on human nature and its possibilities, on society and change. Compare Wordsworth's blank verse with Milton's and that of the pre-Romantic poets and get at the kind of voice that speaks through it here. Compare his ideas of the imagination with those of Coleridge, Shelley, and Keats.

Coleridge (1772–1834). Selections from *Biographia Literaria* (1817), a must. "Rime of the Ancient Mariner": attempt to determine what it is the mariner is working out, what his function is, the relation of his tale to the wedding, the tale's effect upon its hearer; be aware of the religious overtones. Read the great meditative poems, such as "This Lime Tree Bower My Prison," "Frost at Midnight," and "Dejection: an Ode," as ways to Coleridge's personality. Compare his ideas of the imagination with those of Wordsworth, Shelley, and Keats.

Byron (1788–1824). Very sympathetic with neoclassical writers; worth looking for his similarities and differences as stylist, satirist. Determine the contours and follow the development of the Byronic hero from "Childe Harold" to "Don Juan."

Keats (1795–1821). Read selections from his letters together with the poems. Watch for tensions between beauty-dreams-poetry-imagination and the hard realities of the waking state. Trace his developing idea of the nature and function of the poet. The poems repay sensitivity to the rich and functional use of sounds, rhythms, words, images. Work out the meaning and use of negative capability, its relation to Wordsworth and Coleridge's ideas on the imagination.

Shelley (1792–1822). "The Defense of Poetry" a must for deep ethical and esthetic notion of what a poet brings to his audience. A poet of considerable range in form and subject, worth watching for his particular idealism, both political and platonic, his concern with human ills and wrongs, his changing idea of their sources, and his careful and hopeful sense of their cure and of benevolent forces beyond our knowledge.

Prose of the Romantic Period, ed. Carl R. Woodring. Houghton Mifflin, 1961. For guidance, see the introductions.

Scott, Sir Walter (1771–1832), *Heart of Midlothian* (1818), 2nd ed. Holt, Rinehart & Winston, 1948. Take your time with Scott, move at his pace, enter his world; he is the great writer of romance. Be aware of the pattern of excursion and return, movement from safety to danger to final safety, and the social-political-economic-psychological nature of both danger and safety. Determine the values affirmed by the Scott romance. Work out the function of the realistic elements in this romantic form.

Austen, Jane (1775–1817), *Pride and Prejudice* (1813). Macmillan, 1962. Consider the relation in Austen's work between manners and morals. Consider how she uses her careful construction, dialogue, setting, characters, and satire to express a particularly moral view of life. Worth comparison with Scott as standing for a different direction in English fiction.

Edgeworth, Maria (1767–1849), *Castle Rackrent* (1801). Norton, 1965. A further reading in the Romantic period.

VICTORIAN

Basic Readings

Tennyson, Alfred (1809–1892), *Selected Poetry,* ed. H. M. McLuhan. Holt, Rinehart & Winston, 1956. Tennyson is a troubled reflector of the disturbances and uncertainties about religion in the face of the higher criticism and new science. Often a topical poet, he is vitally concerned with the role of the poet and with the relation of poetry-imagination and reality (social, political, and human). Control over sound and rhythm worth studying, worth comparing with Pope, Keats, Milton.

Browning, Robert (1812–1889), *Poems of Robert Browning,* ed. Donald Smalley. Houghton Mifflin, 1956. Discover the particular bite of Browning's poetry, its difference from that of the other Victorians, the kind of experience it tends to include, the voices it is capable of, its usefulness for the dramatic monologue—of which he was a master. Watch for his doctrine of the moment and doctrine of the imperfect as modes of handling the challenges to religion posed by his age.

Arnold, Matthew (1822–1888), *The Portable Matthew Arnold: Poems, Essays, Criticism,* ed. Lionel Trilling. Viking, 1949. Read "Preface to Poems, 1853 edn.," "The Function of Criticism at the Present Time," "The Study of Poetry," "Wordsworth," and selections from *Culture and Anarchy.* Arnold's criticism is essential, one of the most influential critics in the literature. Watch especially for his idea on the value of the best literature and on the role of the critic; work out what he means by culture, disinterestedness, and high seriousness ("The Study of Poetry"). Possible to think of his prose as a response to the isolation, alienation, and sense of deadness and sterility in self and society in the poems.

Dickens, Charles (1812–1870), *Hard Times.* **Fawcett World Library, 1969.** *Bleak House.* **NAL, 1964.** Compare Dickens' methods of characterization with those of Scott, Austen, Thackeray, Eliot; determine in what sense, if any, his characters are "unreal" (or caricatures) and what that means. Be aware of how his plots function to underline his social criticism, and come to grips with the nature and range of that criticism, the solutions implied.

Brontë, Charlotte (1816–1855), *Jane Eyre* **(1847). Macmillan, 1962.** Worth trying to work out relation between author and heroine. An uneven book in terms of construction; determine its sources of power and coherence.

Brontë, Emily (1818–1848), *Wuthering Heights* **(1847). Macmillan, 1962.** Consider the effect of having so much of the novel conveyed through Nelly and Mr. Lockwood. Watch for the elements in people that are significant to Brontë, possibly through comparing characterization in Dickens, Scott, Eliot.

Thackeray, William M. (1811–1863), *Vanity Fair* **(published in monthly numbers in 1847–1848). NAL, 1962.** A novelist of manners; determine Thackeray's attitude toward and his perspective on those manners; establish the dimensions of his reality. Compare his intrusive authorship with that of George Eliot. Note his ability to structure his novel through patterns of human relationships.

Eliot, George (1819–1880), *The Mill on the Floss* **(1860). Macmillan, 1962.** *Middlemarch* **(1871–1872). Macmillan, 1966.** Note Eliot's grasp of communities and of human nature and her own attitude toward existence, both enabling her to present her material in "such a way," as she said, "to call forth tolerant judgment, pity, and sympathy." Compare her as a realistic novelist to Dickens, Thackeray, Austen. Examine the functions of her intrusive authorship.

Hardy, Thomas (1840–1928), *Tess of the D'Urbervilles* **(1891). Houghton Mifflin, 1960.** Define the inner and outer forces at work on Hardy's characters and determine what resources people have in his universe, what kind of stature is possible. Differentiate between natural and social law; be aware of the novel as social criticism; note the use of animals—actual and as figures of speech; compare his use of setting to, say, Eliot's; is the use of coincidence helpful or harmful to the novel?

Conrad, Joseph (1857–1924), *The Heart of Darkness and The Secret Sharer,* **ed. Franklin Walker. Bantam, 1969.** Consider the importance of location of Marlow and his listeners; work out Marlow's position against Kurtz and determine, if possible, Conrad's attitude toward that position.

Conrad, Joseph, *Nostromo*. Modern Library, 1951. Consider the notions of the nature of reality and truth implicit in the use of a number of different consciousnesses centering around a situation. In both books, watch Conrad's testing of ideals and codes of conduct against various challenges and crises.

Wilde, Oscar (1854–1900), *The Portable Oscar Wilde*, ed. Richard Aldington. Viking, 1946. Read especially The Picture of Dorian Gray and The Importance of Being Earnest. Think of this writing as an art of decadence, art for art's sake; be alert to its relation to normal manners, morals, values. Watch for Wilde's ambivalence on these matters, his self-awareness, at the heart of his wit.

Buckley, Jerome H., and George B. Woods, *Poetry of the Victorian Period*, 3rd ed. Scott, Foresman (hard cover), 1965. Read especially selections by Elizabeth Barrett Browning, Daniel Gabriel Rossetti, Christina Rossetti, Meredith, Morris, Fitzgerald, Clough, Swinburne, Thompson, Hardy.

Hopkins, Gerard Manley (1844–1889), *Selected Poems and Prose*. Penguin, 1953. Read introductory material on his "sprung" rhythm, and watch how he uses rhythm, vocabulary, and juxtaposition to get at the "inscape" or particular essence of a person, event, or object through the relation between it and the individuality of himself.

James, Henry (1843–1916), *The Portrait of a Lady*, ed. Leon Edel. Houghton Mifflin, 1956. Watch James's exploration of the nature and boundaries of freedom, his handling of the relation between innocence and experience, America and Europe, sophistication (or "civilization") and corruption. **James, Henry, *The Wings of the Dove*. Penguin, 1974.** Consider the effects of the stylistic refinements of the late James upon the reading experience. (For another novel with an English setting, see *The Spoils of Poynton*, Doubleday, hard cover, 1971.)

Further Reading

Buckler, William E., ed., *Prose of the Victorian Period*. Houghton Mifflin, 1958. Read especially Carlyle, Mill, Huxley, Pater.

Butler, Samuel (1835–1902), *The Way of All Flesh* (1903). Dutton, 1972.

Stevenson, Robert Louis (1850–1894), *Dr. Jekyll and Mr. Hyde* (1886). Airmont, 1964.

Carroll, Lewis (1832–1898), *Alice in Wonderland and Through the Looking Glass* (1865). Macmillan, 1966.

Trollope, Anthony (1815–1882), *Barchester Towers* (1857). Holt, Rinehart & Winston, 1949.

Auden, W. H., and Norman H. Pearson, eds., *Victorian and Edwardian Poets*. Viking, 1952. Read especially the British poets of the Edwardian period by way of moving into the early twentieth century.

TWENTIETH CENTURY

Basic Readings

Shaw, George Bernard, (1856–1950), *Man and Superman* **(published 1903). Penguin, 1946.** *Heartbreak House* **(published 1917). Penguin, 1965.** Work out Shaw's socialist and evolutionist views, but watch especially his effort—through his handling of dramatic convention, through wit, satire, paradox, and discussion—to challenge, upset, criticize his audience.

Synge, John M. (1871–1909), *Complete Plays of John M. Synge.* **Random, 1960.** Read especially *Riders to the Sea* and *The Playboy of the Western World.* Consider the rich language, the interest in the primitive, and the celebration of gusto and imagination as an effort both to revitalize drama and to answer the indifference of nature and the narrowness of man.

O'Casey, Sean (1884–1964), *Three Plays (Juno and the Paycock, The Shadow of a Gunman, The Plough and the Stars).* **St. Martin's, 1966.** Worth working out the dynamics between comedy and tragedy, or pathos, the mixture of genres, in O'Casey's drama. A disputed question: is his dramatic form erratic and poorly structured or calculatedly unconventional and effective?

Beckett, Samuel (1906–   ), *Waiting for Godot.* **Grove, 1954.** *Three Novels by Samuel Beckett (Molloy; Malone Dies; The Unnamable).* **Grove, 1965.** Beware of simple interpretations of Beckett's work. Look for ways in which both style and content express an attitude toward the human condition. One of the great artists of the absurd, defined thus by Ionesco: "Absurd is that which is devoid of purpose . . . cut off from his religious, metaphysical, and transcendental roots, man is lost; all his actions become senseless, absurd, useless."

Osborne, John (1929–   ), *Look Back in Anger.* **Bantam, 1967.** Consider how the play is intended to act upon the audience. To what extent and in what way is the angry young man, the caustic social critic Jimmy Porter, subject(ed) to criticism himself?

Pinter, Harold (1930–   ), *The Caretaker and The Dumbwaiter.* **Grove, 1961.** Pinter has said he is dealing with his characters "at the extreme edge of their living, where they are living pretty much alone," and that after a certain point *The Caretaker* ceases to be funny, "and it was because of that point that I wrote it." Consider the two plays as different ways of getting at some of the absurdity and terror of existence.

Weiss, Peter (1916–   ), *Marat/Sade.* **Pocket Books, 1966.** Powerful play by an artist of the absurd; compare its abundance of dramatic action and characters with the spareness of Beckett; note what it says about sanity, madness.

Yeats, W. B. (1865–1939), *Selected Poems of William Butler Yeats,*

ed. M. L. Rosenthal. Macmillan, 1962. Admire the continual vital development, the self-confrontations, of this poet. Watch and work out as themes: poetry vs. action, Irish nationalism, the antimask (experiencing of one's opposite), the attainment of wholeness of being, the nature and importance of passion and style (peasant and aristocrat valued, middle-class abhorred), age and wisdom, age and wildness, love, remorse, the sources and function of poetry.

Eliot, T. S. (1888–1965), *Complete Poems and Plays, 1909–1950.* Harcourt Brace Jovanovich (hard cover), 1952. Consider the functions of Eliot's complexity, and of his reference to past cultures and works of art, in his own poems about fragmented culture and spiritual sterility. The later poems repay careful reading in their consideration of material and spiritual time and their exploration of religious experience and possibility. Worth reading through his *Selected Essays* **(Harcourt Brace Jovanovich, rev. ed., hard cover, 1950)** for light on his work.

Auden, W. H. (1907–1975), *Selected Poetry of W. H. Auden.* Random, 1971. Consider Auden as a skillful and experimenting craftsman, an intelligent man concerned with analysis of contemporary problems and events, who combines with his careful art an ear for colloquial speech. Watch for influences of Marx in the 1930s and of Freud then and later.

Thomas, Dylan (1914–1959), *Collected Poems.* New Directions, 1971. Keep an eye on Thomas' exploration and concepts of death. In "Fern Hill," "When All My Five and Country Senses See," and others, find his intense concern with aging and with sources of vitality and love. The poems repay close attention to sounds, rhythms, syntax, vocabulary; they are worth the working out they demand.

Hughes, Ted (1930–   ), *Crow: from the Life and Songs of the Crow.* Harper & Row, 1971. Try reading, with care, but without pause, through the book and seeing what effects accumulate. A devastating view of man and God and nature; to what extent does the form control it? Be aware of the part humor plays, work out other aspects of style and attitude—for instance, the frequent flatness of statement.

Joyce, James (1882–1941), *Portrait of the Artist as a Young Man.* Viking, 1965. Worth close study for Joyce's painstaking care for words, for its autobiography, its development of a theory of art.

Joyce, James, *Ulysses.* Random, 1946. Should be read during an unimpeded period of time, and it repays rereading, repays time taken to work out its levels, meanings. Be aware of how Joyce uses various styles and tones, both to get at the nature of human consciousness and to give perspective on a scene or character. See the book as partially a study of objectivity, or objects, things outside oneself, a study by an objective author. Watch for questions of nation, of creativity, of identity, of isolation and of communication, of how one comes to grips with one's personal and national past and one's environment and transcends them.

Lawrence, D. H. (1885–1930), *The Rainbow and Women in Love,* ed. Clarke Colin. Aurora, 1970. Keep on eye on Lawrence's manner of handling a character so as to disclose subconscious experience, the mysteries of existence. Determine the value such experience and mysteries have for him and look for the solutions Lawrence, as a social critic, offers his contemporaries.

Woolf, Virginia (1882–1941), *To the Lighthouse.* Harcourt Brace Jovanovich, 1949. Woolf's narrative decision expresses a belief about how life is experienced—as "a myriad impression—trivial, fantastic, evanescent, or engraved with the sharpness of steel." The arbitrariness of life and death, the passing of time, the difficulty of human relations—where in it all is the viable pattern found, or the eternal, the permanent? Consider the relation of the book as a whole to Lily's art and to Mrs. Ramsay, especially in the dining-room segment.

Forster, E. M. (1879–1970), *A Passage to India.* Harcourt Brace Jovanovich, 1965. Watch for ways to possibly break through the confusion, sterility, or emptiness of life or of conventional manners and attitudes. Think of Forster as a realist, a satirist of manners, with something more penetrating, symbolic, important happening here and there.

Further Readings

Mansfield, Katherine (1888–1923), *Stories,* ed. Elizabeth Bowen. Random, 1956.

Ford, Ford Maddox (1873–1939), *The Good Soldier.* Random, 1951.

Murdoch, Iris (1919–   ), *A Severed Head.* Avon, 1970.

Lessing, Doris (1919–   ), *The Temptation of Jack Orkney and Other Stories.* Bantam, 1974.

Amis, Kingsley (1922–   ) *Lucky Jim.* Viking, 1958.

Orwell, George (1903–1950), *1984.* NAL, 1971.

Stoppard, Tom (1937–   ), *Rosencrantz and Guildenstern Are Dead.* Grove, 1967.

New Poets of England and America: Second Selection, ed. Donald Hall and Robert Pack. NAL, 1962.

WORKS BY CRITICS

Basic Readings

Abrams, M. H., *The Mirror and the Lamp: Romantic Theory and The Critical Tradition.* Oxford Univ. Press, 1953.

Bate, Walter Jackson, *From Classic to Romantic: Premises of Taste in 18th Century England.* Harper & Row, 1961.

Buckley, Jerome, *The Victorian Temper: A Study in Literary Culture*. Random, 1969.

Brooks, Cleanth, *The Well-Wrought Urn: Studies in the Structure of Poetry*. Harcourt Brace Jovanovich, 1956. Penetrating essays on individual poems by a New Critic; concern with the nature of poetry, how and what it communicates.

Bush, Douglas, *Prefaces to Renaissance Literature*. Norton, 1965.

Booth, Wayne C., *The Rhetoric of Fiction*. Univ. of Chicago Press, 1961.

Eliot, T. S., *Selected Essays*, rev. ed. Harcourt Brace Jovanovich (hard cover), 1950. Important both for English literary tradition and for study of modern poetry.

Lewis, C. S., *The Allegory of Love: A Study in Medieval Tradition*. Oxford Univ. Press, 1936. On courtly love and allegory; chapters on Chaucer and Spenser.

Williams, Raymond, *Culture and Society 1780–1950*. Harper & Row, 1966.

Wilson, Edmund, *Axel's Castle*. Scribner's, 1931. The symbolist movement; chapters on Yeats, Eliot, Joyce, and others.

Further Readings

Bloom, Harold, *The Visionary Company: A Reading of English Romantic Poetry*, rev. ed. Cornell Univ. Press, 1971.

Bodkin, Maud, *Archetypal Patterns in Poetry: Psychological Studies of the Imagination*. Oxford Univ. Press, 1963.

Frye, Northrup, *The Anatomy of Criticism*. Princeton Univ. Press, 1957. Influential study of historical, ethical, archetypal, and rhetorical criticism (modes, symbols, myths, genres), by an archetypal critic.

Langbaum, Robert, *The Poetry of Experience: The Dramatic Monologue in Modern Literary Tradition*. Norton, 1963. Effort to find a tradition in which both Romantic poetry and the reactions of the later nineteenth and the twentieth centuries against it are bound together.

Leavis, F. R., *The Great Tradition*. New York Univ. Press, 1963. A study of George Eliot, James, and Conrad as being, with Jane Austen, the great English novelists in a common central tradition.

Lovejoy, Arthur O., *The Great Chain of Being: A Study in the History of an Idea*. Harvard Univ. Press, 1936.

Martz, Louis, *The Poetry of Meditation; A Study in English Religious Literature of the Seventeenth Century*. Yale Univ. Press, 1954.

Steiner, George, *The Death of Tragedy*. Hill & Wang, 1963.

Watt, Ian, *The Rise of the Novel: Studies in Defoe, Richardson and Fielding.* **Univ. of California Press, 1957.** Realism; relation of authors to growth of reading public and to "the new climate of social and moral experience."

Chapter Twenty

FILM
"... sound, lighting, and choice of image"

Editorial Advisor:
William Alexander
Department of English
University of Michigan

INTRODUCTION

Serious study of film—understanding and practicing the art of motion pictures—has grown rapidly at colleges and universities in recent years. Film has developed into one of the most popular new areas of study, with growing interest in its unique powers as an art and its influence as a communications medium.

Film illuminates contemporary life much as masterful stories and plays and pictures have for centuries; studying the art of film can therefore not only enrich your enjoyment of "movies," but also deepen your insight into what it means to be alive.

Opportunities for studying the best in film all too often depend on access to a film center that presents a variety of old and recent films and has an archive where you may pursue studies in depth. Such centers are operating in major cities and at large universities—for example, at the Museum of Modern Art in New York, the University of California at Los Angeles, the University of California at Berkeley, and the Detroit Institute of Art. Access to the archives varies considerably from place to place and is usually restricted, but all are locations for the showing of important films. You may find these centers, or alternatively a film society that organizes screenings, by inquiring locally.

Failing such access, local libraries can sometimes be persuaded to allocate funds for short films. Film societies can be formed; with wise programming, a society might draw large enough audiences to pay for high-quality film rentals. (A reference widely consulted by these societies is: Limbacher, James L., *Feature Films on 8 mm and 16 mm; A Directory of Feature Films Available for Rental, Sale and Lease in the United States*, 14th ed. Bowker, hard cover, 1977.) Short films may be obtained for low rental fees by responsible and interested groups from audiovisual departments of state universities. Some effort in such local institutions as community colleges and high schools may develop ways of presenting films for study and perhaps even uniting funds and equipment for cooperative experiments in film making.

Televised films are of some help for film study. But films made expressly for television differ from movies made for the large screen. Moreover, large-screen films shown on television lose much of their quality because of small screen size, viewing environment, advertisements, inferior sound equipment, and the distortion of subtle lighting effects that television cannot render, not to mention the greater or lesser degree of cutting generally undertaken.

Film history, still in its first century, has had a number of major impulses and moments. (1) the seminal work of Lumière and Méliès toward the turn of the century; (2) the films of D. W. Griffith and the American comic artists of the 1910s and 1920s; (3) the Soviet montage films of the 1920s and early 1930s; (4) the German expressionist and realist films and the surrealist films of the 1920s; (5) the development of social-political documentary in the 1930s; (6) the neo-realists in Italy in the late 1940s and early 1950s; (7) the New Wave in France in the late 1950s and early 1960s, with corresponding vital developments in other countries; (8) the rise of the American independent underground film during and since the 1950s, including work done in video and computer graphics; (9) documentary *cinéma verité* in the 1960s; (10) also in the 1960s, the reaction of the Zagreb artists and others in Europe against the earlier dominant impulse of Disney animation; and (11) the increasing prominence of political and nonpolitical film from Third World countries. You may find the following partial list of major film makers helpful in keeping on the lookout for their work. They are arranged by the genre or type of film for which they seem best known, though some have worked in other genres.

FEATURE FILM   Robert Altman, Lindsay Anderson, Michelangelo Antonioni, Fernando Arrabal, Ingmar Bergman, Bernardo Bertolucci, Robert Bresson, Luis Buñuel, Frank Capra, Marcel Carné, John Cassavetes, Charlie Chaplin, René Clair, Jean Cocteau, Costa-Gavras, Vittorio De Sica, Alexander Dovzhenko, Carl Dreyer, Sergei Eisenstein, Rainer Werner Fassbinder, Federico Fellini, John Ford, Milos Forman, Jean-Luc Godard, D. W. Griffith, Werner Herzog, Alfred Hitchcock, John Huston, Jan Kadar, Elia Kazan, Stanley Kramer, Stanley Kubrick, Akira Kurosawa, Fritz Lang, Joseph Losey, Louis Malle, F. W. Murnau, G. W. Pabst, Pier-Paolo Pasolini, Arthur Penn, Roman Polanski, Gillo Pontecorvo, V. I. Pudovkin, Satyajit Ray, Jean Renoir, Alain Resnais, Tony Richardson, Alain Robbe-Grillet, Roberto Rossellini, Robert Rossen, Alain Tanner, Francois Truffaut, Agnes Varda, Luchino Visconti, Erich Von Stroheim, Orson Welles, Lina Wertmüller, Robert Wiene, Fred Zinnemann.

EXPERIMENTAL   Kenneth Anger, Bruce Baillie, Jordan Belson, Stan Brakhage, Robert Breer, Maya Deren, Ed Emshwiller, Gregory Markopoulos, Hans Richter, Michael Snow, Stan VanDerBeek, Andy Warhol, James Whitney, John Whitney Jr., John Whitney Sr.

DOCUMENTARY Shirley Clarke, Peter Davis, Robert Flaherty, Frontier Films, Joris Ivens, Allan King, Richard Leacock, Pare Lorentz, Albert and David Maysles, Marcel Ophuls, D. A. Pennebaker, Leni Riefenstahl, Dziga Vertov, Frederick Wiseman, Basil Wright.

ANIMATION Walerian Borowczyk, Walt Disney, John and Faith Hubley, Jan Lenica, Norman McLaren, UPA Studios, Zagreb Studios.

The bibliography that follows is intended to give you good basic and advanced reading in a variety of areas. A text on film making and one on still photography are included; these books are helpful to people without the range of equipment generally available to those in film making and photography courses in universities.

Keep in mind that the books listed are important *secondary* material; the primary material is the film. While they can give background, vocabulary, ideas, they cannot by themselves give training in visual literacy and cinematic style. The individual eye and ear must be trained by watching films closely, by seeking opportunities to see films more than once, especially in a setting where individual scenes can be rerun repeatedly, so as to develop sensitivity toward the way film makers use editing, various kinds of movement, angle, distance, sound, lighting, and choice of image to convey their meanings.

BIBLIOGRAPHY

Introductory Text on
Film Language and Technique

Dudley, Andrew J., *The Major Film Theories: An Introduction.* Oxford University Press, 1976.

Giannetti, Louis D., *Understanding Movies.* Prentice-Hall, 1976. This should be the first book read, as an introduction to cinematic style.

History

Mast, Gerald, *Short History of the Movies.* Pegasus, 1971.

Brownlow, Kevin, *The Parade's Gone by. . . .* Knopf, 1968. Excellent study of the silent era in Hollywood by an author who believes the period to be "the richest in the cinema's history" and who attempts to recapture its spirit. History, analysis, interviews.

Leyda, Jay, *Kino: A History of the Russian & Soviet Film.* Hillary, 1960.

Kracauer, Siegfried, *From Caligari to Hitler: A Psychological History of the German Film.* Princeton Univ. Press, 1947.

Armes, Roy, *French Cinema Since 1946,* 2 vols., rev. ed. Barnes, 1970.

Anderson, Joseph L., and Donald Ritchie, *Japanese Film: Art and Industry.* Grove, 1960.

Cowie, Peter, *Sweden,* 2 vols., rev. ed. Barnes, 1969. Swedish film history.

Theory

Eisenstein, Sergei, *Film Form.* Harcourt Brace Jovanovich, 1969. One of the foremost theorists as well as practitioners of film. Important for understanding some of the complexity and possibility of montage.

Pudovkin, V. I., *Film Technique and Film Acting.* Grove, 1970. A major Soviet theorist and film maker; a seminal and suggestive book, stressing importance of editing as the basis of film art, the relation of editing to spectator, to space and time, and so forth.

Kracauer, Siegfried, *Theory of Film: The Redemption of Physical Reality.* Oxford Univ. Press, 1965. One of the most important and provocative books of film theory. Film realism seen as of highest importance: "Films come into their own when they record and reveal physical reality."

Bazin, André, *What is Cinema?* Univ. of California Press, Vol. I, 1967; Vol. II, 1971. One of the foremost theorists; a theory of film realism significantly different from Kracauer's. Vol I: Important essays include "The Ontology of the Photographic Image," "The Evolution of the Language of Cinema," "The Virtues and Limitations of Montage," and "Theater and Cinema." Vol II: See especially essays on "An Aesthetic of Reality," Italian Neorealism, the Western, eroticism.

Balasz, Bela, *Theory of Film: Character and Growth of a New Art.* Dover, 1971. Especially sensitive on uses of sound, editing, and movement of camera and on the ways visual images communicate.

Wollen, Peter, *Signs and Meaning in the Cinema.* Indiana Univ. Press, 1973. Concern with language of cinema, especially sign language, with *auteur* theory as applied to Hollywood directors, with nature and significance of Eisenstein's aesthetics.

MacCann, Richard D., ed., *Film: A Montage of Theories.* Dutton, 1966. A wide-ranging anthology of writing on film.

Bluestone, George, *Novels into Film: The Metamorphosis of Fiction into Cinema.* Univ. of California Press, 1957.

Hurt, James, ed., *Focus on Film and Theatre.* Prentice-Hall, 1974. Good variety of essays on relation between the two arts: acting, directing, staging, aesthetics.

Animation

Stephenson, Ralph, *The Animated Film,* rev. ed. Barnes, 1973. History of animated film, with some initial definition and a few pages on technique. Covers many animators and animated films, not with great depth of analysis, but informative.

Interviews

Samuels, Charles T., *Encountering Directors.* **Putnam, 1973.** Challenging, sometimes brash, encounters between author and major directors from many countries; very good material.

Sarris, Andrew, ed., *Interviews with Film Directors.* **Avon, 1969.** Collection of forty interviews by various interviewers of wide range of major directors.

Books on Major Directors

The reader is advised to order books on directors in whom s/he is interested and to avoid cheap picture-filled texts. What follows is a list of some good books on some major directors.

Armes, Roy, *Cinema of Alain Resnais.* **Barnes, 1968.**

Bazin, André, *Jean Renoir.* **Dell, 1974.**

Brown, Royal S., ed., *Focus on Godard.* **Prentice-Hall, 1972.** Excellent collection of interviews, reviews, essays, commentaries.

Higham, Charles, *The Films of Orson Welles.* **Univ. of California Press, 1970.**

Richie, Donald, *The Films of Akira Kurosawa.* **Univ. of California Press, 1965.**

Salachas, Gilbert, *Federico Fellini.* **Crown, 1969.**

Moussinac, Leon, *Sergei Eisenstein.* **Crown, 1970.**

Truffaut, François, *Hitchcock.* **Simon & Schuster, 1969.**

Wood, Robin, *Ingmar Bergman.* **Praeger, 1969.**

NOTE The *Focus On* books are generally good collections of material on a director.

Hollywood

Powdermaker, Hortense, *Hollywood: the Dream Factory.* **Little, Brown, 1972.** Pre-1950 films; anthropological view of Hollywood and its relation to American society; research into the Hollywood and the American society behind Hollywood films, into the locus of power, taboos, values, economics, and the like.

Wolfenstein, Martha, and Nathan Leites, *Movies: A Psychological Study.* **Atheneum, 1970.** Cultural anthropology and psychoanalysis applied to themes and plots of the 1940s films to discover fantasies, ideals, beliefs of people who produced and saw American films in that decade.

Schickel, Richard, *The Disney Version; The Life, Times, Art and Commerce of Walt Disney.* Avon, **1969.** Strongly critical look at Disney and his audience; a provocative study in popular culture.

Bogle, Donald, *Toms, Coons, Mulattoes, Mammies & Bucks: An Interpretive History of Blacks in American Films.* Viking, **1973.**

Rosen, Marjorie, *Popcorn Venus: Women, Movies and the American Dream.* Avon, **1974.** Images of women in American films and relation of those images to women in America.

Criticism

Kael, Pauline, *Deeper into Movies.* Bantam, **1974.** Most recent book of film reviews by the challenging critic for *The New Yorker.*

Sarris, Andrew, *Confessions of a Cultist: On the Cinema, 1955/ 1969.* Simon & Schuster, **1971.**

Taylor, John R., *Cinema Eye, Cinema Ear: Some Key Film-Makers of the Sixties.* Hill & Wang, **1964.** Essays on Antonioni, Bergman, Bresson, Buñuel, Fellini, Godard, Hitchcock, Resnais, Truffaut.

Bellone, Julius, *Renaissance of the Film.* Macmillan, **1970.** Selection of major critical pieces from the post-Second World War era, chosen from film and nonfilm periodicals, 1948–1968 (predominantly 1960s).

Documentary Film

Barsam, Richard M., *Non-Fiction Film; A Critical History.* Dutton, **1973.** Substantial, considered criticism, helpful descriptions of films. Mainly Great Britian and United States, but also some European.

Ivens, Joris, *The Camera and I.* International, **1970.** Autobiography with much practical and theoretical material by one of world's leading social-political film makers from 1920s to present. Book covers to 1939-40, with notes and addenda up to 1967.

Levin, G. Roy, *Documentary Explorations: Fifteen Interviews with Film-Makers.* Doubleday, **1971.** Includes Basil Wright, Lindsay Anderson, Georges Frangu, Henri Storck, Willard Van Dyke, Richard Leacock, the Maysles brothers, Frederick Wiseman. A good collection.

Rosenthal, Alan, *The New Documentary in Action: A Casebook in Film Making.* Univ. of California Press, **1972.** Probing interviews with prominent film makers, sometimes several from crew of single film, with interest in practical matters of getting the films made. Includes Frederick Wiseman, Albert Maysles, Allan King, Peter Watkins, Don Alan Pennebaker, George Stoney, and Norman McLaren.

Underground, Avant-Garde, Experimental or New American Film

**Renan, Sheldon, *Introduction to the American Underground Film.*
Dutton, 1967.** A thorough history of names, dates, developments up to
1966.

Tyler, Parker, *Underground Film: A Critical History.* Grove, 1969.
A provocative discussion as well as a history; effort to get at "personality" of underground film and its historical traditions and relations;
attempt to define its particular interest in realities, or reality, not found
in commercial cinema.

Sitney, P. Adams, ed., *Film Culture Reader.* Praeger, 1970. Criticism and theory of avant-garde film as it developed in a periodical
closely tied to the movement.

**Battcock, Gregory, ed., *New American Cinema: A Critical Anthol-
ogy.* Dutton, 1967.** Definitions, theory, and criticism of underground
film by critics and film makers.

Youngblood, Gene, *Expanded Cinema.* Dutton, 1970. Exploration
of cinema, video, computer graphics at furthest reaches of their
technology and discussion of their relation to present and future society and to man's present and future communicative capacities. A major
work.

**Sitney, P. Adams, *Visionary Film: The American Avant-Garde.*
Oxford Univ. Press (hard cover), 1974.** This is a major critical work,
serious analysis and good history, a vital grappling with the avant-
garde film.

Genre (just a sampling)

Cawelti, John, *Six-Gun Mystique.* Bowling Green Univ. Press, 1970.
A major study of the western.

McArthur, Colin, *Underworld, USA.* Viking, 1972. Gangster and
thriller films.

Mast, Gerald, *The Comic Mind.* Bobbs-Merrill, 1973. Theoretical
treatment of comedy and comic films and discussions of Sennett,
Chaplin, Keaton, Lloyd, and others.

NOTE   Again, beware of cheap, picture-filled books. Generally good
are the *Focus On* books—*Focus on the Horror Film,* for example.

Scripts

Many filmscripts are available in paperback; look in bookstores or
consult *Books in Print* to order scripts of films you have seen or expect
to see.

Mayer, David, *Eisenstein's Potemkin*. Grossman, 1972. More than a script; a breakdown of the film into shot-by-shot description that makes possible (to a substantial extent) analysis of Eisenstein's editing style.

Film Making

Pincus, Edward, *Guide to Film Making*. NAL, 1969. Very professional and complete introduction to both 8mm and 16mm film making.

Still Photography

Davis, Phil, *Photography*, 2nd ed. William C. Brown, 1975. Solid, professional text for both basic and intermediate levels of photography.

Periodicals

Cineaste. 333 Sixth Avenue, New York, NY 10002. Intelligent, political analysis of political and nonpolitical films. Special interest in Third World and independent American and European political films from Far Left perspective.

Cinema Journal. Publications and Order Department, the University of Iowa, 17 West College Street, Iowa City, IA 52242. Journal of the Society for Cinema Studies; scholarly studies of film. Published twice a year.

Film Comment. 1865 Broadway, New York, NY 10023. Monthly. Serious criticism and reviews, covers contemporary and older film; numbers sometimes devoted to special topics, such as animation and documentary. Published monthly.

Film Culture. G.P.O. Box 1499, New York, NY 10001. The great journal of the independent film. Appearance now sporadic.

Film Quarterly. Univ. of California Press, Berkeley, CA 94720. Serious film reviews and discussion of film makers and films, interviews; perhaps more interest in theory than *Film Comment*.

Quarterly Film Review. Red Grave Publishing, 430 Manville Road, Pleasantville, NY 10570.

Screen. 63 Old Compton Street, London, WIV 5PN, England. Journal of the Society for Education in Film and Television. Very strong interest in film theory; much discussion of film sign language (semiotics).

Film Society

Weiner, Janet, *How to Organize & Run a Film Society*. Macmillan, 1973.

Chapter Twenty-One

PHILOSOPHY
*". . . much more important than
what philosophers have said"*

Editorial Advisor:
Ned Block
Department of Philosophy
Massachusetts Institute of Technology

INTRODUCTION

The major schools of philosophy disagree greatly about what philosophy is and how it should be done; there is even a fair amount of
disagreement within individual schools. This conflict poses a problem
for the beginning student because it is not possible to become familiar
with a number of schools before choosing one to specialize in. Learning
philosophy within one school is hard enough; students therefore have
to pick a shool of philosophy without a thorough basis for their choice.

This section will deal with the problem by staying essentially within
the mainstream of American philosophy, the tradition sometimes
called "analytic philosophy." Most solid philosophical work in
English-speaking countries today is done within this tradition. The
leading contemporary school in Continental Europe is often characterized as "phenomenology." Readers who want an introduction to it
should study the readings referred to in the bibliography's section on
Intentionality.

The major branches of philosophy are metaphysics, epistemology
(theory of knowledge), logic, philosophy of science, philosophy of
language, philosophy of mind, and the fields concerned with value—
ethics, political philosophy, and aesthetics. The divisions between
these branches are somewhat arbitrary; many issues are equally important in a number of different areas. For example, the question of
whether there is a distinction between analytic and synthetic truths is
of basic significance in each of the first six subfields named.

Most undergraduates majoring in Philosophy take one course in
logic, two in history of philosophy, and one in ethics. The first part of
the bibliography lists books typically studied in these four course

areas. In addition, most undergraduate majors take a scattering of perhaps three or four "electives" chosen from a pool of perhaps twenty to forty courses over a four-year period. Because of the large element of choice, the programs of any two undergraduate majors may look quite different. But there is often a great deal of underlying similarity because there is a relatively small number of basic themes that pervade contemporary philosophical work.

The second part of the bibliography presents readings on seventeen topics. These are intended as one possible approach (though by no means the only one) to the central themes in metaphysics, epistemology, philosophy of science, philosophy of language, and philosophy of mind. The topics are not intended to constitute a survey of these fields; such a survey might be useful for cocktail party conversation, but it is no way to learn philosophy. The third part is similarly intended as one approach to the fields concerned with values.

The goal in studying philosophy is not to learn a set of facts, results, or even the statements of important thinkers on various topics; rather, it is to learn a way of thinking about problems, to learn to think philosophically. Students who master the topics in the second and third parts will learn something much more important than what philosophers have said; they will come to understand what philosophy is and how to do it.

In many fields the advice to "begin at the beginning" is reasonable (though unnecessary). But in philosophy it is bad counsel. In some areas, such as chemistry, you must master one body of knowledge before another, thus giving an order to a course of study. In philosophy there are few such cases of "one-way" structure. Every philosophical problem depends for its solution on the solutions of many other philosophical problems. Areas of philosophy are so intertwined that, to a substantial degree, all must be learned together.

Readings in philosophy can only rarely be classified as beginning, intermediate, or advanced. Both introductory courses and advanced graduate courses often call for reading of the same material. Sometimes the most sophisticated philosophical work is written in a simple, straightforward style suitable for beginners. Students just starting out, however, often feel that, though they can understand such straightforward writings, they fail to see the "big picture" that is being presupposed. Unfortunately, much of the material written deliberately for beginners is so oversimplified as to do more harm than good.

You really have no alternative as a beginning philosophy student except to "start in the middle." Any good works that you read in the beginning can be read again at a more advanced level of understanding. When you start doing philosophy for the first time, you will find yourself puzzled about why the authors say what they say, about what their goals are. If you want to learn philosophy, you must jump in, even though at first you find it difficult to understand what is going on. You learn by doing.

BIBLIOGRAPHY

NOTE   You can start with any one of the three parts, or a mixture of all three. Contemporary discussions of the sort outlined in the second and third parts rarely presuppose detailed knowledge of the history of philosophy. You will find that knowledge of contemporary debates will be as much help in understanding the great philosophers of the past as the reverse.

Studies Undertaken
by Most Philosophy Majors

HISTORY OF PHILOSOPHY

Plato

Hamilton, Edith, and Huntington Cairns, eds., *Plato: The Collected Dialogues.* **Princeton Univ. Press (hard cover), 1961.** Inexpensive and best English-language edition of Plato's writings. Has references to critical literature.

The following are two excellent collections of articles on subjects raised in Plato's dialogues.

Vlastos, Gregory, ed., *Plato: A Collection of Critical Essays,* **2 vols. Vol 1:** *Metaphysics, Epistomology;* **Vol. 2:** *Ethics, Politics, Philosophy of Art, Religion.* **Doubleday, 1970.**

Vlastos, Gregory, "The Third Man Argument in the Parmenides." In *Studies in Plato's Metaphysics,* ed. Reginald E. Allen. Humanities (hard cover), 1968.

Aristotle

Two of the best editions of Aristotle's writings are the following collections by McKeon and Ackrill.

McKeon, Richard P., ed., *Introduction to Aristotle.* **Univ. of Chicago Press (hard cover), 1974.** Selections from Aristotle's works.

Ackrill, J. L., ed., *Categories and De Interpretatione.* **Oxford Univ. Press (hard cover), 1963.**

Ross, William D., ed., *Aristotle.* **Methuen, 1964.** Summarizes Aristotle's writings; helpful to read along with the two preceding works.

Moravcsik, J. M., ed., *Aristotle: A Collection of Critical Essays.* **Doubleday (Anchor), 1968.** A good collection of critical articles.

Descartes

Read the "Meditation on First Philosophy," the "Discourse on Method," "Objections and Replies," and the selections from *Principles of Philosophy* in any of three following books.

Wilson, Margaret, ed., *Essential Descartes*. NAL, 1972. Best edition of Descartes' writings.

Anscombe, Elizabeth, and Peter T. Geach, trs., *Descartes' Philosophical Writings*. Bobbs-Merrill, 1972.

Haldane, E. S., and G. R. Ross, eds., *Descartes: Philosophical Works*, 2 vols. Cambridge Univ. Press, 1967.

Good critical articles on issues raised in Descartes' writings can be found in the two following books.

Doney, Willis, ed., *Descartes: A Collection of Critical Essays*. Doubleday (Anchor), 1968.

Sesonske, Alexander, and Noel Flemming, eds., *Meta-Meditations: Studies in Descartes*. Wadsworth, 1965.

Kenny, Anthony, *Descartes: A Study of His Philosophy*. Random, 1968. An excellent extended study.

Leibniz

Read the "Discourse on Metaphysics" and the first half of the "Correspondence with Arnaud" in either of the following two books.

Leibniz, W. Gottfried, *Discourse on Metaphysics*, tr. George Montgomery. Open Court, 1968. Best edition of Leibniz.

Wiener, Philip P., *Leibniz: Selections*. Scribner's, 1971.

Frankfurt, Harry G., ed., *Leibniz, A Collection of Critical Essays*. Doubleday (Modern Studies in Philosophy series), 1972. Critical articles.

Spinoza

Spinoza, Benedict De, *On the Improvement of Human Understanding; The Ethics; Selected Letters*, tr. R. H. M. Elwes. Dover, 1955.

Hampshire, Stuart, *Spinoza*. Penguin, 1961. A delightful work.

Hobbes

Hobbes, Thomas, *Leviathan*, 2 vols., ed. Herbert W. Schneider. Bobbs-Merrill, 1958.

Locke

Locke, John, *An Essay Concerning Human Understanding*, abr. ed., ed. Maurice Cranston. Macmillan (Collier), 1965.

Armstrong, David M. and C. B. Martin, eds., *Locke and Berkeley: A Collection of Critical Essays.* Doubleday (Anchor), 1968. A good source of critical articles.

Bennett, Jonathan, *Locke, Berkeley, Hume: Central Themes.* Oxford Univ. Press, 1971. This book is a must. Read all of it.

Berkeley

The Empiricists. Doubleday (Anchor). Presents the original texts of: Locke, John, *Essay Concerning Human Understanding* (abr. ed.), 1690; Berkeley, George, *Principles of Human Knowledge*, 1710, *Three Dialogues*, 1713; Hume, David, *Enquiry Concerning Human Understanding*, 1748, *Dialogues Concerning Natural Religion*, 1779. Good text for Berkeley and Hume. Do not use for Locke.

Turbayne, Colin M., ed., *Three Dialogues Between Hylas and Philonous.* Bobbs-Merrill, 1954.

Turbayne, Colin M., ed., *Berkeley: Principles of Human Knowledge with Critical Essays.* Bobbs-Merrill, 1970.

Also read articles on Berkeley in the last two books listed under Locke.

Hume

Hendel, Charles W., ed., *Hume: Selections.* Scribner's, 1971. Best edition on Hume. Read *Dialogues Concerning Natural Religion*, and *An Enquiry Concerning Human Understanding.*

Chappell, V. C., ed., *Hume: A Collection of Critical Essays.* Doubleday (Anchor), 1968. Read some of the critical articles along with the Bennett book above.

Kant

Reading Kant is very hard, demanding work.

Korner, Stephen, ed., *Kant*, 2nd ed. Penguin, 1955. Start with this volume; not particularly profound, but it will serve to orient you.

Kant, Immanuel, *Critique of Pure Reason*, tr. Norman Kemp-Smith. St. Martin's, 1929. Read up to and including the *Transcendental Analytic*, and then the *Antinomies of Pure Reason*, Chapter 2, Book 2. When you get stuck, proceed to the next work listed.

Wolff, Robert P., *Kant's Theory of Mental Activity, a Commentary on the Transcendental Analytic of the Critique of Pure Reason.* Peter Smith (hard cover), 1962.

Wolff, Robert P., ed., *Kant: A Collection of Critical Essays.* Doubleday (Anchor), 1968. Critical articles.

To learn more about Kant after getting through the above works, read the following three books.

Strawson, P. F., *Bounds of Sense: An Essay on Kant's Critique of Pure Reason.* Methuen (hard cover), 1966.

Bennett, Jonathan, *Kant's Analytic.* Cambridge Univ. Press, 1966.

Bennett, Jonathan, *Kant's Dialectic.* Cambridge Univ. Press, 1974.

Russell

Russell, Bertrand, *Our Knowledge of the External World.* Humanities (hard cover), 1961. Russell's version of the construction of the external world from sense data.

Pears, D. F., *Bertrand Russell and the British Tradition in Philosophy.* Random, 1971. For extended Study.

Pears, D. F., ed., *Bertrand Russell: A Collection of Critical Essays.* Doubleday, 1972. Collection of articles on all aspects of Russell's work; contains an excellent bibliography of Russell's writings and articles about them.

Wittgenstein

Wittgenstein, Ludwig, *Philosophical Investigations,* tr. G. E. M. Inscombe, 3rd ed. Macmillan, 1973. Start with this. If you get stuck, read the following.

Wittgenstein, Ludwig, *Blue and Brown Books: Preliminary Studies for the Philosophical Investigations,* 2nd ed. Barnes & Noble, 1969. Course notes taken when Wittgenstein was developing the ideas that resulted in the *Investigations*.

Pitcher, George, ed., *Wittgenstein: Philosophical Investigations.* (Doubleday (Anchor), 1966. Critical readings.

ETHICS

Williams, Bernard, *Morality: An Introduction to Ethics.* Harper & Row, 1972.

Aristotle, *Ethics,* tr. J. A. Thomson. Penguin, 1955.

Kant, Immanuel, *Groundwork of the Metaphysics of Morals,* tr. H. J. Paton. Harper & Row, 1964.

The following books are good on Kant's ethics.

Paton, H. J., *Categorical Imperative: A Study in Kant's Moral Philosophy.* **Univ. of Pennsylvania Press, 1971.**

Wolff, Robert P., *Autonomy of Reason: A Commentary on Kant's Groundwork of the Metaphysics of Morals.* **Harper & Row, 1974.**

Mill, John S., *Utilitarianism,* **ed. Samuel Gorovitz. Bobbs-Merrill, 1971.** Contains a number of critical articles in addition to Mill's text.

Smart, J. J., and B. Williams, *Utilitarianism: For and Against.* **Cambridge Univ. Press, 1973.**

Moore, George E., *Principia Ethica.* **Cambridge Univ. Press, 1959.**

Thomson, Judith J., and Gerald Dworkin, eds., *Ethics.* **Harper & Row (hard cover) 1968 (out of print).** An excellent collection of articles.

Foot, Philippa, *Theories of Ethics.* **Oxford Univ. Press, 1967.** Read the articles on the "Ought-Is" debate.

LOGIC

Jeffrey, Richard C., *Formal Logic: Its Scope and Limits.* **McGraw-Hill (hard cover), 1967.** Best book for students working on their own. Read chapters one through seven (omitting five) and the first half of chapter nine. If you master these, you will know what is taught in a good introductory logic course.

Boolos, G. S., and R. C. Jeffrey, *Computability and Logic.* **Cambridge Univ. Press (hard cover), 1974.** Read if you want to continue in logic. Look at diagram (opposite the Table of Contents) which represents the dependencies among chapters. You should pursue your interests constrained by these relations.

Selected Areas of Elective Studies in the Fields of Metaphysics, Epistemology, Philosophy of Science, Philosophy of Language, and Philosophy of Mind

THE NATURE OF MIND

The central issue in philosophy of mind is the nature of mental phenomena and their relation to physical phenomena.

Shaffer, Jerome A., *Philosophy of Mind.* **Prentice-Hall, 1968.** Good introductory text.

Dennett, D. C., *Content and Consciousness.* **Humanities (International Library of Philosophy and Scientific Method Series; hard cover), 1969.**

BEHAVIORISM

Many philosophers and psychologists have taken the view that the meaning of such mental-state terms as *pain* can be analyzed in terms of the kind of behavior we normally think of as resulting from pain, such as wincing or saying "Ouch." Usually, this view is held in its crude form only by psychologists. For examples, see the following two books.

Skinner, B. F., *Science and Human Behavior.* **Macmillan (Free Press), 1965.** Read first few chapters.

Herrnstein, Richard J., and Edwin G. Boring, eds., *Source Book in the History of Psychology.* **Harvard Univ. Press, 1965.** See "J. B. Watson on Behaviorism."

The following three philosophical works defend one or another version of behaviorism.

Carnap, R., "Psychology in Physical Language." In *Logical Positivism,* ed. Alfred J. Ayer. Macmillan (Free Press), 1966.

Malcolm, N., "Wittgenstein's Philosophical Investigations." In *Philosophy of Mind,* ed. Vere C. Chappell. Prentice-Hall, 1962.

Ryle, Gilbert, *The Concept of Mind.* **Barnes & Noble, 1969.**

The following two articles are refutations of behaviorism.

Putnam, H., "Brains and Behavior." In *Analytical Philosophy,* vol. 2, ed. Ronald J. Butler. Barnes & Noble (hard cover), 1965.

Fodor, Jerry A., *Psychological Explanation: An Introduction to the Philosophy of Psychology.* **Random House, 1968.** Chapter 2.

Refutations of behaviorism as a substantive psychological theory are found in the following.

Chomsky, Noam, Review of B. F. Skinner's *Verbal Behavior.* In *Structure of Language: Readings in the Philosophy of Language,* ed. Jerry Fodor and J. J. Katz. Prentice-Hall (hard cover), 1964.

Taylor, Charles, *Explanation of Behavior.* **Humanities (hard cover), 1964.**

MATERIALISM

A recently revived view of the nature of mental phenomena is that they are simply identical to physical phenomena.

O'Connor, John, *Modern Materialism: Readings on Mind-Body Identity.* **Harcourt, Brace Jovanovich, 1969 (out of print).** Contains the major writings on materialism. All the articles are worth reading, but the most important ones are numbers 1, 2, 6, 9, 11, and 14.

FUNCTIONALISM

In an attempt to make something of the spirit behind behaviorism compatible with central state materialism, philosophers have developed *functionalism:* the view that mental events are to be characterized in terms of their causal relations to stimuli, behavior, and other mental events. Read the following articles.

Lewis, David, "An Argument for the Identity Theory"; J. A. Fodor, "Materialism"; H. Putnam, "The Nature of Mental States." In *Materialism and the Mind-Body Problem,* ed. David Rosenthal. Prentice-Hall, 1971.

Block, N., and J. Fodor, "What Psychological States are Not." In *Philosophical Review,* 1972 (journal; consult in a library).

Shoemaker, Sydney, "Functionalism and Qualia." In *Philosophical Studies,* 1975 (journal; consult in a library).

INNATE IDEAS

Whether people have inborn concepts or knowledge or whether all concepts and knowledge are acquired from experience is one of the oldest philosophical questions. There has recently been a resurgence of interest in this topic, along with a sharpening of the issues—all because of the claims by Chomskyan linguists that there is strong evidence indicating that linguistic knowledge is innate.

Stich, Steven, ed., *Innate Ideas.* Univ. of California Press, 1975. A first-rate reader on innate ideas.

Harman, Gilbert, ed., *On Noam Chomsky.* Doubleday, 1974. For further readings.

Hook, Sidney, ed., *Language and Philosophy: Proceedings.* New York Univ. Press (New York University Institute of Philosophy Symposium; hard cover), 1969. For further readings.

PERSONAL IDENTITY

What is it that makes you the same person at the age of twenty that you were at the age of ten? Why should I care more about my future suffering than my past suffering? Is there ever more than one person in one body? These and related issues concerned with personal identity cut across the traditional areas of metaphysics, philosophy of mind, and ethics.

Perry, John, *Personal Identity.* Univ. of California Press, 1975. Excellent collection of articles.

INTENTIONALITY

This topic is interesting in its own right; further, it falls in the area in which analytic philosophy and phenomenology most clearly overlap. What is the relation between thinking and the object of thought? Can this relation be used to distinguish the mental from the physical?

Chisholm, Roderick M., "Intentionality." In *Encyclopedia of Philosophy,* 4 vols., ed. Paul Edwards. Macmillan (Free Press; hard cover), 1973.

Kenny, Anthony, *Action, Emotion and Will.* Humanities, 1963. Read Chapter 9.

Husserl, Edmund, *Ideas.* Macmillan, 1962. Most important phenomenological work on intentionality. To lead up to *Ideas,* read the following three articles in the order listed.

Brentano, Franz, "Psychology From an Empirical Standpoint"; Alexius Meinong, "Theory of Objects." In *Realism and the Background of Phenomenology,* ed. Roderick M. Chisholm. Macmillan (Free Press; hard cover), 1960 (out of print).

Frege, Gottlob, "The Thought." In *Philosophical Logic,* ed. P. F. Strawson. Oxford Univ. Press, 1967.

If you have difficulty with Husserl, try reading the two following books.

Follesdal, D., "Husserl's Notion of Noema"; A. Gurwitsch, "Husserl's Noesis-Noema Doctrine." In *Phenomenology and Existentialism,* ed. Robert C. Solomon. Harper & Row, 1972.

REFERENCE

How do words pick out things? In what ways is naming like describing? What is the relation between the meaning of a term and what the term refers to? This cluster of issues is central to many philosophical problems. Read the following articles in the order given.

Frege, Gottlob, "On Sense and Reference"; Bertrand Russell, "On Denoting." In *The Logic of Grammar,* ed. Gilbert Harman and Donald Davidson. Dickenson, 1975.

Strawson, P. F., "On Referring." In *Essays in Conceptual Analysis.* St. Martin's (hard cover), 1956.

Articles by Quine, Burge, and Kaplan in Part Three of Davidson and Harman (above).

REFERENCE, IDENTITY, AND NECESSITY

Mark Twain is necessarily identical to Mark Twain. However, even though Mark Twain is Samuel Clemens (because the man christened

"Samuel Clemens" wrote and was known to the public under the name "Mark Twain"), if you substitute "Samuel Clemens" for the first occurrence of "Mark Twain" in the previous sentence, you get: "Samuel Clemens is necessarily identical to Mark Twain." But how could this be true? While this puzzle may seem somewhat technical, it gives rise to a host of exciting issues. Once you have mastered the readings on "Reference" (above), read one of the following articles by Kripke.

Kripke, Saul, "Identity and Necessity." In *Identity and Individuation*, ed. Milton Munitz. New York Univ. Press (hard cover), 1971.

Kripke, Saul, "Naming and Necessity." In *Semantics of Natural Language*, ed. D. Davidson and G. Harman. Reidel, 1973. Expensive but available in libraries.

Linsky, L., ed., *Reference and Modality*. Oxford Univ. Press, 1971. Read especially articles by Quine, Kaplan, and Kripke.

EXISTENCE

One basic philosophic issue asks about the reasons for believing in the existence of things—for thinking that a universe of objective reality, including oneself, actually exists. (See also "Realism," below.)

Prior, A. N., "Existence." In *Encyclopedia of Philosophy*, 4 vols., ed. Paul Edwards. Macmillan (Free Press; hard cover), 1973.

Quine, Willard V., "On What There Is." In *From a Logical Point of View: Nine Logico-Philosophical Essays*, Harper & Row, 1961.

Carnap, R., "Empiricism, Semantics and Ontology." In *Semantics and the Philosophy of Language*, ed. Leonard Linsky. Univ. of Illinois Press, 1970.

Another important philosophic issue has to do with the logic of attributions of existence. This issue arises in the following argument for the existence of God: it is part of our conception of God that each property he has, he has in its most perfect form; but existence is more perfect than nonexistence; therefore, God exists.

Frege, Gottlob, *Foundations of Arithmetic: A Logico-Mathematical Enquiry into the Concept of Numbers*. Northwestern Univ. Press (hard cover), 1968. Read sections 46 through 54.

Moore, George E., "Is Existence a Predicate?" In *Philosophical Papers*. Macmillan, 1962.

Pears, D. F., and J. F. Thomson, "Is Existence a Predicate?" In *Philosophical Logic*, ed. P. F. Strawson. Oxford Univ. Press, 1967.

Strawson, P. F., *Introduction to Logical Theory*. Barnes & Noble, 1966. Read pages 190–192.

Ryle, G., "Systematically Misleading Expressions." In *Logic and

Language, Vol. 1, ed. Anthony G. Flew. Barnes & Noble (hard cover), 1951.

Kant, Immanuel, *Critique of Pure Reason.* Dutton, 1972. Read pages B620–B630.

MEANING AND ANALYTIC-SYNTHETIC DISTINCTION

The issue here is whether there are statements (for example, "All cats are animals") which are true merely by virtue of the meaning of the terms, or whether the notion of meaning is a confusion. Katz as well as Grice and Strawson take the first view; Quine and Putnam take the second.

Quine, W. V., "Carnap and Logical Truth." In *The Philosophy of Rudolph Carnap,* ed. Paul A. Schilpp. Open Court (Library of Living Philosophers, Vol. 1; hard cover), 1963. Expensive; consult in library.

Putnam, H., "The Analytic and The Synthetic." In *Scientific Explanation, Space and Time,* ed. Herbert Feigl and G. Maxwell. Univ. of Minnesota Press (Minnesota Studies in the Philosophy of Science, Vol. 3; hard cover), 1962. Expensive; consult in library.

Katz, J. J., "Logic and Language: An Examination of Recent Criticism of Intentionalism." In *Minnesota Studies in the Philosophy of Science, Vol. 6,* ed. Keith Gunderson and G. Maxwell. Univ. of Minnesota Press (hard cover), 1975.

Grice, H. P., and P. F. Strawson, "In Defense of a Dogma." In *Necessary Truth,* ed. R. C. Sleigh, Jr. Prentice-Hall (Central Issues in Philosophy Series; hard cover), 1972.

Putnam, H., "The Meaning of 'Meaning.' " In *Minnesota Studies in the Philosophy of Science, Vol. 6,* ed. Keith Gunderson and G. Maxwell. University of Minnesota Press (hard cover), 1975.

FREE WILL AND DETERMINISM

Much of what I do, I do of my own free will, and I am consequently morally and often legally responsible for such doings. But how is this possible if every state of the universe is a consequence of previous states of the universe in accordance with the laws of physics? There are a number of books on this subject. The following are probably the best.

Berofsky, Bernard, ed., *Free Will and Determinism.* Harper & Row, 1966.

Honderich, Ted, ed., *Essays on Freedom of Action.* Routledge & Kegan Paul (hard cover), 1973. For advanced students.

THE NATURE OF SCIENCE

There are two excellent introductory books.

Hempel, Carl G., *Philosophy of Natural Science.* **Prentice-Hall, 1966.** A short, clear introduction by one of the most eminent of the logical empiricists. Logical empiricism was a movement which emphasized the use of modern logic and held that most traditional philosophical problems were pseudoproblems. It began in Germany in the 1920s and spread to England and America in the 1930s. Hempel's text modifies the early logical empiricist doctrines in the light of the criticisms that have been made.

Smart, John J., *Between Science and Philosophy.* **Random (hard cover), 1968.** Longer than Hempel's book and somewhat livelier.

Brody, Boruch A., ed., *Readings in the Philosophy of Science.* **Prentice-Hall (hard cover), 1970.** The best reader on this subject.

Grandy, Richard E., *Theories and Observation in Science.* **Prentice-Hall, 1973.** One of the best paperbacks on the subject.

See also the sections below, "Alternative Conceptual Schemes, "Realism," and "Explanation."

ALTERNATIVE CONCEPTUAL SCHEMES

Kuhn's work, along with the writings of Polanyi and Hanson, touched off a storm of controversy in the early 1960s. The main issue was whether current scientific theories are closer approximations to the truth than the theories they replaced or whether, on the other hand, current theories represent just one perspective, which is in no objective sense an advance over earlier perspectives. Start with the following.

Kuhn, Thomas S., ed., *Structure of Scientific Revolutions.* **Univ. of Chicago Press, 1970.**

Then see the review of Kuhn's book.

Shapere, Dudley, "The Structure of Scientific Revolutions." In *Philosophical Review,* **Vol. LXXIII, 1964** (journal; consult in library).

Another response to Kuhn follows.

Scheffler, Israel, *Science and Subjectivity.* **Bobbs-Merrill, 1967.** Read Chapter 4.

For expositions of other aspects of the Kuhnian position see the following.

Polanyi, Michael, *Personal Knowledge: Towards a Post-Critical Philosophy.* Read Chapter 6, Section 5.

Feyerabend, Paul, "How to be a Good Empiricist." In *Readings in the Philosophy of Science.* **Prentice-Hall, 1973.**

Other good articles follow.

Goodman, Nelson, "The Way the World Is." In *Problems and Projects.* Bobbs-Merrill (hard cover), 1971.

Quine, Willard V., *Word and Object.* MIT Press, 1960. Read pages 21–25.

Rorty, Richard, "The World Well Lost." In *Journal of Philosophy,* 1972 (journal; consult in library).

Lewis, Clarence I., *Mind and the World Order.* Dover, 1924. Read pages 166–194 and 345–391.

Pepper, Stephen C., *World Hypotheses: A Study in Evidence.* Univ. of California Press, 1970. Read Chapter V (section iv to end), pages 96–114, and Chapter VI.

Smart, John J., *Between Science and Philosophy* (above). Read pages 76–88.

REALISM

The issue here is whether theoretical terms ought to be understood as referring to real things, events, and properties or whether they ought to be analyzed as disguised ways of talking about observations. The readings mentioned above under "Behaviorism" are relevant here, since behaviorism is the chief antirealist view in psychology. The following articles discuss the issue in the context of science as a whole.

Maxwell, G., "The Ontological Status of Theoretical Entities." In Boruch A. Brody, ed., *Philosophy and Scientific Realism* (above).

Maxwell, G., "Theories, Frameworks and Ontology." In R. E. Grandy, *Theories and Observation in Science* (above).

Smart, John J., *Philosophy and Scientific Realism.* Humanities (hard cover), 1963. Read Chapter II (skip pages 29–32).

Russell, Bertrand, "The Relation of Sense-Data to Physics." In *Philosophy of Science,* ed. Arthur Danto and Sidney Morgenbesser. NAL (Meridian), 1960.

EXPLANATION

Hempel, Carl, *Philosophy of Natural Science.* Prentice-Hall, 1966. Read Chapters 5 and 6.

Smart, John J., *Between Science and Philosophy* (above). Read pages 53–75 and 100–112.

Harman, G., "The Inference to the Best Explanation" in *Philosophical Review,* 1965 (journal; consult in library).

Brody, Boruch A., ed., *Readings in the Philosophy of Science.* Prentice-Hall, 1973. Read articles in Part I.

PERCEPTION

There are many issues having to do with perception, the most important is the question of how we can base beliefs about the world on perceptual experiences.

Swartz, R. J., ed., *Perceiving, Sensing and Knowing*. Doubleday (Anchor), 1965 (out of print). Read especially the articles by Moore, Broad, Barnes, Chisholm, Ryle, Firth, and Grice.

Russell, Bertrand, *Our Knowledge of the External World*. Humanities (hard cover), 1961.

Selected Areas of Elective Studies in the Fields of Aesthetics, Ethics, and Political Philosophy

THE NATURE OF ART

What distinguishes something which is a work of art from something which is not? What is the history of the concept of art and the relation between art and the senses?

Tolstoy, Leo, *What is Art?*, tr. Aylmer Maude. Bobbs-Merrill, 1960.

Croce, Benedetto, *Guide to Aesthetics*, tr. Patrick Romanell. Bobbs-Merrill, 1965.

Tillman, Frank A., and Steven M. Cahn, eds., *Philosophy of Art and Aesthetics: From Plato to Wittgenstein*. Harper & Row (hard cover), 1969. Read the article entitled "Aesthetics."

Valery, Paul, "The Idea of Art." In *Aesthetics*, ed. Harold Osborne. Oxford Univ. Press (Readings in Philosophy Series), 1972.

Langer, Susanne K., *Feeling and Form*. Scribner's, 1953.

Kennick, W. E., "Is Traditional Aesthetics Based on a Mistake?" This article is widely reprinted in anthologies.

THE NATURE OF REPRESENTATION

Representation is an important issue, not only in aesthetics, but also in philosophy of mind and philosophy of language.

Wollheim, Richard, "On Drawing an Object." In *Aesthetics*, ed. Harold Osborne. Oxford Univ. Press (Readings in Philosophy Series), 1972.

Steinberg, Leo, "The Eye is a Part of the Mind." In *Reflections on Art: A Source Book of Writings by Artists, Critics and Philosophers*, ed. Susanne K. Langer. Oxford Univ. Press, 1961. An attack on Malraux, with Goodmanite themes.

Gombrich, Ernst H., *Art and Illusion: A Study in the Psychology of*

Pictorial Presentation, 2nd ed. Princeton Univ. Press (Bollingen Series, Vol. 35; A. W. Mellon Lectures in the Fine Arts, Vol. 5), 1961. See chapters I, III, V, VII, VIII, and IX. This book began a sophisticated discussion of these issues. It is exciting but disorganized.

Goodman, Nelson, "Review of *Art and Illusion.*" In *Problems and Projects.* Bobbs-Merrill (hard cover), 1971.

Goodman, Nelson, *Languages of Art: An Approach to a Theory of Symbols.* Bobbs-Merrill, 1968. Read chapters I and VI (section 1).

CONTEMPORARY MORAL ISSUES

Traditional moral theories (discussed in the works in section on Ethics) are now being applied to and tested against a host of current moral issues, such as privacy, abortion, racism, sexism, sexual morality, punishment, civil disobedience, and violence.

Wasserstrom, Richard A., ed., *Today's Moral Problems,* Macmillan, 1974.

POLITICAL OBLIGATION AND CIVIL DISOBEDIENCE

In what situations is it a person's obligation to obey the law and in what situations is it someone's obligation to disobey the law? Theoretical and practical aspects of these issues are taken up in two excellent readers.

Bedau, Hugo A., ed., *Civil Disobedience: Theory and Practice.* Pegasus, 1969. Read especially the articles by Rawls and Wasserstrom in the final section.

Murphy, Jeffrie G., ed., *Civil Disobedience and Violence.* Wadsworth (Basic Problems in Philosophy Series), 1971. A little weak in classical sources, but contains a number of useful articles not found in Bedau's collection.

Pitkin, Hannah, "Obligation and Consent." In *Philosophy, Politics and Society,* Vol. 4, ed. Quentin Skinner. Barnes & Noble, 1972. Excellent article, not yet anthologized.

The Sciences
and Mathematics

Chapter Twenty-Two

BIOLOGY
". . . the marvelous diversity of life"

Editorial Advisor:
Madeleine Swindlehurst
Science Division
Bennington College

INTRODUCTION

". . . Between error and adaptation there is generated the marvelous diversity of life. . . . In material and energy, life stems from the stars, and the flux of life is at one with the ceaseless flux of the universe." Clifford Grobstein, *The Strategy of Life.*

Biology is the scientific study of life. This area has become so broad in recent years that it is often referred to as the biological sciences and encompasses a number of extensive fields—for example, molecular biology, cell biology, developmental biology, genetics, ecology, evolution, botany, physiology, and biochemistry.

Biologists interested in molecular and cell biology study the basic structures of life by means of electron microscopy and a variety of other techniques. Geneticists attempt to describe the action of chromosomes and DNA molecules, which provide the means for passing on inherited characteristics from one generation to the next. The development of a species and its relationship to another and to its environment are explored by biologists specializing in evolution or ecology. The structure and function of the organs and systems of individual living creatures are studied by physiologists.

Because biology has developed so many branches, it is important for student and professional alike to keep the whole in sight. Atoms combine to form molecules, some of which form chains of amino acids, which in turn form proteins, which are utilized by cell organelles, which are constituents of cells, which make up tissues, which make up organs, which make up organ systems, which make up organisms, which interact in biological communities, which change in cycles and which are one aspect of the functioning of biospheres. As summarized by a Nobel Prize-winning biologist, Albert Szent-Györgi, "I have concluded that life is not linked to any particular unit; it is the expression of the harmonious collaboration of all. As I descended through the levels of complexity, I studied simpler units and found myself speaking more and more in the language of chemistry and physics."

Chemistry and physics have proven helpful in describing many mechanisms of life, but they have not provided any ultimate explanation. In the sense that these sciences of largely inanimate phenomena might be said to deal with that which is most probable, biology often seems to concern the improbable. A chemical or thermodynamic reaction essential to the life of a cell may long go undiscovered because it seems highly improbable under the conditions assumed. The beauty of it all is that so many of these reactions take place and all with perfect timing. "Life is a wondrous phenomenon," in Szent-Györgi's words. "I can only hope that some day man will achieve a deeper insight into its nature and its guiding principles and will be able to express them in more exact terms. It is this mysterious quality of life that makes biology the most fascinating of the sciences."

The bibliography which follows presents works that convey the knowledge typically offered undergraduate majors in Biology.

BIBLIOGRAPHY

FOR LEISURE READING:
BIOLOGY AS SCIENCE, HISTORY, AND PHILOSOPHY

Biology is becoming more and more accessible to the general reader through nontechnical books written by leading biologists, many of them Nobel Prize recipients. Such books give a reflective view of biology, not only as science, but also as history and philosophy. They make good reading for anyone with an interest in the complex phenomena of life.

Alland, Alexander, *The Human Imperative*. Columbia Univ. Press (hard cover), 1974. The ethical and existential dilemma of modern man is presented with insight and a sense of urgency.

Boeke, Kees, *Cosmic View: The Universe in 40 Jumps*. John Day (hard cover), 1957. An imaginative pictorial introduction to the concepts of size at different levels of organization—atomic, molecular, cellular, organismal, communal, and cosmic.

Burnet, MacFarlane, *Dominant Mammal*. St. Martin's, 1974. The biology of human destiny, examined with an awareness of the immense complexity of human problems and based on a considerable record of scientific achievement.

Grobstein, Clifford, *The Strategy of Life*. Freeman, 1974. An optimistic book, firmly grounded in the author's belief in the "indomitable force of life." Human destiny appears less fragile than others (Monod, Jacob, or Burnet) would have it. The outlook is one of unity and wholeness. The book can bridge the gap between leisure reading and serious study.

Jacob, Françoise, *The Logic of Life: A History of Heredity*. Pantheon (hard cover), 1973. A tightly argued, well organized exposition concerning the meaning of life that studies its structures, functions, and history.

Luria, S. E., *Life: The Unfinished Experiment*. Scribner's, 1973. The essential discoveries of experimental biochemistry and genetics compressed in a short, rich, sensitive, and highly readable volume.

Monod, Jacques, *Chance and Necessity: An Essay on the Natural Philosophy of Modern Biology*. Random, 1972. Life's logic and evolution is the consequence of its structural and functional organization. Monod's conclusions are as inescapable as are Jacob's. Monod's overview of biology is philosophical, his presentation rhetorical, his final proclamation existential and ethical.

Nilsson, Lennant, *Behold Man: A Photographic Journey of Discovery Inside the Body*. Little, Brown (hard cover), 1973. A pictorial essay describing the human body in exquisite detail and beauty; lavishly illustrated with color photomicrographs, many of them based on advanced optical systems, which make it possible to observe and film parts of the body never before photographed.

Popper, Karl, *Objective Knowledge*. Oxford Univ. Press (hard cover), 1972. Popper proposes to discard common-sense (Aristotelian) logic in favor of bold conjectures. Truth, he argues realistically, can never be found, only searched for. The idea of truth, however, becomes a regulative concept that helps us in the "critical search for what is false in our various competing theories."

Thomas, Lewis, *The Lives of a Cell: Notes of a Biology Watcher*. Bantam, 1975. Based on a series of essays first published in the *New England Journal of Medicine*. The style is artistic and poetic, the point of view unified and visionary.

Von Frisch, Karl, and Otto Von Frisch, *Animal Architecture*. Harcourt Brace Jovanovich (hard cover), 1974. This beautifully illustrated book explores the creative building activities of animals, who frequently surpass the architectural skills of humans.

Watson, James, D., *The Double Helix*. NAL, 1968. The story of the discovery of the structure of DNA, told with unusual candor by one of the scientists who worked along with Francis Crick, Maurice Wilkins, and Rosalind Franklin.

FOR INTRODUCTORY READING
OR BROAD PROFESSIONAL REVIEW

Even if you have had little or no schooling in biology, one group of paperback books can provide you with clear and interesting introductions to the major areas of biological science today. These contain collected articles on the life sciences from *Scientific American* magazine. These anthologies are widely read in introductory college courses; additionally, many graduate students study their more technical passages closely when preparing for oral examinations. Biology professors also often rely on them for broad knowledge outside the professors' specialties in preference to scholarly journals.

Listed below are most of these paperback books that are currently available. They may be ordered at reasonable prices (usually under $6) through bookstores or directly from the house that publishes all of them, W. H. Freeman and Co. (660 Market St., San Fransisco, CA 94104). Many libraries also have the original articles in back issues of *Scientific American* (you can locate the articles under subject headings in the magazine's periodic indexes). However, the illuminating introductions in the books are well worth reading and do not appear in the back issues. Because many authors are represented in each book, the books are identified only by title and year. Some are also listed under broad topics within biology.

Man and the Environment

Food, 1973.

Plant Agriculture, 1970.

The Ocean, 1969.

Oceanography, 1971.

Energy and Power, 1971.

The Biosphere, 1970.

Man and the Ecosphere, 1971.

Ecology, Evolution and Population Biology, 1974.

Science and Society

Science, Conflict and Society, 1969.

Biology and Culture in Modern Perspective, 1972.

Communication, 1972.

Life and Death and Medicine, 1973.

Genetics and Evolution

   Facets of Genetics, 1970.

   Human Variations and Origins, 1967.

Molecular Biology, Biochemistry and Cell Biology

   Organic Chemistry of Life, 1973.

   Bio-Organic Chemistry, 1968.

   The Molecular Basis of Life: An Introduction to Molecular Biology, 1968.

   The Chemical Basis of Life: An Introduction to Molecular and Cell Biology, 1973.

   The Living Cell, 1965.

Developmental Biology

   From Cell to Organism, 1967.

General and Comparative Physiology

   Cellular and Organismal Biology, 1974.

   Vertebrate Adaptations, 1969.

   Vertebrate Structures and Functions, 1974.

Physiological Psychology

   Frontiers of Psychological Research, 1966.

   Physiological Psychology, 1972.

   Psychobiology: The Biological Basis of Behavior, 1967.

   Altered States of Awareness, 1972.

   The Nature and Nurture of Behavior: Developmental Psychobiology, 1973.

   Animal Behavior, 1975.

GENERAL RESOURCES FOR INDIVIDUAL STUDY OF BIOLOGY

Definitions of Terms

Abercrombie, M., *et al.,* *Dictionary of Biology,* 6th ed. Penguin, 1973.

King, Robert C., *Dictionary of Genetics.* Oxford Univ. Press, 1972. Helpful to supplement definitions of terms given in other books.

For Laboratory Practice

An important part of any study of biology is experimentation with and observation of living material. Guides to simple experiments you can do in your home and to college laboratory methods and techniques are listed below. For the laboratory experience typically acquired by college majors in Biology, you would need to take biology laboratory courses at a nearby college.

UNESCO, *700 Science Experiments for Everyone,* rev. ed. Doubleday (hard cover), 1962. Tells how to set up a home laboratory and carry out experiments and projects using readily available materials. Describes many basic and interesting experiments in biology (concerning plants, animals, and the human body) as well as in the physical sciences. Designed for beginners but thoroughly sound; try to overlook its address to "boys and girls."

Turtox Service, *Turtox Service Leaflets.* These leaflets, now numbering about 60, represent a fairly comprehensive set of aids to developing skill in biological methods and techniques. Each describes an experiment or project and lists related supplies and equipment obtainable from Turtox; the series contains, for example, leaflets on *How to Make an Insect Collection, Preserving Zoological Specimens,* and *The Care of Protozoan Cultures in the Laboratory.* The leaflets are nominally priced and available from Turtox Service Dept., General Biological Supply House, 8200 S. Hoyne St., Chicago, IL 60620.

Steele, H. C., *The Departmental Laboratory Assistant in Biological Science: A Book of Principles, Methods and Techniques.* Dorrance, 1966. Useful as a resource book for the student doing laboratory work in college biology.

For Supplementary Reading

Two sources of reading and study materials that you may find helpful to supplement the books listed later are as follows.

Scientific American Offprints and Books Catalog. Freeman. This regularly revised catalog lists several hundred articles from *Scientific American* magazine that are available in separately reprinted form. It also lists books of collected articles bearing on specific topics (like those listed in the section "For Introductory Reading or Broad Professional Review"). You can use this catalog to build tailor-made, ongoing collections of these *Scientific American* articles on any areas of your particular interests in biology. The article reprints can be ordered in any combinations you want and currently cost about 25 cents each.

Categories and descriptions in the catalog are generally informative in themselves. You can get the catalog free on request from Freeman.

General Biology Textbooks. Many general textbooks attempt to offer a comprehensive overview of biology for the beginning student. There are three outstanding ones currently available:

Keeton, William T., *Biological Science,* **2nd ed. Norton (hard cover) 1972.** Laboratory guide also available.

Curtis, Helena, *Biology.* **Worth (hard cover) 1975.** Beautifully illustrated and well written. Student study guide available.

Kirk, David, *Biology Today.* **2nd ed. CRM, Random House (hard cover) 1975.** Set apart from the main text in chapter "interleaf" sections are descriptions of classical experiments and concepts in modern biology—mini-essays written with exemplary conciseness and clarity. Certain topics (notably on human behavior, sexuality and drug use) which were an outstanding feature of the first edition of *Biology Today* have been omitted in second edition.

Clow, Duane J., and N. Scott Urquhart, *Mathematics in Biology: Calculus and Related Topics.* **Norton, 1974.** Presents the mathematical concepts of central importance in biology.

GENERAL BIOLOGY

Introductory

Baker, Geoffrey, and Garland E. Allen, *Matter, Energy and Life.* **Addison-Wesley, 1974.** An introduction to the principles of physics and chemistry for biology students with little or no background.

Swanson, Carl P., *The Cell,* **3rd ed. Prentice-Hall (Foundations of Modern Biology Series), 1969.** A clear introduction to the structure, functions, and behavior of normal cells (the basic functional entities of all living things) and cell organelles, with examples from animal, plant, and microbe kingdoms.

Bonner, David H., and Stanley E. Mills, *Heredity.* **Prentice-Hall (Found. Mod. Biol. Ser.), 1964.** Good on chromosomal and biochemical genetics. Very basic, historical; may be somewhat dated.

Sussman, Maurice, *Growth and Development.* **Prentice-Hall (Found. Mod. Biol. Ser.), 1964.** Another fine small volume.

Bold, Harold C., *The Plant Kingdom.* **Prentice-Hall (Found. Mod. Biol. Ser.), 1970.** An introduction to plant life, presenting up-to-date concepts and principles of biology as illustrated in the study of plants.

McElroy, William D., *Cell Physiology and Biochemistry,* **3rd ed. Prentice-Hall (Found. Mod. Biol. Ser.), 1971.** A very brief and basic introduction to cell biology and biochemistry; a bit limited in scope, with many details purposely omitted.

NOTE All but the first book above are works in the Foundations of Modern Biology Series published by Prentice-Hall. Other books in the series on basic topics in biology include works on man in nature, animal behavior, animal diversity, animal physiology, adaptation, and the life of the green plant. Readers interested in these and new titles in the series may find out about them by requesting current catalogs from Prentice-Hall.

Other series of well-done paperback books on biology in which the reader may be interested are: Modern Biology Series, Holt, Rinehart & Winston; and the Scott, Foresman Series in Undergraduate Biology.

MOLECULAR AND CELL BIOLOGY

Intermediate

Jensen, William A., and Roderic B. Park, *Cell Ultrastructure.* Wadsworth, 1967. A fine collection of electron microscope photographs of animal, plant, and bacterial cells and organelles; a variety of cytological techniques are represented (sectioning, freeze-etching, shadowing, negative-staining, and others).

Loewy, A. G., and P. Siekewitz, *Cell Structure and Function.* Holt, Rinehart & Winston, 1970. Highly readable treatment of cell and molecular biology and biochemistry; develops an appreciation of the importance of physical science to biology. Appealing in style and layout, with clear introduction to basic principles.

Lehninger, Albert, *Bioenergetics.* Benjamin, 1973. Presupposes some basic knowledge of chemistry and general biology; very well written and organized.

Ingram, Vernon, *The Biosynthesis of Macromolecules.* Benjamin, 1972. Explains revolutionary new knowledge concerning DNA, RNA, and protein synthesis, giving the basics needed for more advanced work in modern biochemistry, genetics, and general biology.

Novikoff, Alex B., and Eric Holtzman, *Cells and Organelles.* 2nd ed. Holt, Rinehart & Winston (Modern Biology Series), 1976.

Scientific American, *The Molecular Basis of Life: An Introduction to Molecular Biology.* Freeman, 1968. A good collection of articles from *Scientific American* magazine (listed in a previous section) traces the most important experimental and conceptual developments in molecular biology in recent years with a historical flavor.

Scientific American, *The Chemical Basis of Life: An Introduction to Molecular and Cell Biology.* Freeman, 1973. Issued as a sequel to the work just above; includes some (but not all) of the articles reprinted in that work. Has a new section dealing with cellular regulators and the self-assembly of biological structures.

Hood, L. E., J. H. Wilson, and W. B. Wood, *The Molecular Biology of the Eucaryotic Cell: A Problems Approach.* Benjamin, 1975. Uses a self-teaching approach to the learning of basic principles through data analysis and problem solving. Intended as a companion volume to Wood, Wilson, Benbow and Hood, *Biochemistry A Problems Approach* (see bibliography section "Biochemistry—Intermediate-Advanced").

DEVELOPMENTAL BIOLOGY

Intermediate

Ebert, James D., and I. M. Sussex, *Interacting Systems in Development.* Holt, Rinehart & Winston (Modern Biology Series), 1970. Lucid introduction to the problems of embryology, growth, and differentiation of cells in both plants and animals.

Trinkaus, J. P., *Cells into Organs: The Forces that Shape the Embryo.* Prentice-Hall (Foundations of Developmental Biology Series), 1969. Tells a fascinating and compelling story: how biochemistry, molecular biology, and genetics have contributed to understanding the processes by which complex living creatures develop from one-celled embryos. Interesting related titles in the same series include *Fertilization, Developmental Genetics,* and *Principles of Mammalian Aging.*

Alston, R. E., *Cellular Continuity and Development.* Scott, Foresman (Series in Undergraduate Biology), 1967. Ably treats the functioning of maturing cells. May be supplemented by relevant titles in the same series, such as *Macromolecular Form and Function, The Cellular Role of Macromolecules,* and *Nuclear Control of Cellular Activities.*

GENETICS

Intermediate

Kormondy, Edward J., *Introduction to Genetics A Program for Self-Instruction. McGraw-Hill, 1964.* Takes the student through the introductory aspects of genetics.

Lawson, Chester A., and Mary A. Burmester, *Programmed Genetics;* Vol. I: *The Basic Concepts,* 1963; Vol. II: *Chromosome Behavior,* 1964; Vol. III: *Extension of the Theory,* Heath, 1966. Books in the "programmed instruction" format designed for step-by-step learning by the reader without any help from a teacher; includes some self-tests with which to evaluate progress.

Watson, James D., *The Molecular Biology of the Gene,* 2nd ed. Benjamin, 1970, and 3rd ed. Benjamin (hard cover), 1976. Written for a wide audience ranging from college freshmen through professional biologists (by a codiscoverer of the double-helix structure of DNA, the basic material controlling all inherited characteristics); includes annotated bibliographies at the end of each chapter.

Woese, Carl R., *The Genetic Code: Molecular Basis for Genetic Expression.* Harper & Row, 1967. Can serve as an excellent supplement to Watson's book (above). Gives a more historical, analytical, and philosophical description of the process that led to the elucidation of the genetic code.

Dupraw, E. J., *DNA and Chromosomes.* Holt, Rinehart & Winston (Molecular and Cellular Biology Series), 1970. An introduction to the chromosomal basis of genetics and inheritance. Well-illustrated with diagrams and photomicrographs.

Hartman, Philip R., and Sigmund R. Suskind, *Gene Action.* Prentice-Hall (Foundation of Modern Genetics Series), 1965. A good introduction to molecular and chromosomal genetics. A number of related titles appear in the same series.

Peters, James A., ed., *Classic Papers in Genetics.* Prentice-Hall, 1959. A well-chosen selection, ranging chronologically from Mendel (1865) through Benzer (1955) by way of Johannsen, Sutton, Bateson, Hardy, and others. For each paper, a brief evaluation by the editor is included.

Moore, John A., *Heredity and Development; Readings in Heredity and Development,* Oxford Univ. Press, 1972. Two companion volumes—the first, an explanatory introduction to genetics; the second, an edited collection of supplementary readings cross-referenced conveniently to the first.

Young, Louise B., ed., *Evolution of Man.* Oxford Univ. Press (for American Foundation for Continuing Education), 1970. Collected essays and articles that focus on issues concerning man's control of his activities and his environment, such as eugenics, birth control, pollution, resources depletion, city planning, evolution, and human development.

ECOLOGY

Introductory

Kormondy, Edward J., *Concepts of Ecology.* Prentice-Hall, 1969. A concise introduction to ecology, the branch of biological science dealing with the interrelationships of all forms of life in their environments.

Whittaker, R. H., *Communities and Ecosystems.* Macmillan, 1970. Introductory-intermediate presentation of ecology by a leading ecologist.

Billings, D., *Plants and the Ecosystem.* Wadsworth (Fundamentals of Botany Series), 1964. A general introduction to plant ecology.

Odum, E., *Ecology.* Holt, Rinehart & Winston (Modern Biology Series), 1963. An introduction to general ecology by the pioneer of the ecosystem approach.

Intermediate

Hazen, W. E., ed., *Readings in Population and Community Ecology.* Saunders, 1964. Collected papers by leaders in the field, including Hutchinson, Cole, Dewey, Park, Lindeman, Slobodkin, MacArthur and Whittaker.

MacArthur, R. H., and E. O. Wilson, *The Theory of Island Biogeography.* Princeton Univ. Press (Monographs in Population Biology Series), 1967. Represents a basic step along the theoretical-mathematical path in ecological analysis.

NOTE See also reprints of important papers in ecology, MSS Modular Publications (formerly Warner Modular Publications), 655 Madison Avenue, New York, NY 10021. The series includes such classic papers as Likens and Bormann on nutrient cycling, Fager on diversity, and Margolof on unifying principles.

EVOLUTION

Introductory

Stebbins, G. L., *Processes of Organic Evolution.* Prentice-Hall (Concepts of Modern Biology Series), 1966. Clearly written introduction.

Savage, J. M., *Evolution.* Holt, Rinehart & Winston (Mod. Biology Series), 1969. An alternative introduction.

Keosian, J., *The Origin of Life,* 2nd ed. Van Nostrand Reinhold, 1968. Summarizes a wide variety of work on the problem of how life originated.

Intermediate

Avers, Charlotte, *Evolution.* Harper & Row, 1974. Well-written, very good coverage; gives attention to endosymbiotic theory of eucaryote origin.

Methler, L. E., and T. G. Gregg, *Population Genetics and Evolution.* Prentice-Hall (Foundations of Modern Genetics Series), 1969. A good basic treatment.

Wallace, B., *Chromosomes, Giant Molecules and Evolution.* Norton, 1966. Especially good on giant chromosomes and visible effects of such phenomena as inversions and translocations.

NOTE See also reprints of classic papers on evolution issued by Bobbs-Merrill (papers by Mayr, Glass, Wright, Miller, Wald, Stebbins) and MSS Modular Publications (including papers by Slobodkin, Tomkins, Workman).

Advanced

Grant, V., *Plant Speciation.* Columbia Univ. Press, 1973. Clear, concise, well-written.

Mayr, Ernest, *Animal Species and Evolution.* Harvard Univ. Press (hard cover), 1963. The classic reference on the animal side.

Stebbins, G. L., *Variations and Evolution in Plants.* Columbia Univ. Press (hard cover), 1950. The classic reference on the plant side.

BOTANY

Introductory

Ray, P. M., *The Living Plant.* Holt, Rinehart & Winston (Modern Biology Series), 1972. Up-to-date; concise yet comprehensive.

Steward, F. C., *Plants at Work.* Addison-Wesley (Principles of Biology Series), 1964. Very good introduction to plant physiology.

Fogg, G. E., *Photosynthesis,* 2nd ed. American Elsevier, 1972. Good introduction to the process through which plants convert sunlight and water to food; includes some fine electron micrographs of chloroplasts.

Raven, Peter, and Helena Curtis, *Biology of Plants.* Worth (hard cover), 1970. An unusually good textbook.

PHYSIOLOGY

Intermediate-Advanced

Langley, Leroy L., *Homeostatis.* Van Nostrand Reinhold, 1965. Treats homeostasis as a concept basic not only to biology but also to sociology and psychology.

Brown, Frank A., *et al., The Biological Clock: Two Views.* Academic, 1970. A provocative presentation of two opposing views on the environmental versus the biochemical basis of biological rhythms and cycles in organisms.

Burnett, Allison L., and Thomas Eisner, *Animal Adaptations.* Holt, Rinehart & Winston (Modern Biology Series), 1964. Includes several well-chosen case studies in physiological regulation.

Barrington, Ernest J., *The Chemical Basis of Physiological Regulation.* Scott, Foresman, 1968. Covers the basic functions any organism must carry on in order to survive (respiration; ingestion, digestion, and the intake and use of energy; water balance; temperature regulation).

Hochaka, Peter W., and George N. Somers, *Strategies of Biochemical Adaptations.* Saunders, 1973. A more advanced volume similar in scope to the preceding title.

Scientific American, *Vertebrate Adaptations,* (1969); *Vertebrate Structures and Functions,* 1974; *Cellular and Organismal Biology,* 1974. Freeman. Unusually good sources on general and comparative physiology; clearly written and well-illustrated, these books should be fascinating to any general reader. (They are also listed in an earlier section of the bibliography.)

Burnet, Macfarlane, *Self and Non-Self: Cellular Immunology,* 1969; *Natural History of Infectious Disease,* 1972. Cambridge Univ. Press. Two books by a leading biologist who also writes very well. The first introduces the general reader to the complex subject of immunity to infections. The second is an introductory treatment of the physiology and epidemiology of infectious diseases.

BIOCHEMISTRY

Intermediate-Advanced

Lehninger, Albert L., *Biochemistry: The Molecular Basis of Cell Structure and Function.* Worth (hard cover), 1970, and 2nd ed., 1975. A currently unsurpassed biochemistry text. No really effective substitutes for a good text have yet been introduced.

Bennet, Thomas, and Karl Frieden, *Modern Topics in Biochemistry.* Macmillan, 1966. Will give the beginning student a minimum foundation in biochemistry.

Van Holde, Kensal, *Physical Biochemistry.* Prentice-Hall (Foundations of Modern Biochemistry Series), 1971. A bit heavy on the physical aspects of biochemical techniques and theory, and probably not readily accessible to the untutored student. Requires knowledge of calculus.

Ingram, Vernon M., *The Biosynthesis of Macromolecules,* 2nd ed. Benjamin, 1972. Treats the biochemistry of giant molecules of DNA, RNA, and protein. Another widely respected work on the same subject, is **Wold, Finn, *Macromolecules: Structure and Function,* Prentice-Hall (Foundations of Modern Biochemistry Series), 1971.**

Larner, Joseph, *Intermediary Metabolism and Its Regulation.* Prentice-Hall (Found. Mod. Biochem. Ser.), 1971. Very compact treatment, giving an integrated overview of metabolic regulation. Perhaps attempts too much in too little space; understanding it probably would call for the help of a tutor.

Cohen, George N., *The Regulation of Cell Metabolism.* Holt,

Rinehart & Winston (Molecular and Cellular Biology Series), 1968. Good on detailed descriptions of regulatory enzymes (a bit of a catalog in this respect) and useful in conjunction with Larner's book (above). Neither this nor Larner's book would be very intelligible without a basic biochemistry text.

Bernhard, Sidney A., *The Structure and Function of Enzymes.* Benjamin, 1968. Emphasizes the chemical mechanisms of biological reactions; good introduction to methodology in enzymology.

Wood, W. B., J. H. Wilson, R. J. Benbow, and L. E. Hood, *Biochemistry: A Problems Approach.* Benjamin, 1974. Designed for individual study, without a teacher. Gives a working knowledge of biochemical principles through analysis of experimental data and solution of concrete problems by the reader. Each problem section is cross-referenced to related chapters in widely used biochemistry textbooks, including Lehninger (above) 1970 edition. Briefly outlines basic principles and gives many problems and their solutions. A companion volume to Hood, *et al., The Molecular Biology of the Encaryotic Cell: A Problems Approach* (above, section on "Molecular and Cell Biology").

Steward, M. W., *Immunochemistry.* Wiley (Outline Studies in Biology) 1974. Short but authoritative introduction to the molecular aspect of immune reactions.

Gude, William, *Autoradiographic Techniques.* Prentice-Hall (Biological Techniques Series), 1968. This volume and others in the series give basic introduction to important biological research techniques.

Chapter Twenty-Three

CHEMISTRY
*". . . atoms, molecules, and
their interactions"*

Editorial Advisor:
Dennis R. Aebersold
Science Division
Bennington College

INTRODUCTION

Chemistry is the science that deals with atoms, molecules, and their interactions. The major disciplines undergraduate majors are usually required to study are analytical, inorganic, organic, and physical chemistry. Biochemistry, geochemistry, and petroleum chemistry are also often offered but seldom required. The typical major in Chemistry is expected to acquire at least an introductory knowledge of each of these first four disciplines and to study one or more of them in depth.

Chemistry does not stand alone as a science, and if one is to study anything past the introductory level, a good grounding in mathematics and physics is needed. A bare minimum in physics would include the study of mechanics and of electricity and magnetism at the intermediate level. The student would in addition be well advised to learn some electronics, quantum mechanics, and statistical mechanics. The mathematical minimum requires calculus and the study of differential equations; however, analysis, integral equations, abstract algebra, and complex variables are recommended.

This order of rigor is not essential to a traditional undergraduate Chemistry program. In fact, a knowledge of calculus and introductory college-level physics is all that is needed to read the texts in the bibliography's "Basic List." A knowledge of these texts would be considered by most chemists to be adequate undergraduate preparation in chemistry. However, a college major in Chemistry would also complete about 500 to 1000 hours of laboratory work. Readers who want to develop as full a laboratory knowledge as typical Chemistry majors can take laboratory courses at a nearby college (which are often available to part-time or evening students).

A number of chemists believe that the division of chemical subject matter into disciplines such as those noted above can be improved upon for learning purposes. Classifying the body of chemical knowledge into structure, energy, and kinetics appears to provide a better organization for students. If these areas are studied at the introductory, intermediate, and advanced levels, the student will see all of chemistry in a more coherent light and will avoid the overlap of courses found in many colleges.

Introductory textbooks (including those in the following bibliography) are often written along these lines. Unfortunately, very few intermediate and advanced textbooks have been similarly organized as yet. The consequent shortcoming is unavoidably reflected in the bibliography.

The bibliography opens with two histories of chemistry that may be of interest to readers for general background. After those works, the bibliography has been designed so that thorough study of the works listed in it should result in a good, broad education in undergraduate Chemistry. Most of the problems given as exercises in the books should be worked or understood by the seriously interested reader. Such practice is important because chemists are constantly called upon to solve problems of one sort or another in their work. Readers who wish to proceed still further into chemistry may do so by consulting the bibliographies included in many of the individual works listed here.

BIBLIOGRAPHY

HISTORY OF CHEMISTRY

Reichen, Charles-Albert, *A History of Chemistry* (Vol. 10 in The New Illustrated Library of Science and Invention). Hawthorn (hard cover), 1963 (out of print). For the general reader.

Partington, James R., *A History of Chemistry,* 4 vols. St. Martin's (hard cover), 1961–70. A definitive work; may be too much for the beginner.

BASIC LIST

NOTE   The following works are intended to be read in the order given.

Dickerson, Richard E. *et al., Chemical Principles.* Benjamin (hard cover), 1974.

Skoog, D. A., and D. M. West, *Fundamentals of Analytic Chemistry,* 2nd ed. Holt, Rinehart & Winston (hard cover), 1969.

Morrison, Robert J., and Robert N. Boyd, *Organic Chemistry* 3rd ed. Allyn (hard cover), 1973.

Moore, Walter J., *Physical Chemistry,* 4th ed. Prentice-Hall (hard cover), 1972.

Cotton, F. Albert, and Geoffrey Wilkinson, *Advanced Inorganic Chemistry: A Comprehensive Text,* 3rd ed. Wiley (hard cover), 1972.

Lehninger, Albert L., *Biochemistry: The Molecular Basis of Cell Structure and Function.* Worth (hard cover), 1970.

SUPPLEMENTARY LIST

Thomas, George B., *Calculus and Analytic Geometry.* Addison-Wesley, (hard cover), 1972. Treats the mathematics needed for reading the books in the "Basic List" (above) for those not familiar with it.

Mahan, Bruce H., *University Chemistry,* 2nd ed. Addison-Wesley (hard cover), 1969. A textbook that is especially helpful as a general introduction.

For Reading Next

The following books complement Mahan, *University Chemistry* (above), and can be read in any order; they round out a good introduction to analytical, organic, inorganic, and physical chemistry and biochemistry and provide a sound basis for further study.

Fischer, Robert B., and Dennis G. Peters, *Chemical Equilibrium.* Saunders, 1970.

Gray, Harry B., *Chemical Bonds: An Introduction to Atomic and Molecular Structure.* Benjamin, 1973.

Eyring, Henry, and Edward M. Eyring, *Modern Chemical Kinetics.* Van Nostrand Reinhold, 1963.

Scientific American, *General Chemistry: Readings from Scientific American.* Freeman, 1973.

Kieffer, William F., *The Mole Concept in Chemistry,* 2nd ed. Van Nostrand Reinhold, 1973.

King, Edward L., *How Chemical Reactions Occur.* Benjamin, 1963.

Nash, Leonard K., *Stoichiometry.* Addison-Wesley, 1966.

Mahan, Bruce H., *Elementary Chemical Thermodynamics.* Benjamin, 1963.

Roberts, John D., *et al., Organic Chemistry: Methane to Macromolecules,* rev. ed. Benjamin, 1971.

Roberts, John D., and Casiero, Marjorie C., *Modern Organic Chemistry.* Benjamin (hard cover), 1967.

Harpp, D. N., *et al., Organic Chemistry Problems,* 2nd ed. Benjamin, 1972.

Bobbitt, James M., *et al., Introduction to Chromatography.* Van Nostrand Reinhold, 1968.

Barker, Robert, *Organic Chemistry of Biological Compounds.* Prentice-Hall (hard cover), 1971.

Scientific American, *Organic Chemistry of Life: Readings from Scientific American.* Freeman, 1973.

Scientific American, *The Chemical Basis of Life: An Introduction to Molecular and Cell Biology.* Freeman, 1973.

For Needed Physics Background

The knowledge of physics needed for further study in chemistry as indicated below is explained in the following book.

Feynman, R. P. *et al., The Feynman Lectures on Physics,* 3 vols. Addison-Wesley, 1964.

Intermediate-Level Readings

Malmstadt, H. V. *et al., Module One: Electronic Analog Measurements and Transducers: Text with Lab Summaries,* 1973; *Module Two: Control of Electrical Quantities in Instrumentation,* 1973; *Module Three: Digital and Analog Data Conversions,* 1973; *Module Four: Optimization of Electronic Measurements,* 1974. Benjamin. These books present a very good modern introduction to the electronics used in chemistry.

Waser, Jurg, *Quantitative Chemistry: A Laboratory Text.* Benjamin, 1965.

Bockris, John O., and Amulya K. Reddy, *Modern Electrochemistry: An Introduction to an Interdisciplinary Area,* 2 vols. Plenum, 1973. Presents a new, very modern approach.

Boyce, W. E., and R. C. DePrima, *Elementary Differential Equations and Boundary Value Problems.* Wiley (hard cover), 1969. Covers the mathematics needed for a number of the following works.

Karplus, Martin, and R. N. Porter, *Atoms and Molecules: An Introduction for Students of Physical Chemistry.* Benjamin, 1970. Good on spectroscopy and bonding.

Nash, Leonard K., *Elements of Chemical Thermodynamics,* 2nd ed. Addison-Wesley, 1970.

Nash, Leonard K., *Elements of Statistical Thermodynamics,* 2nd ed. Addison-Wesley, 1974.

Hill, Terrell L., *Introduction to Statistical Thermodynamics.* Addison-Wesley (hard cover), 1960.

Matsen, F. A., *Vector Spaces and Algebras for Chemistry and Physics.* Holt, Rinehart & Winston (hard cover), 1970. Starts easy, ends hard; good references in the bibliography.

Gardiner, W. C., *Rates and Mechanisms of Chemical Reactions.* Benjamin, 1969.

Edwards, John O., *Inorganic Reaction Mechanisms: An Introduction.* Benjamin, 1965.

Pilar, Frank L., *Elementary Quantum Chemistry.* McGraw-Hill, 1968.

Cotton, F. Albert, *Chemical Applications of Group Theory,* 2nd ed. Wiley, 1971.

Chapter Twenty-Four

EARTH
SCIENCES

*". . . rocks, minerals, and the processes
that form and rework these materials"*

Editorial Advisor:
Richard S. Naylor
Department of Earth Sciences
Northeastern University

INTRODUCTION

Geologists study the rocks and minerals of which the earth is composed, the processes that form and rework these materials, and the history of how these processes have acted through time. Though geology draws heavily on the related sciences of mathematics, physics, chemistry, and biology, the field has characteristics and methodologies of its own by which it can be identified as a distinct science. The term *geology* literally means "earth science" and is used in this broad sense.

Oceanography is properly regarded as an earth science, and its methodologies are closely related to geology. The techniques of geology have also been proven applicable to the study of other planets, and it seems quite reasonable to broaden the meaning of "geology" to include the study of planetary surfaces and interiors in general. Meteorology and climatology, in contrast, involve techniques which are not closely related to geology; specialized sciences in their own right, they are not included in this section. And although geography, the study of human interaction with the earth, shares much common ground with geology, the social-science aspects of the discipline are not treated in this section beyond some consideration of environmental and economic geology.

Many of the basic geological concepts are easy to grasp, and considerable progress can be made by the student working alone with minimal guidance. Almost uniquely among the sciences, geology is concerned with time. The serious student should understand this concern, which permeates much of geologic thought. The Principle of Uniformity, the idea that "the present is the key to the past," is also crucial. Geologists believe that by studying contemporary geologic processes and phenomena, they can come to understand the past history of the earth.

A revolutionary synthesis of geologic thought was accomplished in the 1960s with the emergence of a theory of plate tectonics. Plate theory successfully relates continental drift; the distribution of earthquakes, faults, and volcanoes; patterns of ore occurrence; sea-floor geology; and many other aspects of earth sciences which formerly seemed unconnected. Fortunately, many writings on this topic are readily accessible, and reading this material is an excellent way to catch the flavor of current geological thought. Like any theory, it is still being modified as new facts are uncovered. There is considerable disagreement on many details and a limited understanding of some of the basic mechanisms involved, but the overall theory is clear and vital.

More difficult to learn from books alone are many essential practical aspects of geology including the identification, classification, and analysis of rocks, minerals, ores, and fossils. In some cases this process requires sophisticated equipment, and even the uncomplicated methods used in the field are best learned with the guidance of a teacher and access to a good collection of specimens. There is considerable truth to the aphorism that "the best geologist is the one who has seen the most rocks."

The serious student of geology needs a good grounding in differential and integral calculus, general chemistry and thermodynamics, and physics. Some knowledge of electronic instrumentation, economics, statistics, and computer programming is also beneficial. Undergraduates majoring in the interdisciplinary fields of Geophysics or Geochemistry devote as much time to the study of physics or chemistry as to geology.

BIBLIOGRAPHY

**POPULAR (good for a taste of geology,
but not serious study)**

Matthews, W. H., *Invitation to Geology: The Earth Through Time and Space.* **American Museum of Natural History, 1971.** Numerous references to works suitable for digging deeper; easy reading.

Cailleux, André, *Anatomy of the Earth.* **tr. J. Moody Stuart. McGraw-Hill (World University Library Series), 1968.** One man's viewpoint; interesting.

Harris, A. G., *Geology of National Parks.* **Kendall-Hunt, 1975.** Descriptive geology of places you may have visited.

Robinson, G. D., A. A. Wanek, W. H. Hays, and M. E. McCallum, *Philmont County: The Rocks and Landscape of a Famous New Mexico Ranch.* **U. S. Geological Survey (Professional Paper 505), 1964.** Something of a super-merit-badge-pamphlet—popular account based on authors' researches in this area; excellent figures, maps, and explanations.

INTRODUCTORY

Press, Frank, and Raymond Siever, *Earth.* **Freeman (hard cover), 1974.** A text, but essential for starting serious study; comprehensive yet comprehensible summary of modern geology.

Gass, I. G., Peter J. Smith, and R. C. L. Wilson, *Understanding the Earth: A Reader in the Earth Sciences,* **rev. ed. M.I.T. Press, 1973.** Easily understood, very modern, but more restricted coverage than the previous work; written as a text for the British Open University program.

Science Foundation Course Team of the Open University, *Earth History I and II.* **Harper & Row (Open University Dept.), 1974.** One example of a short text (77 pages) used in the basic-science course at the Open University.

Allison, I. S., R. F. Black, J. M. Dennison, R. K. Fahnestock, and S. M. White, *Geology: The Science of a Changing Earth,* **6th ed. McGraw-Hill, 1974.** A standard text; somewhat restricted in coverage but available in paperback.

Cox, D. P., and H. R. Cox, *Geology Principles and Concepts: A Programmed Text,* **rev. ed. Freeman, 1974.** The "programmed" form of presentation is especially designed for step-by-step learning in individual study, but some readers find it tedious.

Peterson, M. S., J. K. Rigby, and L. F. Hintze, *Historical Geology of North America.* **Brown, 1973.** Covers historical geology of the sort taught in courses typically taken by students who have completed first-year geology.

INTERMEDIATE

Rocks and Minerals

Ernst, W. G., *Earth Materials.* **Prentice-Hall, 1969.** An introduction to the basic theory of rocks and minerals.

Practice in identifying rocks and minerals is a basic part of geologic training. The three following guides may be helpful although not written at college level.

Pough, F. H., *A Field Guide to Rocks and Minerals,* **ed. Roger T. Peterson. Houghton Mifflin, (Peterson Field Guide; hard cover), 1953.** Recommended.

Arem, Joel, *Rocks and Minerals.* **Bantam, 1973.** More elementary than Pough.

Pearl, R. M., *Rocks and Minerals.* Barnes & Noble (Everyday Handbook #260), 1969. Also more elementary than Pough.

Structural Geology and Geophysics

Ragan, D. M., *Structural Geology: An Introduction to Geometrical Techniques,* 2nd ed. Wiley, 1973.

Oakeshott, Gordon, *Volcanoes and Earthquakes.* McGraw-Hill, 1975.

Sumner, J. S., *Geophysics, Geologic Structures, and Tectonics.* Brown, 1969.

Clark, S. P., *Structure of the Earth.* Prentice-Hall, 1971.

Geologic Time

Faul, Henry, *Ages of Rocks, Planets and Stars.* McGraw-Hill (hard cover), 1966. Basic material on isotopic dating methods.

Harbaugh, J. W., *Stratigraphy and the Geologic Time Scale,* ed. Sherwood D. Tuttle. Brown, 1968. Basic material on telling time from rocks.

Clark, D. L., *Fossils, Paleontology and Evolution.* Brown, 1968. Basic material on fossils and dating.

McAlester, A. L., *The History of Life.* Prentice-Hall, 1968. Also presents basic material on fossils and dating.

Berry, W. B. N., *Growth of a Prehistoric Time Scale,* ed. Sherwood D. Tuttle. Freeman, 1968. Gives an excellent perspective on the history of the development of geologic time scales.

The following four works provide useful supplementary material on geologic time.

Colbert, E. H., *The Age of Reptiles.* Norton, 1966.

Colbert, E. H., *Evolution of the Vertebrates,* 2nd ed. Wiley (hard cover), 1969.

Cowen, Richard, *History of Life.* McGraw-Hill, 1975.

Nations, D., *Record of Geologic Time.* McGraw-Hill, 1975.

Geochemistry

Ahrens, L. H., *Distribution of the Elements in Our Planet.* McGraw-Hill, 1965.

Wood, J. A., *The Solar System.* Prentice-Hall, 1969.

Sedimentation and Sedimentary Rocks

Allen, J. R. L., *Physical Processes of Sedimentation.* American Elsevier, 1970. Basic material of these phenomena.

Laporte, L. F., *Ancient Environments.* Prentice-Hall, 1969.

Pettijohn, F. J., R. E. Potter, and Raymond Siever, *Sand and Sandstone.* Springer, 1973. Somewhat advanced.

Geomorphology

Bloom, A. L., *The Surface of the Earth.* Prentice-Hall, 1969. A basic treatment of this topic.

Dury, W. H., *The Face of the Earth.* Penguin, 1959.

Tuttle, S. D., *Landforms and Landscapes.* Brown, 1970.

Field Methods (but books are no substitute for practice)

Kottlowski, F. E., *Measuring Stratigraphic Sections.* Holt, Rinehart & Winston, 1965.

Lattman, L. H., and R. G. Ray, *Aerial Photographs in Field Geology.* Holt, Rinehart & Winston, 1965.

Plate Tectonics

Glen, William, *Continental Drift and Plate Tectonics.* Bobbs-Merrill, 1975. A basic introduction to the revolutionary new theory of plate tectonics that was introduced only in the 1960s.

Hallam, A., *A Revolution in the Earth Sciences: From Continental Drift to Plate Tectonics.* Oxford Univ. Press, 1975. Supplementary explanations and historical development of the theory.

York, D., *Planet Earth.* McGraw-Hill, 1975.

Tarling, Don, and Maureen Tarling, *Continental Drift: A Study of the Earth's Moving Surface.* Doubleday, 1971. Also gives supplementary explanations and historical development of the theory.

Scientific American, *Continents Adrift: Readings from Scientific American,* intro. J. Tuzo Wilson. Freeman, 1972. Excellent supplementary readings.

Takeuchi, H., *et al., Debate about the Earth: An Approach to Geophysics Through Analysis of Continental Drift,* rev. ed. Freeman, Cooper, 1970. On paleomagnetism; good reading.

Cox, Allen, ed., *Plate Tectonics and Geomagnetic Reversals.* Freeman, 1973. A more advanced treatment of paleomagnetism.

Wegener, Alfred, *The Origin of Continents and Oceans,* tr. John Biram, Dover, **1966.** Interesting for historical perspective.

Economic and Environmental Geology

Kesler, Stephen, *Our Finite Resources.* McGraw-Hill, **1975.** A basic analysis of pollution and depletion of the environment.

The following five books amplify on basic treatment of economic and environmental geology, first generally and then with respect to specific resources.

Turner, Daniel S., *Applied Earth Science.* Brown, **1969.**

Fagan, John J., Jr., *The Earth Environment.* Prentice-Hall, **1974.**

White, Gilbert F., *Natural Hazards: Local, National, Global.* Oxford Univ. Press, **1974.**

Ruesdisili, L. C., and M. W. Firebaugh, eds., *Perspectives on Energy and the Environment: Issues, Ideals and Dilemmas.* Oxford Univ. Press, **1975.**

Cameron, Eugene N., *The Mineral Position of the United States, 1975–2000.* Univ. of Wisconsin Press, **1973.**

Tank, Ronald W., ed., *Focus on Environmental Geology: A Collection of Case Histories and Readings from Original Sources.* Oxford Univ. Press, **1973.** Supplementary readings.

McKenzie, Garry D., and Russell O. Utgard, eds., *Man and His Physical Environment: Readings in Environmental Geology.* Burgess, **1972.** Further supplementary readings.

Water, Oceans, and Atmosphere

Leopold, Luna B., *Water, A Primer.* Freeman, **1974.**

Scientific American, *Oceanography: Readings from Scientific American,* intro. J. Robert Moore, Freeman, **1971.** Supplementary readings.

Pirie, R. Gordon, ed., *Oceanography: Contemporary Readings in Ocean Sciences.* Oxford Univ. Press, **1973.** Presents additional supplementary readings.

Heezen, Bruce C., and Charles D. Hollister, *The Face of the Deep.* Oxford Univ. Press, **1971.**

Turekian, K. K., *Oceans.* Prentice-Hall, **1968.**

Flohn, Hermann, *Climate and Weather.* McGraw-Hill, **1968.**

Gates, David M., *Man and His Environment: Climate.* Harper & Row, **1972.**

General supplementary readings
(very good for perspective)

Press, Frank, and Raymond Siever, eds., *Planet Earth.* **Freeman, 1974.** Current anthology; designed to supplement the textbook, *Earth*, by the same authors listed in the "Introductory" section.

Cloud, Preston, ed., *Adventures in Earth History: Original Selections from Steno to the Present.* **Freeman, 1970.** Material on evolution of earth; compiled during early stages of the development of plate tectonics.

White, J. F., *Study of the Earth: Readings in Geological Science.* **Prentice-Hall, 1962.** Basic geology; written before plate tectonics.

ADVANCED

Harker, Alfred, *Petrology for Students,* **8th ed. Cambridge Univ. Press, 1962.** Identification of crystalline rocks.

Bowen, N. L., *The Evolution of the Igneous Rocks.* **Dover, 1928.** Old but good; most concepts still valid, although considerable space devoted to criticizing theories no longer current.

Simpson, Brian, *Rocks and Minerals.* **Pergamon, 1966.**

Winkler, Helmut G., *Petrogenesis of Metamorphic Rocks,* **2nd ed., tr. N. D. Chatterjee and E. Froese. Springer, 1967.** Very readable treatment.

Spry, Alan, *Metamorphic Textures.* **Pergamon, 1969.**

Taylor, S. Ross, *Lunar Science: A Post-Apollo View.* **Pergamon, 1975.** Application of geologic studies to the Moon.

Bird, J. M., and Bryan Isacks, eds., *Plate Tectonics.* **American Geophysical Union (1707 L St., N. W., Washington, DC 20036; hard cover), 1972.** Readings on plate tectonics at professional level.

Hart, P. J., ed., *The Earth's Crust and Upper Mantle* **(Geophysical Monographs Series, Vol. 13). American Geophysical Union, 1969.** Readings on geophysics at professional level.

PERIODICALS

Geotimes. **American Geological Institute (2201 M St., N. W., Washington, DC 20037).** Provides a good way of keeping up with news and activities of the geological profession. Issued monthly.

Chapter Twenty-Five

MATHEMATICS
*". . . No laboratory is necessary;
just paper and pencil and patience"*

Editorial Advisor:
Susanna and Helmut Epp
Department of Mathematics
DePaul University

INTRODUCTION

The concept of "higher" mathematics is mysterious to many. Indeed, if mathematics is defined as the study of numbers and geometric laws, it is difficult to conceive that there can be much beyond high-school Algebra and Geometry. Some of what does lie beyond and is studied by college students majoring in Mathematics is outlined here. It represents the quantitative reasoning that is both essential in many aspects of modern life (ranging from scientific research to election forecasting) and enjoyable as one of the oldest disinterested intellectual recreations of humankind.

Mathematics has the advantage of being more suitable for self-study than are the other sciences. The nature of the subject requires clear and unambiguous statements and definite procedures for solving problems. At each stage of learning you can check your mastery of the material by referring to the answers ordinarily found in the back of mathematics books. The convenience of having personal instruction with immediate possibilities for asking questions is clear. Nevertheless, by using more than one book for a given subject (possibly with the help of a public library), you can achieve somewhat the same effect. No laboratory is necessary; just paper and pencil and patience.

The importance of being able to solve problems correctly at each stage cannot be overemphasized. It is therefore important to choose books that include many exercises and to work them. Mathematics is learned by doing. Active participation through solving problems is essential.

However, a purely "cookbook" approach to mathematics can achieve only limited (though legitimate) goals. It is the nature of the subject that the understanding of basic principles enables you to solve problems more effectively. No one enjoys rote memorization of series of formulae. This procedure can largely be avoided by reliance on the remarkable organizing power of abstract concepts.

Brief descriptions of the core branches of mathematics now typically taught by colleges follow. The descriptions have been written to be understandable to anyone who recalls high-school Mathematics. Each description of a branch corresponds to a section of the following bibliography. Introductory comments given at the start of each bibliography section use terms that can probably be understood only after you have learned at least some college Mathematics.

Colleges vary widely in the level of sophistication of their course offerings in mathematics. The program outlined by the readings is intended to chart a middle course in American college practice. Some more advanced topics taught at a few colleges are briefly indicated at the end of this introduction.

College students, of course, also vary, not only in the amount, but also in the type of Mathematics courses they take. The first two years of courses are often much the same for both those who intend to specialize in mathematics and those who need to fulfill basic requirements for further study in other fields. After that point, Mathematics majors are usually required to take a certain number of courses to get a degree, and they will choose them according to their own tastes and desires to prepare themselves for various future professions. Thus, it is important to realize that no Math major would read all the books on the list—just one per topic as a main text, with a few others, perhaps, consulted for reference. More are listed to give you a range of choice.

Many additional titles could have been included, for a large number of books in print treat the topics addressed. Of necessity, only one or a few books are given on each topic; often these are the ones generally regarded as classics. Actually, most mathematical material is fairly standardized. While there are differences among books, few are unredeemably bad. A student who works carefully from almost any text, solving problems from it diligently, will become fond of it by the end. You may find it helpful, particularly in studying on your own, to use Schaum outlines where available alongside a text because of their large number of worked exercises.

MATHEMATICAL DISCIPLINES

General Mathematics and History

College students are not usually required or even urged to read books of general and historical interest (although there is some current feeling to change this practice). Since you will be working on your own, however, these books are given in the hope they may provide some of the inspiration and perspective customarily provided by mathematics professors.

Precalculus

Many colleges offer beginning Mathematics courses that cover topics which mathematicians generally consider most appropriate for study in high school. High schools and high school graduates, however, differ widely in levels of mathematics covered. Such courses are given in colleges under the guise of "College Algebra and Trigonometry," which is usually high-school Algebra and Trigonometry taught very quickly.

Calculus

Calculus was invented (discovered?) by Newton and Leibniz— to treat problems which arose primarily in the course of an attempt to develop laws of motion that applied equally to the action of mechanical forces on earth and to their action on planets, stars, and other astronomical bodies throughout the universe. The success of these efforts was the major scientific triumph of the seventeenth century.

Among the problems with which calculus could accordingly deal were: (1) finding the velocity and acceleration of a moving body (like a cannon ball or pendulum weight) at any given instant; (2) finding the tangent to a curve (making it possible to determine at any instant the speed and direction of planets or other bodies moving in noncircular orbits); (3) finding the maximum or minimum values of a mathematical "function" (useful in telling how far out in space a comet ranges); and (4) finding the lengths of curves (for instance, computing the length of the orbit of a planet around the sun).

Other current uses of calculus are legion. They range from finding areas of two-dimensional figures or volumes of solids of many different shapes to finding the age of ancient statuettes using the law of radioactive decay, figuring the price at which to sell dresses or shoes for maximum profit, figuring bank-account interest that is continuously compounded, or proving that Apollo command modules must travel in elliptical orbits around the moon. And these example are just for starters.

Ordinarily, in introductory Calculus courses in college, you would study the varieties of calculus called "differential" and "integral" and how techniques in them can be applied to "infinite series" (such as 1/2 + 1/4 + 1/8 . . .). These studies deal with equations having only one unknown—one "variable" or "real variable."

After this initial study, several paths are open. You can continue on to the study of calculus of several variables, or you can leave calculus temporarily for other branches of mathematics. Many mathematicians recommend a brief study of the branch called "linear algebra" at this point as preparation for the study of multidimensional calculus. In fact, Advanced Calculus textbooks often include some elementary linear algebra.

Advanced Calculus or
Calculus of Several Variables

Most quantities that need to be determined in engineering or science are influenced by several varying factors or several variables, rather than by only one. The calculus of several variables is, as you might expect, more complicated than the calculus of just one variable, but it has even wider applications in engineering and the sciences. Studies in such advanced calculus are important in many advanced technological areas—for example, in electromagnetism, which underlies the generating of electricity and all radio waves.

Differential Equations

Some college Mathematics majors follow courses in the calculus with courses in differential equations. Many physical laws are expressed as differential equations—for example, Newton's second law of motion, the laws governing the behavior of electrical circuits and of chemical reactions, the laws of thermodynamics (that is, those that have to do with heat flow), and the laws governing the growth of bacteria. The planet Neptune was discovered as a result of predictions made by examining certain differential equations.

Introduction to Analysis or
Foundations of Analysis

Seventeenth- and eighteenth-century mathematicians were by and large content to work with the calculus on an intuitive level, without demanding rigorous definitions for the basic concepts. It was not until the nineteenth century that mathematical analysis of these and other concepts was placed on a sound logical foundation. Bolzano, Cauchy, Dedekind, and Weierstrass worked out in a precise way what was meant by such mathematical concepts as real numbers, limits of functions and sequences, continuity, and infinite series. In the later nineteenth century Cantor founded modern set theory (a theory met in simple form today by children learning the "New Math" in schools). Cantor also rigorously established the basic facts about cardinality (or size) of sets. These topics are often covered superficially in introductory Calculus courses. They are then returned to in greater depth later—sometimes as a separate course, sometimes as part of a year-long Advanced Calculus course.

Complex Variables

Perhaps the most beautiful mathematical subject an undergraduate encounters is the theory of a function of a complex variable, pioneered by the French mathematician Cauchy. Deep insights into the relations among the functions learned in calculus are revealed by the extension of the functions from the system of real numbers to the systems of "imaginary" or "complex" numbers (numbers containing a term involving $\sqrt{-1}$ as a factor; these were originally called imaginary because the square root of minus one is not one of the ordinary numbers we use in everyday life, the "real" numbers). Moreover, the theorems of the subject possess a characteristic elegance. Far from being a useless abstraction (as the term "imaginary" would imply), the theory of functions of a complex variable is one of the most useful branches of mathematics. It has important applications in such fields as hydrodynamics, aerodynamics, heat flow, and the theory of elasticity.

Geometry

Three types of geometry are generally taught in colleges. The first, Analytic Geometry, is usually included as a part of the Basic Calculus sequence. In plane analytic geometry, such geometric figures as straight lines, circles, and ellipses are plotted on "Cartesian" coordinates (in which a horizontal line is usually the "x-axis" and a vertical line is the "y-axis"). When geometric figures are described in terms of coordinates, techniques of ordinary high-school Algebra can be used to study them.

The second kind of college Geometry is not unlike high school Geometry in method, for it starts with stating axioms and drawing conclusions based on them. Such a course is often taken by persons planning to teach high-school Mathematics. These courses soon become ones in "non-Euclidean" geometry, though, often by introducing Lobaschewski's demonstration of the independence in logic of Euclid's parallel axiom from the other nine axioms of Euclidean geometry. (As now usually taught, the parallel axiom states that, for a given line and a given point not on it, you can draw through the point one and only one line parallel to the given line). The courses then go on to study what "geometry" results when Euclid's other axioms are retained but the parallel axiom is dropped.

Differential Geometry is the third type often offered for undergraduates. It applies calculus to the study of curves (such as parabolas) and of surfaces (such as those of spheres or cones). It can be very abstract. Einstein used differential geometric ideas in his theory of relativity. Since that time, the subject has become increasingly important in various branches of physics.

A fourth type of geometry that is seldom offered for undergraduates at present is Projective Geometry. This beautiful subject originated in the study of perspective for realistic painting and drawing. It enjoys periodic revivals in college programs and is a field of active research in modern mathematics.

Topology

Topology is an outgrowth of geometry. Very roughly, it is the study of the geometric properties retained by an object when it is reshaped by being bent, stretched, or squeezed but not cut or broken. For example, a doughnut and a coffee cup with a handle are considered equivalent in topology. (One can be mapped to the other in a way that sends nearby points to nearby points and does not collapse any two points together. In other words, if you have a doughnut made of some very flexible clay, you can reshape it without cutting to look like a coffee cup).

The Moebius band is a well-known figure analyzed in topology. You can easily make a model of the band by taking a strip of paper, twisting it once and pasting the ends together to form a ring. Your band will then appear (on small sections) like an ordinary two-sided surface, but taken all together, it will have only one side, as you can find by tracing it with your finger or trying to paint its "outside" and its "inside" different colors. And if you try to cut it in two along the middle of the strip, it stays in one piece after you have cut it all the way around.

Topology does not have the wealth of applications of some other branches of mathematics, but it proves useful for settling basic questions that arise in other branches of mathematics which do have many important applications.

Probability and Statistics

Probability and statistics are often offered as a one-year sequence for college students, for many of the theoretical ideas and calculations in probability are important in various uses of statistics. Probability is, of course, the fascinating branch of mathematics used to calculate the likelihood or frequency with which chance events will occur—how often you will get a seven when rolling dice, for example. Probability and statistics are a popular option for mathematics majors. Students in many other fields such as economics, psychology, sociology, engineering, and education, are increasingly viewing knowledge of these fields as necessary to the understanding of much of the work in their own.

Most study in statistics concerns how to draw conclusions based on the analysis of samples. Examples of typical applications for such study are as follows. A decision may be made to recommend drug A over drug B for a certain disease because, when the two drugs were given to random samples of patients with that disease, a significantly larger fraction of those who took drug A recovered. Or a lawsuit may be brought against a company for short-weighting based on the fact that a random sample of the company's products weighed significantly less than specified on the label. In both these cases conclusions are drawn about an entire group (all patients with the disease; all products made by the company) based on information gathered from only a sample of the entire group. In mathematical statistics, the theory of probability is used to calculate precisely what the odds are that such conclusions will be correct or incorrect. Probability theory is also employed to determine how large a sample must be taken to attain a desired degree of accuracy or "confidence." (Results of "80 per cent confidence," for example, means that the specified results would be realized in 80 out of every 100 occurrences on the average.)

Computer Programming and Numerical Analysis

Many college mathematics departments offer courses in computer programming that attract students with a wide variety of study interests. Programming can be learned without any prior study of college-level mathematics. Mathematics majors often elect to master some kinds of programming, and computers have become widely used in recent years to illustrate many mathematical principles with realistic examples. Books on programming that include many sample solutions to exercises make it possible to learn programming without a computer (though using one is, of course, helpful).

Computers can be programmed to perform calculations only by means of "algorithms"—explicit, step-by-step directions by which the computer system carries out the necessary operations. "Numerical Analysis" is the branch of mathematics in which such algorithms are studied. It has been developing rapidly with the speedy growth of the whole field of electronic computers. In this field different algorithms can be compared for such properties as efficiency and accuracy (the more efficient requires the least number of individual calculations; the more accurate produces the least error in the final result). Numerical Analysis calls for some prior learning in such branches as Advanced Calculus, Differential Equations, and Complex Variables.

Linear Algebra and Modern Abstract Algebra

In essence, Linear Algebra is the study of methods for obtaining simultaneous solutions to systems of "linear" equations (like the equations in x and y that are solved simultaneously in high-school Algebra, except that college Linear Algebra deals with ways for solving such equations for any number of unknowns). Two approaches to linear algebra are taken in college courses. In one approach, students get a quick, elementary understanding of the basic facts for use in Advanced Calculus courses they are taking. In the other approach, Linear Algebra is developed in a more leisurely and complete fashion as a separate course that gives a general introduction to modern abstract mathematical concepts and reasoning.

Algebra is used in all branches of mathematics, in that symbols are manipulated according to arithmetic laws. By modern algebra or Modern Abstract Algebra, however, mathematicians today usually mean the axiomatic study of those properties which relate to basic algebraic operations, such as addition and multiplication, of familiar objects, like the integers (whole numbers), rational numbers (fractions), complex numbers ($a + bi$, for example) and polynomials ($2 x^3 - 8 x^2 + 1$). For example, addition and multiplication can both be carried out within the system of integers, but division of two integers is not always possible within the system ($1 \div 2$ is not an integer). Similarly, the equation $x^2 - 4 = 0$ can be solved for integer values of x ($+2$ and -2), but the similar equation $x^2 + 1 = 0$ can only be solved by using complex number values for x ($+i$ and $-i$). The abstract conceptual approach of modern algebra exploits similarities between structures. For example, the division of one polynomial by another to give a polynomial quotient and a remainder is seen to be in all essentials the same as the division of one integer by another to give an integer quotient and a remainder. Because of this similarity, the ring of polynomials can be shown to share many further properties with the ring of integers. The axiomatic approach leads to examining mathematical systems of quantities in which such laws as $ab = ba$ or $a(bc) = (ab)c$ may fail. Such seemingly idle speculations have, in fact, found important applications in such areas as crystallography and nuclear physics (quantum mechanics).

Other Topics

Other topics are sometimes offered for college students, depending usually on the specialities of faculty members. Some are given here for readers possibly interested in study on their own beyond the scope of the bibliography. These include graph theory, combinatorics, theory of automata, theory of computability and Turing machines, general mathematical logic, assembly language and data structures (for those planning careers in computer science), operations research (used in sophisticated management of any system—industrial, business, governmental), partial differential equations, and calculus of variations. Colleges with unusually advanced programs may also offer undergraduate course work in such topics as Lesbegue integration, functional analysis, and differentiable manifolds.

BIBLIOGRAPHY

NOTE This booklist must begin with a disclaimer. There are undoubtedly many excellent texts which were not included, either because they did not seem to be quite the right level, or for reasons of space, or simply for lack of acquaintance. In addition, there is some bias in the list toward "classics" in each field and toward paperback books for reasons of economy and ease of purchase. In many instances, virtually any book which covers the desired topics will serve the student well.

GENERAL MATHEMATICS AND HISTORY

Kline, Morris, ed., *Mathematics in the Modern World*. Freeman (Readings from *Scientific American*), 1968.

COSRIMS, ed., *The Mathematical Sciences: A Collection of Essays*. M.I.T. Press, 1969.

Boyer, Carl B., *History of Mathematics.* Wiley, 1968.

Saaty, Thomas L., and F. J. Weyl, *The Uses and the Spirit of the Mathematical Sciences.* McGraw-Hill, 1969.

Kasner, Edward, and James R. Newman, *Mathematics and the Imagination.* Simon & Schuster (hard cover), 1940.

Newman, James R., ed., *The World of Mathematics.* 4 vols.; vol. 1: *Men and Numbers,* vol. 2: *The World of Laws and the World of Chance;* vol. 3: *The Mathematical Way of Thinking;* vol. 4: *Machines, Music and Puzzles.* Simon & Schuster, 1956–1960.

Kramer, Edna, *The Nature and Growth of Modern Mathematics,* 2 vols. Fawcett World Library, 1974.

Aleksandrov, A. D., *et al.,* eds., *Mathematics: Its Content, Methods, and Meaning,* 3 vols., 2nd ed., tr. S. H. Gould, M.I.T. Press, 1969. These exceptionally well-written volumes form excellent minitexts with good motivation for each of the major fields of mathematics.

Kline, Morris, *Mathematical Thought from Ancient to Modern Times.* Oxford Univ. Press, 1972.

Courant, Richard, and Herbert Robbins, *What is Mathematics?* Oxford Univ. Press (hard cover), 1941.

Behnke, H., *et al., Fundamentals of Mathematics,* 3 vols.; vol. 1: *Foundations of Mathematics: The Real Number System and Algebra;* vol. 2: *Fundamentals of Mathematics; Geometry;* vol. 3: *Fundamentals of Mathematics: Analysis,* tr. S. H. Gould. M.I.T. Press, 1974. Translated from German.

Bourbaki, Nicolas, *Elements of Mathematics,* 3 vols.; vol. 1: *General Topology: Part 1,* 1966; vol. 2: *General Topology: Part 2,* 1967; vol. 3: *Theory of Sets,* 1968. Addison-Wesley (hard cover). Heavy going but elegantly complete.

PRECALCULUS

For precalculus study, virtually any text called College Algebra and Trigonometry or having a similar title will prepare the student for calculus. Some specific books of this kind are noted below. In addition, a number of programmed texts (designed for self-study) on algebra and trigonometry are available as, for example:

Sowokowski, Earl, *A Precalculus Course in Algebra and Trigonometry,* 5 "modules," Prindle, 1973; and Davis, Thomas A., *Algebra and Trigonometry,* 4 vols., Harcourt Brace Jovanovich, 1972.

Spiegel, Murray R., *College Algebra.* McGraw-Hill (Schaum's Outline Series), 1956.

Ayres, Frank, Jr., *Trigonometry.* McGraw-Hill (Schaum's Outline Series), 1954.

Ayres, Frank, Jr., *First-Year College Mathematics.* McGraw-Hill (Schaum's Outline Series), 1958.

Fisher, Robert C., and Allen D. Zieber, *Integrated Algebra & Trigonometry, with Analytic Geometry,* 3rd ed. Prentice-Hall (hard cover), 1972.

CALCULUS

As the readings below will make clear, the idea of limit is at the heart of calculus. The derivative is a limit of a quotient of functions, the (Riemann) integral is a limit of sums, and infinite series are limits of sequences of partial sums. Students in first-year Calculus college courses usually learn differential calculus first and then integral calculus, followed by infinite series. If the course continues into a second year at an introductory level, such topics as partial differentiation, multiple integration, and vector analysis are usually covered. These courses develop proficiency in techniques of differentiation, methods of integration, and tests for convergence of series. The courses also acquaint students with applications of techniques and principles at each stage.

The number of calculus books is infinite. Almost any text you pick up will be adequate. The following four are in some way distinctive.

Thomas, George B., *Calculus with Analytic Geometry,* 4th ed. Addison-Wesley, 1968.

Apostol, Tom M., *Calculus, Vol. I,* 2nd ed. Xerox (hard cover), 1967. Many schools use this book for their Honors Calculus course; it is a beautifully written book, with excellent problems. For students willing to work hard, there is no single undergraduate text from which they will benefit more. *Vol. II* treats functions of several variables.

Shenk, Al, *Calculus and Analytic Geometry.* Goodyear, (hard cover), 1977.

Bonic, Robert, and Gabriel V. Hajian, *Freshman Calculus.* Heath (hard cover), 1971. Written by several teachers in collaboration with students. A helpful *Guide Book* to this text is available.

Courant, R., and John F. Courant, *Introduction to Calculus & Analysis, Vol. I.* Wiley (hard cover), 1965. A good classic treatment.

Ayres, Frank, Jr., *Calculus,* 2nd ed. McGraw-Hill (Schaum Outline Series), 1967.

ADVANCED CALCULUS OR
CALCULUS OF SEVERAL VARIABLES

Advanced Calculus courses in college normally include learning to compute partial derivatives and understanding their significance, evaluating double and triple integrals, and finding maxima and minima for funtions of several variables. The courses then go on to vector functions and Green's, Stokes', and the divergence theorems. These topics are especially important in the study of electromagnetism and hydrodynamics.

Taylor, Angus E., and Robert W. Mann, *Advanced Calculus,* 2nd ed. Xerox (hard cover), 1972.

Buch, R. Creighton, *Advanced Calculus,* 2nd ed. McGraw-Hill (hard cover), 1965.

Apostol, Tom M., *Mathematical Analysis,* 2nd ed. Addison-Wesley (hard cover), 1974.

Goldberg, Richard R., *Methods of Real Analysis.* Xerox (hard cover), 1964.

Wilson, E. B., *Advanced Calculus.* Dover, 1969 (out of print).

Spiegel, Murray R., *Advanced Calculus.* McGraw-Hill (Schaum's Outline Series), 1963.

Spiegel, Murray R., *Vector Analysis.* McGraw-Hill (Schaum's Outline Series), 1959.

DIFFERENTIAL EQUATIONS

College courses taken after Advanced Calculus may deal with differential equations—equations involving a function and one or more of its derivatives. The unknown in a differential equation is not a number but a function (for example, one defining the variation of the temperature of a body over time, or describing the motion of a planet over time). To solve a differential equation means to find a function which satisfies the equation. If the function depends on only one variable, the equation is called an ordinary differential equation. If it depends on several variables (so that partial derivatives must be taken), it is called a partial differential equation.

Agnew, R. P., *Differential Equations,* 2nd ed. McGraw-Hill, 1960 (out of print). A classic, traditional elementary treatment.

Coddington, Earl A. and N. Levinson, *Theory of Ordinary Differential Equations.* McGraw-Hill (hard cover), 1955. Another classic, rigorous treatment of traditional topics. INTERMEDIATE to ADVANCED.

Ince, Edward L., *Ordinary Differential Equations.* Dover, 1953.

Tennenbaum, Morris, and Harry Pollard, *Ordinary Differential Equations.* Harper & Row (hard cover), 1963. A traditional treatment with a very large number of applications.

Pontayagin, L. S., *Ordinary Differential Equations.* Addison-Wesley (hard cover), 1962. Advanced, qualitative treatment; gives an idea of the modern direction of the subject.

Smale, Stephen, and Morris Hirsch, *Differential Equations, Dynamical Systems and Linear Algebra.* Academic, 1974. An even more contemporary treatment. ADVANCED.

Ayres, Frank, Jr., *Differential Equations.* McGraw-Hill (Schaum's Outline Series), 1952.

INTRODUCTION TO ANALYSIS OR FOUNDATIONS OF ANALYSIS

The content studied in this area of undergraduate Mathematics normally includes complete and systematic definitions of such concepts as real numbers, limits of functions and sequences, continuity, infinite series, set theory, and the cardinality of sets. Undergraduates are often given a superficial treatment of these topics in beginning Calculus courses and then return to study them later in more depth, either in a separate course or as part of a year-long advanced calculus course.

Kaplansky, I., *Set Theory and Metric Space.* Allyn (hard cover), 1972. A very well-written, excellent foundation for study of higher mathematics.

Rudin, Walter, *Principles of Mathematical Analysis,* 2nd ed. McGraw-Hill (hard cover), Classic; gives theoretical basis of calculus.

Olmstead, Hohn M., *Intermediate Analysis: An Introduction to the Theory of Functions of One Real Variable.* Prentice-Hall (hard cover), 1956. Also a classic that gives theoretical basis of calculus.

Lipschutz, Seymour, *Set Theory and Related Topics.* McGraw-Hill (Schaum's Outline Series), 1964.

Goffman, Casper, *Real Functions,* Vol. 8, rev. ed. Prindle (hard cover), 1967. INTERMEDIATE to ADVANCED.

COMPLEX VARIABLES

The theory of a function of a complex variable concerns functions which are defined on and take their values in the system of complex numbers—numbers of the form $a + bi$, where a and b are real numbers and $i = \sqrt{-1}$. Among the topics studied in it are complex integration, Cauchy's formula. Cauchy-Reimann equations, power series, conformal mappings, and an introduction to the theory of Riemann surfaces. The subject is one of the most useful branches of mathematics and has application in many areas of science.

Churchill, Reul V., and James W. Brown, *Complex Variables and Applications,* rev. ed. McGraw-Hill (hard cover), 1974.

Hille, Einar, *Analysis,* 2 vols. Blaisdell (hard cover), 1964, 1966 (out of print). INTERMEDIATE.

Ahlfors, Lars Walerian, *Complex Analysis: An Introduction to the Theory of Analytic Functions of One Complex Variable.* McGraw-Hill (hard cover), 1953 (out of print). INTERMEDIATE.

Knopp, Konrad, *Theory of Functions,* 2 vols. Dover, 1945. There are accompanying problem books. INTERMEDIATE.

Spiegel, Murray R., *Complex Variables.* McGraw-Hill (Schaum's Outline Series), 1964.

GEOMETRY

Three types of geometry are often taught in colleges—analytic, non-Euclidean, and differential. Since analytic geometry is usually included as part of the introductory calculus courses, works treating it are accordingly listed in the "Calculus" section. Non-Euclidean geometry—the study of geometries with different axiom systems from ordinary Euclidean geometry—is introduced in the works by Eves and Coxeter (below). Differential geometry is the study of such geometric objects as curves and surfaces with the use of calculus. While it can be very abstract (as in the study of differential manifolds), it is usually taught as a course concerning differential properties of curves and surfaces—including, for example, the concepts of curvature and geodesics.

Eves, Howard, *Survey of Geometry,* 2nd rev. ed. Allyn (hard cover), 1972. Good coverage of different topics.

Moise, Edwin H., *Elementary Geometry from an Advanced Standpoint,* 2nd ed. Addison-Wesley (hard cover), 1974. Well written.

Seidenberg, Abraham, *Lectures in Projective Geometry.* Van Nostrand Reinhold (hard cover), 1962.

Struik, Dirk J., *Differential Geometry,* 2nd ed. Addison-Wesley (hard cover), 1961. A classic, accessible introduction to the subject.

Coxeter, H. S., *Introduction to Geometry.* Wiley (hard cover), 1969.

Artin, Emil, *Geometric Algebra.* Wiley (hard cover), 1957. INTERMEDIATE to ADVANCED.

Lipschutz, Seymour, *Differential Geometry.* McGraw-Hill (Schaum's Outline Series), 1969.

Spivak, Michael, *Calculus on Manifolds.* Benjamin, 1965. Good short account from modern viewpoint.

Ayres, Frank, Jr., *Projective Geometry.* McGraw-Hill (Schaum's Outline Series), 1967.

TOPOLOGY

Typically, an Introductory Topology course involves studying set theory first, then becoming familiar with a large number of topological spaces. Students next examine various properties that the spaces may or may not have: separation axioms, connectedness, compactness, and neighborhood bases of various cardinalities. The students may also study some algebraic topology, which applies knowledge of the structures of modern algebra to the study of topological spaces. The course may further discuss the classification of surfaces in Euclidean three-space according to genus and introduce the basic ideas of the fundamental group and/or the homology groups of a space.

Mendelson, Bert, *Introduction to Topology,* 3rd ed. Allyn (hard cover), 1975. Unusually well written.

Hu, Sze-Tsen, *Introduction to General Topology*. Holden-Day (hard cover), 1966.

Kelley, John L., *General Topology*. Van Nostrand Reinhold (hard cover), 1955. ADVANCED.

PROBABILITY AND STATISTICS

Often probability and statistics are taught together as a one-year sequence on the undergraduate level, with the distributions studied in the probability segment reappearing in the statistics segment to calculate various probabilities involving statistical data.

In the mathematics of probability the fundamental assumptions have been axiomatized. Probabilities are seen to be certain set functions on "probability spaces," and the subject can be studied in a mathematically precise way. "Random variable," a central concept in probability, is the term used to identify a quantity that may have various values under given conditions with specific probabilities. If a coin is tossed three times, for example, the number of heads that result from the three tosses (none, one, two or three) is a random variable. Probability theory demonstrates that in this case the probabilities of getting 0, 1, 2 or 3 heads are 1/8, 3/8, 3/8, and 1/8 respectively. A table summarizing this information is called a probability distribution; in the example given, the table would appear as follows.

Number of heads	Probabilities
0	1/8
1	3/8
2	3/8
3	1/8

When the number of possible values taken by the random variable is finite or countable (as in the case above), the distribution is called *discrete*; otherwise the distribution is called *continuous*. The "expecta-

404   COLLEGE ON YOUR OWN

tion" associated with a random variable measures its value on the average; the "variance" measures the amount of variability in the values.

Undergraduates study different kinds of probability distributions—binomial, hypergeometric, Poisson, exponential, normal—as well as joint and marginal distributions, independence of random variables, sums of random variables, and multivariate distributions. Having learned the basic concepts of probability, students can apply the tools of mathematical analysis to establish many facts about probabilities such as Chebyshev's theorem and the Central Limit Theorem.

Topics in statistics usually studied by undergraduates after probability include theory of estimation, unbiased estimators, maximum likelihood estimators, confidence intervals, the power of a test of hypothesis, likelihood ratio test, goodness of fit, regression and correlation, analysis of variance, and multivariate statistics.

Larson, Harold J., *Introduction to Probability Theory and Statistical Influence*, 2nd ed. Wiley, 1974. Very clear treatment; with answers to exercises at the back of the book.

Goldberg, Samuel, *Probability: An Introduction*. Prentice-Hall (hard cover), 1960.

Gnedenko, Boris V., and Alexander Y. Khinchin, *An Elementary Introduction to the Theory of Probability*, 5th ed., tr. Leon F. Boron, Dover, 1961.

Feller, William, *An Introduction to Probability Theory and Its Applications*, 2 vols., 2nd ed. Wiley (hard cover), 1971. This book probably inspired most of the people working in the field in this country. INTERMEDIATE.

Hoel, Paul, *et al.*, *Introduction to Probability Theory*. Houghton-Mifflin, 1971; *Introduction to Statistical Theory*. Houghton-Mifflin, 1971. Answers are given to all exercises.

Dwass, Meyer, *Probability and Statistics*. Benjamin (hard cover), 1970.

Breiman, Leo, *Probability and Stochastic Processes: with a View Toward Applications*. Houghton-Mifflin (hard cover), 1969; *Statistics: with a View Toward Applications*. Houghton-Mifflin (hard cover), 1973.

Tanur, Judith, *et al.*, eds., *Statistics: A Guide to the Unknown*. Holden-Day, 1972. Essays by well-known researchers describing (to the layman) some important uses of statistics. An excellent accompaniment to the study of statistics.

Naiman, Arnold, *et al.*, *Understanding Statistics*. McGraw-Hill (hard cover), 1972. A statistics book for the non-mathematician; very elementary and readable. Someone wishing to study mathematical statistics can benefit from reading through this kind of text to get the basic ideas and applications.

Spiegel, Murray R., *Statistics.* McGraw-Hill (Schaum's Outline Series), 1961.

Lipschutz, Seymour, *Probability.* McGraw-Hill (Schaum's Outline Series), 1968.

Lipschutz, Seymour, *Finite Mathematics.* McGraw-Hill (Schaum's Outline Series), 1966.

COMPUTER PROGRAMMING AND NUMERICAL ANALYSIS

Techniques of computer programming can be learned without any background in college Mathematics by studying manuals like those listed below. Many such manuals are available, and they frequently include sample program solutions to problems, so that access to a computer is not absolutely necessary to learn programming—although it is, of course, desirable.

The study of algorithms, on which computer programming is based, belongs to a branch of mathematics called numerical analysis. Topics often studied in college courses in it include numerical solution of matrix equations, finding the roots of equations of a real or a complex variable, numerical integration, and solution of differential equations.

Andree, R., *et al., Computer Programming: Techniques, Analysis and Mathematics,* rev. ed. Prentice-Hall (hard cover), 1973. Fortran IV.

Cress, R., *et al., Fortran IV with Watfor and Watfiv,* rev. ed. Prentice-Hall 1970.

Albrecht, R. L., et al., *Basic.* Wiley, 1973.

Forsythe, Alexandra I., *Computer Science: A First Course,* 2nd ed. Wiley (hard cover), 1975. This book is exceptionally well written. It seems intended for high school use, but it is an excellent introduction to the subject at any level.

Stark, Peter A., *Introduction to Numerical Methods.* Macmillan, 1970. Also very well-written, understandable text; covers numerical analysis topics in greater depth than Forsythe's.

Ralston, Anthony, *A First Course in Numerical Analysis.* McGraw-Hill (hard cover), 1965. One of the classics in the field.

Dorn, William S., and Daniel D. McCracken, eds., *Numerical Methods with Fortran Four Case Studies.* Wiley, 1972. Somewhat more advanced than Stark.

Scheid, Francis, *Introduction to Computer Science.* McGraw-Hill (Schaum's Outline Series), 1970.

Scheid, Francis, *Numerical Analysis.* McGraw-Hill (Schaum's Outline Series), 1968.

LINEAR ALGEBRA AND
MODERN ABSTRACT ALGEBRA

In essence, linear algebra concerns methods of obtaining simultaneous solutions to systems of linear equations. Study in it includes consideration of abstract finite and infinite dimensional vector spaces (even over arbritrary fields). A system of linear equations is seen to be equivalent to a linear transformation from one vector space to another. The rational and Jordan canonical forms separate linear transformations on a space into equivalent classes. Students in Linear Algebra courses also explore what happens when a vector space is equipped with an inner product.

Modern algebra is usually understood to mean the systematic study of such structures as groups, rings, and fields. College courses in it generally deal with the laws of algebraic operations with respect to such things as the sets of integers (which form a ring), rational numbers, real and complex numbers with ordinary addition and multiplication (each of which are fields), the integers with modular arithmetic, matrices, vectors, groups of transformations, rings of polynomials, and the quaternions and Cayley numbers. Courses sometimes also include Galois theory (the study of the solutions of an algebraic equation was shown by Galois to be related to the permutation group of roots of the equation). Elementary Number Theory, which used to be a common undergraduate course, is now usually studied as a part of abstract algebra.

Shields, Paul C., *Elementary Linear Algebra.* Worth (hard cover), 1973. Readable elementary treatment; many proofs are done only for $n = 2$.

Zelinsky, Daniel, *First Course in Linear Algebra,* 2nd ed. Academic, (hard cover), 1970. Readable.

Nering, Evar D., *Linear Algebra and Matrix Theory,* 2nd ed. Wiley (hard cover), 1970.

Hoffman, Kenneth, and Ray Kunze, *Linear Algebra,* 2nd ed. Prentice-Hall (hard cover), Somewhat more theoretical than the above; good basis for further mathematical studies.

Halmos, P. R., *Finite Dimensional Vector Spaces.* Krauss Reprints, 1947. Slightly more abstract than Hoffman and Kunze (above).

MacLane, Saunders, and G. Birkhoff, *Algebra.* Macmillan (hard cover), 1967. Combines linear algebra and abstract algebra.

Herstein, I. N., *Topics in Algebra,* 2nd ed. Wiley, 1975. Beautifully written, excellent introduction to abstract algebra.

Paley, Hiram, and Paul M. Weichsel, *Elements of Abstract Linear Algebra.* Holt, Rinehart & Winston (hard cover), 1972.

Fraleigh, John B., *A First Course in Abstract Algebra*. Addison-Wesley (hard cover), 1967.

McCoy, Neal H., *Fundamentals of Abstract Algebra*. Allyn (hard cover), 1972.

McCoy, Neal H., *Theory of Numbers*. Macmillan (hard cover), 1965.

Vinogradov, Ivan M., *Elements of Number Theory*, tr. Saul Kravetz. Dover, 1954.

Lipschutz, Seymour, *Linear Algebra*. McGraw-Hill (Schaum's Outline Series), 1968.

Ayres, Frank, Jr., *Modern Algebra*. McGraw-Hill (Schaum's Outline Series), 1965.

Baumslag, Benjamin, and B. Chandler, *Group Theory*. McGraw-Hill (Schaum's Outline Series), 1968.

Ayres, Frank, Jr., *Matrices*. McGraw-Hill (Schaum's Outline Series), 1962.

Chapter Twenty-Six

PHYSICS

*". . . explaining phenomena
from the cosmic scale down to
the level of the atomic"*

Editorial Advisor:
James Currin
Division of Natural Sciences
State University of New York
College at Purchase

INTRODUCTION

Interest in physics, both as a major field of study and as an avenue for elective study, has undergone great fluctuations since the end of the Second World War. The identification of physics in the public mind with the goals of national power and prestige, together with large infusions of federally provided funds into universities starting after the war and continuing through the early years of the space program, resulted in a precipitous rate of growth. This spurt began to level off in the 1960s, followed by an equally precipitous decline connected with widespread public disillusionment, especially among young people, with these national goals. It is still too early to tell whether the current preoccupation with an "energy" crisis will lead to a new period of growth in the study of physics.

The general perception of physics as an aspect of public policy, significant as it may be, is not particularly helpful in approaching the subject as an academic and intellectual discipline. Being in the broadest sense the study of inanimate nature, the subject does not reflect any of the divisions of humankind, whether political or ethnic, and major contributions have been made by investigators from nearly all civilized countries. There is no doubt that this international quality has served to animate the discipline, and that it has contributed to the intellectual unity of all peoples, however much it may have simultaneously increased the dangers inherent in their political and ideological divisions.

At the beginning the student of physics should put aside rather commonly held notions that the subject is mysterious and abstruse. Physics has its origin in those primitive sense perceptions by which human beings apprehend the external world: (1) the sense of spatial extension, (2) the sense of time duration, (3) the sense of tactile pressure or "touch," and (4) the sense of heat and cold. (The senses of smell and taste may safely be left to the chemists.) From these sense perceptions physics abstracts the qualities of distance, time, force, quantity of heat, and temperature, which are susceptible to precise definition through quantitative measurement. And these magnitudes, augmented by the quantity of electric charge, compose the quantitative subject matter of physics and may be used to delineate its major subject areas.

GEOMETRY

Normally thought of as a branch of mathematics, geometry (insofar as it treats actual measurements of length) is a physical science. As such it was the first to be given rigorous study and the first to achieve an elegant synthesis, codified in the geometry of Euclid and the remarkable theorem of Pythagoras. (Einstein, the greatest modern "physical geometer," considered Pythagoras his boyhood inspiration.)

At the practical level, familiarity and facility with geometry and trigonometry as taught in most high schools is essential to anyone undertaking the study of physics, and nearly all introductory texts assume such preparation on the part of the reader.

STATICS

Statics is a topic that combines geometry with the measurement of force. Its history goes back to Archimedes, who discovered the principle of the lever. Its simplest results, which are of great practical utility, apply to the so-called simple machines: the lever, pulley, inclined plane, screw, crank, gear, and the like (with which the student who has studied physics in high school will already be quite familiar). Statics also treats introductory forms of the concepts of work, the product of force and linear displacement, and potential energy, as well as the first inkling of the great principle of the conservation of energy.

CHRONOMETRY AND KINEMATICS

The science that deals with the accurate measurement of time intervals is *chronometry*. Unlike geometry, which offers three spatial dimensions, it opens few possibilities for theoretical elaboration and does not by itself play a very significant role in an understanding of physics. However, the combination of measurements of time and length gives rise to the science of *kinematics*, the study of motion. Here the concepts of velocity and acceleration are introduced. It was by means of a rigorous critique of kinematics that Einstein achieved the first results in his theory of relativity.

DYNAMICS

The decisive step of relating the measurements of force, length, and time was taken by Isaac Newton through his celebrated laws of motion. In particular, the second law defines the change in momentum of a moving body to be the product of the force and the length of time during which the force acts. Newton further defined the inertial mass by expressing the momentum as the product of the mass and velocity. This simple scheme, which many physicists today profess to find nearly self-evident (after the fact), has provided the foundation for all the advances in physics of the modern era. It explains phenomena from the cosmic scale down to the level of the atomic.

While Newton's scheme is simple, its application to a given system is not self-evident. All but the most workaday examples are attended by considerable mathematical complexity. Accordingly, by far the greater portion of the student's effort in learning physics is spent in working problems at various levels of difficulty in Newtonian dynamics. At an early stage in this process the student requires the more subtle mathematical tools provided by the calculus (invented by Newton).

CALORIMETRY

The science that relates the measurement of quantity of heat to temperature changes is called *calorimetry*. It also will already be familiar to readers who have taken high-school Physics. Its operative principle is the "conservation of heat." (Historically the principle stems from the "caloric" theory of the eighteenth century, which treated heat as a conserved fluid, the "caloric," whose quantity determined the temperature of a substance). Although we now recognize the caloric theory as a special case of energy conservation, it is still of much practical utility in the laboratory, and the student should become thoroughly familiar with the simple method of calculation it affords.

THERMODYNAMICS

Just as the consolidation of Newton's dynamics was the most significant activity of eighteenth-century physics, by far the most important achievement of nineteenth-century physics was the development of the science of thermodynamics. It unified the "conservation of heat," of calorimetry and the "conservation of work" of statics into a single principle, "the conservation of energy." That latter principle has become the foundation of contemporary physics.

The first law of thermodynamics states that although the quantity of heat added to a system and the quantity of work done on a system are not separately conserved quantities, their sum may be described as the increase of the system's energy. This energy will therefore not change if the system is closed. This remarkable principle applies equally to all systems in nature, from heat engines to the nucleus of the atom. The second law of thermodynamics goes on to say that although a given quantity of work is done on a system and an equal amount of heat emerges, the reverse process is not possible. This process introduces a fundamental assymmetry in time for physical processes and leads to the definition of a new quantity, entropy (from the Greek, *tropos,* way). Entropy is characteristic of all physical systems and must increase during any real process occurring in a closed system.

ELECTRODYNAMICS

Of all the major subject areas that a student must confront at an early stage, electrodynamics is the one that presents the most difficulty. For this reason, an introductory treatment usually emphasizes currents and their interactions in electrical circuits from a practical point of view, leaving the detailed treatment of the interaction forces between charged particles to a later presentation at a more advanced mathematical level.

The fact of the existence of electric charge leads to two distinct types of forces: an electric force between stationary particles, described by Coulomb's law, and a magnetic force transmitted between charged particles that are moving. The ratio which the magnetic force between two moving particles bears to the electrical force is the same as the ratio of their velocity to a fixed constant with the dimensions of velocity.

In the mid-1800s James Clerk Maxwell, building on the experimental researches of Michael Faraday, showed that electromagnetic waves would be propagated in free space at this constant velocity, which was quite close to contemporary measurements of the velocity of light. Thus Maxwell had established light as an electromagnetic phenomenon. Maxwell's tour de force created the most severe difficulties, however, when attempts were made to understand and incorporate it within the structure of Newtonian dynamics. Maxwell's theory led naturally to a fundamental "speed limit" for the universe—the velocity of light waves. But Newtonian dynamics, as then understood, contained not the slightest hint of any such limitation. It was with this conflict that Einstein grappled at the turn of the century.

RELATIVITY

When the prospective student of physics sees the term "relativity," it will more than likely evoke either some sort of paradox about space travelers being time-distorted or some banality such as "space and time are relative to the observer" (or perhaps merely "relative to each other"). This is the result of the emphasis in popularizations of Einstein's work (including those by Einstein himself) on the revision in customary notions about time (particularly simultaneity) that an understanding of the theory makes necessary.

Although physicists (and writers of text books in physics) enjoy treating these puzzles, the puzzles tend to obscure the real importance of relativity in the structure of physics. Einstein was able to encompass the most important concepts of energy, momentum, and mass (derived from Newtonian laws of dynamics) and of the velocity of light (derived from electromagnetism) into a single structure. That structure, Einstein's theory of relativity, combines into one consistent mathematical analysis the theories of both "mechanical" and electrodynamic phenomena.

The most succinct and characteristic expression of Einstein's theory is in the equation

$$E^2 - p^2c^2 = m^2c^4$$

where E is the energy, p the momentum in the mass, and c the velocity of light. (The equation is a less restricted form of the familiar $E = mc^2$.)

This wonderful equation unifies and makes comprehensible two centuries of developments in physics. For the student it can serve as a sort of plateau in his study of the subject from which he can view in relative comfort the difficult path he has taken. It also represents probably the most comprehensive level of understanding that can be expected from a program of self-study. The principal developments in physics since Einstein's early work have been to apply this type of physics to the submicroscopic world. Before this could be done, a revolution even more far-reaching than relativity had to take place.

QUANTUM THEORY

As long as we deal with systems of larger than atomic dimensions, the processes by which energy and momentum are exchanged between systems may be analyzed by means of Newtonian forces that allow us to think of energy and momentum as continuously variable quantities. When, however, we wish to deal with fundamental processes on the atomic and subatomic level, it is found that these exchanges do not take place continuously but instead occur in discrete units called *quanta*. The scale of this fundamental "currency" of energy exchange is fixed by a constant of nature known as the "quantum of action," or Planck's constant.

It is by now customary to introduce quantum ideas in first-year college physics textbooks, so that the student may, at an early stage, gain some appreciation of the fundamental processes occurring between elementary particles. Detailed description of these processes, however, requires a complex theory—the quantum theory, which was developed during the first quarter of the twentieth century. Because of its highly mathematical nature, quantum theory is not introduced in its generality until the student has a thorough understanding and mastery of classical Newtonian concepts. Normally this implies that the student will not begin a systematic study of quantum theory before late undergraduate or even graduate years.

There is, however, a great body of factual material concerning atomic and nuclear phenomena with which any student of physics should have a considerable familiarity. Although it is conceivable that physics could be studied with profit purely as an intellectual exercise, much as "pure" philosophy might be, the subject, like philosophy, takes life only from consideration of actual phenomena. In the realm of classical mechanics students' everyday experiences, supplemented by their imagination, probably provide enough "reality" for an adequate understanding of the concepts; but in the atomic and nuclear domain, unless students have studied the factual information elicited by often elaborate experiments, they have nothing upon which their imaginations may feed. They have nothing real to think about, and the study of theories of phenomena of which they have no direct knowledge becomes an arid exercise indeed.

These remarks also apply to the physics of condensed matter (a branch of the field that includes solid-state physics). Specialists in this area attempt to understand the electromagnetic, thermal, and mechanical properties of matter in bulk by application of the methods of quantum mechanics to the collective behavior of the atoms and molecules of which it is composed. Some of the most exciting and technologically significant developments in postwar physics have occurred in this area.

BIBLIOGRAPHY

GENERAL FIRST READINGS

The following works represent a selection of general readings that provide orientation in the field.

Koestler, Arthur, *The Watershed: A Biography of Johannes Kepler.* Doubleday, 1960.

Einstein, Albert, and Leopold Infeld, *The Evolution of Physics.* Simon & Schuster, 1968.

Bernstein, Jeremy, *Einstein,* ed. Frank Kermode. Viking, 1973.

Asimov, Isaac, *Understanding Physics,* 3 vols., Vol. 1: *Light, Magnetism and Electricity;* Vol. 2: *Motion, Sound and Heat;* Vol 3: *The Electron, Proton and Neutron.* NAL (Signet Science Series), 1969.

Park, David, *Contemporary Physics.* Harcourt Brace Jovanovich, 1964.

Rogers, Eric M., *Physics for the Inquiring Mind: The Methods, Nature and Philosophy of Physical Science.* Princeton Univ. Press (hard cover), 1960.

Born, Max, *The Restless Universe,* 2nd ed. Dover, 1951.

Holton, Gerald J., *Introduction to Concepts and Theories in Physical Science,* 2nd ed. Addison-Wesley (hard cover), 1973.

Holton, Gerald J., and D. H. Roller, *Foundations of Modern Physical Science.* Addison-Wesley (hard cover), 1958. Treats such fields as chemistry, astronomy, and the earth sciences in addition to physics.

INTRODUCTORY TEXTBOOKS SURVEYING THE FIELD

The following six works are college-level introductory texts that survey the whole field. You can pick any one of these for systematic study and do some reading in one or two of the others.

Atkins, Kenneth R., *Physics,* **2nd ed. Wiley (hard cover), 1969.**

Ford, Kenneth W., *Basic Physics.* **Xerox (hard cover), 1968.** Answers to exercises booklet also available.

Orear, Jay, *Fundamental Physics,* **2nd ed. Wiley (hard cover), 1967.** Orear's *Programmed Manual of College Physics (Wiley, 1968)* is also available.

Miller, Franklin, Jr., *College Physics,* **3rd. ed. Harcourt Brace Jovanovich (hard cover), 1972.** Instructor's manual also available.

P.S.S.C. (Physical Science Study Committee), *College Physics.* **Heath (hard cover), 1968.**

Freeman, Ira, *Physics: Principles and Insights,* **2nd ed. McGraw-Hill (hard cover), 1973.** Study guide and instructor's guide also available.

Three more demanding textbooks, using methods of the calculus, are listed below. You may use one as a substitute for or supplement to study in any of the six books above.

Sears, Francis W., and M. W. Zemansky, *University Physics,* **4th ed.** *Part 1, Mechanics, Heat and Sound; Part 2, Electricity and Magnetism, Light and Atomic Physics.* **Addison-Wesley (hard cover), 1970.**

Halliday, David, and Robert Resnick, *Fundamentals of Physics,* **rev. ed. Wiley (hard cover), 1974.**

Ford, Kenneth W., *Classical and Modern Physics: A Textbook for Students of Science and Engineering,* **3 vols. Xerox, (hard cover) Vols. 1 and 2, 1972; Vol. 3, 1974.** Answer manuals also available.

The following is a masterful survey of the whole range of physics, which you can use to supplement any of the introductory texts above.

Feynman, R. P., et al., *The Feynman Lectures in Physics,* **3 vols.** Addison-Wesley, 1964. Exercise booklets for each volume also available.

WORKS ON SPECIFIC BRANCHES OF PHYSICS

The following works are still on the introductory level; they treat specific branches of physics in somewhat more detail.

Berkeley Physics Laboratory, *Berkeley Physics Course,* **5 vols.; Vol 1:** *Mechanics,* **1965 (out of print); Vol 2:** *Electricity and Magnetism,* **1965; Vol. 3:** *Waves,* **1968; Vol. 4:** *Quantum Physics,* **1971; Vol. 5:**

Statistical Physics, 1967. McGraw-Hill (hard cover). Solutions manuals also available.

French, A. P., *Special Relativity* (1968), *Newtonian Mechanics* (1971), *Vibrations and Waves* (1971); A. P. French and Edwin Taylor, *Quantum Physics.* Norton (M.I.T. Introductory Physics Series, (forthcoming; 1978).

Taylor, Edwin F., and John A. Wheeler, *Spacetime Physics.* Freeman, 1966. Answer booklet also available.

ADVANCED WORKS

Presented below are books that treat specific branches of physics in greater depth and at a somewhat more advanced level (about the junior- and senior-year level).

Lorrain, Paul, and Dale R. Corson, *Electromagnetic Fields and Waves.* Freeman (hard cover), 1970. Answer book also available.

Synge, John L., and B. Griffith, *Principles of Mechanics,* 3rd ed. McGraw-Hill (hard cover), 1959.

Zemansky, M. W., *Heat and Thermodynamics; An Intermediate Textbook,* 5th ed. McGraw-Hill (hard cover), 1968.

Landau, Lev D., and Eugene Lifshitz, *Shorter Course of Theoretical Physics,* 3 vols.; Vol. 1: *Mechanics and Electrodynamics,* 1972; Vol. 2: *Quantum Mechanics,* 1974; Vol. 3: *Macroscopic Physics,* 1975. Addison-Wesley (hard cover).

Books that deal with atomic and nuclear phenomena on an advanced undergraduate level follow.

Dicke, Robert H., and James P. Wittke, *Introduction to Quantum Mechanics.* Addison-Wesley (hard cover), 1960.

Born, Max, *Atomic Physics,* 8th ed., tr. John Dougal. Hafner (hard cover), 1969. Old but a classic.

Semat, Henry, and J. Albright, *Introduction to Atomic and Nuclear Physics,* 5th ed. Holt, Rinehart & Winston (hard cover), 1972.

Oldenberg, Otto, and W. G. Holladay, *Introduction to Atomic and Nuclear Physics,* McGraw-Hill (hard cover), 1967.

Eisberg, Robert, and Resnick, Robert, *Quantum Physics of Atoms, Molecules, Solids, Nuclei and Particles,* John Wiley and Sons, 1974.

PERIODICALS

There are several Periodicals through which readers may keep generally up-to-date on new developments in the field.

Physics Today, American Institute of Physics, 335 East 45th Street,

New York, NY 10017. Very readable, with many timely articles of general interest.

American Journal of Physics, American Institute of Physics, 335 East 45th Street, New York, NY 10017. Devoted to matters of interest in the teaching of physics. Some articles are on the undergraduate level.

Scientific American, 415 Madison Avenue, New York, NY 10017. From time to time contains articles about current developments for the general reader with some scientific awareness.

ABOUT THE AUTHORS

GAIL THAIN PARKER was born in Chicago, Illinois. She holds a B.A. from Radcliffe and a Ph.D. from Harvard. From 1969-1972 she served as Assistant Professor of History and Literature at Harvard, and from 1972-1976 she served as President of Bennington College. Ms. Parker is the author of two books and numerous articles on topics ranging from Jonathan Edwards to women's history to the future of higher education. Currently Ms. Parker is serving as a member of the National Board of Consultants of the National Endowment for the Humanities and she is also working on a book on higher education.

GENE R. HAWES was born in Chicago, Illinois, and is a Phi Beta Kappa graduate of Columbia University. For two decades, he has been the author of a bestselling college directory, *New American Guide to Colleges*. Past books of his include *How to Get College Scholarships, Open Education* and *Making College Count* (with Ewald B. Nyquist). Mr. Hawes has also written articles for *Saturday Review, Esquire, Town & Country, Nation's Schools* and *NEA Journal*. Currently Mr. Hawes is a Principal of The Hudson Group, Inc., a firm of senior authors and editors based in Pleasantville, N.Y.